Hans Wallach ON PERCEPTION

BF 311
.W 2667
1976

Hans Wallach
ON PERCEPTION

Quadrangle/The New York Times Book Co.

INDIANA
UNIVERSITY
LIBRARY
AUG1 0 1977
NORTHWEST

In memory of
Phoebe Kasper Wallach

Copyright © 1976 by Hans Wallach. All rights reserved, including the right to reproduce this book or portions thereof in any form. For information, address: Quadran-
gle/The New York Times Book Co., 10 East 53 Street, New York, New York 10022.
Manufactured in the United States of America. Published simultaneously in Canada
by Fitzhenry & Whiteside, Ltd., Toronto.

Book design: Mary M. Ahern

LIBRARY OF CONGRESS CATALOGING IN PUBLICATION DATA

Wallach, Hans, 1904–
    On perception.

    Includes bibliographies and index.
    1. Perception. I. Title.
BF311.W2667   152.1'4'08   73–79938
ISBN 0–8129–0480–X

Contents

PERCEPTION

                1. On size-perception in the absence of cues
                    for distance
                    (with Virgil V. McKenna)   129

                2. The role of slant in the perception of shape
                    (with Mary E. Moore)   133

                3. The constancy of stereoscopic depth
                    (with Carl Zuckerman)   139

                4. On constancy of visual speed   149

Chapter VIII   The role of memory in visual perception

                1. Some considerations concerning the relation
                    between perception and cognition   161

                2. The memory effect of visual perception of
                    three-dimensional form
                    (with D. N. O'Connell and Ulric Neisser)   170

                3. Recognition and the localization of visual
                    traces
                    (with Pauline Austin Adams)   184

                4. On memory modalities
                    (with Emanuel Averbach)   189

Chapter IX   On perceived identity

                1. The direction of motion of straight lines   201

                2. Circles and derived figures in rotation
                    *(with Alexander Weisz and Pauline
                    Austin Adams)*   217

PERCEPTUAL LEARNING

Chapter X   Adaptation based on cue discrepancy

                1. Informational discrepancy as a basis of
                    perceptual adaptation   235

                2. Modification of stereoscopic depth-
                    perception
                    (with Mary E. Moore and Linda Davidson) 261

Preface

I have selected for this book that part of my work which is of current theoretical interest. The last part of the book (Chapters X and XI) deals with perceptual adaptation and tells coherent stories. But the rest is concerned with a great variety of subject matter. For the most part, this is a reflection of the many processes that make up perception, and that, in turn, is simply the consequence of the great heterogeneity of the physical facts and events which we can perceive. To a minor degree it reflects the manner in which I have worked, pursuing a problem as long as the work yielded worthwhile results and then shelving it until a new idea promised progress.

Chapter I presents my work on neutral color, first reported in "Brightness constancy and the nature of achromatic color" (1948). Later work is, however, included and the scope of the chapter is greatly enlarged. Lightness or value of chromatic color is treated, the modes of appearance of color are related to the modes of appearance of neutral light, and the latter are given a critical place among the color vision phenomena. The chapter also replaces my article in *Scientific American,* "The perception of neutral color" (1963). Both these articles have been available in collections of readings and as reprints. But they do not tell the whole story as I see it now.

Chapter III brings together a number of experiments that represent a challenge to the theory of stereoscopic vision.

For many years the effectiveness of accommodation and convergence as distance cues has been under debate. Chapter IV resolves that issue. Further measurements on the effectiveness of accommodation and convergence in distance perception can be found in Chapter X, selections 5 and 6.

In Chapter V, I present my current views on visual motion perception. This chapter, therefore, supersedes my article in *Scientific American,* "The perception of motion" (1959).

In Chapter VII, selection 2, the question is raised whether there is such a thing as shape constancy, that is, whether the slant of a surface is taken into account in the perception of its shape. Although it seems not at all evident that such a constancy process is required to account for the perceived shapes of slanted surfaces under ordinary circumstances, a clear answer is provided. Experimental results are presented that demonstrate such a process in operation.

The work reported in Chapter VIII, selections 3 and 4, is more timely now than when it was first published. The question of brain localization is now more important than ever and the technique employed in the experiment reported in selection 3 should be useful in research on hemispheric functions. The basic idea of selection 4 is that of memory coding. One of its results, namely that verbal material is visually coded, is also still an issue, and the experimental technique employed may find new applications.

The two selections in Chapter IX are closely related. Because it was available only in a German publication, my work on the direction of motion of straight lines is now accessible virtually for the first time (selection 1). The explanations used in this selection play a central role also in the explanation of the phenomena described in selection 2.

Chapter X brings together my more important work on adaptation based on cue discrepancy, which is centered on the process assimilation hypothesis. A comprehensive statement of this hypothesis and a discussion of its consequences is contained in Selection 9.

Chapter XI contains my work on the constancy of visual direction and a selection on a newly discovered similar compensation process. An interpretation of such compensation processes is presented in selection 9 and new experiments that support this interpretation are reported.

Much of the work presented in this book was done in collaboration with numerous assistants and associates who were entrusted with the actual performance of the experiments. I am deeply indebted to them, not only for carrying the burden of data collecting but also for the creative contributions they made at every step of our work, to the searching for methods and the trial and error that this search entailed, to the planning of the procedures, and to the evaluation of the results. Their names appear as co-authors of those articles. I also want to thank the nameless hundreds of willing subjects who refrained from trying to second-guess us and made our experiments succeed.

I would like to acknowledge here the role that support of basic research on the part of the federal government has played in the progress of my work. Of the 49 articles I have published since 1939, 16 were produced in the first 20 years of that period. Since 1959 when my work first received federal support, I published 33 articles; of the latter, 23 are represented in this volume.

This book represents a substantial part of my life's work. It should therefore be an occasion for expressing my gratitude to those who have set me on my way. As Wolfgang Kohler's assistant in my first year as a graduate student I learned to observe with an open mind and to translate theoretical questions quickly into experiments. In the years after my arrival at Swarthmore College, Edwin B. Newman helped me with the technical problems of my early work. He taught me much about research and made me learn what an American psychologist was then expected to know. I am also deeply grateful to Max Wertheimer, whose confidence in my ability encouraged me during the first hard years on the psychological scene in the United States.

Finally, I want to name the two men who, in different ways, had more effect on my work than anybody else. For 36 years Otto Hebel has built the apparatus for my experiments. Without his technical skill and his inventiveness and without his endless patience with the half-baked ideas I brought to him, much of my work would have been impossible. I feel more grateful to him than I can express. Of similar importance has been the work of Karl Duncker. His monograph, "On Problem Solving," has been a guide for my thinking and has strongly influenced the manner in which I have worked.

Introduction
by Carl Zuckerman

Hans Wallach's colleagues, and several generations of students who have admired his scientific work for many years, will welcome the publication of this collection of his research papers. It represents a unique record of almost four decades of experimentation and thought about the psychology of perceptual experience and related aspects of memory function. Anyone who has wondered about how we become aware of the properties of the external world—in Kurt Koffka's phrase: "Why do things look as they do?"—will obtain great intellectual satisfaction as he finds many problems of perception analyzed and clarified by ingenious experiments and probing conceptualization.

Hans Wallach was born in Germany in 1904. In 1926 he began graduate work in psychology at the University of Berlin. His studies were interrupted a year later but in 1931 he was able to return on a part-time basis and completed his work in 1934. In the following year, after the required publication of his thesis, he was awarded the Ph.D. degree.

These were the brilliant years of Gestalt psychological theory and research. Wolfgang Kohler was the Director of the Psychological Institute at the University of Berlin; Max Wertheimer, the founder of Gestalt psychology, was there until 1929. Together with Kurt Lewin they provided an atmosphere of great intellectual challenge and excitement. Wallach's thesis—an experimental study of the direction of perceived motion—was published in the *Psychologische Forschung,* the journal for Gestalt-inspired research. Unfortunately,

Wallach's paper, like much of the material found in the *Forschung,* has remained little known in this country. For the present volume, the author has prepared a summary of the main results of this important investigation. Before leaving Germany he discovered the head-movement principle in the localization of sounds.

In 1936 Wallach moved to the United States and for a number of years he was Kohler's Research Associate (in 1935 Kohler had resigned his position at Berlin and emigrated to America) at Swarthmore College in Pennsylvania. One outcome of their collaboration was a monograph on figural after-effects (1944), which gave rise to a great deal of research and theoretical controversy. This work is not represented in this book for reasons to be discussed below. Kohler continued to investigate figural after-effects and attempted to discover the cortical correlates of perceptual experience while Wallach returned to the kind of psychological study of perception which he had pursued in his thesis work. He became Instructor in 1943, Assistant Professor in 1945, Associate Professor in 1947, and Professor in 1953. In the academic year 1954–1955 he was a member of the Institute for Advanced Study at Princeton. He was a Visiting Professor at the Graduate Faculty of the New School for Social Research for many years, beginning in 1947. Wallach remains at Swarthmore College, teaching a seminar in perception and actively engaged in research. A visit to his laboratory is an exciting experience—there are many intriguing demonstrations of perceptual phenomena, two or three research assistants busy at work on new experiments, and he is there, always ready to discuss the progress of scientific research and still as curious as ever about the mysteries of mental functions. New ideas for experiments are constantly erupting and his plans for future research leave no doubt that significant discoveries are forthcoming. He has inspired and influenced many of his students, and among them are a number of well-known contributors to various areas of psychological research.

How can one characterize Wallach's scientific style? He is not a grand theorist who attempts to construct a general "theory of perception," neither is he a pure empiricist devoted to the collection of facts and data. He starts with a problem and attempts to solve the problem by finding the laws or principles which determine or explain a psychological phenomenon. And problems are chosen with some idea as to their significance for the understanding of perceptual processes. One of the main directions of his research lies in the search for the relevant stimulus conditions for a particular perceptual experience. This is one of the oldest traditions in the study of perceptions. Isaac Newton demonstrated that the perception of hue is correlated with the specific degree of what he called the "refrangibility" of the light which strikes the eye. In the nineteenth century, Wheatstone proved that one important stimulus condition (or "cue") for the perception of depth was retinal disparity—the fact that each eye gets a slightly different image of a three-dimensional scene or object. Knowledge of the stimulus provides, in a certain important sense, an explanation for perceptual experience. For example, it is possible to say that we see depth *because* of retinal disparity.

As the reader will find, Wallach has made important discoveries with reference to stimulus conditions. We know that we see a particular hue because of the spectral composition of the light that gets to the eye. But what determines whether a surface will be seen as white, gray, or black? Using very simple apparatus, Wallach found that the stimulus for the perception of neutral color is relational; that is, a surface will look white not because it reflects lots of light to the eye. It looks white because it reflects more light than any neighboring or adjacent surface. An object or surface looks black not because it reflects little light to the eye but because it reflects much less light than do adjacent surfaces. In the simplest case—with two adjacent areas visible—the specific neutral color depends on a *ratio* of light intensities. The relational property of the stimulus is important for the explanation of several well-known phenomena. Neutral color constancy—the fact that a white surface under dim illumination continues to look white and a black object still looks black in bright illumination—can be readily understood. If the illuminating light falls not only on the object in question but also on the surrounding area the ratio of light intensities is not changed. It is the ratio not the absolute amount of light reflected to the retina from a particular object which determines a particular gray. If the ratio is unaltered by a change of illumination, no change of perceived neutral color should occur. With the publication of this volume, Wallach's theory of neutral color constancy should be clearly understood. It is not as some textbooks describe it, a "contrast" theory. Rather, both constancy and contrast are explained in the same way—in terms of the stimulus for neutral color. Moreover, other perceptual phenomena such as the modes of appearance of colors and the lightness aspect of chromatic colors follow as a necessary consequence of the ratio principle.

Other examples where the elucidation of the stimulus properties leads to an understanding of various perceptual phenomena are to be found in the papers on the kinetic depth effect and in the discussion of motion perception.

Other psychologists, in particular, J. J. Gibson, have also stressed the importance of stimulus conditions. But Wallach does not agree with Gibson's position that everything necessary to explain a perceptual experience is to be found in the stimulus (or in Gibson's words: all the information necessary for perception is contained in the stimulation). As one can see, Wallach often refers to situations where the stimulus conditions are ambiguous. The stimulation "permits" several possibilities; why then does one perception arise and not other possible ones (see the paper on the direction of movement and the one on perception of motion). For an explanation, one has to go beyond the stimulation. Unlike Gibson, Wallach does so. He refers to central processes: in some cases his Gestalt training shows and he speaks of perceptual organization and selective principles in order to explain the "disambiguation" process; in others he relies on memory traces. In both, of course, the stimulation is seen as insufficient. Another example of the inadequacy of Gibson's view is the cue-conflict situation which Wallach uses so inventively to study perceptual functions. Obviously the phenomenal outcome of such a conflict cannot be understood on the basis of the stimulus information alone. And finally, consider the instances of what seems to be problem solving in perception, where perception and thinking are intimately linked. (See the paper on sound localization and the paper on the direction of motion.)

In the past decade the major part of Wallach's research has been directed toward problems of perceptual learning. He has analyzed a variety of cue conflict situations and has studied in detail the process of adaptation to artificially altered stimulation. In the twenty or so papers written during this period Wallach seems to be mounting a bold attack on the hitherto invincible fortress of perceptual function in order to lay bare it's secrets. The reader will be impressed by the imaginative experimentation, the sheer ingenuity of the apparatus, and the techniques for measuring perceptual effects and the clarity and originality of the thinking.

Each paper in this series contributes to the solution of old problems and opens up new questions for study. I believe, for example, that this research is leading to a reformulation and elucidation of the ancient nativism–empiricism issue. For centuries philosophers and psychologists have argued about the origin of our perceptual capacities—are they based on innate mechanisms or are they the outcome of learning processes? Now we are able to see the inadequacy of both views; the empiristic position does not explain what directs the learning while traditional nativism cannot account for the enormous flexibility of the perceptual system revealed in Wallach's research.

The controversy can be resolved if we assume as innately given not a system of fixed pre-wired mechanisms but rather directive principles or rules. Consider the problem of position constancy for example (or in Wallach's terminology, the constancy of visual direction). When we move our head, let us say 20° to the right, the retinal image of the scene moves across the retina 20° to the right. In spite of the retinal movement, we do not perceive motion in the visual field. If there were fixed innate mechanisms which would correct for or cancel this particular head movement-caused retinal displacement, it would be difficult to explain the rapid re-acquisition of position constancy when lenses are worn which change the relationship between head movement and visual field displacement.

In several experiments Wallach has changed the direction and extent of retinal image displacement dependent on head movement and has demonstrated a rapid relearning of visual direction constancy. This flexibility can be understood if we assume that the organism is equipped with a perceptual rule: discount any image movement which begins and ends with the movement of the head (or for displacement of the entire body in space). This rule (Wallach calls it a co-variance principle) can explain the constancy of visual direction under normal conditions. It can also account for the re-achievement of constancy when different head–retinal movement relationships are imposed experimentally as in Wallach's investigations and in the dramatic experiment of Stratton more than 80 years ago. Rock[1] has suggested a similar rule—which he calls the concomitance principle—to account for the facts of position constancy.

Similar reasoning is applicable to other aspects of perceptual experience, for example, stereoscopic depth. Most theoretical models of stereoscopy assume a fixed relation between the amount of retinal disparity and the degree of perceptual depth. The fact, however, that stereoscopic depth can be rapidly modified in a cue conflict situation, and in addition, that the same disparity can lead to more or less seen depth depending on the registered distance of the depth interval from the eye argues against a fixed relationship. A plausible solution would be that disparity is an innate cue for depth but that the exact calibration for the extent of seen depth is dependent on learning. This view contributes to the understanding of problems in perceptual development. Bower[2] has pointed out that as the baby grows, the interocular distance increases and therefore, the disparity cue is

[1]Irvin Rock, *The Nature of Perceptual Adaptation* (New York: Basic Books, 1966).

[2]T. G. R. Bower, *Development in Infancy* (San Francisco: W. H. Freeman, 1973).

constantly changing. Only a system capable of re-calibrating itself could adapt to these growth-produced changes. How this calibration process occurs is a task for future research. Reference to Wallach's work will be of great value.

As I stated above, the figural after-effect research is not included here. The principal aim of that work was to construct a brain model of perception. It can be readily seen from the content of this book that Wallach analyzes perceptual experience on the psychological level—he rarely speculates about neuro-physiological processes, neither does he search for neural principles in order to explain perception. In a certain sense, therefore, the figural after-effect investigation does not fit in with the main direction of his scientific work.

Wallach's published reports are concerned with problems in perception and memory function. Those of us who have studied with him at the New School for Social Research do not think of him only as a perception psychologist. We have had the privilege of hearing his stimulating and original ideas about issues in the fields of motivation and emotion, problem solving, and creative thinking. We are certain that Wallach would have made important contributions to whatever field of psychology he had chosen to work in. Meanwhile, we are happy that this volume is now available to students of perception and of psychology in general. In it they will find a rich store of intriguing experiments and fruitful ideas which will remain valuable for years to come.

Perception

On color perception

Although the relation between the stimulus variables and the experience of hue is complicated, it is possible to ascribe the experience of hue to the properties of the stimulating light mixture. To be sure, one cannot infer the nature of the stimulus mixture from the experienced hue, but one can predict the hue of a perceived color if the properties of the stimulating light are known along with the state of adaptation of the eye. No similar relation exists between the experience of a neutral color (of a white or gray or a black) and a property of the stimulating neutral light mixture. It is true that neutral color depends in some fashion on the intensity of a stimulating neutral light mixture. If one changes the intensity of the light that is reflected by a gray paper disk which is fastened to a white wall, one will thereby change the quality of the perceived gray. (This can be done, for instance, by projecting a circular beam of light on the disk in such a way that the edge of the beam coincides with the edge of the paper disk.) Because it receives additional light, the disk will now reflect a higher light intensity, and this will indeed cause the color of the disk to be a lighter gray. Nevertheless it is impossible to state that light of such and such an intensity will always produce a dark gray and light of another intensity will produce a light gray, even if the influence of the current adaptation of the eye could be correctly estimated.

The fact is that neutral color depends on differences in the intensity of light stimulation received at different parts of the retina. Such differences normally exist owing to the variety of surfaces of which the visual field is composed. The gray disk just mentioned does not change color because light of higher intensity is received in its retinal image, but because the intensity received from the surface of the disk is changed in relation to the light intensity received from the white wall, which happens to form the surroundings of the disk. If additional light were projected on both the disk and the surrounding wall surface, the disk would also reflect more light, but its color would not appreciably change because the relation of light intensity received from the disk to that received from the wall would remain unaltered.

It is not only the particular quality or value of a neutral color, however, which depends on the difference in the intensity of stimulation received from the area in which the color is seen and the intensity received from the surroundings. That any neutral color is seen at all also requires the presence of differential stimulation. This fact becomes quite clear when one studies the result of homogeneous stimulation of the retina with neutral light. It has long been known that if an observer faces a completely uniform field, be it total darkness or an evenly illuminated homogeneous plane surface, the colors that he sees are not the ordinary neutral colors that are visible on objects. If the plane surface is brightly illuminated, he may see it as a white fog. With the illumination more moderate, the impression is still different from that produced by a white surface that is surrounded by other neutral colors. The color that the homogeneous field causes lacks the density of a smaller whole surface. But there is also a difference in function. When the light intensity of the homogeneous field is lowered its peculiar color fails to change to gray; it becomes merely dimmer. A large decrease in illumination is needed to cause a more radical change, but even then the field becomes dark rather than gray.

In order that ordinary neutral colors be perceived it is necessary that light of different intensity stimulate different regions of the retina. However, differential stimulation will not necessarily lead to the perception of neutral colors. It is essential that the differences in the intensity of stimulation in different retinal areas be not too great. The appearance of the moon at different times is an example. When seen in a blue sky in full daylight, the moon looks white. Under these conditions the eye receives somewhat more light from the direction of the moon than from the surrounding blue sky. The light of the latter consists of scattered sunlight; the dark interstellar space is beyond. While the bluish light of the sky originates in the sun, it has its immediate source everywhere in the atmosphere. Thus, bluish light of the sky comes also from the direction in which we see the moon and therefore is added to the light that the moon reflects. Thus, no matter what the intensity of the latter may be, the light that comes from the direction of the moon must be more intense than the light from the surrounding sky. As the sun goes down, the light available for scattering by the atmosphere diminishes and the intensity of the bluish light decreases everywhere. Only the light that the moon itself reflects remains unchanged. In absolute terms the light received from the direction of the moon decreases because of the diminished contribution of light of atmospheric origin. Relatively speaking, however, that is, in relation to the intensity of the surrounding sky, the light from the direction of the moon becomes more intense. As a consequence the moon seems to become brighter and brighter. First a little glow appears to be added to the white surface. Then, as the light of the sky is further reduced, the moon appears more strongly luminous and long before the sky looks quite dark all whiteness has disappeared and the moon looks brilliantly bright. At that time the intensity of the light received from the moon is many times brighter than that from the atmosphere. The whiteness of the surface which was seen with moderate differences between the intensity of the light from the moon and from its surroundings gives way to a luminous appearance when that difference is enhanced.

The same observation can be made when in a darkened room a circular spot of light is projected on a white wall. This spot will look luminous rather than white. When the intensity of the light spot is reduced, for instance by reducing the brightness of the lantern light, or by replacing the white wall with a gray screen, the spot will merely become dimmer, but it will continue to look luminous, for it is still very much brighter than its almost completely dark surroundings. In order to cause the spot to look white the surroundings must be made much brighter. This can be done by projecting from a second lantern a ring of light whose inner edge coincides with or is close to the contour of the spot. A good opaque white appears in the spot when the light intensity of the ring is one half that of the spot. When the intensity of the ring is lowered stepwise, first some luminosity appears on the white disk, then the luminosity becomes more brilliant and finally the whiteness disappears altogether. As in the case of the moon, only moderate intensity differences between the critical area and its surroundings will lead to a real white, that is, a neutral surface color. An arrangement such as the one just described represents the simplest condition of stimulation that will produce a white surface color. In addition, it seems important that under the same simple conditions a given area may simultaneously look white and luminous. However, before these observations are evaluated we have to describe the simplest stimulus conditions for the other neutral colors, namely, the grays and black.

The same luminous spot which can be transformed into a white surface when it is surrounded by an area of lower light intensity can be changed into a gray when it is surrounded by an area of higher intensity. For instance, when the ring of light which surrounds the spot has an intensity twice as great as that of the spot, the latter assumes a light gray color. It will look medium gray if the ring is four times as intense as the spot and the gray will become darker as the intensity of the ring is further raised. A good black will appear in the spot at a ratio of approximately 20:1. Thus, the statement that neutral colors depend on differences in the intensity of stimulation is true over the full range of values. With the light intensity of the spot constant, variation in the light intensity in the surrounding area serves to produce the whole range of neutral colors in the spot.

The colors that are produced under these conditions have all the characteristics of neutral colors seen under ordinary circumstances. They are completely opaque and solid and have all other properties of surface colors, with only one exception; they need not have microstructure. A light spot on a homogeneous screen which a moment ago looked completely luminous will, when it is now surrounded by a ring of a four-times-higher light intensity, display a completely opaque and homogeneous medium gray. Microstructure is neither a regular attribute of experienced surface color nor a necessary stimulus condition for the perception of a surface color as has frequently been claimed. Ring and spot may, for instance, be projected on a sheet of milk glass and observed from the other side. For the perception of surface color, mere differential stimulation is sufficient. The very frequent association of surface color with microstructure under ordinary conditions is merely accidental.

Neutral Color and Luminosity

So far we have concerned ourselves only with the appearance of the spot in the combination of ring and spot. In the presence of appropriate stimulation from the ring, the spot will assume the character of a neutral surface color. The question is what happens to the ring when the spot is added, and when the intensity of the spot is varied. If the light in the spot is of lower intensity than the light of the ring, its addition causes little change in the ring. With or without the light of the spot the ring looks merely luminous. However, when the light of the spot is more intense than that of the ring (a condition that causes the spot to be white or luminous) the ring assumes a most unusual appearance: it looks a seemingly translucent gray. This seems to be an experience which can be evoked only under these and similar artificial conditions. When the light intensities are reversed, that is, when the lower intensity of light is in the spot, a completely solid and opaque gray appears in the spot. But when the lower intensity is in the ring, the ring is simultaneously gray and luminous. One of the reasons for the different appearance of the gray when it is in the ring is the fact that the area of the ring is larger than the area of the spot. That size of area plays a role here can be demonstrated under the condition where the gray appears in the spot. A strong reduction in width of the more intense ring such that its area is less than half that of the spot will cause the gray in the spot to appear similarly luminous. A way in which to produce a luminous gray is to make the more intense area too small to exert its full influence. But there is a second reason. Luminous grays will also occur when the contact between two areas of different intensity in an otherwise dark field is altered. One can give the two areas of different light intensity the shape of two congruent oblongs lying side by side in contact with each other. Here the less intense area will show a gray that is less opaque than when it is a disk surrounded by a ring, because only on one side is it adjacent to an area of high intensity. If one moves the oblongs apart so that a dark gap appears between them, the gray one will become even more luminous. A diminished contact or the introduction of an interval between the areas of different intensity seems to interfere with the influence which they have on each other, and the surface color character will be less pronounced.

The manner in which this influence diminishes as it spreads over larger distances can be directly observed when in the spot-ring arrangement only half of the ring is visible. This can be easily achieved by intercepting with an opaque screen an appropriate part of the projector beam which casts the ring. The spot, which is only half surrounded by a ring section that is, e.g., more intense, and which with the other half borders directly on the dark remainder of the visual field, now assumes an uneven appearance. In that part which protrudes into the section of the ring it shows a gray as solid and opaque as that observed when the ring is complete. On the other hand, the gray does not seem to reach to the other pole; there the spot has a luminous cap. Between these two extremes, the density of the gray changes gradually, allowing, as it were, more and more luminosity to show. As yet, it is not known whether distance as such is responsible for the diminishing density of the gray across the spot or whether the gray process that takes place in the interval is the cause for the reduced influence of the ring section in the distant parts of the spot. More research is needed before we will know the nature of the interaction process which underlies the influence that causes neutral surface color to be seen instead of luminosity.

Whereas a luminous gray occurs only when the influence of the more intense area on the less intense one is diminished, a luminous white can appear also in a spot that is completely surrounded by light of another, in this case, lower intensity. As we have seen above, it is merely necessary to increase somewhat the intensity difference between spot and ring in order for the white to become luminous. This is one aspect of the basic difference in the functioning of white and gray. We have seen that when two areas of different stimulus intensity exert their influence on each other, the area of lower intensity will be gray and the area of high intensity will be white. However, the correspondence between white and gray goes no further. When the *difference* in intensity is varied, the value of the gray changes; the gray may even turn into black. If the spot is more intense, it will show no color other than white. An increase in the intensity difference will cause a different kind of quality, that is, luminosity, to appear in addition to the white and a further increase will merely cause luminosity to become stronger.

There can be no doubt that neutral colors must be the result of an interaction process in the nervous system. The fact that the very occurrence of neutral color depends on differential stimulation and that the value of a gray color depends largely on the ratio of the pertinent stimulus intensities requires this conception. If, for instance, a medium gray arises in a spot because it is surrounded by a ring of an intensity four times as high, the underlying process in the spot must be determined by two quantities: the intensity of the stimulation which is received from the spot itself and the intensity of stimulation received from the ring. Some sort of interaction must subsequently go on such that the intensity in the ring makes itself felt in the spot. The nervous process which is the correlate of the experienced neutral color is the result of two conditions: of the condition that results from the stimulation received from the spot and of an influence which the stimulation received from the ring exerts on that condition. To this correlate of experienced neutral color we shall refer with the term "surface color process."

We have seen that stimulation by neutral light may also result in a very different experience, namely that of luminous appearance and that this luminosity can occur simultaneously with a gray or a white. It seems that luminous appearance occurs where conditions for interaction are absent, as in the case of the homogeneous field, or unfavorable, as in the case of a luminous gray. The existence of a luminous gray is of great importance. It shows that the gray colors do not result from a simple interaction process in which intensity difference and proximity have parallel effects, as, for instance, lateral inhibition. In order that a particular gray be perceived two things have to happen: In the first place, a "surface color process" must take place, whose presence or absence and the degree to which it is present depends on the degree of contact between regions of different intensity of stimulation or on the relative size of the region of higher intensity. Secondly, when conditions for a surface color process exist, a gray will be perceived that depends roughly on the intensity ratio of the regions, but the density of that gray, the degree to which it is present, will depend on the degree of contact between the regions and on the sizes of their areas. A simple hypothesis about the relation between luminous appearance and surface color process that allows for their simultaneous presence in the same area would assume that luminous appearance is the outcome of stimulation by neutral light whose effect on the nervous system does not participate in a surface color process. While the latter results from differential stimulation, luminous appearance depends directly on the intensity of stimulation received from the area in which it is seen. It, therefore, occurs where intensity differences are absent or where they are too large, as in the case of a bright spot in dark surround, or where conditions for a diminished surface color process exist. As we have seen in connection with the luminous gray, such conditions are a reduced common border between the areas of different intensity, their separation by a spatial interval of low intensity or a strong difference in area size. Replacing the sharp border between areas of different intensity with an intensity gradient is still another condition that diminishes interaction and hence the surface color process.

This hypothesis which regards luminosity that occurs in combination with neutral color as a residual process sheds some light on the basic difference in the functioning of gray and white. When an area is of an intensity lower than that of the surroundings, it will look gray or black and in that case the ratio of the two intensities will largely determine the color value. If, on the other hand, the area is of higher intensity, it will look white and a change in the ratio will not affect the color as such. There will, however, be a change in the area of the white as the difference between the intensity of this area and the intensity of its surroundings increases in favor of the former. The white area will, in addition to white, also look luminous. Here, too, we may consider luminosity as the result of that part of the neural representation of stimulation in a given area which does not participate in a "surface color process." A lowering of the intensity of the surroundings in relation to the intensity of the area that looks white may cause the influence exerted in the latter to be diminished to a point where it is insufficient to involve in a surface color process all of the process that represents the stimulation in that area, leaving some of it free to function as a luminous process.

Much attention to the luminous appearance of neutral color has been given in this report for two reasons. In the first place, I feel that any neurophysiological theory of neutral color perception which does not take these facts into account is doomed to failure. Secondly, I believe that these observations furnish the explanation of those instances when we seem to perceive illumination.

Quantitative Relations

It has become amply clear that neutral colors are the outcome of an interaction process that requires stimulation by at least two different intensities of light in neighboring retinal areas, and that, in the case of gray and black, the particular value that results depends in some fashion on the difference between these light intensities. What is the quantitative aspect of this dependence? In the case of the spot and ring arrangement in which the higher light intensity is in the ring, the particular gray that is seen in the spot depends largely on the ratio between the intensity of the ring and that of the spot. Such were the results of experiments with two such spot and ring arrangements, in which the intensity in one of the spots was variable to allow the observer to match the colors that emerge in the spots. In one of these experiments, for instance, the ring in one of the arrangements received the full light of one of four matched lantern beams, while the light falling into the spot was reduced to 50%. In the other arrangement the ring received an intensity of 12.5% and the spot was varied until the observer was satisfied that the grays appearing in the spots looked the same. The average match for five observers was 6.7%, which is rather close to the proportionate value of 6.25%. The fact that the matching intensity was slightly higher than the proportionate value means, of course, that a spot of an intensity of 6.25% looks slightly too dark.

Not always is the deviation from proportionality such that the spot of lower intensity shows a slightly darker gray. Where the intensities of ring and spot in one arrangement were again 100% and 50% and the less intense ring was 25%, the gray in the spots was the same when the second spot had an intensity near the proportionate value of 12.5%. Or, with the same intensities in the brighter arrangement (100% and 50%) a ring of 50% required a spot of 23.6% instead of 25% (average for ten observers). Here, the proportionate intensities in the less intense ring and spot pattern appeared as too light a gray to the majority of *S*s. However, where the intensity difference between ring and spot was large, the less intense pattern produced a slightly darker gray. These deviations from proportionality in most of these cases did not merely show up in the measurement; they were large enough to lead to visibly different grays when arrangements with equal ratios were presented. Nevertheless, they were small compared to the total effect which these experiments demonstrate. This can be made vivid when one transforms the difference in the absolute light intensities which stimulate the eye in a pair of matched spots into a color difference. To quote still another result, if one surrounds spots of the intensities 29.4% and 8.3% with rings 100% and 25% intensity respectively, they will produce the same grays. But if one surrounds the same spots with equal rings, say, of 60% intensity one spot will appear a light gray and the other one as a very dark gray.[1]

Experiments of this kind can be done with a less elaborate set-up. The crucial point is that it does not matter by what means the four different light intensities that are needed here are produced. For a simple demonstration it suffices to fasten a light gray sample on a white background to a wall and, not too far from it, a properly chosen dark gray sample on a medium gray background. By means of a cardboard slide with two holes, one projection lantern can be made to throw two beams of light on the wall such that one illuminates the light gray sample and an enclosing portion of its white background and the other only the dark gray sample and a part of its medium gray background. Under these conditions the intensities reaching the eye will be approximately 40% surrounded by 80% of the lantern light under one beam and 10% surrounded by 20% under the other beam. The observer will perceive the two gray samples as the same color, a light gray. As in all experiments of this kind, success depends entirely on the restricted illumination. When the projection lantern is turned off and the room is lighted, the samples and their background are seen with their true color. Light reflected by the other visible surfaces, in particular by the wall to which the samples and their backgrounds are fastened, are responsible for this.

[1]The same sort of experiments were done with a better technique at the end of the last century by Hess and Pretori. (Messende Untersuchungen über die Gesetzmässigkeit des simultanen Helligkeits-Contrastes, *Graefe's Archive für Ophthalmologie,* 1894, 40, 1–24). This work became known to me only in recent years. For more on my experiments see Brightness constancy and the nature of achromatic colors. *Journal of Experimental Psychology,* 1948, 38, 310–324.

It has roughly the same effect as surrounding spots of different intensity by rings of the same intensity.

There is still another way to do experiments which demonstrate that the value of a gray color depends largely on the ratio of the two intensities involved. One can use identical samples in each of the two arrangements, say a dark gray on a medium gray background, and use, for further differentiation in intensity, the illuminating beams. If two projectors are used and the beam on one of the arrangements is four times as intense as the beam on the other arrangement, the light which the former reflects will be of the same intensities as the lights that would be reflected by a light gray sample on a white background illuminated by the weaker beam. Again both samples will look the same, namely, light gray; the backgrounds will look luminous.

These experiments make it clear that the neutral colors that result from differential stimulation in two adjacent areas in an otherwise dark field depend largely on the proportion in which the stimulating light intensities stand. For a wide range of absolute intensities, a ratio of 2:1 of two such light intensities will cause a light gray, a ratio of 4:1 a medium gray and one of 20:1 a black. What will happen when this ratio is further enhanced?

Under ordinary circumstances the intensity of light reflected from adjacent regions of the visual field will rarely exceed a ratio of 20:1. This ratio usually occurs when an objectively white surface is adjacent to a black one. The spot and ring arrangement makes it possible to increase this ratio considerably. This can be done by fastening a black cardboard disk to the screen at the place where the spot falls. For a given illumination a black cardboard will reflect only about one-sixteenth of the amount of light which a white screen will reflect. If now an intensity ratio for ring and spot is used which when projected on an all-white screen causes the spot to appear black, the fact that the light of the spot is reflected by a black surface instead of a white one further enhances this ratio by a factor of 16. By these means a ratio of more than 200:1 can be achieved.

The color which is seen in the spot under these conditions is hard to describe because it is different from any color one has seen before. It resembles to some degree a black velvet, but what under ordinary conditions appears to be the characteristic quality of velvet occurs on the spot with a much greater pronouncedness. The color is very soft and at the same time very intense and deep.

The Temporal Course of the Interaction Process

A way to investigate the interaction process as such would be to study the temporal conditions of the emergence and disappearance of neutral colors. Unfortunately, very little has been done in this direction. When a ring of higher intensity is added to a light spot that has been visible for some time, one becomes aware of the added ring and the emergence of gray in the spot simultaneously. When, on the other hand, the ring is suddenly extinguished, the gray in the spot seems to linger on for a brief time which at the most seems to be about one half second. It seems impossible to observe the exact moment when it disappears, because one cannot see it vanish. Rather, one seems to be suddenly aware that it has disapppeared and that now the spot looks luminous again. In this respect the experience resembles one which occurs under certain circumstances when the sensation of one's own motion disappears. This can be observed when one is turned at a moderate constant speed on a smoothly revolving chair. Though blindfolded, one becomes aware that one rotates when the chair is set in motion; at that time acceleration causes vestibular stimulation. When the rotation of the chair has reached a constant rate the sensation of rotation still continues although vestibular stimulation ceased when acceleration ended. After a lapse of 5 to 15 sec., one will feel oneself at rest, though the chair goes on rotating at a constant rate. Here, too, one cannot observe the moment when felt motion stops. Rather, one is suddenly aware that it has stopped, that is, one finds oneself at rest. To be sure, the magnitude of the delay involved in the two cases is very different; the felt motion lingers on much longer than the gray in the spot. They have, however, this in common: a perceptual quality which is related to a specific condition of stimulation outlasts this stimulation.

More instructive than the disappearance of neutral color is its change from one value to another when the change is caused merely by an alteration of the intensity of stimulation in the surroundings. When the intensity of a ring which surrounds a spot of lower intensity is suddenly raised and then lowered, the darker gray color which comes in with the increase in the intensity of the ring seems to outlast very slightly the lowering of the intensity in the ring.

Retinal Rivalry of Neutral Colors

When retinal rivalry of neutral colors is explored in the light of our observations on the functional nature of neutral colors, rather striking results are obtained. It is a well-known fact that when two figures of equal form but different color are stereoscopically combined the colors will show retinal rivalry if they are strongly different from each other. This is true of neutral colors as well as of chromatic colors. Thus, a light gray and a dark gray, one presented to the left and the other to the right eye, will show retinal rivalry as will a white and a black visible on some gray background. Under ordinary conditions such differences in color go hand in hand with differences in stimulation. However, in the arrangements reported here stimulation with light of a given intensity may lead to very different experienced colors dependent on the stimulation that takes place in the surroundings. The same spot of light may thus be made to look black, gray, white, or luminous. This makes it possible to raise the question of whether rivalry depends ultimately on the difference in the perceived colors or on the difference in stimulation. Can one, for instance, prevent rivalry between a dark gray and a light gray by using equal intensity of stimulation for the two pertinent areas and by applying different intensities in their surroundings? Some typical results of such experiments will be reported.

Two ring-spot arrangements were projected on the same wall at some distance from each other and an arrangement of four mirrors, two of them directly in front of the observer's eyes enabled him to see one ring-spot arrangement with the left and the other one with the right eye. In the first experiment to be reported the two rings were of equal and rather high intensity. The spot for the left eye was of an intensity one half that of the rings and the spot for the right eye showed only one twelfth of the intensity of the rings. This made the left spot a light gray and the right spot a very dark gray. When the two arrangements were stereoscopically combined, retinal rivalry resulted. The color of the spot changed periodically from darker to lighter and back to darker. However, when both rings were eliminated so that the spots adjoined directly the dark surrounding field no rivalry was detectable. Each spot seen by itself looked luminous, the left one bright and the right one dim, and when they were stereoscopically combined the resultant spot was of intermediate brightness and completely fused. It appears that a given difference in the intensity of stimulation may lead to rivalry when it is transformed into a color difference, while it may lead to fusion when it appears as a difference in the brightness of luminous areas. It is interesting to note that rings of the same intensity were used to cause different colors to appear in the spots. Thus, the addition of the rings as such could not augment the difference in the patterns of stimulation for the two eyes. Only the change in the resultant psychological processes can be responsible for the rivalry.

In the experiment just described the areas in which rivalry could occur consisted of spots of different intensity. Whether or not rivalry did occur depended on the intensity of stimulation in the surround of the spots. A dark surround caused the spots to appear luminous and to fuse, whereas a surround of higher intensity than that of either spot caused them to differ in neutral color and to rival. Under either condition, however, the surrounds were homogeneous. In our next experiment, the spot intensities were equal and different surrounds were used to make them appear different in color. When the ring for the left eye had an intensity one and a half times as high as the intensity for the spot which it surrounded and the ring for the right eye was nine times as intense as its spot, rivalry occurred consistently. In monocular view the spot for the left eye looked light gray and the spot for the right eye, dark gray. Since the stimulation received in the two spot regions was the same, and since the surrounds appeared luminous and did not rival, the difference in the surface color process must have been responsible for the rivalry.[2]

The Relation of Neutral Color Perception to Chromatic Color

When samples of all colors that are derived from a given hue are assembled and are arranged in such a way that the most similar ones are everywhere next to each other, they will fill a plane which, in the case of the majority of hues, will be of roughly triangular shape.

[2]For more detail see Wallach and Adams, Binocular rivalry of achromatic colors. *American Journal of Psychology,* 1954, 67, 513–516.

The most desaturated samples will form a sequence so similar to the series of neutral colors that it seems adequate to include this series; it forms then one side of the triangle. The most saturated sample will be located in the tip opposite the neutral series. In this triangle, value or lightness varies parallel to the neutral series and saturation at right angles to it. When all the different hues are arranged according to their similarity, they form a closed series called the color circle. With each hue goes a triangle which accommodates all the shades and tints derived from it. All these triangles have the series of neutral colors in common. They can therefore be arranged in space around this series as a common axis. When in such an arrangement the triangles are put in the order of the color circle, a solid results within which there is a place for all colors such that all shades and tints of all hues are arranged according to similarity.

Inasmuch as the series of neutral colors is the axis of the color system, it should be obvious that the rules of interaction must play an important role in the perception of chromatic colors also. It should be expected that the value or lightness of a chromatic color depends on interaction conditions. That this is true can be easily demonstrated. When, in the dark, a spot of reddish yellow light is projected on a neutral surface surrounded by a ring of neutral light of a much higher intensity, the spot takes on the appearance of a dense brown. Similar transformations can be obtained with other chromatic lights. Surrounding a disk of a particular hue with a ring of neutral light of a higher intensity will produce a dark shade of that hue.

Modes of Appearance of Color

It has long been known that stimulation with colored light can cause a number of qualitatively different impressions. The blue of the sky looks certainly different from the color of a paper reflecting blue light of the same degree of saturation. It lacks the opaqueness and the well-defined localization of the latter; such colors have been called "expanse colors." Presumably because of this difference in mode of appearance, a particular blue of the sky cannot be matched with any sample from the color solid, while this can be done for the blue paper. All the colors which have a place in the color solid are of the same mode of appearance, which is called "surface color."

Different from both expanse color and surface color is aperture color. It appears in a small opening in a screen in which the color of a chromatic surface some distance beyond the screen is visible. It looks like a transparent colored film stretched across the aperture. Like expanse color, it lacks the opaqueness of surface color, but like the latter it is well localized, forming a thin, seemingly transparent layer which fills the aperture. In addition to these, there are, of course,the luminous colors of chromatic light sources. Traffic lights and the golden or red color of the sun at different elevations can serve as examples.

Stimulation with neutral light also gives rise to different modes of appearance. In fact, the difference between neutral color and luminosity which was described earlier is as striking as that between some modes of appearance of chromatic color. There can be no doubt that neutral color belongs with the chromatic surface colors. Like the chromatic surface colors they are opaque. Besides, there is complete continuity between the chromatic surface colors and the colors of the neutral series; the most desaturated chromatic colors are very similar to neutral colors of the same lightness. That chromatic surface colors are subject to interaction effects has already been stated.

All the other modes of appearance of chromatic color, luminous, aperture, and expanse colors, are related to luminosity. The same conditions which give rise to luminous appearance in areas of neutral color cause these modes of chromatic color. This is obvious in the case of luminous color. A strong intensity difference between the stimulation received from a light source and from the surrounding region exists in the case of neutral and of chromatic sources alike. That aperture colors, functionally speaking, also belong to the luminous colors cannot be guessed from reading the literature on this subject. Yet, simple observations make it clear that aperture conditions as such are really irrelevant and that intensity relations are essential. A good aperture color is produced when a well-illuminated, fairly homogeneous chromatic surface appears in a hole in a light screen which is kept in moderate illumination. Merely raising the illumination of the screen will transform the aperture color into a surface color. The hole will now look like a piece of colored paper pasted on the screen surface. The same observation can be made in an easy way by using the color of the blue sky as a source of colored light. When, with the sun at low elevation, one looks up at the sky through a small hole in the center of a large white cardboard, the blue of the sky visible in the hole will appear as an aperture color, that is, it will look like a bright transparent film in the plane of the cardboard. If next, one changes the orientation of the cardboard in such a way that it catches the full light of the sun, it is difficult to recognize the hole; there is now in the center of the cardboard a bluish gray patch, an opaque surface color. The emergence of a strong gray component which accompanies here the change in the mode of appearance makes the qualitative change very great. It is due to the fact that even a deep blue sky is a source of rather desaturated blue light. As long as the sky appears as an expanse color, one is not readily aware of this, but when stimulation by light from the sky is surrounded by stimulation by light of higher intensity and therefore becomes involved in an interaction process, its high content of neutral light is transformed into a gray component and becomes conspicuous. These observations leave no doubt that aperture colors correspond to the luminous appearance that appears in neutral areas of limited extent. Like such luminosity, they occur when the stimulus intensity of the area in which they are seen is greater than the intensity of the surrounding area. When this relation is reversed, chromatic surface color will be perceived.

That expanse color must also be classified as a luminous color is easy to show. Expanse color is perceived in an extended region of uniform stimulation. The very absence of intensity differences in such a region will restrict interaction processes to its border and for the rest, only luminosity will be seen.

It seems likely that the shape of the upper part of the color solid, where the light colors (tints) are located, is related to the mode of appearance of color. This shape, of course, reflects the fact that light tints are always rather desaturated, and the more so the lighter they are. But if it is true that the lightness or value of chromatic colors depends on the interaction conditions, what happens to a highly saturated color when it is subject to interaction conditions that would transform a less saturated sample of the same hue into a light tint? The answer is that it would become a luminous color. The upper conical surface of the color solid simply represents the border between surface color and luminous color where the underlying interaction functions are concerned.

The partially conical shape of the lower surface of the solid requires, of course, a different explanation. It reflects the fact that, for most hues, saturated dark shades do not exist. An exception are the yellow-orange hues whose dark shades, the browns, can appear highly saturated. As mentioned earlier such colors can be produced by surrounding spots reflecting highly saturated light of yellow-orange hue with rings of neutral light of higher intensity. If, on the other hand, saturated spots of the other hues are being surrounded by rings of higher intensity, the chromatic spots do not only get darker but also lose saturation. Why this should be so is not clear, and the partial conical shape of the lower part of the color solid remains unexplained.

Constancy of Neutral Color

Our discussion of neutral colors took its start from the conditions of stimulation which appear to be essential to bring about the experience of these colors. In most of the observations and experiments reported, the objective arrangements that caused the patterns of stimulation were quite artificial and very different from the objective conditions under which neutral colors are normally perceived. There is nothing wrong with this. In visual perception the psychologist's main task is to understand the relation between the pattern of stimulation and the resultant perceptual experiences. What the perceptual processes achieve in enabling us to deal with our physical environment is, comparatively, a secondary question. However, not under all circumstances is concern with the physical objects which cause the pattern of stimulation of secondary importance. Early in the investigation of a perceptual problem, the nature of the stimulation that corresponds to a particular experienced property may not yet be known and, under these circumstances, the interest in the relation between a perceptual experience and the features in the physical environment to which it pertains is of a very different sort. With the pertinent stimulation conditions as yet unknown it may indeed be necessary to begin with an investigation of the relation between the perceptual experience and the objects in the physical environment to which it refers. This happened in the case of neutral color. In psychology they pose a problem that was for many decades discussed under the name of brightness constancy.

In the final analysis, the problem of brightness constancy is centered about the fact with which we began our discussion of neutral color. It is the fact that there is no fixed relation between the intensity of stimulation on the one hand and the neutral color which this stimulation evokes on the other hand. This fact emerges strikingly when one considers the properties of the surfaces of physical objects that correspond to the neutral colors of the perceived objects. These properties consist in the capacity of a surface to reflect a fixed fraction of the light that illuminates the surface. Thus, a surface that is normally seen as white reflects about 80% of the light that falls on it, a surface that looks medium gray reflects 20% and one that looks black about 4%. The condition of the surface that varies here is called reflectance. Except for extraordinary conditions which are seldom encountered, a surface whose reflectance is 80% will always look white and one of 20% reflectance approximately medium gray, etc., and for that reason we do not hesitate to call a physical surface white or gray or black, that is, to regard these qualities as properties of the objects around us. This correspondence between reflectance and perceived color prevails in spite of the fact that the intensity of illumination in which a surface of given reflectance is seen may vary widely from one occasion to another. Reflectance being what it is, a change in the intensity of illumination will cause a proportionate change in the intensity of the light that the surface reflects and that causes the stimulation in the eye on which the perceived color of the surface depends. Were there a fixed relation between the intensity of the reflected light that ultimately stimulates the eye and the perceived color, a surface of given reflectance would sometimes look gray, sometimes white, and sometimes black dependent on the variations in the intensity of the illuminating light. The fact that this is not so but rather that perceived color corresponds to the reflectance of the object surface is referred to by the term brightness constancy. A number of problems in perception have been dealt with under the name of "constancy"; besides brightness constancy, size constancy and shape constancy have been widely discussed. In an abstract way these problems are all similar and have therefore evoked similar attempts to solve them. The term constancy refers to a situation where a perceived quality or property is in better correspondence with a property of the physical object than with the stimulus variable by which the physical property is represented. Size constancy, for instance, refers to the relation between the perceived size of an object and its physical size. The size of the image on the retina may vary widely, because it depends also on the distance from the observer at which the object is given. However, the perceived size is highly independent of these variations of the retinal image and corresponds closely to the objective size. Thus, the notion of a perceptual constancy is a rather complex one. It involves, first, the relation between a perceived property and the property of the physical object which corresponds to it, second, the relation between that perceived property and the pertinent stimulus variable, and, finally, a comparison of these two relations. If in the first relation a better agreement prevails than in the second, we speak of perceptual constancy.

In each perceptual constancy an extraneous factor operates which has an influence on the stimulus variable. In the case of size constancy, for instance, not only the size of the object but also the distance between the object and the observer determines retinal size and thereby contaminates the size of the retinal image as a representation of the size of the object. It is for this reason that the task to explain a constancy has been regarded as equivalent to explaining how the influence of the particular contaminating factor is compensated for. This has been essentially the approach to size constancy, although the terminology used often differs from mine. Evidence that a compensating process operates in shape constancy, too, is presented below in Chapter VII, selection 2.

In the case of brightness constancy illumination is the contaminating factor. If our environment were so constructed that illumination were always and everywhere the same, the light reflected by the surface of an object and thus the intensity of the stimulation received in the retinal image of the object would unequivocally represent the reflectance of that surface. But illumination varies widely, and since a particular reflectance causes a particular *proportion* of the illuminating light to be reflected, the intensity of the reflected light per se is a rather poor indicator for the reflectance of the object. Yet, the intensity of the reflected light is the only message from the object which the eye receives. No wonder then that from Helmholtz down, the problem of brightness constancy has been understood as the problem of how the intensity of illumination is taken into account in the perception of neutral color.

No specific problem in perception has given rise to more experimental research than this one. Of the many experiments demonstrating brightness constancy, one by David Katz best represents this effect as it occurs under ordinary circumstances. In this experiment two identical gray samples are placed in different illuminations; one in direct illumination of a light source and the other in shadow where it receives only the light reflected by walls and ceiling. The samples are presented on a uniform background of different color; a white background is preferable. Under these circumstances the sample in the shadow appears as a somewhat darker gray than the sample in full illumination. However—and this is the important fact —the gray is not as dark as it would have to be if the difference in color corresponded to the difference in illumination. If, for instance, the full illumination is four times as strong as the light that is received by the shadowed sample, the latter should look dark gray when the sample in full illumination looks light gray, and this just does not happen. The two grays will look much less different and, to the degree to which this is the case, constancy is said to prevail in the situation. If they looked altogether the same, constancy would be called complete. However, for reasons which will become clear later, under conditions of Katz's experiment constancy is never complete.

Katz's arrangement can be used to pin down by measurement the degree of constancy which it yields. This is done by replacing, say, the shadowed gray sample which appears to be darker by a lighter one whose apparent color will match the color of the sample in full illumination; the result of this procedure is called "constancy equation." When this is achieved the shadowed sample will still reflect light of a lower intensity than the one in full illumination. Since now they are perceived as the same color, the difference in the light intensity that they reflect is completely compensated by the constancy effect and therefore can be said to measure it. The actual determination of the two light intensities is, of course, a physical measurement and is best done with a photometric device. However, an alternative procedure used by Katz can also be employed: A screen which is uniformly illuminated is placed between the observer and the samples. Two small holes are cut in the screen in such locations that through each the observer can see a part of the surface of one of the samples but not its edge. When so viewed, the shadowed sample looks very dark and it must be replaced by another one of still higher reflectance so that the two colors match again. The new differences in the reflectance (called "reduction equation" by Katz) in comparison with the match attained by the "constancy equation" also measures the constancy effect.

The screen with the two holes, called a reduction screen, supposedly has the desired effect, because it prevents the observer from appreciating the different illuminations in which the two samples are visible. With the arrangement in full view the observer can see the shadow on one of the samples and this presumably enables him, or rather his perceptual processes, to take this special condition of illumination into account and to correct for it to some degree. When the samples are viewed through the reduction screen, the perceived colors are supposed to depend only on the light that the samples reflect without any correction entering in.

Another impressive experiment in the area of brightness constancy was first described by Gelb. An instructive demonstration can be based on it. In a dimly lighted room, a dark sample, black or dark gray, is suspended by a pair of wires a good distance in front of a light colored wall. A narrow beam of light from a projection lantern illuminates the samples in such a way that it does not strike any other surface visible to the observer. This can be achieved by arranging the light beam obliquely to the surface of the sample so that the part of the beam not intercepted by the sample produces a light spot on the wall far to the side of the sample, where it can easily be hidden from the observer by a screen. By making the light from the lantern intense enough, the sample can be made to look white and its color reverts to dark when the lantern is turned off. This is a vivid demonstration of the gross changes in color that may occur when illumination is changed under conditions which do not allow constancy to operate, presumably because the illumination provided by the lantern beam cannot be recognized as such. When a slip of white paper is held up in front of the sample so that it is also illuminated by the lantern beam, the color of the sample becomes much darker. Presumably, the white paper, now brilliantly luminous in appearance, makes the special illumination of the sample visible and causes constancy to be, at least, partially restored. A more satisfactory way of restoring constancy consists in holding up a white screen in back of the dark sample and letting it intercept the part of the beam which previously had reached the wall. Now the dark sample is surrounded by white in equally bright illumination and that makes the sample appear more pronouncedly dark than when the slip of white paper is used. Of this, more will be said later.

This arrangement lends itself to further instructive variations. One may say that under constancy conditions a change in illumination will *not* lead to a change in the perceived color, whereas in the absence of constancy it will. There is no constancy when the dark sample alone is presented under special illumination. Therefore, when this illumination, for which no constancy effect compensates, is altered, the color of the dark sample should change and that is indeed the case. By lowering the intensity of the lantern beam, e.g., with neutral density filters, one can change the color of the sample through the whole range from white to its true dark color, as the intensity of the beam is changed from the high value needed to make the sample white all the way down to zero. If, on the other hand, a white background for the sample is visible in the light of the beam, the same changes in the intensity of the beam have almost no effect on the perceived color of the sample; it remains dark throughout. Supposedly, a change in the intensity of the beam is now seen only as a change in the perceived illumination. In the juxtaposition of white and a dark color, the latter becomes immune to changes in illumination and remains constant.

An interesting question arises in connection with the first part of this demonstration when the sample alone is visible in the light of the beam: How is the particular color determined which results from a certain intensity of the beam? It can be shown that this color depends a good deal on the general illumination of the room. When for a certain intensity of the lantern beam the sample looks, for instance, light gray, raising the general illumination of the room will change this color to medium or even dark gray. This occurs in spite of the fact that with a higher general illumination the sample, too, receives more light and consequently reflects more. However, in relation to the light reflected from the other surfaces in the room, particularly from the wall against which the sample is seen, the light reflected by the sample has become less intense. Thus, it appears that the light which the sample in special illumination reflects is evaluated in terms of the general illumination of the room.

All these observations can be understood in terms of the traditional conception, that brightness constancy results from taking illumination into account and correcting for the influence which it has on the light that a surface reflects. However, this kind of explanation has its limitations. In the experiment under discussion, a black sample looks black, when it is given a white background that is also illuminated by the bright light of the beam. The white background which looks very bright presumably makes the special illumination visible, which, in turn, causes the constancy effect. However, when a medium gray background is used instead of the white one, the background may again look white provided the beam is made bright enough; the sample, however, will now look gray instead of black. Constancy seems to take place only in part. What is remarkable here is that these colors do not change when the intensity of the lantern beam is lowered to a certain limit. Just as in the case of the combination of white and black, the combination of objective gray and black is immune to changes in illumination, but the perceived colors that remain constant here in spite of changes in illumination are not the right ones; they are white and gray instead of the gray and black objectively given.

There is a basic difficulty with the constancy explanation which assumes that registering the given illumination plays a central role: the illumination is actually never directly given. It is true that in many instances we have an experience of illumination. But this experience raises as much of a problem as does the perception of color. There is only one stimulus variable for both the perceived color and the perceived illumination, namely, the intensity of the light that each surface in the given field reflects. As we have seen, this intensity is the product of both the reflectance of the surface and the intensity of the illumination. If the seen illumination were found to be in agreement with the objective illumination, in principle the same problem would arise which we face regarding the perceived colors. In order to account for the agreement between color and reflectance, we must assume that the illumination is somehow known and in order to account for an agreement between the perceived illumination and the objective illumination we must assume that the reflectance of at least one of the surfaces on which that illumination is supposedly visible is known. But there was, for a long time, no study that raised the issue whether perceived illumination is in agreement with the objective illumination.

A quite different approach to the problem of brightness constancy becomes possible on the basis of our considerations of the nature of neutral color. There we had come to the conclusion that a neutral color is seen when at least two different intensities of light stimulate the retina in neighboring areas, and that the value of the gray seen under these conditions depends mainly on the ratio in which these two intensities stand to each other. If, in the case of two areas of different stimulus intensities, the perceived colors depend on a relation between these intensities rather than on their absolute values, it seems difficult to accept the traditional explanation of constancy that implies a dependence of the seen color on a single stimulus intensity, though one corrected for illumination. There is even a strong resemblance between Katz's demonstration of constancy and the experiments reported earlier in which a dependence of colors on the ratio between two stimulating light intensities was demonstrated. This resemblance becomes apparent when, in Katz's experiment, one considers only the intensities of light that issue from the display. Let us, for the sake of having a specific example, assume that the illumination of the shaded portion of the set-up is one-fourth that of the direct illumination, and that identical light gray samples of 40% reflectance on a white background are used. It is now easy to compute the relative values of the light intensities which these surfaces reflect. Assigning the value of 100 units to the light intensity of the full illumination, we find that the gray sample in full illumination reflects 40 units and its white background 80 units, whereas the sample and its white background in the shaded portion, where illumination is only one-fourth of full strength, reflect light of 10 and 20 units respectively. If these two pairs of stimulating intensities were the only ones given in an otherwise dark field and were a good distance apart, the pattern of stimulation would be essentially the same as one caused by two ring and spot arrangements that produce light grays. With that set-up, when one ring is given the intensity of 80 units and the spot inside it the intensity of 40 units, a ring of 20 units intensity had to be combined with a spot of approximately 10 units to produce the same gray. Hence, the two gray samples in the modified Katz demonstration could be expected to look alike, in other words, nearly complete constancy would result.

Quite generally, when a pair of different reflectances, one surrounding the other, is homogeneously illuminated, the surrounded one should be seen as the same color when the strength of the illumination is varied within wide limits. This is due to the fact that reflectance is defined as the proportion of the illuminating light that is reflected. Hence a pair of reflectances will always emit two light intensities that stand in the same proportion to each other, no matter what the intensity of the illumination. Nearly complete constancy should result, as complete as the results of interaction processes conform to the proportionality rule. Then, why is constancy incomplete in Katz's experiment? This is because in Katz's experiment the shaded portion of the display is not spatially separated from the part that is in full illumination. This brings the interaction process caused by the lights reflected by the shaded gray sample and by its surround, the shaded white, under the added influence of the process representing the white background in full illumination. That such a remote influence would indeed make that gray darker can readily be demonstrated with ring and spot arrangements. When the intensities in one ring and spot pattern are 100 units and 50 units and in the other pattern 50 units and 25 units, the same light grays will appear in the two spots. But if now the ring of 50 units intensity is surrounded in turn by another ring of 100 units intensity, the spot of 25 units intensity will show a considerably darker color. This new gray will not be quite as dark as one which is seen in a spot of an intensity of 25 units which is directly surrounded by a ring of 100 units intensity, but it will be decidedly different from the light gray in the 100 and 50 unit arrangement. Thus, there are no major obstacles against understanding the outcome of Katz's experiment on the basis of the characteristics of the interaction process on which the perception of neutral colors is based.

The same is true of the observations with Gelb's arrangement that were reported. Let us first take up the case of a dark sample visible against the background of a white wall in a dimly lighted room; it can be made to appear white or gray by putting it under special illumination. The color of the sample will depend here on the relation between the intensity of light that it reflects under the special high illumination, and the intensity of the light the wall reflects, which is only under the dim general illumination. If, for instance, the special illumination which is provided by the lantern is seven times as high as the general illumination, the sample will receive eight times as high a total illumination as the white wall which, in the observer's visual field, surrounds it. If we assume that the sample has a reflectance of 5% and the wall a reflectance of 80%, the intensity of the light which the sample actually reflects will be one half of the intensity reflected by the wall, since the sample receives eight times as much light as the wall. Therefore, the sample will look light gray. A change in the intensity of the special illumination will, of course, change the intensity of the light that the sample reflects and alter the proportion between that intensity and the intensity of the light reflected by the wall which remained unaffected by that illumination change.

When "constancy is restored" by giving the sample a white background that intercepts the beam of the special illumination, the sample will look very dark because it reflects one sixteenth of the intensity of the light which the white background reflects. This proportion between the intensity reflected by the sample and the intensity reflected by its immediate surroundings remains unaltered when the intensity of the special illumination is changed; the white will still reflect 80% and the sample 5% of the altered illumination, leaving the ratio of the reflected intensities one sixteenth. This explains why, in the juxtaposition of white and black, the colors are immune to changes in illumination. This is not only so for white and a near black but must be true also for a combination of white and gray. As long as both stand in the same illumination, the ratio between the two intensities that they reflect remains constant as that illumination varies, and, inasmuch as the perceived color of the area of lower intensity depends mainly on that ratio, that color remains constant.

This makes it clear in what way the proportionality rule predicts complete constancy. A combination of any gray or black surface with a white surface can be taken from one illumination into another without an effect on the perceived colors, because a change in illumination does not alter the proportion of the two light intensities that are reflected. It is, however, necessary that one of the surfaces is white. When this is not the case, peculiar results are obtained. An example is the modification of Gelb's experiment already reported where a black sample and its medium gray background are both visible in the special illumination of the lantern beam. It will be remembered that here the black looks gray. Yet, within a certain limit, the perceived color remains constant without being correct. These facts, however, follow directly from the proportionality rule. The color of the sample will remain constant, again because the proportion between the intensities that the sample and its background reflect remains constant. It will be medium gray because this proportion is four to one, since the background has a reflectance four times as high as the sample (20% and 5% respectively).

I believe that all facts of brightness constancy can be explained in a similar manner, that is, on the basis of the proportionality rule and perhaps of further characteristics of the interaction process that causes the perception of neutral colors. To be sure, accurate prediction of color values is not yet possible in the case of complex constancy situations, because so little is known about interaction of three or more stimulus intensities. But to know that the proportionality rule predicts complete constancy and to realize why in practical situations as exemplified by Katz's experiment constancy must remain incomplete, goes a long way toward understanding brightness constancy. This approach assumes that the perceived neutral colors depend directly on the patterns of stimulation, that is, the stimulus intensities and their spatial arrangements which affect the interaction among the nervous processes caused by them. They are not supposed to be influenced by recognized illumination, awareness of transparency, and the like.

Brightness Contrast

It is a consequence of this approach that there is no essential difference between brightness constancy and brightness contrast. In the past, contrast and constancy were sharply distinguished. Contrast was regarded as the outcome of some sort of interaction process, but constancy was assumed to be of an entirely different nature. Now we propose that both are to be understood as the result of the rules of the interaction process that produces neutral colors.

The chart used to demonstrate contrast consists usually of a half black, half white surface with a small medium gray sample fixed to the center of each half. The gray on the white background will then look somewhat darker than the gray on the black background. This effect can be measured by replacing the gray sample on the white background with a lighter one that matches the sample on the black background. In order to interpret the contrast effect with the help of the proportionality rule, we first simplify the situation by reducing the number of different light intensities that can influence the appearance of each gray. This is done by cutting the chart in half and by placing the black half and the white half a good distance apart in a darkened room, illuminating each half individually with a lantern beam. Under these conditions, the gray sample on the white half will be seen as a medium gray because that light that it reflects has an intensity of one-fourth of that of the light that the white background reflects. The latter will appear luminous, because the area of lower intensity, the gray sample, is too small to exert a noticeable influence in the surrounding high-intensity region. On the black half, the gray sample will appear white, because it reflects a higher light intensity than the surrounding black background. The latter will look luminous gray. It will appear gray because it reflects one fifth of the light intensity that the gray sample reflects, and it will be luminous because of the smallness of the area of higher intensity, namely of the sample, that causes the surface color process in the area of the black background.

When now the two halves are put back together but are still kept in restricted illumination, not much change occurs in the white half. But the black half is strongly affected, for it comes under the influence of the high intensity of light which the now adjacent white background reflects. As a consequence, the black background becomes very dark while still looking a bit luminous. The gray sample changes from white to gray; its color also is influenced by the area of high intensity which is now adjacent to the black, though not quite as much as if it were in direct contact with it, as is the gray in the white half of the chart. It is this difference in the degree of influence that the white part of the chart exerts on the two gray samples which is the reason for the contrast effect. This can be demonstrated by varying the size of the black background. The larger its size, the greater will be the separation of the gray sample in its center from the area of high intensity, namely, the white background area, and the lighter will the gray look. No corresponding effect is obtained for the gray on white when the size of the white background is varied.

If now the restricted illumination is replaced by a general illumination of the room, further changes occur. The most conspicuous is that the luminosity of the white and the black backgrounds disappear, because they are now surrounded by other lighted surfaces which provide enough interaction to involve in surface color processes all the processes that represent the intensity of stimulation in these areas. In addition, the difference between the gray samples may be further diminished, because further areas of higher intensity may come into existence in the surroundings of the black background.

The Perception of Illumination

We have already made it clear that the perception of illumination is not relevant to the issue of constancy. However, illumination, too, is sometimes perceived and this fact must now be explained. It will be recalled that the perception of illumination involves the same problem as the perception of neutral color. There is only one stimulus variable representing both: Unless the reflectance is known the illumination in which it is visible remains undefined, while in order to know the reflectance the illumination must be given. Under these circumstances it is questionable whether the strength of illumination on a homogeneous surface can be accurately perceived.[3] In the following, I am concerned only with the qualitative aspects of perceived illumination.

I believe that the quality of luminosity which arises under certain interaction conditions is the basis for the experience of illumination. There are two conditions under which luminosity occurs: (1) The area of highest intensity in a sizeable region of the visual field will look either white or luminous or both, dependent on the difference in the light intensity received from it and from the surrounding areas: the larger the difference, the stronger the

[3]Correct perception of illumination on patterned surfaces was obtained by J. Beck (*Journal of Experimental Psychology,* 1959, 58, 267–274 and *Journal of Experimental Psychology,* 1961, 61, 368–375). Whether gradients of intensity that typically occur at the borders between regions of different illumination function as cues in perceiving strength of illumination is not known.

luminosity. (2) Other areas will look luminous when conditions exist which interfere with interaction and therefore diminish the influence of surrounding light intensities. Where perception of illumination occurs, one of these conditions should exist.

To be sure, not under all circumstances will luminosity give the impression of illumination. A strongly luminous area of limited size and with a sharp outline will look like a source of light; a spot of light projected on a wall in a dark room is an example. A luminous gray as it can be produced in the ring-spot arrangements rather looks translucent; light from behind seems to shine through it. Larger luminous areas, however, usually look as if light fell on a surface, particularly when they show a brightness gradient. As I see it, these differences are not caused by specific interaction conditions. Luminosity is the common factor in all of these different impressions, and only *it* is the product of a primary perceptual process. The different impressions to which it gives rise are caused, I believe, by effects of past experience, and this applies also to perceived illumination. But since luminosity is the basis for all of these impressions, it should be possible to show that conditions under which the impression of an illumination arises are also conditions under which luminosity is produced.

The most important among the conditions that cause luminosity by interfering with interaction are intensity gradients and large area size. Intensity gradients ordinarily occur in accordance with the penumbra principle: the edge of a shadow cast by a distant object, with the source of illumination extended rather than a point, will be a gradient of intensity. The lack of opaqueness of a shadow was recognized long ago and so was its cause, the penumbra. Functionally speaking, a shadow is a region of lower intensity in which little surface color develops and the luminous process dominates. In this connection, a weak shadow is most instructive. It can be produced by illuminating a surface with two equal light sources from different directions and by putting a shadow-casting object in the path of one of them. The ratio of the light intensity in the shadow to that in its surround is then 2:1 and, without the penumbra, would produce a light gray. But no gray is seen; the shadow looks merely diffusely dark.

The brighter of two areas of not too different intensities that are separated by a gradient instead of a sharp outline will also be luminous (instead of white), and this may cause one to see light falling on a surface. Whether this will actually happen or whether the darker area will be seen as a shadow will depend on the spatial arrangement. When the less intense area is surrounded by the more intense area a shadow will be seen, and when the spatial relations are reversed, the surrounded brighter area will be seen as a spot of light. The rules pertaining to Figure and Ground are here in operation: the penumbra is seen to belong to the surrounded area. When, for this reason, it is part of the darker area, a shadow is perceived, and when it belongs to the brighter area, a spot of light is seen. This belonging of the penumbra to one of the two areas that it separates and not to the other is a revealing example of the Figure and Ground phenomenon.

The kinetic depth effect

The problem of how three-dimensional form is perceived in spite of the fact that pertinent stimulation consists only of two-dimensional retinal images has been only partly solved. Much is known about the impressive effectiveness of binocular disparity. However, the excellent perception of three-dimensional form in monocular vision has remained essentially unexplained.

It has been proposed that some patterns of stimulation on the retina give rise to three-dimensional experiences, because visual processes differ in the spontaneous organization that results from certain properties of the retinal pattern. Rules of organization are supposed to exist according to which most retinal projections of three-dimensional forms happen to produce three-dimensional percepts and most retinal images of flat forms lead to flat forms in experience also. This view has been held mainly by gestalt psychologists.

Another approach to this problem maintains that the projected stimulus patterns are interpreted on the basis of previous experi-

Written in collaboration with D. N. O'Connell. Reprinted from *Journal of Experimental Psychology,* 1953, 45, No. 4, 205–217.

ence, either visual or kinesthetic. However, such empiricistic assumptions do not explain much, unless it is made clear how those previous experiences come about whose influence is supposed to account for the current perception. Kinesthetic form perception itself presents far more complex problems than does three-dimensionality in vision, and recourse to kinesthesis appears at present quite futile. Retinal disparity can of course account for that previous visual experience insofar as Ss with binocular vision are concerned. Whether in the absence of binocular vision, e.g., in congenitally monocular Ss, head movement parallax can fully play the role of binocular parallax appears doubtful. It seems that all we have left to account for an original experience of three-dimensional form in monocular Ss is the assumption that certain patterns of retinal stimulation will naturally produce experience of solid form. However, once it is assumed that perception of three-dimensional form can follow directly from retinal stimulation because of spontaneous organization of visual processes alone, there is no point in postulating an influence of past experience.

Unfortunately it appears that no one has succeeded in formulating rules of spontaneous organization adequate to predict which pattern of retinal stimulation will lead to perceived flat figures and which one will produce three-dimensional forms. We have made a vain attempt of our own and have become convinced that the three-dimensional forms perceived in perspective drawings, photographs, etc. are indeed in a matter of previous experience.[1] In this situation the search for a visual process which can account for an original perception of three-dimensional form in monocular vision becomes imperative. Such a process will be described in this paper.

When one moves about, the retinal image of solid objects lying to the side of one's path not only expands but also distorts, because the objects are seen successively from different directions. More specifically, a retinal image distorts under these conditions as if the corresponding object were rotated through a certain angle in front of the eye of a stationary observer.

This fact suggests a simple technique for the investigation of the perceptual results of these distortions. An object is placed between

[1]Evidence supporting this point of view will be reported in Chapter VIII, selection 2.

a punctiform light source and a translucent screen and is rotated or turned back and forth. Its shadow is observed from the other side of the screen. The shadow-casting object is placed as close to the screen as possible, whereas the distance between the light source and object is made large. Owing to this arrangement isometric projection is closely approximated. The shadows of a great number of three-dimensional forms, solid or wire-edged, will be perceived as three-dimensional under these circumstances. The shadows of some forms will look three-dimensional *only* in such a moving presentation; that is, in none of the positions through which such a form passes during rotation will it cast a stationary shadow which looks three-dimensional. With such forms one can study this effect in isolation. It will be referred to by the term "kinetic depth effect." It is important because it answers our problem: It appears that the kinetic depth effect can cause a genuine perception of three-dimensional form in a monocular *S* whenever he moves and keeps looking at an object which does not lie directly in his path.

Similar set-ups have been used before by Miles (3) and Metzger (2). Miles presented to *S*s the shadow of a two-bladed fan wheel in rotation, the shaft of which was parallel to the screen on which the shadow was formed. His *S*s reported a large number of different motion patterns, most of them involving depth, but no attempt was made to find out whether the object that was seen in motion was a good representation of the fan wheel whose shadow was presented. Metzger also was not primarily concerned with the perception of three-dimensional form which such a set-up can yield. In fact, he investigated with great thoroughness the effects of a very special kind of arrangement which is not favorable to the emergence of stable three-dimensional forms. He had arrangements of vertical rods rotate about a vertical axis and showed their shadows in a low oblong aperture which hid the ends of the rod shadows from view. As in Miles's experiment the motion patterns seen by a given *S* during an extended period of inspection were very changeable. Moreover, naive *S*s mostly differ among each other as to whether the first movement process which they perceive is in three dimensions or takes place in a plane. Suggestion has a strong influence, in the course of longer observation as well as initially. We shall see below that the patterns of line shadows which Metzger presented to his *S*s do not contain the condition essential for the kinetic depth effect.

The depth observed in Lissajous figures (1, 4) is the result of complex effects and will be discussed in later paper.

Experiments to Define Conditions of Kinetic Depth Perception

EXPERIMENT 1: ROTATION OF SOLIDS

One of the figures which we presented to many Ss was a solid block in the shape of a roof with sloping gables, as shown in Figure 1A. This was rotated continually about its longest axis. Figures 1B and 1C show two of the forms of the shadow during rotation. When any one of the three figures is shown stationary to a naive S, it is described as a two-dimensional figure. When the solid is slowly rotated so that the shadow undergoes continuous deformation, S sees a three-dimensional solid in rotation. The direction of the seen rotation may or may not coincide with that of the object behind the screen, and this is in agreement with the conditions of stimulation which give no clue of the object's real direction of rotation. Which one of the two directions of rotation is seen seems entirely a matter of chance, and with prolonged observation S usually experiences a number of spontaneous reversals of the direction of rotation. Occasionally an S sees for long periods reversals after each rotation of 180°.

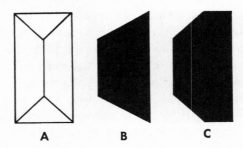

A   **B**   **C**

Fig. 1. Solid form (A) used in Exp. 1, and two samples (B, C) of its shadows

In experiments like this the impression of three-dimensional form is so natural that many *S*s who are not psychologists are not astonished by their observations. They correctly assume that behind the screen is just such an object as they see. Only after reversals of the direction of rotation have occurred to they begin to wonder.

Where the kinetic depth effect takes place, a rigid three-dimensional form in rotation is seen instead of the distorted two-dimensional figure given on the shadow screen. The distorting two-dimensional shape may occasionally be *seen* after prolonged exposure of the same kinetic presentation, or when one looks from a sharply oblique direction at the screen. The *S*'s experience of a continuously flowing form seems to him abnormal or unusual, although this is exactly what is given on the retina.

The essential difference between this two-dimensional experience and the three-dimensional form which is usually seen seems to be that the latter is unchanging and rigid instead of ever changing and flowing. The changes in the shape of the retinal image are accounted for by a perceived rotation of the three-dimensional object, whereas in the two-dimensional process the seen movement distorts the form itself. As far as we can see, the distortions of the perceived two-dimensional form agree closely with the changes of the retinal image. But the perceived three-dimensional form is not determined merely by what is presented on the retina at a given moment. A single one of the projections of the shadow-casting object which make up the changing shapes of the shadow does not look three-dimensional. Only the sequence of changing shapes gives rise to the seen three-dimensional form. In other words, a single projection causes a three-dimensional form to be seen only because it was preceded by a number of other projections. By itself, it simply does not convey enough data about the three-dimensional form which it represents. The seen three-dimensional form is richer in structure than any single projection and it is built up in a temporally extended process. The individual retinal image determines only which aspect of the turning three-dimensional form appears to be given at the moment. Thus, perceptual experience far surpasses what one should expect of a process determined by momentary stimulation and seems to a higher degree a product of the immediate past than of stimulation occurring at a given moment.

EXPERIMENT 2: PARTIAL ROTATION OF WIRE FIGURES

Experiments of the kind just reported differ in two ways from the realistic situations in which the kinetic depth effect occurs. In the first place, a shadow-casting object is put through a complete rotation and produces a pattern of distortion on the screen which corresponds to that obtained when under natural viewing conditions an *S* moves completely around an object, which is hardly ever done. In the second place, in the shadow of a solid object an edge of the three-dimensional form is visible only for a comparatively short period, namely as long as it forms a contour of the shadow, whereas in the realistic situation it usually can also be seen when it passes across the front of the figure. We therefore performed quantitative experiments with wire figures which of course show all edges continuously, and had them turn back and forth through an angle of only 42°.

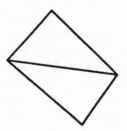

Fig. 2. The wire "parallelogram" used in Exp. 2

Figures 2 and 3 each show projections of two of the wire figures used. The figure represented in Figure 2 can best be described as a parallelogram containing one diagonal, which was bent along this diagonal so that the planes of the upper and the lower half formed an angle of 110° with each other. The other figure (Figure 3A) consisted of a piece of wire twice bent to form part of what might be described as a triangular helix. Figure 3B shows a view from the top. These figures were turned back and forth through an angle of 42° at a rate of one cycle per 1.5 sec. and their deforming shadows were shown to individual *S*s one at a time for as many periods of 10 sec.

as were necessary to obtain a clear report. After each 10-sec. exposure, *S* was asked for a report.

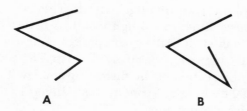

A   **B**

Fig. 3. The wire "helix" used in Exp. 2 (A) and its appearance from the top (B)

In the case of the parallelogram (Figure 2) all of 50 *S*s sooner or later during the exposure periods reported seeing a three-dimensional figure turning back and forth apparently very much like the wire figure behind the screen, except that it sometimes appeared to *S* in its inverted form. In the case of the "helix" 48 of the same 50 *S*s reported a three-dimensional form like the wire figure and 2 *S*s saw a flat zigzag line which distorted before their eyes, a process which corresponds to the changing pattern of stimulation. Evidence that the three-dimensional forms which were perceived were due to the kinetic depth effect and that none of the projections represented in the deforming shadow by itself would have been seen as three-dimensional was obtained in the following way. To a new group of 22 *S*s five such projections of each figure were presented individually in random order. They were the projections of the two extreme positions at which the figures stopped and started to turn the other way and of three intervening positions chosen to be at about 10° of rotation apart. None of these stationary projections looked three-dimensional to any one of the 22 *S*s. Positions intermediate between the ones presented resembled them so closely that it seems impossible that they would lead to a radically different perceived form.

Often the turning wire figures were seen three-dimensionally immediately upon presentation. Of 16 *S*s for whom time records were taken 11 reported the "parallelogram" in the correct three-dimensional shape after the first 10-sec. exposure period. In the case of the "helix" only 4 of 16 *S*s reported its shape correctly after the first exposure. The reason for this difference is yet to be investigated.

Once it has occurred, the three-dimensional impression is so strong that one cannot voluntarily see the two-dimensional figure which is given on the screen. It has been mentioned that the perceived three-dimensional figure may resemble the inverted form of the wire figure rather than that figure itself. This is to be expected, inasmuch as a three-dimensional figure and its inverted form have identical projections, such that a given projection is always a representation of both, a figure and its inverted form. The added fact that with prolonged observation of the distorting shadow the perceived three-dimensional figure may spontaneously invert in Necker cube-like fashion is also a consequence.

EXPERIMENT 3: ROTATION OF A TRUNCATED CYLINDER

A systematic investigation of the kinetic depth effect resulting from rotation of a solid was attempted in the following manner.

A cylinder which is rotated about its axis casts a shadow which does not change in any way, but any cut that is taken off the cylinder and which is not at right angles to its axis produces a characteristic deformation of its shadow. A large number of wooden cylinders, about as high as wide, were made and cuts were varied systematically. The solid forms which were produced in this fashion were shown in complete rotation to Ss who had no previous experience with our studies.

The results can be summarized in the following way: (a) Shadows whose only deformation consists in an expansion and contraction in one dimension will look flat; a dark figure is seen which periodically becomes wider and narrower. An example is the shadow of a rectangular block which is rotated about an axis parallel to a set of edges. (b) Shadows which display contour lines that change their direction and their length will appear as turning solid forms. The roof-shaped figure described above (Exp. 1) is an example; the shadow contour produced by an edge of a gable tilts and changes its length simultaneously (compare Figures 1B and 1C). (c) Curved contours which are deformed without displaying a form feature which identifies a specific point along the curve are seen as distorting, often even if for some reason the shadow is seen as a three-dimensional form. This peculiarity is in disagreement with our description of the kinetic depth effect and has delayed our work for years. It is now clear that the perceived distortions of deforming curved contours are not related to the kinetic depth effect at all. They will be dealt with in a later paper.[2]

EXPERIMENT 4: ROTATION OF STRAIGHT RODS

When it became clearly recognized that shadows which display contour lines that change their direction and length will appear as turning solid forms, we checked whether this would also apply to single lines. Will a detached line which changes its direction on the screen and its length at the same time display a kinetic depth effect, i.e., will it appear to tilt into depth in such a way as to account for its shortening? The following experiments show that this is the case.

When a rod is fastened to the end of a vertical shaft at an angle of, say, 45° and is rotated about this shaft, the shadow which it produces tips from side to side. From a tilt of 45° toward the left, the shadow rights itself and goes through the vertical into a tilt of 45° toward the right and back through the same positions. At the same time it shortens and lengthens periodically. Its end points move on horizontal lines across the screen. This process is invariably seen as a motion in three dimensions, as nearly as one can tell exactly like the real movement of the rod behind the screen, a rotation describing a conical surface about a vertical axis.

This set-up lends itself to a variation which is interesting because the three-dimensional motion which is perceived is a different one from that which the rod behind the screen undergoes. The shaft on which the rod turns is tilted toward or away from the screen by 15° or 20°. This changes the pattern of expansion and contraction of the rod shadow completely; its end points now move on elliptic paths on the screen. Only rarely does the rod motion seem to describe a circular cone like the real movement of the rod behind the screen. In most cases a movement is seen in which the movement component of tilting toward or away from S is much smaller than the lateral movement component such that the surface described is that of an elliptic cone. Whereas the real rod goes in one rotation from a tilt toward S into a tilt away from him, the perceived motion of the rod is restricted either to a changing forward tilt or to a

[2]See Chapter IX, selection 2.

changing tilt away from S. Either one of these two different move-ments can of course be perceived because, like a three-dimensional figure and its inverted form, they would if they were objectively given produce the same projection.

It seems that what distinguishes in these experiments perceived movement from the two-dimensional process which is given on the screen and therefore on the retina is the fact that the perceived rod is seen with a constant length. Tilting into depth is seen instead of shortening. Inasmuch as the rod as a whole must anyway be seen to move, this tilting motion is only a modification of a necessary pro-cess and not an added change, which is what a perceived stretching and shrinking would amount to. Thus a tendency to see one motion instead of the two simultaneous movements of the two-dimensional process (a tipping from side to side, and a stretching and shrinking) may be held responsible for the depth effect. Another possibility would be a selective principle according to which a line of constant length is seen rather than a changing one. No decision between these two possibilities can be made on the basis of our present results.

EXPERIMENT 5: ROTATION OF T AND Δ FIGURES

It is important to realize that a shadow line must undergo both a displacement and a lengthening or shortening in order to produce a kinetic depth effect. Both these changes must be given together. A change in length alone is not sufficient to produce a reliable kinetic depth effect. This is shown in the following experiment.

A piece of 1/16-in. wire 4 in. long was fastened at right angles to a vertical shaft of the same diameter so that the two formed a figure of T shape. When this form was turned back and forth about the vertical shaft through an angle of 42°, the shadow of the horizon-tal wire formed a line of 105-mm. length which periodically con-tracted to a length of 75 mm. and expanded again. We presented it with a rate of one period per 1.5 sec. for 10 sec. to 24 Ss.

Eighteen of 24 Ss saw a line in the plane of the screen expanding and contracting and only 6 Ss perceived the line turning in the third dimension. Had the horizontal wire been in a oblique position with respect to the axis of rotation so that its shadow had shown a dis-placement in addition to the change in length, the kinetic depth effect would have been obtained with the majority of the Ss, as the experiment with the oblique rod would predict.

Because of its importance we had the experiment with the T figure repeated by another E and obtained the same result: Of 40 Ss, 30 saw the horizontal line expand and contract in the plane of the screen and 10 saw it turn.

These results must be compared with those of a different wire figure which does produce a kinetic depth effect under identical conditions. Comparable data come from a shadow presentation of an equilateral triangle. Its sides consisted of wires 5 in. in length, and one of them was tilted by 15° against the horizontal. When this figure was turned back and forth, the shadow of one of its sides changed from a slope of 45° to one of 57° and thus presented conditions favorable to the kinetic depth effect. Of 20 Ss who observed the triangle for 10 sec. 17 reported a turning in depth and only 3 expansion and contraction. (With such a plane figure the kinetic depth effect consists, of course, in the perception of a plane figure that turns into depth.) This score is to be compared with that for the T figure where only one-third of the Ss saw a turning. The difference is reliable at the .001 level of confidence.

Still, the 6 and 10 Ss who saw the T figure turning in depth need be accounted for, if our claim is correct that they are not the outcome of a genuine kinetic depth effect. Here the following result is significant. When the T figure was presented *following* the presentation of the triangle, 15 out of the 17 Ss who saw the triangle turn saw the T figure turn also. (Three Ss who saw the triangle expand and contract reported the same for the T figure.) In other words, when a figure that Ss saw turning preceded the presentation of the T figure, a large majority of Ss saw it turning also. This shows a strong influence of a previous perception on the manner in which the T figure is seen, for only one-third of the Ss saw the T figure turning when it was given as a first presentation. This difference is significant at the .05 level of confidence. We suggest that in the case of these latter Ss some such influence of a previous experience, though a more remote one, has been at work also.

We are inclined to conclude that a line which changes in length but is not displaced at the same time does not give rise to the kinetic depth effect. This agrees well with the already reported finding that a solid shadow which expands and contracts only one dimension will not show the kinetic depth effect either.

The Accuracy of Kinetic Depth Perception

When we described the kinetic depth effect in complex figures, we stated that the change in the retinal image is accounted for in percep-tion by a rotation of a three-dimensional form. This implies, of course, that a *real* form which is like the perceived one would in rotation produce a sequence of retinal images very similar to that actually given, or in other words, that the perceived form resembles closely the shadow-casting object. That this is the case has been confirmed by many *S*s to whom the shadow-casting object was di-rectly shown immediately following the kinetic presentation.

For more stringent confirmation several methods were used: In the case of the "helix" (Figure 3), *S*s were asked to bend a piece of wire into the shape of the figure which they saw turning on the screen. Only *S*s who reported seeing a three-dimensional form turn-ing back and forth were given this test. Of 29 *S*s, 13 made good reproductions, 12 fair ones, and only 4 *S*s made poor reproductions. Eleven of the 12 *S*s whose reproductions were fair were later asked to make another reproduction while they looked *directly* at the turning wire figure. Of these only 7 were able to make good repro-ductions and 4 made only fair ones under these conditions. Al-together there were 8 *S*s who could make only fair reproductions when they viewed the figure directly.

In the case of the parallelogram (Figure 2), the accuracy of per-ception by virtue of the kinetic depth effect was checked by showing *S* four similar wire figures and asking him to pick out the one that matched best the form he saw turning on the screen. As mentioned earlier, the bend in the shadow-casting figure amounted to an angle of 110° between the planes of the two triangles which made up this figure. This angle is, of course, characteristic of its three-dimensional form. If this angle were 180°, the wire figure would be plane. In our four models the bend amounted to angles of 95°, 110°, 125°, and 140°, respectively. The one with the 110° angle was an exact copy of the shadow-casting figure; the other three models had the same height as the standard and were made to produce projections on the frontal plane which were identical with the projection of the standard. The four models were inserted in a wooden block and handed to *S.* The choices of 30 *S*s who had previously reported seeing the three-dimensional figure were 8, 17, 4, and 1 for the 95°, 110°, 125°, and 140° figure, respectively. Only one *S* found it impossible to make a choice. It is unfortunate that we did not include one more model with a still sharper angle, but even so the data give a rough idea of the accuracy of the perception of three-dimensional form which is based on the kinetic depth effect.[3]

EXPERIMENT 6: ROTATION OF LUMINOUS ROD

Another attempt to obtain a measure of the accuracy with which depth perception functions by virtue of the kinetic depth effect was made employing a straight line which rotated in an oblique plane. When a line is turned in a frontal-parallel plane about its midpoint, the end points of its retinal projection move on a circle. However, when it rotates in an oblique plane, its retinal image changes in length as it turns, and its endpoints move on an elliptic path. Therefore, when in the dark a luminous line is rotated in a frontal-parallel plane about its midpoint and is exposed from behind an elliptic aperture, its retinal projection will be the same as that of a line which turns in an oblique plane, for the aperture causes the line to be visible with the same changes in length. If the motion of the line that rotates in an oblique plane can be correctly perceived with the help of the kinetic depth effect alone, then the line rotating behind an elliptic aperture should also appear to rotate in an oblique plane, because the two lines produce identical stimulation so far as the kinetic depth effect is concerned. Other cues for depth perception as, for instance, retinal disparity, would give rise to experienced rotation in an oblique plane only in the first case. Thus when the rotating line behind the aperture is presented to a naive *S* and he perceives it turning in a properly oblique plane, one can be sure that this is due to the kinetic depth effect. By this procedure, as by the use of the shadow screen, the effect can be studied in isolation; other cues for depth perception would tend only to prevent the line from turning in an oblique plane.

[3]It should be noted that a turning by 42° produces only a moderate distortion of the shadow. Its width which is most strongly affected suffers a reduction of only 27%.

A ½-in. lucite rod, approximately 23 in. long, served as light source for the luminous line. Its ends were flat and finely ground to admit a maximum of light. They were inserted in metal caps which contained hidden flashlight bulbs and also served as mountings. The light from these bulbs made the lucite rod appear to glow evenly over its whole length. The rod was inserted in a U-shaped sheet-metal trough of proper length and attached by the mountings. A bushing was fastened to the back of the trough at its midpoint and attached to the horizontal slow shaft of a reduction gear motor, so that the lucite rod could be turned in a vertical plane. The trough and rod were covered by a long strip of cardboard into which was cut an aperture 22 in. long and ⅛ in. wide. Through this aperture part of the rod's surface was visible. In front of this apparatus was a frame to which cardboards with different elliptic apertures could be attached parallel to the plane of rotation of the rod. Three different elliptic apertures were used. They were 40 cm. long and 35 cm. wide, 39.5 cm. long and 28.9 cm. wide, and 40 cm. long and 20.6 cm. wide, respectively. They produced projections of the turning luminous rod identical with the projections produced by a luminous line that turns in a plane forming an angle of 29°, 46°, and 59°, respectively, with the plane of the aperture. They were attached with the large axis of the elliptic opening in vertical position.

The S was seated in front of this apparatus at a distance of 9 ft. He had before him a small table covered with a light gray cardboard. A metal rod was joined at right angles to a shaft which was fastened vertically to the table, so that the rod could be swung around in a plane parallel to the table top about an inch above it. A degree scale was marked out on the cardboard by which the position of the rod could be read. With the help of the rod, S could indicate the position of the plane in which the luminous line seemed to turn. A darkroom amber bulb illuminated this arrangement in such a way that S could see the rod but not the scale markings and that the remainder of the room was completely dark. After each setting of the rod E asked S to close his eyes and then read the scale with a flashlight.

During testing E asked S to look at the luminous line before him and close one eye, and that eye was covered. The luminous line which, when presented in the appropriate elliptic aperture, produced the projection of a 46° tilt was set into clockwise rotation at a rate of one revolution in 10 sec. When S reported that it turned in an oblique plane, he was asked to turn the measuring rod before him into a position parallel with that of the luminous line in rotation. This was repeated with the 59° and the 29° apertures, and thereafter the three apertures were used twice more in random order for the purpose of practice. Neither in this practice period nor later during the experimental trials was *S* told whether his settings were correct or not correct. No time limit was set on the presentation of the revolving line and *S* made his setting when he felt ready. After a rest period of 3 or 4 min. the experimental series began. It consisted of nine presentations, that is, each one of the three apertures was presented three times in random order.

The means and *SD*'s of the 15 means of the three measurements for each of the three degrees of tilt were 14.9 (*SD* = 6.6), 44.0 (*SD* = 3.4), and 59.8 (*SD* = 4.4) for the 29°, 46°, and 59° tilt, respectively. There was *no* overlap between the means of the settings by individual *S*s from one tilt to another, and there was *no* overlap between the individual settings which a given *S* made for the three tilts.

Where projections of tilts of 46° and of 59° were presented, the averages for all *S*s came close to the expected values. However, in the case of the 29° tilt, the average of 14.9 deviates significantly from this value; only one individual setting out of 45 is as high as, or exceeds 29°.

Why this is so is not clear. However, it should be pointed out that the change in length which a line turning with a 29° tilt undergoes amounts only to 12.5% and one of 14.9° tilt (the value of the average) only to 3.4%. In other words, a tilt of 14.9° produces a change in length that is very likely below the limen. Yet, that does not necessarily mean that those *S*s who gave settings of 15° or lower did not receive effective stimulation for a tilt. Whereas the small angles of tilt (due to the negligible change of the cosine function in this range of values) probably do not lead to a change in length sufficient to produce a kinetic depth effect, settings of such low values do not indicate that no tilt was perceived when these settings were made. In experience, a tilt of 15° is of distinct significance, and objectively conditions of stimulation of 29° were given.

It would have been important to find out whether these results can be improved by making the luminous line wider. To make it wider would have the advantage that the contraction of the line would be given by a change in its proportions, that is, in figural terms, rather than by a change in its absolute length. Improved results would indicate that change in proportions is effective in producing the kinetic depth effect. Unfortunately, this variation could not be done with the present set-up, because a wider line would have shown up the intersections with the elliptic aperture by their changing obliqueness. A more expensive manner of presentation would be needed.

Other Factors in Kinetic Depth Perception

EXPERIMENT 7: THE EFFECT OF ANGLE CONSTANCY

Such a variation of the experiment might have contributed to the solution of the following problem. It has been reported that shadows of solid blocks will produce the kinetic depth effect only if they have contours which are displaced and change their length simultaneously. Should we assume then that the presence of such contours solely accounts for the kinetic depth effect in complex forms, imparting their depth to the whole figure, or do complex forms produce such an effect in their own right? Just as we have considered the possibility that a line is seen to move into the third dimension to account for the given change of its retinal image while it is perceived with constant length, we might assume a tendency to see in general rigid, unchanging forms instead of the given distorting shapes. For the present this question must remain unanswered.

Fig. 4. The figure used in Exp. 7

However, a question which can be considered a part of the question just raised was actually put to a test. Most shadows of turning figures do not only display contours which are displaced and change their length; their angles also change. Is there a separate tendency for angles to remain constant which produces kinetic depth effects?

To answer this question we used a figure which consisted of three rods all meeting in one point under angles of 110° and forming a wire-edged representation of an obtuse corner (Figure 4). When this figure was turned back and forth through an angle of 42° and its shadow was shown to 56 *S*s who before had seen its stationary shadow as two-dimensional, 53 *S*s reported seeing a rigid obtuse corner. In this presentation two of the three dark lines forming the shadow were not only displaced but also underwent considerable changes in length.

Entirely different results were obtained when the length of the shadow lines was made indefinite. To achieve this, the shadow screen was covered with a cardboard with a circular aperture where the shadow of the corner figure fell on the screen. The size of the aperture was so chosen that the ends of the shadow lines were always hidden from *S*. Thus, only movement of the corner point, angular displacements of each of the three lines, and changes of the angles which they formed with each other were visible. As the corner point shifted sideways, one of the lines seemed to move far-ther under the aperture edge and another one seemed to pull out from under it, and the length of all three of them seemed indefinite.

All 22 *S*s employed in this experiment reported seeing a flat figure which distorted. Had the kinetic depth effect occurred, the *S*s would have seen instead a rigid three-dimensional form with constant angles. However, no such effect was observed where changes in the length of the lines which constituted the figure were not given, because that length was indefinite. We may conclude that a displacement of lines which is linked only with a change of angles does not give rise to the kinetic depth effect; displacement of lines and change in their length is needed. The question remains unan-swered whether length must be understood only in absolute terms, or whether change in proportion has an effect of its own.

EXPERIMENT 8: VARIATION OF DISTANCES BETWEEN OBJECTS

Not only are the retinal images of solid objects deformed when one moves about, the same is true to various degrees of the projection of the whole environment. That the objects which make up the environment are seen arranged in three-dimensional space and with unchanging distances between each other may also result from a kinetic depth effect. Just as some of the contours of solid objects produce appropriately changing retinal projections when the objects are seen from different angles, the projections of many of the intervals between objects change their length and their direction when one moves about. That this has the effect of producing visual depth can be demonstrated with the shadows of an arrangement of several objects on a rotating platform.

We used spheres supported by thin vertical rods because the shadow of a sphere in rotation does not change its shape and will therefore not produce a kinetic depth effect of its own. Four spheres of 1 3/16-in. diameter were arranged at the corners of a square concentric with the platform. The four rods were all of different height so that all the intervals between the shadows of the spheres were periodically oblique when the platform turned and changed length and direction simultaneously. The lower part of the screen was covered so that the shadow of the turntable itself was hidden. The arrangement was turned at a rate of one revolution in 5 sec. and was exposed to individual Ss for 20 sec.

Under these circumstances all 30 Ss who took part reported the spheres to move in three dimensions. Twenty-four Ss saw the spheres in a rigid spatial arrangement which turned about its center just like the actual arrangement behind the screen. The others saw them move in open single file in snakelike fashion into depth. In this latter motion only the shorter intervals between spheres are rigidly maintained, and each sphere changes direction of rotation with each excursion; but there can be no doubt that this is an incomplete form of a kinetic depth effect. It should be mentioned that 15 of the 30 Ss had no other experience with these shadow experiments except for another experiment with the spheres which will be reported below. It is apparent that the kinetic depth effect will readily yield a perception of a rigid spatial arrangement of unconnected objects.

EXPERIMENT 9: VARIATION OF DISTANCES BETWEEN OBJECTS

The arrangement of Experiment 8 offers still another opportunity to check on our finding that a line must change both in length and in direction in order to produce a kinetic depth effect. From our experiments with solid blocks and with the T figure we concluded that a shadow which merely expands and contracts in one dimension will not give rise to the effect. Here we set out to show that the same is true for intervals between objects; we modified the experiment with the spheres to correspond to these experiments.

All the rods were given the same height so that the spheres were aligned on a horizontal line and the intervals between the shadows changed in length only. This arrangement was shown to the same 30 Ss and under exactly the same conditions that prevailed in Experiment 8, but was presented prior to it. The fact that the T figure proved so susceptible to the influence of previous perceptions made this sequence advisable. The experiment with the luminous rod which has been reported at length was done with the same Ss in between the two experiments with spheres.

As in the case of the T figure, only a minority of the Ss now saw movement in three dimensions, namely 10 out of 30. The difference between this result and that of Experiment 8 is reliable at the .03 level of confidence. Of the 15 naive Ss, 12 saw the shadows move back and forth in the plane of the screen, 1 S reported movement in three dimensions, and 2 saw in the beginning of the observation period the plane and later the three-dimensional version. For the other group of 15 Ss who had observed the shadows of some wire figures before, the numbers were: 8 flat, 2 three-dimensional, and 5 first flat and later three-dimensional. When these results are compared with those of the previous experiment where imaginary lines connecting sphere shadows changed both in length and in direction, it becomes again apparent that these are essential conditions for the kinetic depth effect and that a mere expanding and contracting of retinal distances is insufficient.

This is the reason for our view that Metzger's work (2) is not directly concerned with the kinetic depth effect. He exposed shadows of arrangements of vertical rods whose changing patterns presented Ss with rectangular intervals which changed in width only. No other deformations were visible, because no marks were distinguishable along the shadow lines, and the latter ended only at the edges of the aperture in which they were given. As with the aligned spheres, no reliable depth effects are produced spontaneously in naive Ss with such an arrangement. Whether Metzger's work contributes to an understanding of the kinetic depth effect remains to be seen when more of the nature of the effect is known.

EXPERIMENT 10: EFFECT OF SET

In our experiments the kinetic depth effect results in two perceptual characteristics: (*a*) a turning in the depth dimension and (*b*) three-dimensionality of form. However, when the effect is observed under realistic conditions, namely when by moving about one obtains a changing retinal projection for a stationary solid object, no turning is perceived. The reason for this is that the object remains in unaltered relation to its environment with respect to which *S* perceives himself moving.[4] Thus, only three-dimensionality and rigidity of form, seen instead of the deforming two-dimensional pattern which is given on the retina, are here the overt manifestations of the kinetic depth effect.

The fact that under realistic conditions the object remains in unaltered relation to its environment needs some consideration, because this is not so in our experiments. There the deforming shadow of the object denotes a turning while the environment, that is, the screen on which the shadow is shown, remains stationary. Under realistic conditions, on the other hand, both the object and its environment are given retinally with deformations which denote a turning in relation to *S*. The kinetic depth effect transforms the deforming retinal projection of the environment into a three-dimensional structure, and once this has happened, the perception of the object as a three-dimensional form is probably facilitated. That such a facilitation is likely to take place is indicated by experimental results which show a strong influence of preceding exposures on the readiness with which the kinetic depth effect occurs.

The following results may serve as an example. When the "helix" (Figure 3) was shown following the presentation of one or two figures which readily show the kinetic depth effect, all of 18 *S*s saw it as three-dimensional during the first 10-sec. exposure. This is to be compared with results in Experiment 2 according to which

[4]This statement is incorrect. There is a different reason, as shown in Chapter XI, selection 8.

only 4 out of 16 naive *S*s gave a clear report of three-dimensional form for this figure after the first 10-sec. exposure.

The question of how this influence is exerted must remain open. It is conceivable that it consists merely in a set to see a turning in the depth dimension. However that may be, the influence is a strong one.

If such an influence is effective between succeeding exposures of different figures as shown, it should be expected to work also within a given visual field. Under realistic conditions, once the environment of a given object is perceived as a rigid spatial structure which changes its orientation with respect to the moving *S*, such an influence should facilitate a kinetic depth effect for the object. There are several reasons why the environment should easily be seen in this fashion. To mention only one: the environment will usually contain familiar features which would cause the facilitating influence of previous experience with similar situations to operate. Thus we have good reason to believe that the kinetic depth effect takes place more readily under realistic conditions than it does in our shadow-screen experiments.

Summary

When a three-dimensional form, solid or wire-edged, is turned behind a translucent screen and its shadow on the screen is observed, the shadow will appear as a rule as a three-dimensional rigid object which turns, quite similar to the physical object behind the screen. This happens notwithstanding the fact that *S* actually looks at a plane figure which is being deformed.

One condition seems to be essential for the occurrence of this effect: the shadow must display contours or lines which change their length and their direction simultaneously. If this condition is not fulfilled, a plane distorting figure like the one on the screen is perceived unless an influence of previous perception operates.

This effect is believed to operate widely under ordinary circumstances. When one moves about, objects near one's path are successively seen from different angles, and this change in orientation of the object to *S* is the same as occurs when the object is turned by an equivalent angle. Thus, the object's retinal projection undergoes the same deformations as do shadows in our experiments, and the same perceptual processes should result.

References

1. Fisichelli, V. R. Effect of rotational axis and dimensional variations on the reversals of apparent movement in Lissajous figures. *American Journal of Psychology,* 1946, 59, 669–675.
2. Metzger, W. Tiefenerscheinungen in optischen Bewegungsfeldern. *Psychologische Forschung,* 1934, 20, 195–260.
3. Miles, W. R. Movement interpretation of the silhouette of a revolving fan. *American Journal of Psychology,* 1931, 43, 392–405.
4. Philip, B. R., & Fisichelli, V. R. Effect of speed of rotation and complexity of pattern on the reversals of apparent movement in Lissajou figures. *American Journal of Psychology,* 1945, 58, 530–539.

On the definition of retinal disparity

Sometimes progress is made in perception simply by an inquiry into the nature of the relevant stimulus condition. Even in vision we cannot take it for granted that by now all relevant stimulus conditions are correctly described. Not long ago, for instance, successive revisions of our notions about the stimulation for visual movement have made two major illusions of motion, induced movement and Brown's transposition principle, understandable and have led to a more coherent picture of motion perception.[1] This paper attempts a similar step in the field of stereoscopic depth perception by proposing a revision of the concept of retinal disparity.

Retinal disparity is usually assumed to be effective through the stimulation of corresponding and noncorresponding points on the retinae. We propose to hold the difference in the monocular patterns themselves responsible for stereoscopic depth rather than the differences in the location on the retinae of the individual elements that make up the patterns. We assume, in other words, that retinal disparity has its effect because of differences in the configuration of the

Written in collaboration with Judith Lindauer. Reprinted from *Psychologische Beitrage,* 1962, 6, 521–530.

[1]Karl Duncker, Ueber induzierte Bewegung. *Psychologische Forschung,* 1929, 180–259; also, in the present volume, Chapter V.

two monocular patterns and not because individual points or lines of these differ in their location on the retinae of the two eyes.

The alternatives can be illustrated with an arrangement of two vertical rods of which the left one is a bit more distant from the observer than the right one. In the retinal projections of this arrangement the rod images are slightly farther apart in the left eye than in the right eye. According to the classical interpretation, the depth effect takes place because, as one of the rods is fixated, the images of the other one will fall on noncorresponding points and this difference in their location on each retina will cause this rod to be placed at a depth different from that of the fixated rod. Our interpretation simply credits the fact that the distance between the images of the rods differs in the two eyes—this difference being significant only in so far as it affects the figural properties of the two monocular patterns.

To support the interpretation of retinal disparity in terms of configuration, we shall present four different experiments which demonstrate characteristics of stereoscopic depth perception not compatible with the classical view but which follow naturally from the configurational interpretation. Disparities amounting to a certain value may be incorporated in different pairs of monocular patterns so chosen that the resulting configurational differences between the patterns are conspicuous in varying degrees. Stereoscopic depth effects should then vary according to the conspicuousness of these differences. Our experiments employed different methods of varying conspicuousness and various manifestations of the resulting differences in the depth effect.

I

Our first experiment used additions to the monocular patterns to make the given disparity more conspicuous. On a mirror stereoscope a horizontal line 35 mm. in length was presented to the left eye and a similar line 38 mm. long to the right eye at distances 40 cm. from each eye, for an observation time of 15 sec., and a description was obtained from the subject. Next, a different pair of stereoscopic charts was presented to him. As shown in Figure 1 each one showed the longer and the shorter line. On the left-eye chart a 38-mm. line

Fig. 1.

was added below the 35-mm. line and for the right eye a 35-mm. line was added in corresponding fashion. Again observation time was limited to 15 sec. Whereas only 5 out of 33 observers reported depth effects in the case of the single line, 25 of the same observers saw the double lines slanting into depth at opposite angles. This large increase in the incidence of depth reports when the double lines were presented is obviously due to the fact that adding the second lines makes the difference in length of the upper, as well as the lower, lines conspicuous. Whereas for the single line there is only the difference in the distance between the end points that can cause a depth effect, in the case of the double lines the differences in length are represented also in the configuration that end points on either side form with each other. The more conspicuous disparity produces a more potent depth effect. It is a well-known fact that the stereoscopic effect takes time to develop when, instead of real three-dimensional arrangements, stereograms drawn on paper are viewed. A tendency of lines to stay in the plane of the paper can easily be observed. It is probably by operating against this tendency that the difference in the potency on the depth effect causes our striking result.[2]

II

Our second experiment was designed to show that a disparity which produces a distance difference of a fixed amount is more effective when the length to which the increment is added is small than when it is large. It is obvious that any given increase in distance produces a more striking change when the distance to which it is added is small than when it is large. If, for instance, a pair of vertical lines

[2]This result is important in connection with Wilde's Punktreiheneffekt (K. Wilde, *Psychologische Forschung*, 1949/51, 223–262). Linschoten's failure to confirm Wilde's result (J. Linschoten, *Strukturanalyse der binocularen Tiefenwahrnehmung*, Groningen, 1956, pp. 242–244) is due to the fact that in his own experiments he changed Wilde's patterns from two to one row of dots.

is presented on the stereoscope so that the distance between them differs by a small amount, the difference between the monocular patterns should be more conspicuous when the lines are close to each other than when they are far apart, and as a consequence the resulting disparity should be more effective. That this is the case can be demonstrated with a somewhat more complex arrangement. It consists of a scene composed of eight vertical rods, the ground plan of which is shown in Figure 2a. The rods are arranged in three frontal-parallel planes indicated by three horizontal lines in the illustration. Since the distances between these planes are equal and the scene is observed from a relatively large distance, all disparities between neighboring rods are, in close approximation, equal. As this scene is viewed by the observer (Figure 2b), the distance between rod 2 and rod 3 is considerably smaller than the distance between rod 3 and rod 4. Thus, although they are geometrically the same, the disparity between rod 2 and rod 3 should be more effective than the disparity between rod 3 and rod 4. The disparity between rods 2 and 3 might have the result that the perceived location of rod 3 is farther forward than its real position would warrant. The total arrangement of rods is designed to make such an effect noticeable, should it exist. The peculiar asymmetrical situation of rod 3 is duplicated by the situation of rod 6, except that in its case the more effective disparity would place it farther back than its real situation would warrant. Thus, if these effects exist, rods 3 and 6 should not be seen in the same frontal-parallel plane, but rod 3 should appear nearer than rod 6. This was indeed the case; the difference in depth between rods 3 and 6 was quite conspicuous. To obtain this effect it was necessary to eliminate all other cues for the three-dimensional arrangement of the rods. The base to which the rods were fastened and their upper ends remained hidden from the observer. The rod scene was therefore viewed through an aperture in a screen as indicated in Figure 2b. It was also preferable to keep the rods dark and view them against an illuminated background.

It was possible to measure the effect by moving rod 6 forward until it appeared to be in the same frontal-parallel plane as rod 3, and such experiments were undertaken. Rod 6 was mounted so that it could be moved continuously at right angles to the frontal-parallel plane in which the three tiers of rods were arranged. A small fixation mark, suspended on a thin wire that remained invisible, ap-

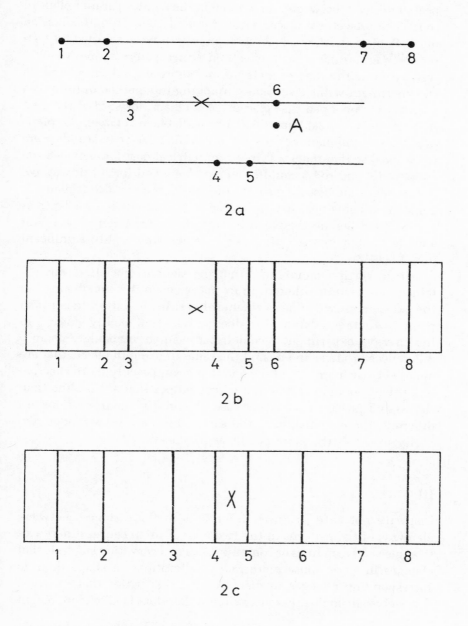

Fig. 2. 1:3 scale except for rod diameters which were 3 mm.

peared midway between rods 3 and 6 in the frontal-parallel plane of rod 3. The subject was placed at a distance of 2.5 m. from the fixation mark. Subjects with good stereoscopic vision were selected by testing them for ordinary depth effects on a mirror stereoscope. Matches were made with different methods and showed good agreement. In an experiment with 10 subjects employing the method of limits, an average was obtained that placed rod 6 1.8 cm. forward of rod 3 (at point A in Figure 2a), that is 36% of the distance between the plane of rod 3 and the plane of rods 4 and 5. When the critical rods were rearranged so that rod 3 was in a symmetrical position between rod 2 and rod 4 and rod 6 could be moved back and forth midway between rods 5 and 7 (see Figure 2c) with the depth of rod 3 unchanged, a match was obtained that placed rod 6 at exactly the same depth as rod 3. The difference between the match in this latter experiment and the match in the critical experiment was highly significant $(p < .0001)$.[3]

It is worth remembering that the sizable effect that was obtained here is quite different in its nature from the one obtained in the experiment with the horizontal lines. In the latter, the crucial point is whether a depth effect does, or does not, readily emerge. In the present experiment, geometrically equal binocular distance differences produce, in one and the same line, depth effects that are opposed to each other, and the one that is supposedly more effective has a stronger influence on the perceived position of that line than the less effective one. In either case, though the manifestations are different, the explanation is the same: the more conspicuous disparity produces the more potent depth effect.

III

Disparity not only produces differences in the distances between elements of the patterns in the two eyes, it often causes differences in angles between lines or contours. Casual observation suggests that changes in angle cause more radical alterations in shape than do corresponding changes in distance, and disparities that manifest themselves in angle differences should therefore lead to more potent

[3]The authors are grateful to Mr. John Hay for collecting these data during the academic year 1953/54.

depth effects. The remaining two experiments are concerned with this prediction.

In the first one the resistance of the stereoscopic depth effect to contradictory knowledge about the given depth interval is tested. Two different wire arrangements were viewed through a telestereoscope, a device that enhances stereoscopic depth by increasing binocular parallax. Ours increased the effective interocular distance by 7.6 cm. One wire arrangement consisted of two vertical rods 3.4 cm. apart, the other of three rods forming an isosceles triangle with the 10 cm. long base in vertical position and a height of 4.5 cm. In the case of the triangle, the base was continuous with the supporting shaft. The parallel rods were actually joined at the top and at the bottom forming a tall oblong, one vertical side of which was continuous with the supporting shaft. The oblong was viewed through a wide rectangular aperture 12.5 cm. high so that only parts of the vertical rods were visible. Either one of these arrangements were viewed first with its plane slanting 30 degrees against the line of sight. Subjects were asked to give estimates of the distance either between the parallel rods or between the tip and the base of the triangle by adjusting the length of a thin brass rod which could be lengthened or shortened. Since these distances occupied a position forming an angle of 60 degrees with the frontal-parallel plane, these estimates amounted to judgments of stereoscopic depth. Since the wire arrangements were viewed through the telestereoscope, the distances were, of course, overestimated.

Next each wire arrangement was revolved once about its supporting shaft at the rate of 10 r.p.m. By bringing the wire arrangement twice into the frontal-parallel position such a revolution revealed its true shape. The wire arrangement was then put back into its original position and another depth estimate was made. 14 subjects viewed the triangle and made one estimate before and one after seeing it revolve and another group of 14 subjects went through the same procedure with the parallel rods.

At issue was whether the second depth estimate showed an influence of the experience of the true shape of the wire arrangement gained during the revolution. This was the case with the parallel lines but not with the triangle. The average depth estimate for the parallel lines was 5.35 cm. before and 4.43 cm. after the revolution and the mean reduction in depth of .92 cm. was significant at the .001

level. For the triangle, on the other hand, the estimates remained practically the same, 6.01 cm. before and 5.91 cm. after the viewing of the revolving arrangement, the mean depth change amounting to only .1 cm. (p = .6). The difference between the mean depth changes for the two arrangements was significant at the .005 level. Thus, the enhanced stereoscopic depth produced by the telestereoscopic viewing remained unchanged in the case of the triangle where disparity manifested itself in angle differences, but yielded in the case of the parallel rods, which presumably produced the less potent depth effect.

IV

Our last experiment demonstrates the relative potency of disparity that manifests itself in angle differences by bringing disparity in conflict with perspective depth cues. A preliminary experiment had shown that the pattern of Figure 3a transmits perspective cues so strong that they readily overcome the effect of an opposing retinal disparity. Ordinarily the right one of the two vertical lines is seen farther back in space than the left one. When this pattern was presented on a mirror stereoscope with a disparity that would tend to put the right vertical line into the nearer position, only three out of 20 subjects saw depth in accordance with disparity; the remaining 17 reported the right line farther back in space.

Next we transformed the distance disparity into one which manifested itself in an angle difference by replacing the disparate vertical lines with sloping ones which formed an inverted V (Figure 3b), giving the lower ends of the lines the same disparity as that of the parallel lines. We hoped that the greater potency of an angle disparity might cause a majority of observers to see the depth according to stereoscopic cues. The perspective cues proved, however, to be still dominant; only four out of 19 subjects saw depth in accordance with disparity.

Therefore we made a change in the patterns designed to decrease the effectiveness of the perspective cues. As shown in Figures 3c and d, the parallel lines were brought to the same level and the legs of the angle were made equally long, so that the perspective arrangement tended to keep the two critical lines at the same depth.

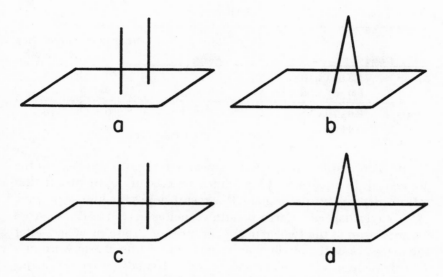

Fig. 3a-d.   In the left eye charts the distance between the vertical lines was 6.5 mm. This distance amounted to 8 mm. in the right eye charts. Note that the mirror stereoscope produces pseudoscopic depth.   The distance from the eye was 40 cm.

Disparity no longer had to overcome the opposite perspective depth, but would cause a depth difference where perspective cues did not indicate one. The purpose of the experiment still was to show that a disparity that manifested itself in an angle difference was more apt to overcome contradictory perspective cues than a disparity, identical in amount, that produced only distance difference.

Two groups of subjects were used, each consisting of 26 young adults. Subjects were first tested for stereoscopic vision by having them view a pair of stereoscopic charts showing side by side a vertical line and a circle between which a disparity existed. Only a subject who reported the correct depth difference within 15 sec. was admitted to the experiment. Each pair of critical charts was then exposed for 15 sec. after which the subject was asked to look away and describe what he had seen. Group A was first presented with the angle chart and following this with the parallel lines chart and for Group B this sequence was reversed. Table 1 summarizes the results.

A comparison of the first critical exposures for the two groups shows that more subjects reported depth in the case of the angle disparity than in the case of the distance disparity (19 out of 26 vs.

TABLE 1

| | | Number of *S*s reporting | |
		Depth	No depth
Group A	Angle Charts	19	7
	Parallel Charts	9	17
Group B	Parallel Charts	10	16
	Angle Charts	14	12

10 out of 26), a difference which proved to be significant beyond the
.01 level (Chi square = 6.315). Since reports of depth meant that
retinal disparity was dominant, this result shows the higher potency
of the angle disparity. Corresponding conclusions can be drawn from
a comparison of the two critical exposures of Group A. When, after
the exposure of the angle charts, the parallel line charts were presented, the number of subjects for whom retinal disparity was dominant dropped from 19 to 9, a change significant at better than the .001
level.

It is interesting that the reverse sequence in the case of Group
B did not produce as great a change in the opposite direction (a drop
from 16 to 12 subjects only). In fact, the difference in amount of the
two changes was significant at the .06 level. Since the two critical
exposures followed each other with little interruption, the temporally second exposure could be under the influence of a set produced
by the first, which would tend to prevent a change in experienced
depth. Inasmuch as Group A proceeded from the disparity dominated to the perspective dominated condition and provided a large
number of subjects who changed while Group B underwent the
reverse sequence and showed only a few changes, it appears that set
operates when it serves to maintain the influence of perspective
cues, but not when it would favor retinal disparity. However that
may be, the experiment as a whole provides strong evidence for the
greater potency of angle disparity.

Summary

It is proposed that retinal disparity is effective through the differences in the configuration of the two monocular patterns as such
rather than through the differences in location on the retinae of

individual points or lines. Four experiments are reported in support of this thesis which show that the effectiveness of retinal disparity varies with the conspicuousness of the difference in configuration which the disparity produces.

1. When an addition was made to a simple distance disparity such that the two monocular images showed a striking form difference, the frequency with which stereoscopic depth was reported within a limited observation time was substantially raised.

2. A number of vertical rods were so arranged that two disparities identical in amount had opposite depth effects on a critical rod. One of the disparities existed between rods a short distance apart in the retinal projection, producing a conspicuous distance difference in the two eyes, while the other, existing between more distant rods, produced a less conspicuous binocular difference. The former was shown to have a stronger effect on the position of the critical rod than the latter.

3. When a depth effect resulting from an artificially enhanced disparity between parallel lines was contradicted by experience with the objective depth, it yielded measureably. If, on the other hand, such a disparity manifested itself in a difference between angles, it remained unchanged.

4. Subjects were presented with two pairs of stereoscopic charts displaying disparities of identical amount of which one manifested itself as a difference in distance between parallel vertical lines and the other as a difference in angles between converging vertical lines. Additional lines on the charts conveyed perspective cues for distance which contradicted the depth effect that could have resulted from the disparities. A majority of subjects saw depth according to disparity in the case of the angle difference, while this was true of only a minority in the case of the distance difference.

The use of size matching to demonstrate the effectiveness of accommodation and convergence as cues for distance

The work to be reported was undertaken to clarify the role of accommodation and convergence as distance cues. Size perception rather than distance perception as such was used as an indicator for the effectiveness of these oculomotor cues for distance. This has become an accepted procedure, probably because size matching is easier for Ss than distance matching. The work of Heinemann, Tulving, and Nachmias (1959) and of Biersdorf, Ohwaki, and Kozil (1963) are examples. When the perceived sizes of objects located at different distances from S are matched, the accuracy of these matches measures the accuracy with which the available distance cues represent the different distances. This is so because the perceived size of an object depends on its registered distance as well as on the size of its

Written in collaboration with Lucretia Floor. Reprinted from *Perception & Psychophysics,* 1971, 10, 423–428. Copyright © 1971 Psychonomic Society, Inc.

retinal projection. Accurate size perception is described by Emmert's law, according to which, for an image of a given size, perceived size is proportional to registered distance of the object causing the image.[1] Where distance cues are available, perceived size then becomes a measure of the effectiveness of these cues.[2]

An investigation of the effectiveness of oculomotor adjustments as cues for distance requires that all other distance cues be eliminated from the test situation, and, since we cannot be quite sure what properties of the experimental condition can serve as distance cues, this is not an easy task. A good way to go about this is to let *S* see the test object through spectacles or other optical arrangements that simultaneously alter the accommodation and convergence needed to produce sharp and fused images to the test object. Under these circumstances, extraneous distance cues will contradict the effect of the given oculomotor cues, for they will represent the true object distances. Size matches in agreement with predictions made on the basis of the altered oculomotor cues would prove the operation of only that kind of distance cues, while certain systematic errors may reflect the operation of extraneous cues that represent the true object distance.

Techniques of this sort have been used by Gogel (1962) and by Wallach and Zuckerman (1963). The latter seem to have been the first to obtain results showing that these oculomotor adjustments can serve as fairly adequate distance cues. They altered by optical means these oculomotor adjustments in equivalent amounts and obtained size estimates that approximated predictions derived from the altered oculomotor cues. In 1966, Leibowitz and Moore published an extensive experiment with optically altered accommodation and convergence, which demonstrated the investigative power of the cue alteration technique. They provided optical arrangements that required *S*'s eyes to view test objects with a number of combinations of accommodation and convergence that corresponded to distances

---

[1]Registered distance is a theoretical term denoting the representation of distance in the nervous system usually resulting from the available cues for distance. Registered distance must be distinguished from apparent or judged distance, which is often affected by conditions other than cues for distance.

[2]In the absence of distance cues, *S,* asked to make size matches, in effect matches image sizes.

either larger or smaller than the true distances of the test objects. These artificial distances, which the authors call "equivalent" distances, thus depended on the true distances of the test objects *and* on the alterations in accommodation and convergence produced by the lenses and prismatic effects employed in the optical arrangements. *S* had to match the apparent size of the test objects by adjusting the size of a comparison object located at a distance of 200 cm. and seen directly. The sizes of the test objects whose true distances varied between 400 and 10 cm. were so chosen that they all produced identical image sizes. Therefore, if accommodation and convergence provided effective distance cues and if there were no extraneous distance cues operating, the matching sizes should be found to be proportional to the "equivalent" distances of the test object. The results showed that this was so only within limits: where the "equivalent" distance differed much from the true distance of the test object or where the true distances were large, the obtained matches deviated strongly from the theoretical values. Both kinds of deviations were such that they could have resulted from extraneous cues for the true distances of the test objects.

Of the experiments to be reported by us, Experiment 1 showed that results did not improve when, under our experimental conditions, distance cues other than accommodation and convergence were eliminated and were thus prevented from interfering with the effect of the optical arrangements. Poor results were obtained also when, under the same conditions, size matches between test objects at different distances were made with normal viewing, that is, without optical arrangements. In Experiment 2 the size estimation technique used by Wallach and Zuckerman produced good results with normal viewing, with conditions the same as in Experiment 1. Experiment 3 cleared up this discrepancy and, together with Experiment 4, established accommodation and convergence as fair cues for distances up to 2 m. In Experiment 5, results are reported that provide evidence that our experimental conditions did succeed in eliminating all distance cues other than accommodation and convergence.

Experiment 1

Our first experiment was similar to that of Leibowitz and Moore and was designed to eliminate all distance cues other than accommodation and convergence with the hope that we would obtain matches that corresponded to the "equivalent" distances. There was one further difference: both the standard test object and the comparison object were viewed through spectacles that altered the accommodation and convergence with which they were given. There was also a match in which both objects were viewed without glasses. Extraneous distance cues were eliminated in the following manner: the objects were luminous diamonds viewed in complete darkness through an aperture in a large screen that hid all light reflected from floor and furniture. *S*'s head was held at a fixed distance from the diamonds and could only turn to face one or the other. The diamonds remained dark while *S* turned his head and only one lit up when the head had reached the position for which the diamond's center was in *S*'s median plane; it remained lit only as long as the head was kept still.

The standard test object was always at a distance of 120 cm. from *S*'s eyes and the comparison object at 60 cm. Seen from *S*, they were located at eye level and 20 deg. apart. The standard diamond measured 12 cm. on the diagonal. Two different spectacles were used. The "near" glasses consisted of 5-diopter prisms oriented to force an increased convergence on the eyes and of a pair of lenses whose strength in the case of *S*s with near normal interocular distance amounted to —1.5 diopters. These lenses would induce an increase in accommodation corresponding to the convergence change caused by the prisms. For these glasses, equivalent distances amounted to 42.9 cm. for the 120-cm. distant object and to 31.6 cm. for the one at 60 cm. The "far" glasses were equipped with 2.5-diopter prisms, forcing divergence of the eyes and .75-diopter positive lenses; they caused equivalent distances of 1,200 and 109 cm. The spectacles, hence, altered the *ratio* of the test object distances implied by the oculomotor adjustments caused by the glasses. While that ratio was 2:1 for normal viewing, it was only 4:3 for the near glasses and 11:1 for the far glasses, and thus led to very different theoretical predictions for size matches.

Preliminary experiments performed with a technique similar to the one just described had given results that strongly deviated from theoretical values derived from Emmert's law and the altered oculomotor cues. This seemed to contradict a result obtained by Wallach and Zuckerman (1963) with a different procedure. In attempting to explain this discrepancy, we hypothesized that oculomotor cues operate best when oculomotor adjustment has just changed in response to an altered viewing distance. To test this hypothesis, two lightboxes, each exhibiting a thin vertical line, 9 cm. long and .05 cm. wide, were added. Each was placed beyond one of the diamonds so that from S's vantage it was visible just to the side of it. The line that appeared next to the standard diamond was twice as far from S as the standard, namely, 240 cm. and the one next to the variable diamond was correspondingly placed at 120 cm. distance. The lightboxes exhibiting the lines were so wired that either both could be made to stay dark or that one of them was lit when the test diamond with which it belonged was visible. During trials in which the lines were visible, S was under instruction to look back and forth between the test object and the line before giving a judgment.

EQUIPMENT

The diamond-shaped test objects were cutouts attached to the front of lightboxes equipped with milk-glass faces. The brightness of the diamonds' surfaces was so chosen that they were clearly visible but not so bright that irradiation noticeably blurred their contours, even after one's prolonged stay in the dark. A variable aperture operated by a screw and a crank provided the size variations of the comparison diamond.

Locating of S's head and elimination of movement parallax was achieved in the following manner: S wore a welder's headgear which could be attached to a vertical shaft, an arrangement that permitted only a turning of the head and prevented all other kinds of head displacement. Fixed to the shaft was a horizontal bar which turned with the head. Stops for its angular displacement were so set that a head turning had to terminate in either one of the two positions in which the head's median plane was aligned with a center of a test diamond. Microswitches were mounted near the stops in such a way that on the bar's approach it caused a switch to make contact less than 1 deg. of angular displacement before the stop was reached. Each switch operated the light for the corresponding diamond and, in the case of the trials at which the lines were present, also the line that belonged with it.

In Experiments 1 and 3, the spectacles consisted of trial frames into which lenses and prims in appropriate combination were inserted. In the case of prisms, the equivalent distance also depends on the interocular distance. Therefore, the lenses we used in combination with the two sets of prisms were appropriately varied, and equivalent distances were computed for individual *S*s. The means of the individual equivalent distances for the *S*s who participated amounted in the case of the near glasses to 41.8 and 31.1 cm., not much different from the previously stated values of 42.9 and 31.6 cm. that were computed on the basis of 1.5 lens diopters.

PROCEDURE

In order to obtain a match between the apparent sizes of the standard and the variable test diamonds, *E* varied the objective size of the latter, specifically the length of its diagonal, in steps of .1 cm. For half of the 16 *S*s, *E* set this length so that the variable diamond seemed clearly too large, made it smaller by one step, and asked *S* to make a comparison by turning his head back and forth between the two stops that caused the test diamonds to light up. *E* went on in this fashion until *S* judged the two sizes as equal. For the other eight *S*s, the variable diamond was initially adjusted to appear too small, and this applied to all five trials of which this experiment consisted. Thus, for half of the *S*s only the upper limit of the range of equality was always obtained and for the other half only the lower one. This was done to keep the experiment from becoming too long. It caused, of course, an increase in variability which, however, did not interfere with the significance of our results.

There were three experimental conditions: in the "normal" condition, *S* wore no glasses; in the other two, he wore either the near glasses or the far glasses. Under the first two conditions, *S* made two matches, one with the added vertical lines and the other without them. For half of the *S*s all matches were made first with the lines and then, still for the same condition, without the lines, and for the other eight *S*s this order was always reversed. In the case of the far glasses, the lines could not be used because the 240-cm. distance of one of the lines could not be increased by .75 lens diopters.[3] All

---

[3] A distance of 240 cm. normally requires an accommodation of .42 diopters, which cannot be diminished by .75 diopters.

experiments began by having S make two practice matches with the near glasses, with the three experimental conditions immediately following. Of the six possible sequences of these conditions, four were actually used. The two that started with the near glasses were omitted, because the near glasses were used in the practice matches.

RESULTS

As presented in Table 1 under the heading Experiment 1, results were obtained that were far from the matches to be expected, if accommodation and convergence were fully effective as cues to distance. The mean match of 8.7 cm. obtained for the normal viewing condition was closer to the value of 6 cm. expected if Ss were matching the sizes of retinal images—the result that would have been expected in the absence of all distance cues—than to a veridical match of 12 cm. The same was true of the mean match of 6.9 cm. made with the near glasses, where a value of 8.2 cm. should have been obtained, had the accommodation and the convergence forced by the glasses been fully effective in representing the equivalent distances of the two diamonds.[4] The matches obtained under normal

[4]The matching size of 8.2 cm. under the assumption of complete constancy was computed in the following manner: The equivalent distance of the far object (D_{ef}) amounted to 42.9 cm. and the one for the near object (D_{en}) to 31.6 cm. These values were obtained by transforming the real distance into lens diopters, adding 1.5 (the diopter strength of the near glasses), and transforming the result back into the corresponding distance values. According to Emmert's law, the perceived size of the far object is proportional to its image size times D_{ef}, and, since that image size is proportional to its objective size (12 cm.) over its objective distance (120 cm.), the perceived size is proportional to

$$\frac{12}{120} \cdot D_{ef}.$$

The corresponding formula for the near object is

$$\frac{x}{60} \cdot D_{en}$$

where x is the size of the variable near object whose size we want to predict. Since our S's task was to match the two perceived sizes.

$$\frac{12}{120} \cdot D_{ef} = \frac{x}{60} \cdot D_{en}$$

When the values given above are substituted for D_{ef} and D_{en}, $x=8.2$. The equivalent distances for the far glasses are computed by subtracting .75 lens diopters from the diopter values of the objective distances of the test objects.

conditions (8.7 cm.) and with the near glasses (6.9 cm.) were significantly different from each other (p<.01). Changing accommodation and convergence between simultaneously visible objects at different distances, which happened when one of the lines lit up together with a diamond, did not improve the matches substantially. The same mean matches were obtained with and without the line (Table 1).[5] Whether a match was begun with the diamond apparently too large or with a diamond that appeared too small had little effect. In the normal condition, the mean for the eight Ss who were first shown the diamond too large was 8.5 cm. and for those who were first exposed to the smaller diamond it was 8.8 cm. For the near glasses, the corresponding values were 7.2 and 6.6 cm. and for the far glasses they were 8.5 and 7.3 cm. The far glasses seem to have been completely ineffective. Whereas the expected match should here have been much larger than the match under the normal condition, it actually did not even reach that value. This result will be discussed with those of Experiment 3, where a quite similar result was obtained for the far glasses.

Though this experiment did show a significant influence of the oculomotor adjustments on perceived size, the results were no improvement over those obtained by Leibowitz and Moore. But the deviation of the mean matches from the expected values toward image size matching can no longer be ascribed to extraneous distance cues, for it also occurred under normal conditions; here the presence of extraneous distance cues would have had the opposite effect of favoring the expected match. Hence we turned to the question of how image size influenced our results. Experiment 2, which employed a size estimation technique, provided part of the answer.

Experiment 2

The same setup was used as in Experiment 1 except that the two diamonds were given the same fixed size of 8.5 × 8.5 cm. S's head was again attached to the switch device that caused the appropriate diamond and line to light up only as long as the head remained in one position, but now E controlled which one of the two diamonds

[5] The negligible difference obtained under the normal conditions was opposite to the expected direction.

TABLE 1

Mean Sizes in Centimeters of Near Object When It Matched Far Object

| Conditions of Viewing | Expected for | | Experiment 1. Two Diamonds | | | Experiment 3 | Significance of Difference Between Experiments 1 and 3 | |
	Complete Constancy	Image Size Match	With Line	Without Line	Combined	Oblong and Triangle	t	p
Normal	12	6	8.6	8.7	8.7 ± .50	11.0 ± .58	5.29	< .001
Near Glasses	8.2	6	6.9	6.9	6.9 ± .28	8.1 ± .46	4.58	< .001
Far Glasses	66	6	—	7.9	7.9 ± .60	9.9 ± 1.51	2.88	< .01

would do so. *S* gave his estimates by changing the length of an adjustable rod to match the apparent length of one of the diamond sides which was objectively 8.5 cm. for either. A small lamp near *S*'s hands enabled him to see the adjustable rod. There were four different presentation sequences: either the near or the far diamond was presented first and, of the two estimates made for each diamond, the one with the line present was made either in the first or second place. No glasses were used in this experiment.

Again, the presence of the line had no effect. The average of the mean estimates for the near and the far diamond made with the line was 7.28 cm. and without the line it was 7.35 cm. The mean estimate for the diamond at 120 cm. distance (7.13 ± .83 cm.) was smaller than the mean estimate for the one at 60 cm. distance (7.50 ± .70 cm.), and this difference was statistically significant (p < .05). But the difference was very small compared to the matching result for the normal condition in Experiment 1. While in that case the constancy ratio (objective size of matched near object/objective size of far object) amounted to .725, the constancy ratio in the present experiment (estimate of far size/estimate of near size) was .95.

This result showed that accommodation and convergence can serve well as cues for distance. The poor results obtained in Experiment 1 seemed to be caused by some factor operating in matching tests. We assumed that it consisted in a tendency to match image sizes, which interfered with the result of size perception that takes distance into account. We therefore tried to find a form of matching test where this tendency would not operate. Instead of presenting two figures of identical shape for size matching, we presented two figures of different shapes and asked *S* to match the length of two lines in the different figures by adjusting the size of one of them.

Experiment 3

The same equipment was used as in Experiment 1 except that the diamond of standard size was replaced by an oblong 18 cm. high and 8.5 cm. wide, and the variable diamond was changed into a triangle by covering its lower half. Thus, changing the size of the triangle did not alter its shape. Because in Experiments 1 and 2 the lines proved to have no effect, they were omitted. *S*'s task was to match the horizontal base of the triangle to the 8.5-cm. width of the oblong.

To protect our results against possible extraneous effects connected with the shapes of these figures, half of our *S*s made the match with the triangle in the near position, at a distance of 60 cm. and with the oblong 120 cm. from the eyes, and the other half with the triangle 120 cm. distant and the oblong at the distance of 60 cm.

We first tried this setup for the normal viewing condition and, when it proved successful, went on and used the near and far glasses also. Therefore, different groups of 16 *S*s participated in the two parts of this experiment. Since this, together with the omission of the matches made in the presence of the lines, shortened *S*'s task considerably, an individual trial now consisted in obtaining the upper as well as the lower limit of equality and recording as *S*'s match the average of these two values. Again, the sequence of presentation was appropriately varied from *S* to *S*.

In the case of the normal viewing condition, the matching length of the base of the triangle was 8.2 cm. when it was in the near position and 9.8 cm. when it was in the far position. There are two reasons why the latter matching length was higher. First, because of a lag in constancy, any far object looks somewhat smaller than it should, and, compensating for this, the matching size of the triangle when it is in the far position is larger than when it is in the near position. To make the two matching lengths comparable, the result of the match between the near oblong and the variable triangle in the far position (8.5 to 9.8 cm.) must be transformed into one where the length in the far object is chosen to be 8.5 cm. We therefore ask what value of length in the near object would stand in the same ratio to the standard length of 8.5 cm. as does 8.5 to the matching length of 9.8 cm. obtained when the triangle was the far object ($x/8.5 = 8.5/9.8$). The result of this transformation is an equivalent length in the near object of 7.4 cm. With the mean match for the triangle in the far position so transformed, our two matches were 8.2 to 8.5 for the triangle in the near position and 7.4 to 8.5 when the triangle was the far object. There was, then, still a difference. It was due to the effect of the figure shapes on the apparent lengths of the lines that were compared. Specifically, it was due to the Mueller-Lyer illusion, which operated in the triangle and diminished the apparent length of its base. It was precisely to eliminate the effect of such errors that we presented to half of our *S*s the triangle in the near position and to the other half in the far position. Since, as it must compensate for the illusion, the matching length of the triangle base was always larger than it should have been, the effect of the illusion was to produce too large a matching near length when the triangle was the near object and too small a matching near length when the triangle was the far object. The true mean match, then, is the average of (1) the matching length obtained with the triangle in the near position and (2) the equivalent matching length computed from the match made with the triangle in the far position. This average was 7.8 cm. for a standard of 8.5 cm. and was thus close to objective equality. The constancy ratio of .92 computed from these values is not much different from the constancy ratio of .95 obtained in Experiment 2.

To make the reported match of 7.8 to 8.5 cm. comparable with the corresponding result from Exeriment 1 as presented in Table 1, it must be transformed once more to conform to the standard length of 12 cm. of the far object, the basis for all data in this table. The transformed value of the matching length in the near object is computed from $x/12 = 7.8/8.5$ and amounts to 11.0 cm. It is found in Table 1 under the heading Experiment 3.

In the case of the near glasses, the mean matches actually obtained were 6.0 cm. for the triangle in the near position and 13.1 cm. for the triangle in the far position, and the true matching length computed in the same manner as before was 5.8 cm. This result can be appreciated only in the context of Table 1, where it can be compared with the value expected for complete constancy and with the match obtained for the diamonds. For this purpose, it also must be transformed to correspond to the standard length of 12 cm. This was done by multiplying the true match of 5.8 cm. by 12/8.5. The resulting value of 8.1 cm., found under the heading Experiment 3, is close to the one expected for complete constancy. For the far glasses, the actual matches were 6.8 and 10.0 cm., respectively, and the true matching length came to 7.0 cm., which transformed to 9.9 cm.

In the case of the normal viewing condition and when the near glasses were used, the transformed values obtained from the mean matches between triangle and oblong (11.0 and 8.1 cm.) were much nearer to the veridical match of 12 cm. and to the expected match of 8.2 cm. than the corresponding values obtained from matching two diamonds. The difference of the mean matches obtained with the different pairs of test objects was highly significant, as the statistical data presented in the last columns of Table 1 show.[6] This outcome confirms our explanation of the poor results obtained by the ordinary matching method: a tendency toward matching the sizes of the retinal images of the compared objects has a strong influence on these matches. Such a tendency does not seem to operate in our new method, where lengths of lines that are parts of different shapes are being matched, nor will it have an influence in a brief size estimation test. In speaking of a tendency toward matching the sizes of the retinal images, we do not mean to favor a particular explanation of this tendency. It may be due to an effect that assigns the same distance to similar shapes, which then, through the operation of Emmert's law, will cause these shapes to appear of equal size when their image sizes are equal; or it may be due to a tendency to match image sizes as such; or it may operate for still another reason.[7]

In the case of the far glasses, though the difference between the mean matches obtained under the two conditions was significant, the use of different shapes did not improve the results markedly. There seems to be a good reason why we might not expect the far glasses to be fully effective. The equivalent distance for the 120-cm. distant test object is here 1,200 cm. and the size of the experimental room known to our Ss could not accommodate such a distance. On the other hand, the match of 9.9 cm. that was actually obtained implies a registered distance of 180 cm. for this object, still a small distance compared to the space known to our Ss to be available. Twice the distance would have fitted into the room. A matching size of 20 cm. of this object could have resulted from such a registered distance. A match much larger than 9.9 cm. was thus compatible with the known size of the room. We therefore prefer another explanation. We believe that oculomotor adjustments do not serve as distance cues for large distances. We do not, however, assume that states of convergence caused by the larger object distances are less accurate. We can see no reason for such an assumption. But in the

[6]t was obtained in the case of the normal viewing condition by changing the average matches made by individual Ss into constancy ratios, which then served as raw scores. For the matches obtained with glasses, individual average scores in the triangle and oblong condition were transformed to conform to the standard length of 12 cm. and then treated as raw scores to compare with the matches of Experiment 1.

[7]The stated explanations were proposed recently by Gogel (1969) and by Rock and McDermott (1964) in another context.

case of larger object distances, a difference between two states of convergence corresponds to a much larger difference in distance than where short distances are concerned. (This is a consequence of the fact that the degree of convergence is inversely proportional to distance.) The small convergence angles are therefore not associated with well-defined distances, and this, we believe, interferes with the establishment of the learned connections between small convergence angles and registered distance.

Experiment 4

Because of the importance of Experiment 3, we repeated part of it with a new group of Ss and larger distances of the test objects. We obtained matches under normal viewing conditions with the oblong and triangle at distances of 100 and 200 cm., with 12 Ss participating.

The mean matching length of the base with the triangle in the near position was 8.2 cm. It was 11.3 cm. when the triangle was in the far position, from which the equivalent value was computed as 6.4 cm. The true matching length for the near position, the average of 8.2 and 6.4, was therefore 7.3 cm. for a far length of 8.5 cm. The constancy ratio amounted to .86±.096.

Experiment 5

A large part of the evidence in this report stems from comparisons made without the glasses. It therefore seems worthwhile to present further evidence for the absence of extraneous distance cues from our experimental conditions. Such cues would, where normal viewing conditions were employed, contribute to the veridicality of the matches and the size estimates. The new evidence was obtained by obtaining size estimates under two conditions, one with glasses and the other without them, causing the same oculomotor adjustment. To bring this about, the object distances were so chosen that an equivalent distance of a test object seen through the glasses was the same as an actual distance of the normally viewed object. In the absence of extraneous distance cues from the tests, mean size estimates made under two such conditions should be the same.

Two spectacles were used. One was identical with the near glasses employed in our experiments and caused the eyes to increase

accommodation and convergence by the equivalent of 1.5 lens diopters. The other, a different pair of far glasses, forced a decrease of
oculomotor adjustments equivalent to 1.5 lens diopters. Two test
distances were selected because they were 1.5 lens diopters apart,
namely, 33.3 and 66.7 cm. Wearing the near glasses, our *S*s made size
estimates of an object 66.7 cm. away, which made its equivalent
distance 33.3 cm. These estimates could then be compared with estimates of an object actually 33.3 cm. distant and viewed without
glasses. Similarly, an object 33.3 cm. away was viewed through the
far glasses, and the resulting estimates could be compared with those
obtained with normal viewing of an object 66.7 cm. distant. The
objects were two diamonds, but they were not of equal size. Instead,
their sizes were so chosen that they produced the same image size.
This made easier the critical comparisons ultimately to be made,
namely, of size estimates that were obtained with the same oculomotor adjustments but were of objects actually located at different distances. The diagonal of the nearer diamond was 6 cm. and that of the
one twice as far away was twice as long. As in Experiment 2, *S* gave
his size estimate by changing the length of an adjustable rod to
match the apparent length of a diagonal. Because *S*s wore glasses for
some of the size estimates, they made the adjustments of the length
of the rod by touch only. In all other respects the experimental
conditions were the same as in our other experiments for which the
present one served as control. The order of presentation of the four
experimental conditions was varied. Twenty-four *S*s participated.[8]

The results are given in Table 2. As can be seen, the mean size
estimate obtained when the diamond at 66.7 cm. distance was seen
through the near glasses was the same as the mean estimate for the
diamond at 33.3 cm. seen without glasses. Inasmuch as the retinal
images of the two diamonds were the same, identical size estimates
imply identical registered distances. The same applies to the other
two conditions where oculomotor adjustments were for the same
distance, namely, 66.7 cm. The obtained mean estimates were quite
similar also. Since extraneous distance cues would counteract the
effect of the glasses by causing registered distance and therefore size

[8]We are grateful to Dr. Karl Josef Frey for making this experiment available to
us.

estimates to be more veridical, the close agreements of the mean size estimates within the pairs of conditions that produced the same oculomotor adjustments demonstrates absence of extraneous distance cues.[9]

TABLE 2

Mean Tactile Size Estimates in Centimeters of Two Diamonds Yielding Identical Image Sizes

Size	Actual Distance	Condition	Equivalent Distance	Oculomotor Adjustments for	Size Estimates	Difference
12	66.7	Near Glasses	33.3	33.3	8.03	.01 ± .41
6	33.3	No Glasses		33.3	8.02	
6	33.3	Far Glasses	66.7	66.7	12.17	.59 ± 70
12	66.7	No Glasses		66.7	12.76	

Conclusions

We would like to draw two conclusions from our results: (1) A tendency toward making image sizes equal operates in experiments where the sizes of figures of identical shape are being matched. This tendency competes with the given cues for distance and makes them appear less effective than they really are. (2) Under conditions where both accommodation and convergence respond to the same distance, these oculomotor adjustments serve as fairly good cues for distances of at least up to 2 m., but this can be demonstrated with size matching only if the tendency toward image size matching is prevented from operating.

Image size matching has often been obtained when all cues for distance had been eliminated. This fact has been attributed either to a capacity to perceive size according to the size of the retinal image (Rock & McDermott, 1964) or to a tendency to perceive the objects to be matched at a common distance (mainly Gogel, 1969). Our results are compatible with either one of these explanations.

[9]The mean size estimates obtained under normal viewing conditions can be used to compute a constancy ratio. It amounts to .80, considerably lower than those obtained in Experiments 3 and 4. We ascribe this to the estimation procedure of adjusting the length of the rods by touch only.

References

Biersdorf, W. R., Ohwaki, S., & Kozil, D. J. The effect of instruction and oculomotor adjustments on apparent size. *American Journal of Psychology,* 1963, 76, 1–17.

Gogel, W. C. The effect of convergence on perceived size and distance. *The Journal of Psychology,* 1962, 53, 475–489.

Gogel, W. C. The sensing of retinal size. *Vision Research,* 1969, 9, 1079–1094.

Heinemann, E. G., Tulving, E., & Nachmias, J. The effect of oculomotor adjustments on apparent size. *American Journal of Psychology,* 1959, 72, 32–45.

Leibowitz, H., & Moore, D. Role of changes in accommodation and convergence in the perception of size. *Journal of the Optical Society of America,* 1966, 56, 1120–1123.

Rock, I., & McDermott, W. The perception of visual angle. *Acta Psychologica,* 1964, 22, 119–134.

Wallach, H., & Zuckerman, C. The constancy of stereoscopic depth. *American Journal of Psychology,* 1963, 76, 404–412. In the present volume, Chapter VII, selection 3.

V

Visual perception of motion

The farther natural science has developed the greater has been
the discrepancy between the picture of the world which it has presented us and the world we experience through our senses. The
physical world consists mostly of processes: molecules move and
collide or they swing and rotate while forces hold them together;
other dynamic processes make up chemical bonds; electrons move,
revolve and spin, causing fields and all manner of radiation; nuclei
are held together by mysterious forces, and at the other end of the
scale, a living organism is an intricate array of a huge number of
chemical processes. As opposed to this, the external world as we
experience it through perception is mostly static. It consists mainly
of forms and qualities. It is the qualitative nature of so many experiences that most strongly contrasts with the real nature of the physical world. All sorts of physical processes cause qualitative
experiences in perception as, for instance, colors, tones, noises, the
sensations of cold, warm and hot. The inner-organic processes also
present themselves to the mind as qualities, like pain and other

Reprinted from G. Kepes, ed., *The Nature and the Art of Motion.* New
York: George Braziller, 1965.

feelings. Even dynamic processes within the mind are often experienced in a qualitative manner as, for instance, yearning, frustration or mourning.

I suspect that, while it fascinates a few, this discrepancy in general helps to alienate the humanistically oriented individual from physical science. Yet the artist who fashions physical objects knows enough to be free of such an attitude. He realizes that to a large part the discrepancy is due to the medium of light, which connects our eyes with the physical objects we see. Some of the discrepancies, on the other hand, arise with the perceptual processes and this is why they interest us here. More often than is usually realized, our perceptual experience is influenced by the nature of the psychological processes that lead up to it. To be sure, much of this "creativity" serves to make perceptual experience truer than the intake of the eye would warrant: the tri-dimensionality of the environment, lost in the projection on the retina, is restored to visual experience, and correction is made for the effect of distance on projective size. An integrative process causes veridical form perception to emerge from a sequence of different views of an object, each of which by itself is insufficient to transmit all the information that serves to define the object's shape. Color perception is so organized that the lightness of the perceived colors is more in keeping with the reflectances of surfaces than with the light intensities which they happen to reflect under the prevailing illumination. But not all characteristics of perceptual experience that are due to the manner of operation of the perceptual processes serve to make perception more veridical than the conditions of stimulation which cause them. Some are simply peculiarities which are without any apparent sense and which happen to contribute toward the discrepancy between perceptual experience and our knowledge of the physical world. The term peculiarity may seem oddly disparaging, considering that I am talking about part of our primary reality, but I think it is used with justification.

One of the most interesting examples of such a peculiarity of perception is the manner in which we experience visual movement. There is an essential difference between motion as we experience it and motion as the physicist describes it. While to the physicist motion is primarily displacement of an object in relation to other objects—which object is displaced and which serves as a frame of reference is here merely a matter of description—visually perceived motion has no such relative aspect; it is felt to be entirely the affair of the moving object and may be described as a temporary attribute of that object. Even though we certainly can make ourselves aware of the displacement of a moving object in relation to other objects in the field, this awareness is by no means a genuine part of the perceived motion, which remains solely a property of the moving object.

It would be tempting to ascribe this discrepancy to the manner in which physical movements are represented in the stimulation that reaches the eye. Is not motion perceived when an object changes its position in relation to the observer, causing the eyes to pursue it? Since this need not involve another visual object, absence of a relative aspect from perceived motion would be in accord with the conditions of stimulation. Matters are, however, not so simple. Displacement of a visual object relative to the observer is not the only condition that leads to perception of motion, and is not even the most important one. Displacement of one object in the field of vision in relation to another one is also a cause of perceived motion. One may wonder how this effect could ever be demonstrated, since displacement of an object in relation to another object must always involve a displacement of at least one object with respect to the observer. The evidence comes from measurements of the threshold for movement under different conditions. Everybody is familiar with the fact that a physical movement may be too slow to lead to perceived motion. When an object that undergoes slow displacement is observed for an extended period, one may notice that it changes its position but the impression of motion may be absent. The objective velocity will have to be raised for experienced motion to emerge. The velocity at which this just barely happens is the threshold. It is fortunate that the threshold for motion is lower when an object moves in relation to another visual object than when it moves alone in the field of vision. In other words, in the presence of a stationary object a smaller velocity suffices to cause an impression of motion than when only the displacement between the moving object and the observer mediates the fact of movement. When, for example, in a completely dark room a single luminous dot is moved and observed, its velocity can be gradually reduced until the displacement is no longer perceived as motion. If then a second, stationary dot lights up near the moving one, motion will again be seen as long as the two dots do not move too far apart. Observations like this show that there are two different causes for the visual perception of motion. One condition of stimulation consists of the displacement of a seen object in relation to the observer; to this we shall refer with the term "angular displacement." The other condition of stimulation consists of the displacement of one object in relation to another object in the field of vision, henceforth called "object-relative displacement." The latter can be separately studied by using motion velocities below the threshold for angular displacement, the former by presenting the moving object in an otherwise homogeneous field.

Motion perceived on the basis of object-relative displacement alone presents an interesting question. Perceived motion, we have seen, consists in a specific attribute being temporarily inherent in an object; we call an object at rest when this attribute is absent. Thus, in experience, motion and rest are absolutes. When angular displacement is too slow to be effective, no information is imparted as to which of the objects in the visual field is actually displaced with respect to the observer. Therefore, we cannot expect that the object that moves relative to the observer will always be the one that is seen to move. This gives rise to the question: how will perceived motion and rest here distribute themselves among the objects that are being displaced relative to each other? When in an otherwise homogeneous visual field one object moves toward another object, either one, or even both, may be seen to move. The perceptual result of such an arrangement is as varied as its ambiguity would cause one to expect. But when conditions of stimulation are so arranged that one of the two objects surrounds the other or forms its background, the resultant experience is always the same: the surrounded object is seen to move in a direction identical with that of its displacement in relation to its surround, and the surrounding pattern is seen at rest. This rule is rather strict and pervasive. Under ordinary circumstances, it would cause object-relative displacement to add its effect to that of angular displacement: an object that is being displaced in relation to the observer will also be displaced in relation to the stationary objects of the visual environment, and since the latter will usually form its surround it will be seen to move on object-relative grounds also.

But because of the rule, object-relative displacement may lead to illusory motion. This will happen to an object that is at rest relative to the observer while its surround is in motion. As the surrounded object it will still appear to move. We have here, in fact, the scheme of a well-known illusion of movement. It can be observed, for instance, when the moon is visible among drifting scattered clouds. The moon then appears to move in a direction opposite to that in which the clouds move. The clouds function here as the surrounding object and the moon as the surrounded one. Another example of this sort of illusory motion may be equally familiar to the reader: a pole standing in a steadily moving stream which carries along on its surface leaves or other debris; the pole appears to drift upstream.

This illusion, which is commonly called "induced movement," occurs because object-relative displacement prevails over angular displacement in causing experienced motion, where the two would tend to produce different effects. The pole, being stationary in relation to the observer, appears to move only on account of its displacement in relation to the surrounding pattern; that it does appear to move attests to the potency of object-relative displacement as a cause of perceived movement.

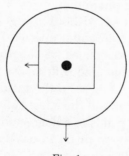

Fig. 1.

The very nature of object-relative displacement as a cue for motion perception has interesting consequences and leads to unexpected phenomena. Imagine, for instance, an arrangement of three figures inside each other: a small disk is surrounded by a larger outline square which, in turn, is surrounded by a still larger ring. Because they are projected, the ring and the square can be displaced independently of each other. Objectively, the ring moves slowly downward, the square to the left and the disk is stationary. What movements will be perceived? Owing to angular displacement, the ring will be seen to move downward; the square, being displaced in relation to the ring obliquely upward and to the left, will be seen to move in that direction, and the disk will be seen to move to the right, for this is its displacement relative to the square.

That object-relative displacement is the more potent of the two conditions that cause perceived movement, becomes quite clear when the causes of motion speed are investigated. Speed is the attribute of perceived motion that we use in judging the velocity of physical motion, the impression of swiftness or slowness of movement. In 1927, J. F. Brown made a discovery which was at the time completely unexpected. For reasons which need not concern us here he had his subjects observe the speed of a small black disk that was seen moving through a bright aperture while the rest of the room was dark. There were, in fact, two such movement fields, with aperture and disk in one field twice the size of those in the other field. When the subjects compared speeds of the disks' motions and by changing the velocity in one of the fields made the speeds appear equal, it was found that the velocity in the larger field had to be almost twice as great as in the smaller field to produce such a speed match. The transposition phenomenon, as Brown called it, held for a wide range of velocities without a significant change in the velocity ratio that produced equal speeds. It was also possible to make the difference in the sizes of the movement fields much greater. For the very large size differences the ratio of matching velocities does not come as close to the ratio of the field sizes as it does for smaller differences, but the effect of field size on speed is still very great. This effect depends to a degree on dark room conditions. When the comparisons were made in daylight, the velocity ratios deviated more strongly from the size ratios. The explanation is undoubtedly that in daylight additional frames of references beyond the aperture edges become visible which are not transposed in size as the apertures are: the outer edges of the aperture frames, for instance, which happened to be equal in size. That this is the right explanation can be shown by covering the normally homogeneous aperture frames with identical patterns; this reduces the velocity ratio still further.

Today, the transposition phenomenon is readily understood.

When perceived motion can result from displacement of an object in relation to another object, it is only sensible to expect that speed can depend on some property of object-relative displacement also. Let us for the moment assume that the transposition phenomenon occurs in ideal form, namely, that velocities have to be transposed in exactly the same ratio as the field sizes in order to produce equal speeds. Doubling both the size of the field and the velocity of the moving disk, for instance, would then leave the speed unchanged. The time that it takes a disk to traverse its aperture from end to end would also remain unchanged. Thus, rather simple relations result from the assumption of ideal transposition ratios. One might, for instance, say that speeds are equal when the objective displacement covers in unit time equal fractions of the aperture path. Speed would depend on the relative rate of displacement, where displacement is measured on a scale that depends on the size of the movement field in which it occurs. The transposition phenomenon may simply mean that, where motion is perceived on the basis of object-relative displacement, there is no general scale available in reference to which a rate of displacement could find definition. Instead, the distance that the moving object traverses in unit time is defined in terms of the scale of the movement field in which it takes place.

At this point it becomes necessary to talk briefly about the perception of form. The fact that we perceive form as such is probably the most important characteristic of visual perception, for the visual patterns that reach the eyes consist merely of an array of different brightnesses and colors. Having been part of our experience as far back as we can remember, form perception is so much taken for granted that few realize that it is the product of the perceptual processes, rather than directly given in the visual input. Yet the fact that it is possible to render some essential properties of a scene by means of an outline drawing should make this evident. All the primary data of color and shading are here eliminated, and by means of a single differentiation in brightness an experience of form is transmitted which is often equivalent to that produced by viewing the natural scene. An outline drawing directly establishes an experience that organizing processes, in the presence of a natural environment, extract from the given color pattern.

The fact that form as we experience it is not directly given in visual stimulation, but is rather a product of the mind, has many interesting consequences. Most widely known of these is the ambiguity of plane patterns, which is connected with the reversibility of figure and ground. One of the properties of form that is relevant to our discussion of motion is the fact that a visual pattern can be changed in size without changing the form which it causes in experience. Form perception may have a bearing on the perception of motion because the displacement of an object relative to its surround can be regarded as a change in the form that the object and its surround taken together make up. The motion of our disk through its aperture offers a simple example. Disk and aperture edge together show different forms dependent on the various positions that the disk passes on its movement through the aperture. Object-relative displacement may thus be taken to mean form change, and inasmuch as form is not affected by change in size, proportionate displacements in transposed movement fields would represent identical form changes. Thus, when the velocities of the disks are in the same proportion as the corresponding field sizes, the displacements produce form changes at equal rates, and this is most probably the reason why they tend to produce equal speed. The fact that in Brown's experiments the results merely approach the ideal proportionate values is easily understood. Brown had his disks move with velocities which made their motion effective through their angular displacement also, and to the degree to which speed depends on angular displacement it should be expected to approach veridicality. We shall return to this point later.

The interpretation of object-relative displacement as form change, which explains the transposition principle, is further supported by an entirely different fact. This fact is related to another property of form perception: the strange dependence of experienced form on the orientation of the given pattern relative to the upright of the visual field. Tipping a square by 45 degrees leaves its shape geometrically unaltered but its perceived form changed; it will look so different that it commands a different word in the English language. It can be shown that this dependence of form on orientation is reflected in motion perception.

When two bright dots in an otherwise dark field are displaced in the same direction and at the same rate, no motion will be seen if the velocity is below the threshold for angular displacement, for the distance between the dots does not change and no object-relative displacement occurs. There is still another way to displace two points so that the distance between them is not changed: to have them revolve about each other, or simpler yet, to have one point move about the other on a circular path. This arrangement, however, involves a change in orientation. The pair of points, being related to each other in experience, produces in every position it assumes a different impression of direction. If change in orientation is equivalent to object-relative displacement, motion should be perceived even when the velocity of the point on the circular path is slowed below the threshold for angular displacement, and this is indeed the case. A mere change in orientation of a rigid pattern causes perceived motion at the slow rate at which object-relative displacement alone is normally effective. Only the notion that perceived movement depends on form change offers an explanation of this fact.

Strong evidence, then, argues that movement perceived on grounds of object-relative displacement is mediated by form perception and is based on form change. Two properties of form perception —the invariance of form under transformation in size, and the dependence of form on orientation—were found to be characteristics of motion perception also.

The realization that one of the two conditions of stimulation for motion leads to perceived movement by way of form perception makes the next question to be taken up only more interesting: what exactly is the relation between the two conditions, angular displacement and object-relative displacement? There are two facts that throw light on the matter.

The first of these has to do with Brown's transposition phenomenon. The experiments that yielded this finding are interesting in still another way: they cause the two conditions of stimulation to be in conflict with each other. With the two movement fields at equal distances from the observer, angular displacement by itself should yield veridical speeds, that is, speeds should appear to be equal when the objective velocities are the same. If, on the other hand, the speed for perceived motion depended merely on the rate of form change, speeds in the transposed movement fields should appear matched when the velocities are exactly in the same proportion as the field sizes. The actual results obtained are the outcome of both conditions of stimulation taking effect simultaneously, and can serve as an indication of the relative effectiveness of the two conditions. The fact that the velocity ratios approach those of the field sizes and are far from being veridical indicates a preponderance of the effect of object-relative displacement.

The other fact that is relevant here leads to more striking conclusions. Numerous arrangements of objective movement are known where a given displacement leads to two perceived movements seen simultaneously. In every case, one of the two perceived movements results from that component of the actual displacement which is given through an object-relative displacement, while the other perceived movement corresponds to what remains of the actual displacement after that component has been subtracted. We shall discuss two specific examples.

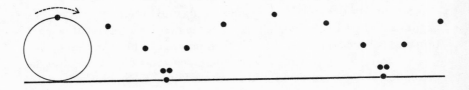

Fig. 2.

The first example, although somewhat complicated, is presented because it has received much attention in the past. A wheel rolls on a horizontal rail in the dark. A small point of light is fixed to the face of the wheel near its rim and is the only object visible. Its objective motion will describe a well-known curve of successive arches, called cycloid, which results from vectorial addition of two simple motion paths, a circular one produced by a point revolving about a center, the wheel's hub, and a straight one, of the translatory motion of the wheel as a whole. The observer perceives the situation as it is, motion through a path of repeated arches. But when a second point of light is added near the wheel's rim diametrically across from the first, the arch-shaped motion paths will cease to be seen. Instead the two light points will appear to revolve about each other and in addition to move together on a straight horizontal path. For each light point the actual cycloid path is now broken down into the two mentioned components. Why does this happen? It has been argued that revolution of the two points about each other plus a translatory motion of the pair is a simpler process than the alternative one where two arch-shaped motion paths penetrate each other. But there is a less speculative interpretation possible: the revolution of the two points about each other is given by object-relative displacement, while the translatory motion of the pair is given by angular displacement alone. If the objective movements were slowed down below the threshold of an effective angular displacement, only the revolution would be seen (even if cycloid motion had been perceived at higher velocities).

Fig. 3. **A** shows the actual motion paths in Johansson's experiment. **B** shows the experienced motion.

Our other example is one from a number of further instances of simultaneously perceived movements which were discovered by Gunnar Johansson. Here two dark spots on a light background moved in straight lines, one vertically downward and the other horizontally to the left so that their movement converged on a point, and then they returned over the same paths to the starting positions. Thus the combined motion paths formed an L. The observer invariably saw the two spots move straight toward each other on an oblique path until they met and then back on the same slant. At the same time they also seemed to move as a group obliquely down to the left and then back up to the right. Of the two simultaneous motions, the movement of the spots toward and away from each other was much more conspicuous. In fact, only about 65% of the observers reported the second motion spontaneously; the others had to be questioned and then "confirmed its presence without hesitation."

It is easy to see what goes on here. Each spot's motion path gives rise to two component movements. One motion of each spot is along the line connecting their extreme end positions; the other is at right angles to this line. The first results from the displacement of the spots in relation to each other, in which they approach each other, overlap for a moment and recede again. The second corresponds to the residual component of the motion path which is effective as a displacement relative to the observer only. By no stretch of the imagination can it be argued that the separation into two component movements results here in a simpler process. On the contrary, single motion of each spot corresponding to its objective horizontal or vertical displacement would be by far simpler. Only one explanation makes sense here: the oblique motion of the spots toward and away from each other is given through object-relative displacement (and would be the only motion seen if velocities were slowed down to the point where angular displacement is ineffective); the other corresponds to the residual angular displacement.

This explanation fits all instances where objects are seen to undergo two movements simultaneously. If it is accepted, these instances show a striking prevalence of motion based on object-relative displacement over motion based on angular displacement. In such instances object-relative displacement comprises only part of the total displacement, whereas angular displacement represents the displacement in its entirety. Thus, neither one of the two perceived motions corresponds to the total angular displacement, while one does correspond to the object-relative displacement. The perceptual process based on the latter pre-empts, so to speak, the given displacement and the second perceived motion corresponds to the residual displacement. The motion process that is caused by object-relative displacement is truly predominant.

Little is known about the manner in which angular displacement leads to perceived motion, and this is probably the reason why there is at this time no further light on the relationship between the two conditions of stimulation that give rise to perceived motion. Allowing ourselves some speculation, we might be inclined to ascribe the fact that motion is perceived as an attribute of a moving object, rather than a relative displacement, to the existence of angular displacement as an effective condition of stimulation. Angular displacement is relative only in respect to the viewer himself; as a visual object the moving thing is unique. And since there can be little doubt that angular displacement appeals to a phylogenetically older perceptual mechanism, the idea that angular displacement is responsible for the peculiar way we perceive motion has a certain force.

On the other hand, that motion is perceived as a temporary attribute of an object is in keeping also with the way object-relative displacement operates. As we have seen, object-relative displacement takes effect by the route of form perception. There is a parallelism in form perception to the peculiar manner in which relative displacement is treated in motion perception, namely, the phenomenon of figure and ground. Of two areas of different color, one surrounding the other, the surrounded area is usually seen as figure; that is, the border-line between the two areas becomes the surrounded area's boundary, limits it, and gives it shape, while the surrounding area does not appear to be bounded by that border-line, derives no shape from it, becomes ground. Similarly, in a relative displacement between an object and the surrounding pattern, the surrounded object attains the attribute of motion, and the surround is perceived at rest. Both phenomena are arbitrary as far as the conditions of stimulation are concerned and reflect the creative nature of our most basic perceptual process.

POSTSCRIPT

The work of J. F. Brown, which was discussed above, has been misrepresented in several secondary sources. Citing O. W. Smith and L. Sherlock (A new explanation of the velocity-transposition phenomenon. *American Journal of Psychology,* 1957, 70, 102–105), they attribute the transposition phenomenon to the impression of rhythmic speed that might develop as evenly spaced rows of dots enter and leave the movement field. When, in transposed movement fields, the distances between dots are also transposed as they in fact were, transposed fields would produce equal rhythmic speeds. This explanation apparently overlooks Brown's second publication (The visual perception of velocity *Psychologische Forschung,* 1931, 14, 199–232), where all earlier experiments were repeated with only one dot visible at a time. This was done for the expressed purpose of excluding an impression of rhythmic speed. The same results were obtained as before. It was also found that the transposition phenomenon occurred over a wide range of absolute velocities, a fact that is sometimes overlooked.

An Explanation of the Visual Perception of Motion

My treatment of motion perception leaves two problems unanswered: Why are there two conditions of stimulation that lead to perception of visual motion, angular displacement and object-relative displacement? And what is the basis for the rule that, given an object-relative displacement, it is the surrounded object that is seen to move? My answer is that both are the product of the simplest kind of learning, the substitution of one stimulus condition for another.

To say that object-relative displacement acquires its capacity to evoke motion perception through stimulus substitution, that is, through pairing with angular displacement, implies that the latter has primacy as a condition of stimulation for motion perception. To argue this point it is necessary to acknowledge that angular displacement may be mediated by two different stimulus events: image displacements and ocular pursuit movements. After a moving object has drawn one's attention, its displacement is given by pursuit movements. But it is the initial displacement of the object's image across the retina that attracts attention. Or when a stationary object begins to move, its image is first displaced and only later is its motion relative to the observer given through ocular pursuit. To find that image displacement and pursuit movement intimately share in mediating angular displacement does not require that we ascribe to them the same degree of primacy. At present, it seems that image displacement operates like a sensation and pursuit movement does not. Prolonged exposure to the same image displacement has results analogous to those of a true sensation. Prolonged exposure of a retinal region to the same color stimulation causes the saturation of the perceived color to diminish and a negative afterimage to develop. Prolonged exposure of a retinal region to continuous pattern displacement causes the speed of the perceived motion to diminish and an aftereffect of motion with opposite motion direction to develop. Pursuit movements cause no such aftereffects. These facts suggest that image displacement is the primary condition of stimulation that causes motion perception.

It seems most likely that every pursuit movement as well as every change in its direction forced by a change in the direction of the object motion is preceded by an image displacement. This regular sequence of events would favor a learning process through which the capacity to evoke motion perception is transferred from image displacement to pursuit movement. Similarly, object-relative displacement is very often paired with angular displacement. In a great majority of occasions for motion perception, an object in angular displacement is seen among stationary objects or viewed against a stationary background; object-relative displacement is here simultaneous with angular displacement. Again, simple stimulus substitution would render object-relative displacement capable of evoking motion perception.

Accounting for the effectiveness of object-relative displacement as a stimulus for perceived motion in this fashion solves a further problem. As pointed out above, object-relative displacement under ordinary conditions leads to veridical motion perception because of the rule that an object that is being displaced relative to other objects that form its surround will be seen to move while the other objects will appear to be stationary. It is only by virtue of such a rule that the relativity of object-relative displacement can be overcome and the temporary attribute of motion can be assigned. As long as motion perception caused by object-relative displacement is regarded as a basic process, this rule is an ultimate fact also. But if object-relative displacement is assumed to have acquired the capacity to evoke motion perception through pairing with angular displacement, the rule naturally results from that learning process. For, under the conditions in which such learning can take place, namely, when the moving object is seen against the background of the stationary content of the visual field, the object that is perceived to move by virtue of its angular displacement is, in fact, the surrounded one.[1]

Finally, this proposed etiology of the various stimulus conditions for visual motion perception explains the nature of perceived motion which consists in a temporary attribute of an object. I regard image displacement across the retina as the primary stimulus condition for motion perception. As previously stated, perceived motion that results from image displacement has the characteristics of sensations in that it is subject to two adaptation effects that are typical of other sensations. But the parallelism between motion perception and, say, color perception does not end here. Just as a color quality is ascribed to the object in whose image the chromatic stimulation

[1]For a more detailed discussion of some of these considerations see Chapter X, selection 1.

occurs, so the temporary attribute of moving is ascribed to the object whose image shifts across the retina. When, through stimulus substitution, other conditions come to evoke motion perception this qualitative aspect is, of course, maintained.

The role of head movements and vestibular and visual cues in sound localization[1]

In a previous paper[2] the writer has demonstrated that a distinct localization of sound exists for directions which do not fall into the horizontal plane but lie above or below at varying elevations, in other words that a discrimination of directions with respect to above and below and front and back is possible as well as discrimination

Reprinted from the *Journal of Experimental Psychology*, 1940, 27, no. 4, 339–368.

[1]The writer wishes to express his gratitude to Prof. W. Koehler and to Dr. Mary Henle for their help in preparing this manuscript.

[2]Ueber die Wahrnehmung der Schallrichtung. *Psychologische Forschung*, 22, 238–266 (I). A short English report on the same work has been published in the *Journal of the Acoustical Society of America*, 1939, 270–74 (II). The two papers will be referred to as I and II respectively. In the present paper the writer has attempted to present the material in such a way that it can be understood without knowledge of the previous papers. While paper II lacks theoretical discussion it may be useful for a quick reference to previous experimental results.

with respect to right and left which has been studied for many years. It was found that only a head movement during the presentation of the sound affords an adequate discrimination of sound direction in the dimension of above and below and thus makes localization complete. This is probably the reason why sound localization with respect to above and below has not been demonstrated in the laboratory at an earlier time. The paper referred to gives an analysis of the manner in which a complete perception of a sound direction is achieved with the help of a head movement. The binaural cues on which sound localization is primarily based do not suffice to characterize a sound direction completely. Yet, during a head movement the binaural cues as produced by the sound direction are altered, and the particular form of this change can in each case strictly determine the given sound direction. This is thoroughly discussed in the article mentioned. Experiments are reported in which perceived sound directions were synthetically produced in accordance with the head movement principle, which was thus verified. It is obvious that the change which the primary factors undergo due to the head movement can characterize a sound direction only if the exact kinematic properties of the particular head movement are taken into account. Two sets of sensory data enter into the perceptual process of localization, (1) the changing binaural cues and (2) the data representing the changing position of the head. It is the latter with which this paper is concerned. The manner in which they are secured is the object of this investigation.

I. The Role of Head Movement in Auditory Localization

It has been shown that the binaural cues for sound localization, time difference and difference of intensity, convey the angular distance of the given sound direction from the axis of the ears. Thus, they only determine how far from the median plane, on the left or on the right side, the given source of sound is located. Whether it lies in front or in the rear, above or below the horizontal plane, remains undetermined, and the same is true of the amount of its elevation. The angular distance of the given sound direction from the aural axis which is actually determined by the binaural cues has been called the lateral angle (ψ), and it is treated in this paper as if it were a directly given sensory datum.³ This lateral angle can be counted from either pole of the aural axis. If it is 90°, the sound direction lies in the median plane of the head. It follows that *the binaural cues determine merely a range of directions, any of which would, if actually presented, produce the same binaural stimulation.* It is significant that such a range of possible directions for a given sound is never perceived. We hear a sound that appears for the most part in one definite direction. It has been shown that this is due to head movements during the perception of the sound. A motion of the head will, in most cases, alter the position of the aural axis and at the same time change the angle between the latter and the given sound direction. It will be seen shortly that this change of the lateral angle can define the direction of the source of sound; and actually the perception of the proper direction is achieved through a head movement affording such a change of the lateral angle.

In order to show that the change of the lateral angle with the head movement can define a direction, we shall consider a number of particular cases. We shall at first assume that the head is turned about a vertical axis, so that the displacement of the aural axis occurs in the horizontal plane. If the given direction lies in the same plane, the angle between this direction and the aural axis (the lateral angle) changes by the amount of the displacement of the aural axis. This is obviously no longer true when the given direction is not in the horizontal plane, but is above or below. While in the case of the horizontal direction the lateral angle is measured within the horizontal plane, in the case of an elevated direction the angle between this direction and the aural axis extends in an oblique plane. It can easily be seen that this angle is affected to a lesser degree by a shift of the aural axis in the horizontal plane than is the lateral angle in the case of a horizontal direction. If the reader finds himself unable to visualize these spatial relations, the following consideration will lead to the same conclusion.

Take the case in which the direction is exactly vertical. The direction then exactly coincides with the axis of the head move-

---

³This is the terminology employed in paper II. In paper I, the term lateral angle refers to the complement of the angle ψ and is called ϕ. ϕ is thus the angular distance of the sound direction from the median plane and was chosen to represent the lateral angle for historical reasons. The motive for changing to ψ was the greater ease with which the angle ψ can be visualized.

ments, and the displacement of the aural axis will not alter the lateral angle at all. It remains 90° throughout the head movement. This is the extreme case. For all other directions the lateral angle will be changed by a displacement of the aural axis. A direction may be given 60° above the horizontal plane, and, before the head movement starts, exactly in front. At this stage, the lateral angle amounts to 90°. When a movement of the head by 90° brings the direction in the lateral position, the lateral angle will amount to 60°, the aural axis still lying in the horizontal plane with the direction 60° above it. A 90° shift of the aural axis thus brings about a 30° change of the lateral angle. For a horizontal direction, on the other hand, a like displacement brings about a 90° change of the lateral angle, as we have seen, while for the vertical direction the lateral angle does not change at all. These three cases are sufficient to suggest what can be learned directly from a visualization of the spatial relations, namely, that the amount by which the lateral angle changes varies with the elevation of the direction. For a given head movement this change is maximal when the direction lies within the horizontal plane, and decreases as the direction approaches the vertical.

Thus the angular distance of the direction from the horizontal plane (angle of elevation) varies with the rate of change of the lateral angle and is determined by it. For a given lateral angle, there are however in most cases four directions, which have the same angular distance from the horizontal plane: in front and in back, above and below. Of these, the two in front are distinguished from the two in back by another feature of the change of lateral angle, the direction, viz., the sign, of the change. When the head is turned to the left a direction in front will shift toward the right side of the head. For the same head movement, a direction in back will shift toward the left side of the head. That is to say, for a direction in front the lateral angle decreases toward the right, for a direction in back it decreases toward the left, and the two directions may thus be distinguished, although both may have the same elevation, and consequently the lateral angle will change for both at the same rate. Only one ambiguity remains: two directions in symmetrical position with respect to the horizontal plane, one above and the other below, are so far not distinguished.

These considerations concerning the rate and the direction of the change of lateral angle are independent of the particular spatial orientation of the head movement. The angle of elevation does not, of course, refer to the horizontal plane as such, but to the plane in which the aural axis is displaced by the head movement, which in the particular case we chose coincided with the horizontal plane. Our considerations apply as well to such a case as a movement about a horizontal axis, that is, a tilting of the head from side to side. Here the aural axis shifts in a vertical plane, the "angle of elevation" extends toward the front or the rear, and above and below now play the same role as front and back did in the case in which the head was turned. They are distinguished from one another through the direction of the change which the lateral angle undergoes due to the tilting motion.

When, upon a movement of the head about a vertical axis, two directions remain which are both consistent with the given change of lateral angle, one above and the other below the horizontal plane, a subsequent tilting of the head, or any motion which contains the tilting as a component, can distinguish between the two possibilities. In fact, natural head movements are rarely accurate revolutions about a constant axis; they must rather be described as revolutions with varying axis. This does not interfere with the qualification of the head movement for procuring a change of lateral angle which can determine a sound direction to the extent indicated above. But the displacement of the axis which occurs during the head movement probably suffices to remove the ambiguity which would result from an accurate revolution about a constant axis.[4]

We have found a number of different movements of the head to be effective in sound localization. The most frequent natural head movement is a turning of the head upon which a tilting to the side is gradually superimposed as the motion approaches the end of the excursion. In the synthetic production of sound directions which were previously reported, a revolution about a vertical axis, in which all components of tilting to the side had to be strictly excluded, was successfully used. In another group of these experiments the head movement was even more artificial; it consisted of a tilting of the head from side to side. With such unnatural movements most accurate localizations were achieved. We are probably justified in saying that any movement of the head which involves

---

[4]For a more detailed discussion of this point *cf.* I §7.

an angular displacement of the aural axis can be effective in sound localization. That a head movement which does not involve such a displacement of the aural axis must be ineffective is evident. No change of lateral angle can result from it. Such a head movement is a revolution about a horizontal axis extending from the left to the right, as it occurs in a straight nodding. It is, of course, also ineffective as a component in a kinematically more complicated natural head movement. Briefly, any head movement may be effective to the extent to which it contains as a component a revolution about an axis which lies in the median plane of the head.

The tests which will be reported in the next section are performed with synthetically produced sound directions. The manner in which sound directions can be synthetically produced has been thoroughly discussed in a previous paper; thus only a general outline will be presented in the following.

In experiments on synthetic production, the binaural stimulation which a given objective sound direction would have produced is brought about without actual presentation of this sound direction. We have seen that for a given position of the head the binaural stimulation which is produced by a given sound corresponds to quite a number of directions. All directions which have the same lateral angle produce the same binaural stimulation. Thus, so far as binaural cues are concerned, any one of these directions can be substituted for any other one. Where the lateral angle of a given direction changes in a characteristic way during a head movement, this direction can be replaced by a series of other directions which together present the same changing lateral angle. For every position through which the aural axis passes the lateral angle can be ascertained, and an equivalent direction can be substituted for the given direction. In practice one need not even consider an infinite number of such positions because a differential threshold exists in discrimination of the lateral position of a sound. Of two positions of the head for which the lateral angle is merely subliminally different, only one need be taken into account. We find it sufficient to consider separate positions which are as much as 3° apart. For the synthetical production of a certain sound direction, a definite head movement must be selected. Separate positions through which the aural axis passes during this head movement are chosen 3° apart from each other, and for each of these positions the lateral angle of the direction which is to be produced is ascertained. Thereupon, for each of these positions a direction can be selected among those which have the specific lateral angle ascertained for this position. In this way a series of directions is obtained which are equivalent to the direction which is to be produced, if each is presented at the moment when the head in its movement passes through the position to which it belongs. For the presentation of each of these different directions at the proper moment, the head of the observer is attached to a switch with 20 contact points. Each of these contact points is connected with a loud-speaker. In a particular experiment the switch permits only that movement of the head which is chosen in planning the experiment. It is always a revolution about a constant axis lying in the median plane of the head. During such a movement a contact spring slides over the contact points one after another, thus connecting each loud-speaker in turn. With every 3° displacement of the aural axis the center of another contact point is passed. The position of head and aural axis at the moment when the center of each contact point is passed can easily be ascertained, and the corresponding loudspeaker is placed in the direction which has previously been chosen to present the proper lateral angle for this particular phase of the head movement. When all the loudspeakers are arranged in this manner, the apparatus achieves precisely what is necessary for the synthetic production of the sound direction. While the head is moved, directions are presented which are equivalent to the direction to be produced. Together they present the same sequence of lateral angles which the synthetic sound direction would bring forth if it were actually given. In such experiments the physically given sound directions differ widely from the synthetic directions which are perceived.

In previously reported experiments the twenty loudspeakers which presented the sound were arranged in front of the observer, while the synthetic direction was, for instance, in back of or above the observer's head. In another experimental arrangement the observer perceived a sound directly in front, while all the actually presented directions lay above his head, distributed from left to right. Localization functioning on a basis other than the head movement principle should lead to the perception of sound in the directions actually presented or in their general neighborhood. If

nevertheless the synthetic direction is perceived, one can be sure
that it is solely on the basis of the head movement principle.

II. Passive Displacement of the Aural Axis

So far we have consistently used the term head movement. Yet,
according to the discussion in Section I any change of position of the
head which involves an angular displacement of the aural axis, no
matter how it is brought about, must suffice to procure a characteristic change of lateral angle. In the abstract, it should not matter
whether an observer turns his head actively, or turns on his heel,
or swings passively on a revolving chair, if the same displacement
of the aural axis results. We have already pointed out, however, that
two sets of sensory data enter into the perceptual process of sound
localization, the changing binaural cues which represent the change
of the lateral angle and the data which characterize the displacement
of the aural axis. Without the latter, the change of lateral angle has
no significance for sound localization. The nature of the stimulation
which represents the displacement of the head will vary with the
manner in which the displacement is achieved, and therefore this
manner may be very significant. In fact, any stimulation which is
capable of coöperating with the binaural cues in sound localization
should be investigated. For this reason the various ways in which
the head can be displaced will now be examined.

Three kinds of sensory data may represent a displacement of the
head: proprioceptive stimulation from the muscles engaged in active
motion, stimulation of the eyes, and stimulation of the vestibular
apparatus. Usually all three are present, but in experimentation one
or another may be excluded, and thus the significance of each kind
may be examined. However, one of them, the vestibular stimulation,
cannot be eliminated where spatial displacement of the head is involved; it will be always present. It should therefore be investigated
first.

In order to eliminate the optical cues for his motion and the
proprioceptive stimulation which would result from active bodily
movements, the observer was blindfolded and placed on a revolving
chair on which he could be turned about a vertical axis. A back rest
and a foot rest as well as a rest for the chin served to decrease the

slight stresses which arise when the acceleration is conveyed through the body from the parts in contact with the chair. Except perhaps for stimulation resulting from these stresses, the observer was made aware of the chair's and his own movements only through the function of the vestibular apparatus. The sounds which were to be localized under these circumstances were presented in exactly the same way as in the experiments on synthetic production. This was necessary because of the existence of a secondary factor in sound localization, the effect of the pinnæ,[5] which has no connection with the head movement principle, and which might possibly have affected the results. By presenting a synthetic sound direction, a differentiation between the effect of the head movement and the effect of this secondary factor becomes possible.

In the experiments we shall report here the displacement of the head was a revolution about a vertical axis. The loudspeakers were arranged in a single row in the horizontal plane, *i.e.,* the same plane in which the aural axis was displaced. The first test made with passive displacement and with blindfold was the synthetic production of a horizontal direction in back, with the row of loudspeakers in front. For this experiment the loudspeakers had to be arranged at distances of 6° from each other, the angles measured from a point which in the actual experiment coincided with the center of the observer's head.

It can easily be shown that this arrangement is suitable for the synthetic production of the desired direction: For a certain position of the head, the direction to be produced may lie straight in back. To this position of the head a position of the switch may correspond in which the contact spring touches exactly the center of a contact point. The loudspeaker which is connected with this contact point is placed straight in front of the observer. Thus its direction is equivalent to the desired direction, for in the case of both directions the lateral angle is 90°. Now we assume that the observer turns his head 3° to the right. This displacement turns the switch by one contact, and at the same time brings the desired direction in back closer to the right pole of the aural axis. The lateral angle of the desired direction decreases by 3° and is 87° for the resulting position of the head. The loudspeaker which is connected with this new contact

5 *Cf.* I §18 and II p. 273.

point must be placed in a direction which has a lateral angle also of
87°. When this is done, its position is 6° to the right of the previously
placed loudspeaker, that is, 3° closer to the right pole of the aural axis
on account of the change of lateral angle, plus another 3° because the
aural axis itself is displaced to the right by 3° with respect to the
position for which the first loudspeaker was placed. The center of the
following contact point is reached after another 3° of displacement
of the aural axis; the lateral angle of the desired direction in back
decreases again by 3°, and again the corresponding loudspeaker must
be fixed in a position 6° to the right of the one placed just before, that
is, 3° to account for the changed position of the aural axis and another
3° to account for the decrease in the lateral angle. The same procedure is, of course, applicable to the placing of all the following
loudspeakers in the row and can also be applied to those which lie
to the left of the loudspeaker placed first. Each is 6° distant from the
next.

In an actual experiment when the observer's head is turned to
the right by a certain angle, the sound will shift to the right by twice
that angle, appearing in one loudspeaker after another, and when the
head is turned to the left, the sound will be displaced to the left in
the same manner. Thus, as the head is turned back and forth the
sound slides through the row of loudspeakers at twice the rate of the
rotation of the head. To stress again the essential point: This sliding
sound will present to the observer the same sequence of lateral
angles which characterizes the desired direction in back, no matter
how quick or how wide the excursion of the head may be, provided
that it occurs within the range of the switch. With 20 contact points
3° apart, the switch allows a maximum displacement of the head of
60°, and stops on the switch confine the head movement to this
range. The 20 loudspeakers 6° apart cover an angle of 120°, and this
is the corresponding maximum displacement of the sound.

Before the observer was seated, the position of the revolving
chair was carefully adjusted so that its axis of revolution was in line
with the axle of the switch which was, of course, in these experiments, also in a vertical position. After the observer had been placed
on the chair, he adjusted his posture until his head could be fastened
to the switch; for the switch had to remain in its position relative
to the chair, and only its height above the floor could be altered.
When the head was fastened, the chin rest was moved up and was

fixed in the proper position. Then the observer was blindfolded. In all experiments reported in this paper, orchestra or piano music from victrola records was presented. When the music was turned on, it issued from one of the loudspeakers. From which one it came depended upon the accidental position of head and switch at the moment. The experimenter began to turn chair and observer back and forth, and the physical sound underwent the corresponding shifts. After a few excursions, interrupted by short pauses, the music was interrupted, and the observer was asked from where he had heard it.

All five observers who took part in this experiment heard the sound in the desired direction in back. When the experiment was varied in such a way as to bring the loudspeakers in back of the observer, the result was again positive for all observers: the sound appeared in front. As a further check, the switch was so constructed that the mechanical connection between the attachment of the head, on the one hand, and the switch proper, on the other hand, could be interrupted. In this case the contact spring remained at rest and one particular loudspeaker was constantly connected, while the observer was turned back and forth as before. When this was done during the presentation, the place of the perceived sound changed immediately; now it appeared in the direction of the sounding loudspeaker.

In the synthetic production, the sound was not only perceived on the reverse side in all cases, but in 9 of the 10 trials its direction was also exactly horizontal. Only in one case did the sound appear 25° above the horizontal plane. It will be shown below that under the conditions in question this direction could not possibly have been distinguished from a horizontal direction, and that it likewise represents a satisfactory result.

The positive results of these tests show clearly that sound localization based on the head movement principle is possible, even if the observer is passively turned and blindfolded. Yet they do not enable us to make an estimate of the accuracy with which the localization is achieved under these conditions. Firstly, localization within the horizontal plane, the only one we have as yet demonstrated, seems to be generally favored. If, for some reason, the data given for the localization of an elevated direction are inadequate, the sound is usually heard in a horizontal direction. Secondly, under our experimental conditions, the displacement of the aural axis occurs strictly in the horizontal plane. It has previously been pointed out that sound directions near the plane in which the aural axis is displaced (the equatorial plane of the head movement) are poorly defined. The reason for this fact is purely geometrical. In order to ascertain numerically how much the lateral angle of an elevated direction changes with a given head movement, one makes use of the following formula

$$\sin (90° - \psi) = \sin \beta \cdot \cos \delta,[6]$$

where ψ stands for the lateral angle (the angle between the sound direction and the aural axis), δ for the angle of elevation of the given direction above the plane in which the aural axis is displaced, and β for the angle by which the aural axis is displaced within this plane. According to this expression, the rate at which ψ changes with changing β is largely dependent upon the cosine function of the angle δ. Now the cosine function shows little change for the angles between 0° and, say, 30°. Applied to the present case this means that for directions of smaller elevation the rate of change of the lateral angle is practically the same over a considerable range of directions, and a direction which is determined by such a rate of change will be poorly defined in spatial terms. This, incidentally, furnished the explanation for our accepting a 25° elevated direction as a satisfactory result in the experiment under discussion. The rate of change for this direction is not different enough from the one which characterizes a horizontal direction to afford a discrimination. It may be added that under ordinary circumstances these conditions do not constitute a real difficulty for sound localization. As noted above, natural head movements are revolutions with varying axis, and with an approach of the axis toward the given direction conditions for a sharp determination of this direction improve rapidly.

In order to determine how accurately a blindfolded and passively moved observer can localize, and especially how his achievements compare with results under normal conditions, a direction was synthetically produced which had an elevation of 60° above the horizontal plane—in back when the loudspeakers were in front, or vice versa.

[6] *Cf.* I p. 245, where $\delta = 90° - \psi$.

The arrangement of the loudspeakers followed the same general procedure as that employed in the first experiment. As the desired 60° direction, one in back of the observer's seat was chosen. That contact point on the switch was ascertained which was connected when this direction fell into the median plane of the observer's head; and the corresponding loudspeaker was placed straight in front of the observer. A displacement of the aural axis by 3° would change the position of the switch so that the next contact would be closed. At the same time the aural axis would come somewhat nearer the desired direction, and the lateral angle would decrease. Yet this decrease would not amount to a full 3° as in the first experiment. An elevated direction, we have seen, corresponds to a change of lateral angle which is smaller than the displacement of the aural axis by which it is caused. Just how great this change will be can be computed from the formula given above. We let β equal 3° and substitute for δ the value 60°, that is the elevation of the desired direction above the horizontal plane, the plane in which the aural axis is displaced. Thus we obtain for ψ the value 88° 30'. Once we know the value of the lateral angle, the loudspeaker corresponding to the contact point in question can easily be placed. The loudspeaker which was placed first had a median position; its lateral angle was 90°. If the displacement of the aural axis is clockwise, the new loudspeaker must be placed to the right of the first one, that is, closer to the right pole of the aural axis; for a clockwise displacement brings the desired direction in back nearer to this pole. In order to determine its exact place we have to take into account the fact that, because of the displacement, the first loudspeaker is no longer in a median position. It now lies 3° to the left of the median plane, that is 93° from the right pole of the aural axis. Thus the new loudspeaker must be placed 4° 30' to the right of the one placed first in order to make its lateral angle 88° 30'. In other words, of the 4° 30' angular distance between the two loudspeakers, 3° account for the different positions of the aural axis when one or the other speaker is connected, and 1° 30' account for the change of lateral angle which takes place when the head passes from one position to the other.

The position of the next loudspeaker may be found in the same way. β has here the value 6°, while δ, of course, remains 60°, and the result obtained for ψ is 87°. For the corresponding position of the head the first loudspeaker lies 6° to the left of the median plane, while the new one must be placed $90° - \psi = 3°$ to the right of the median plane, i.e., $\beta + 90° - \psi = 9°$ to the right of the loudspeaker placed first. This loudspeaker is the starting point with reference to which the other loudspeakers are placed. In this manner all the loudspeakers on the right of the first are arranged. Those on the left side are to be arranged in the same way, with the qualification that here all angles refer to the left pole of the aural axis. When the head of the observer is fastened to the switch he must face the first loudspeaker directly, while the position of the switch must be such that this loudspeaker is connected.

In the actual test the procedure was exactly the same as in the first experiment. The experimenter turned chair and observer swiftly back and forth so that the velocity of the displacement approximated the speed of active head movements. Here again the observer could face the loudspeakers and have the desired direction in back, or vice versa. It seems that the situation in which the desired direction is to appear in front is more favorable, because directions in front are psychologically better defined than directions in back. Thus, most of the tests were done in this manner.

With elevated directions there is always the problem of how the observer is to indicate the direction of the sound. He can give an estimate of the elevation in degrees or he can point in the direction of the sound. Neither method is very accurate, and constant errors probably occur in both. The observer was allowed to choose between the two methods and encouraged in the use of both at the same time. Where both data are available they are indicated in the table. With one exception the 15 observers had only one trial.

The results are given in the first column of Table 1. The observers are listed in the order of their success in this experiment. The results of the first 6 are satisfactory, and the remaining judgments are too low.

With each observer a variation of this experiment was performed. The blindfold was removed from the observer's eyes, the experimenter gave the impression of changing the apparatus so as to suggest quite a different experiment, and then proceeded just as he had done before. The results are listed in the second column of the table. Without the blindfold, 13 of the 15 observers showed quite satisfactory results. This means that 7 observers showed a definite improvement over their performance when blindfolded. The two

TABLE 1

Subject	Blindfolded	Not Blindfolded
I	b . . . . 60° p, 60° est	same
II	b . . . . 60° est	60° est
III	b . . . . 55° p, 50° est	same
IV	b . . . . 60°–80° est	52° p
V	f . . . . 65° p, 80° est	same
V	b . . . . 55° p	same
VI	b . . . . 50° p, 60° est	60° p, 60° est
VII	f . . . . 45°–50° est	same
VIII	b . . . . 45° p	65° p
IX	f . . . . 40° p, 40° est	60° p
X	b . . . . 35° p	41° p
XI	b . . . . 30° est	70° est
XII	f . . . . 30° est	50°–60° est
XIII	b . . . . 20° p	70° p
XIV	b . . . . 10°–20° est	53° p
XV	b . . . . 10° p	64° p

Desired direction = 60°
b = loudspeakers in back.
f = loudspeakers in front.
p = subject points in the direction of sound image.
est = subject estimates its elevation.

who did not give satisfactory results (VII and X) were tested again with the chin rest removed so that active head movements became possible. The results showed no change of the direction they perceived. Apparently these subjects belonged to that large group who generally underestimate the elevation of any steep direction. The constancy in the results of these observers makes this interpretation plausible.

Two facts emerge from these results: Firstly, a sizable number of observers is able to localize sound adequately with passive displacement of the head and with exclusion of sight, that is, largely on the basis of vestibular stimulation. Secondly, all observers when passively moved are able to localize if vision is *not* excluded at least as well as they would do with active head movements. Under the given experimental conditions the first fact is quite remarkable. A revolution of the head strictly about a vertical axis does not entail a change of the direction of the gravitational force relative to the vestibular apparatus; only forces of acceleration give rise to stimulation of the vestibular system. This means that no direct cues for the position of the head at a given moment are obtained in the vestibular system. Even the velocity of the displacement of the head can only indirectly be derived from the stimulation; for only acceleration and not velocity as such can stimulate the vestibular apparatus. In whatever manner the displacement of the head is functionally represented in the process of sound localization, whether as a sequence of positions or as a rate of change,[7] the original sensory data have to undergo a transformation. These circumstances together with the fact that here the vestibular data are to be evaluated quantitatively raise a new problem in the field of vestibular function. The following considerations may help to form an estimate of the accuracy with which the vestibular data must represent the actual head movement in order to make possible the localizations which were obtained in this experiment.

As can be seen from the figures given above, in this experiment the loudspeakers close to the original one are 4½° apart. Roughly this is also true of the others. Since the contact points on the switch are 3° apart, the shift of the sound direction actually presented is 1½ times as great as the corresponding displacement of the head. In the experiment first reported the shift of the sound is twice as great as the displacement of the head, and the image of the sound appears horizontally opposite the loudspeakers. Another case which we may consider here is the one in which the image of the sound is directly overhead. As will be seen below, in this case the shift of the sound actually presented is as great as the displacement of the head. In short, if the ratio of the displacement of the sound to that of the head is 1, the sound image is straight above; if the ratio is 1½, the image is elevated by 60°; and if the ratio is 2, it is horizontal. A simple calculation shows that in the present case, where the ratio is 1½, an overrating of the actual displacement of the head by 50% due to insufficient sensory data would make this ratio 1, and accordingly the sound image would appear straight above; whereas an underrating of the actual displacement by 25% would make the ratio 2, and

[7]With respect to the achievement of sound localization these two possibilities are equivalent.

the sound would appear horizontal. Thus, in this case an underrating of a displacement of the head affects the perceived direction more strongly than an overrating of the same order.

An examination of the table shows that practically all the inadequate localizations which occurred were too low. This may be explained by the asymmetry with which inaccurate sensory data for the displacement of the head affect the perceived direction. In spatial terms, an inadequately determined direction may thus have a better chance of being heard below the desired direction than above. However, the simple assumption that with vision excluded the displacement of the head is underrated rather than overrated could also account for this finding, and in the experiment to be reported next, this latter explanation seems to be the proper one.

A sound image vertically above the observer was synthetically produced. In this case the arrangement of the loudspeakers is especially simple. A sound direction vertically above is characterized by the fact that the sound remains within the median plane when the head turns about a vertical axis; the lateral angle remains 90°. Thus, during such a displacement, the lateral angle does not change at all, and the rate of change is, of course, also zero. In order to duplicate these conditions in a synthetic experiment, the sound actually presented in the horizontal has to shift in such a way as to maintain a constant lateral angle of 90°. This is the case, when the actually presented sound is always either straight in front or straight in back of the observer's head. One achieves this by giving the loudspeakers angular distances of 3° from each other, the same as the angular distances of the contact points on the switch. While the observer's head is being attached, the switch is in a position which connects the loudspeaker straight in front or back. Under these conditions the actually presented sound is located in the median plane for any position of the head. When the head is thus attached, the experiment can proceed in the same way as the one reported above.

Of the 10 subjects who took part in the experiment, two were unable to localize the sound in the region overhead, even under favorable conditions. One of them always heard it in the rear about 60° high, and the other one horizontally in front or in back. The results for the other 8 subjects are as follows: 90°, 90°, 90°, 80°, 75°, 75–70°, 70°, 70°; here 90° represents the vertical, the other angles refer to directions slightly in back of the vertical. Thus, when blindfolded, 3 of the observers heard the sound in the desired direction, and the others localized it from 10 to 20° too far back. When the blindfold was removed, they all had the image of the sound vertically above. Again all deviations from the desired direction corresponded to an underrating of the displacement of the head; and since here misrepresentation of the actual displacement of the head in either sense leads to the same amount of deviation in spatial terms, we can safely adopt underrating of the displacement as the explanation. A simple calculation shows that an underrating of the displacement by 25% accounts for a deviation of 20° toward the back, which is the maximum which occurred in this experiment. In another respect this experiment confirms the result of the preceding one: There are subjects who can adequately localize merely on the basis of vestibular cues derived from acceleration, and with the others inaccuracies are restricted to what corresponds to a misrepresentation of the displacement by 25%. With the aid of vision, moreover, passive displacement is just as effective as active head movements.

The distinctly directed deviations from the desired direction which were found in these experiments seem to me of particular interest for the theory of sound localization. They obviously cannot be regarded as the result merely of an indistinct perception. In a purely geometrical sense there are two ways in which the elevation of a direction can be characterized by the behavior of the lateral angle during a displacement of the aural axis. One way is that the amount of change of the lateral angle referred to the displacement of the head as such characterizes the perceived direction, as has just been discussed. The value of this quotient would here directly determine the process which corresponds to the perceived direction.

The other way was brought out in the discussion of the maximal differences in the change of lateral angle which may occur with different elevations of a source of sound: the range within which the lateral angle of an elevated direction can change depends upon the elevation above the plane in which the aural axis is displaced. The greater the elevation of the sound direction above this plane, the smaller the range of variation of the lateral angle. For a head movement about a vertical axis, for instance, the lateral angle for a direction elevated 60° above the horizontal plane varies only within a range of 30°. An extreme case is the vertical direction; its lateral angle does not vary at all. No matter how far the head is displaced, the smallest value which the lateral angle of an elevated direction can assume is obviously the same as its angle of elevation above the plane in which the aural axis shifts. Thus the limiting value of the lateral angle can directly define the elevation of a direction. This constitutes the other way in which the elevation of a direction might be characterized by the behavior of the lateral angle.

It is clear from the outset that the second principle cannot alone be responsible for sound localization. Long before head movements produce the limiting value of the lateral angle, accurate sound localization may be achieved. The question is rather whether the second principle—which *geometrically* is strictly connected with the first —plays a secondary role in sound localization. In other words, are geometrical relations so fully represented in the process of sound localization that, because the first principle holds, the second—its geometrical corollary—must also hold?

In this connection, the most interesting case is that of the vertical direction because here the second principle could yield as strict a determination as the first. If we say that a sound is heard above because its lateral angle does not change at all but remains 90° throughout, this statement as such could be interpreted in terms of both principles. In terms of the first we might say that the lateral angle does not change, and in terms of the second that it remains *90°*. Either one of the arguments would suffice to characterize the direction. But the question is whether both principles are actually involved in the process. Here the experiment which we have just reported is decisive. When visual cues for the displacement of the head are excluded, the perceived direction is often definitely too low. Since these deviations always disappear when the blindfold is removed, they seem to be due to the insufficiency of available data for the displacement of the head, more specifically to the fact that the displacement of the head is underrated. The sound is heard at an elevation of 70° or 80°; and yet the actually presented sound is given in the median plane, *i.e.,* with a lateral angle of 90°. If the second, the limiting, principle were effective, this could not occur. We must therefore conclude that this second principle plays no role in the process of sound localization. It is merely the *amount* of the change of the lateral angle referred to the displacement of the head which is effective in determining the elevation.

III. The Selective Principle

Before further experiments are reported in which sound localization
is based on *visual* cues, it seems advisable to discuss briefly a general
selective principle which is implied in all sound localization. This
principle becomes particularly obvious in experiments in which
sound directions are synthetically produced. Why is it, one may ask,
that the desired direction is heard instead of the actually presented
sequence of directions? Obviously because this direction is at rest
whereas the actually presented sound shifts in space while the head
is being displaced. Apart from this selective principle, the actually
presented sequence of directions and the direction which is perceived are, according to our previous discussion, entirely equivalent.
They produce, with the head movement in question, exactly the
same temporal pattern of binaural stimulation. We know that almost
every lateral angle can be represented by a number of different
directions, and that a given sequence of lateral angles can thus
be represented by a nearly endless variety of patterns of subsequent directions. But in a given case this sequence of lateral
angles, no matter how it is produced, gives rise to one percept
only, that of a *stationary* direction which is compatible with the
sequence.

For the sake of simplicity we shall confine this discussion to
sequences in which each succeeding direction is contiguous with its
predecessor, i.e., cases where the presented sound shifts steadily and,
moreover, in a plane. Even in this simplest case it may be hard to
visualize the spatial relations which result from the circumstance
that both the presented sound and the head are displaced. The task
becomes easier if one chooses the head as frame of reference. With
reference to the head, all directions which realize a given sequence
of lateral angles are displaced during the head movement, the actually perceived one as well as the others. Objectively, the perceived
direction is distinguished from the others only by one fact. The
perceived direction is covariant with further objects which are
given in our environment by other senses and which are, of course,
also displaced with reference to the head when the head is being
turned. We thus arrive at the following formulation of the principle
of rest which I believe to be the most adequate: Of all the directions
which realize the given sequence of lateral angles, that one is per-

ceived which is covariant with the general content of surrounding space.

It is significant that the principle of rest must apparently be regarded as the limiting case of a more extensive principle which, although not overt in ordinary sound localization, seems to indicate the general way in which the selection is made. This broader principle was demonstrated in synthetic production of sound directions when sequences of lateral angles were presented for which no stationary direction existed. It was named the principle of least displacement. If a sequence of lateral angles is presented to which no stationary direction corresponds, the sound is perceived in the region where it has to undergo the smallest displacement in space while realizing the given sequence of lateral angles.

Suppose a sound direction vertically above is to be synthetically produced by means of a sound that shifts in the horizontal plane. In this case the arrangement of the head switch and the loudspeakers must be such as to leave the actually presented sound in the median plane of the head. This is the condition which must be fulfilled if the desired vertical direction is to be obtained. Consequently the angular distances of the contact points and of the loudspeakers will have to be the same, and if the head is fixed to the switch in such a way as to connect at the start the loudspeaker straight in front, the sound travels about during the head movement so that it is at any moment straight in front of the head. If, on the other hand, the head and the switch are connected, when the loudspeaker in question lies, for instance, 25° to the right, the sound will, during the head movement, always remain 25° to the right of the median plane of the head, i.e., at a lateral angle of 65°. No stationary direction corresponds to this sequence. The only case in which a sound at rest can be produced with a constant lateral angle is that in which this angle amounts to 90°. Here, it will be remembered, the sound image appears in the direction of the axis of the revolution of the head. When the lateral angle remains constant at 65° the sound is perceived at an elevation of about 65° to the right of the median plane, that is, as close as possible to the axis of the displacement. Here it moves about in correspondence with the displacement of the head.

It is obvious that at any lower elevation the shift in space necessary for the realization of the given sequence of lateral angles would be greater. The closer the sound to the axis of the revolution, the smaller is the displacement of the sound image in space. In accordance with the principle of least displacement, the sound is actually perceived in maximal proximity to that axis.[8]

IV. Rotation of the Visual Field

In Section II of this paper, experiments were reported in which both proprioceptive stimulation resulting from active head movements and visual cues for the displacement of the head were excluded. Quite substantial achievements in sound localization were shown to occur when only vestibular stimulation was thus admitted. If visual cues for the displacement of the head were added to the vestibular stimulation, they improved the achievements and even made them optimal. The question will now be examined of whether visual data *alone* can represent the displacement of the head in sound localization.

In order to eliminate vestibular stimulation, it seems to be necessary to keep the observer physically at rest and bring about a psychological state of motion by means of induced ego-movement. When an observer is placed inside a revolving screen he will, after a while, no longer perceive the surrounding screen in motion; rather he will feel himself rotating in a direction opposite to the objective movement of the screen. The question is, of course, whether with respect to sound localization the optically produced state of phenomenal movement is functionally equivalent to real movement; in other words, whether optical stimulation can replace vestibular stimulation.

The revolving screen used in this experiment was made of white cloth which hung down from the edge of a large wheel fixed in a horizontal position underneath the ceiling. It thus formed a hollow cylinder 43 in. in diameter. On the inside it showed vertical black stripes on a white ground, 2¼ in. wide and 6¾ in. apart. Wheel and screen were turned by a motor at various speeds.[9] When an observer was placed in this small compartment he soon felt himself

[8]Another experiment in which the principle of least displacement determines the result is reported in I §22.

[9]One revolution in 7 sec. proved to be a comfortable rate for the screen which was used.

turning in the opposite direction, and soon afterwards the screen appeared to be at rest. When now the observer looked down at the floor, he saw it turning in his own direction and at the same rate. The spontaneous transition from rest to motion was often quite disagreeable, but once the screen had come to phenomenal rest, as a rule no giddiness was felt. When the state of complete ego-movement was attained, there was never a spontaneous change back to the first state in which the observer is at rest and the screen moves. The transition to ego-movement was facilitated when some object was placed inside the screen upon which the observer could let his eyes rest. The observer was instructed to look steadily at a vertical rod which was placed before him and as close as possible to the screen. Soon after the screen began to turn the rod showed induced movement in the direction opposite to the movement of the screen; and gradually the observer felt himself joining in this motion until after a while, with the cessation of the phenomenal movement of the screen, the state of induced ego-movement became complete. Thus the momentary giddiness which often accompanies the transition to ego-movement could be eliminated.

A sound which remains in the median plane when the head is turned will be perceived in the direction of the axis of the displacement. If this axis is vertical, a sound objectively straight above the head would fulfill this condition. But the same condition is satisfied when a sound which shifts about in the horizontal plane remains throughout in a median position with reference to the head. If induced ego-movement can be substituted for an actual displacement of the head, the same effect can be obtained in an experiment with the revolving screen. A loudspeaker is placed at some distance beyond the screen straight in front of the observer whose head is kept in a constant position by a chin-rest. When now during induced movement a sound is presented in the loudspeaker, the above conditions for hearing a sound vertically above are given: the head of the observer "turns" about a vertical axis, and at the same time the sound remains always in a median position with reference to the head. In this situation the sound is actually heard vertically above. Thus it is shown that induced ego-movement can be substituted for a physical displacement of the head.

The great simplicity of this form of the synthetic experiment lies in the fact that instead of two displacements, that of the head and that of the sound, only the screen is actually moving. In the state of induced ego-movement the revolving screen represents the resting space, and all the objects which are physically at rest are therefore represented in the same state of motion as that in which the observer who is also physically stationary feels himself. The floor of the room and the rod in front of the observer are, as reported above, perceived in this state of motion. The loudspeaker would move about in the same manner, if the observer could see it. Had the distribution of motion and rest which the observer perceives in the state of induced ego-movement been objectively given, this experiment would be an exact duplication of an ordinary synthetic experiment: the head of the observer is displaced about a vertical axis, and the source of sound undergoes a corresponding displacement, so that it always remains in a median position.

Of 15 observers who participated in this experiment, 3 were unable, even under ordinary circumstances, to localize a sound presented objectively overhead. The remaining 12 perceived the sound as vertically above the head, either immediately or shortly after the beginning of the presentation. In the few moments during which it stayed in the horizontal plane it seemed to move about with the observer. When a sound was presented exactly to the side, it likewise travelled phenomenally with the observer, remaining always in the same position with reference to him. Yet, in this case, it remained in the horizontal plane. A sound direction which coincides with the aural axis is strictly determined by the binaural cues alone, just as the pole of the globe is sufficiently defined by its latitude, and needs no longitudinal determination. No other direction produces the same binaural cues, and thus no other direction could replace it.

If the loudspeaker was placed obliquely to the side, say, 30° from the median position, the sound was heard obliquely above where it seemed to move about with the observer. From the above analysis, it is clear that this is an analogue of the experiment on the principle of least displacement which was reported in Section III. All these observations can be made in immediate succession, when the loudspeaker is slowly carried around from a position straight in front of the observer to one on his side. The sound which is at first heard directly overhead descends slowly to a horizontal position.

There is still another experiment which can be performed with induced ego-movement. It corresponds to the first experiment reported in this paper, where a sound actually presented in front was perceived in back, and vice versa. This reversal of front and back was brought about when the actually presented sound direction was displaced by twice the angle of the displacement of the head. When induced ego-movement is substituted for a physical displacement of the head, the same relation of the displacement of the head and of the presented sound can be brought about. During induced ego-movement, it will be remembered, the observer and a stationary sound will be felt in the same state of motion. In order to give the sound *twice* the displacement of the observer it must in addition be physically displaced in the direction in which the observer feels himself turning, and this at a rate which is equivalent to the rate of the observer's subjective motion. If we assume that the subjective rate of motion is (in the opposite direction) the same as the objective rate of the screen, the sound must be objectively displaced with an angular velocity equal to the angular velocity of the screen, but in the opposite direction. Thus, in order to obtain by means of induced ego-movement the reversal of front and back, we must rotate the screen as well as the source of sound about the observer, the screen in one direction and the sound in the other direction, but both at the same rate.

In order to rotate the sound about the observer, a small dynamic loudspeaker with permanent magnet was fixed to the end of a long arm which could be swung in a circle about the observer. The seat for the observer was fixed on a vertical column consisting of 1½ in. steel tubing mounted on a heavy iron base. The arm which carried the loudspeaker was rigidly fastened to a wooden block which turned on two ballbearings about the column between the base and the seat. The block carried a pulley by means of which the arm was turned around. The outer end of the arm was bent up to bring the loudspeaker to the level of the observer's head. Mounted on the base was a reduction gear motor which, through a rubber belt, set pulley, block, arm and loudspeaker in rotation. A heavy lead fly wheel on the main shaft of the motor kept it running at a constant speed. This whole device was placed within the revolving screen with the arm projecting out under the lower edge. The distance from the head of the observer to the loudspeaker was 150 cm. The current for the loudspeaker was carried to the moving parts by two iron wires which, fixed to the block, dipped into circular grooves filled with mercury which were cut into a bakelite block fastened to the base.[10]

The procedure in an experiment was the following. After the observer had been placed on the seat inside the screen, the loudspeaker was made to turn around him. When the proper rate of rotation was reached, the screen was set in motion at a rate previously determined to match the speed of the revolving loudspeaker. The screen turned to the right while the loudspeaker shifted to the left. Soon the observer would find himself in rotation to the left, while the screen appeared to be at rest. Then the sound was presented. Had the observer localized it in the loudspeaker from where it actually came, he would have perceived it moving around in the same direction in which he felt himself moving, only twice as fast. But this never happened. Rather the localization of the sound was always reversed with respect to front and back. The observer heard it straight in front when the loudspeaker actually passed the median plane in back of him, and vice versa. For some observers the sound was definitely at rest, and they felt themselves passing it as they turned about, just as if they were turning on a revolving chair and were passing again and again a stationary source of sound. Others could not decide whether the sound moved or remained stationary. Often it was heard moving slowly to the right, that is in the direction opposite to the subjective rotation of the observer and the objective displacement of the loudspeaker. Irrespective of such differences, all 20 observers who took part in this experiment showed the reversal of front and back. When asked "How does the sound behave with respect to you?" all observers reported that it shifted to the right, that is, in the direction opposite to the actual displacement of the sound. This fact is necessarily connected with the reversal of front and back. The binaural cues strictly determine the position of the sound with respect to left and right. Thus the sound is invariably heard on the left when the loudspeaker is on the left and on the right when the loudspeaker is on the right. Suppose now that the loudspeaker travels objectively, for instance, from a position on the left side to a position in back. Since at the same time the phenomenal sound moves from the left to the front, the reversal of the direction of revolution follows.

[10]The writer is indebted to Prof. E. B. Newman for designing this apparatus.

It may be well to consider how the general selective principle which was discussed in Section III applies to this experiment. Are the directions in which the sound is perceived covariant with the general content of surrounding space? More specifically: Is the sound in its reversed positions covariant with the screen? Let us call the physical position of the loudspeaker when it is straight in back of the observer position 1. In this position the sound is heard straight in front. When in its objective revolution to the left the loudspeaker has shifted by 90° from its position in back to the right side of the observer (position 2), it is actually heard in this position. Meanwhile the screen, too, has been displaced by 90°, and since its rotation is to the right, the part, which was in front when the loudspeaker was in position 1, is now also to the right of the observer. During the next quarter revolution the loudspeaker shifts from the right side to the position straight in front (position 3). At the same time the perceived direction changes from the right side to the position straight in back. Yet the part of the screen which just lay in the direction 90° to the right is now likewise straight in back, because the screen, too, has undergone another displacement of 90°. In the same fashion positions of the screen and of the perceived sound continue to coincide for the remainder of the revolution. Thus we see that the direction of the reversed sound remains always the same with reference to the screen. The selective principle applies to this experiment.

In the state of induced ego-movement the screen appears at rest and consequently the perceived direction should also be perceived at rest. This was actually the case with those observers who reported that they seemed to pass a stationary sound in their apparent rotation. Others, however, heard the sound moving in the direction opposite to their own rotation. This observation cannot be explained in terms of our previous discussion. Purely geometrical considerations lead to the conclusion that the reversed sound direction is covariant with the screen. If the sound is heard in a reversed direction, as is actually the case, this direction must always coincide with a particular part of the screen. However, if in spite of this covariance a moving sound is perceived instead of a stationary one, we have a new problem before us. This problem belongs to the psychology of movement rather than to sound localization.

A last point remains to be mentioned. The reversal of front and back can often be shown to occur when the observer is not yet in the state of induced motion. The stimulus condition alone which eventually results in phenomenal movement of the self apparently suffices to produce the reversal of front and back. Here it should be remembered that, as far as visual stimulation is concerned, the situation in which a subject is actually turning in a stationary screen is entirely equivalent to the situation in the present experiment where the screen turns and the observer remains physically at rest. It seems that a visual stimulation, which is equivalent to that resulting from rotation of the subject, produces the corresponding effect on sound localization, and that this effect occurs regardless of whether the phenomenon of ego-movement accompanies this stimulation.

In Section III two alternative formulations of a general selective principle were offered. The evidence which has just been cited favors one of them. It now seems doubtful that phenomenal rest as such is the factor which distinguishes one direction from all the others which are compatible with the presented sequence of binaural cues. Covariance with the general content of surrounding space, however—whether it is perceived at rest or not—can still be regarded as decisive for the selection of the perceived direction.

Summary

Experiments of synthetic production of sound directions have been reported which show that either vestibular cues or visual cues can replace head movements as such. In one group of experiments the blindfolded subject localized the sound while he was passively turned on a revolving chair, and in the other group the subject observed the direction of sound while seated inside a revolving screen. The results indicate that (a) fairly accurate representation of the actual displacement of the head is furnished by vestibular stimulation and that (b) visual stimulation, equivalent to that which actual displacement of the head would give, suffices to determine the direction of sound.

On the constancies

1. On Size-Perception in the Absence of
Cues for Distance

It is generally accepted that the veridical perception of size requires adequate cues for the distance of the object from O. When
distance-cues are eliminated, attempts to match the size of similar
objects at different distances produce equations such that the
matched objects subtend equal visual angles, i.e. produce retinal
images of equal size.[1] While the absence of veridical size-matches

Written in collaboration with Virgil V. McKenna. Reprinted from *The
American Journal of Psychology,* 1960, 73, 458–460.

[1]William Lichten and Susan Lurie, A new technique for the study of perceived
size. *American Journal of Psychology,* 63, 1950, 280–282; E. L. Chalmers, Monocular
and binocular cues in the perception of size and distance. *American Journal of Psychology,* 65, 1952, 415–423; A. H. Hastorf and K. S. Way, Apparent size with and
without distance cues. *Journal of General Psychology,* 47, 1952, 181–188.

under these conditions is only to be expected, the regular occurrence of equated retinal images presents a problem. There are no other indications that there is immediate awareness of image-sizes or that one can react to them directly. That these image-matches occur may, however, be of great importance for the theory of size-perception.[2] In the absence of distance-cues, image-size alone may be able to determine perceived size. It is, therefore, essential to ask whether these matches really are significant facts in the perception of size. How persistent are they? Will they prevail when, without introducing conditions for veridical matches, the experimental situation is altered? We made such a change by arranging that, when two objects were to be compared, only one was presented devoid of cues for distance; the viewing conditions for the other provided the best cues for distance compatible with the necessary dark-room conditions.

Method

The standard stimulus-object was a luminous square 8 X 8 in., cut into a black cardboard that covered the face of a light-box. It was placed 108 in. from O's eye and on a level with it. It was viewed monocularly through two circular apertures one behind the other and so aligned with the standard object that, looking through them, O could see the standard object but nothing else. The experimental room was completely dark. The comparison-objects, squares of white cardboard against a black background, were presented one at a time inside a large box into which O could see with both eyes through an aperture of appropriate size. A lamp in the box illuminated its interior, but not enough light escaped through the aperture to affect the darkness of the experimental room. A headrest in front of the aperture served to fix the distance from the eyes to the comparison-object, which was placed against the far wall of the box. The distance between the eyes and the comparison-object was 27 in., one quarter that of the standard object. Thus, a square of 2 in. produced a retinal image as large as that of the standard square. The 25 comparison-objects ranged in size from ½ to 14 in. Twenty-six undergraduates served as Os.

[2] A. S. Gilinsky, The effect of attitude upon the perception of size. *American Journal of Psychology*, 68, 1955, 173–192.

The method of limits was used for the matches. Ascending and descending trials were alternated within the experiment and from *S* to *S* with regard to initial trials. Two ascending and two descending trials completed a matching experiment. The first ascending trial always started with the ½-in. square and the second with the ¾-in. one. The first descending trial began with the 14-in. square and the second with the 13-in. one. Each trial was continued until *O* had given smaller, larger, and equal judgments.

For 16 of the *O*s, a control experiment followed the darkroom-matches. The light in the room was turned on, the screens with the circular apertures were removed, and *O* was allowed to view the standard square binocularly. One ascending and one descending trial then were given under these constancy-conditions.

Results

Under reduction-conditions, only 7 of 26 *O*s made matches in which the retinal image sizes were approximately equated. The judgments of a majority, 17 *O*s, were strongly influenced by the size of the comparison-object. For ascending trials, which began with small objects, they judged small objects equal to the standard; for descending trials, which began with large objects, they judged large objects as equal. For this group of *O*s, the mean of their matches in ascending trials was 2.05 in., and in descending trials it was 9.6 in. Since the *O*s who showed this difference between ascending and descending trials were in the majority, there was also a large mean-difference between ascending and descending judgments for the whole group of 26 *O*s. This difference amounted to 5.2 in. Of the remaining two *O*s, one gave consistently large matches that averaged 7.8 in. and the other intermediate equality-judgments ranging from 4 to 5.5 in.

In the control experiment, where constancy-conditions prevailed, the difference between ascending and descending judgments was, of course, much smaller. The mean for ascending judgments was 7.94 in., and for descending judgments 9.33 in., close to the true size of the standard object, which was 8 in. square. The difference between ascending and descending judgments in the control experiment was reliably smaller ($p < 0.005$) than that obtained under reduction-conditions.

The experiment was repeated with a five-cornered nonsense-figure instead of the square and with a different group of *O*s. Essentially the same result was obtained as before. Only 2 of 10 *O*s equated retinal-image sizes in ascending trials.

Conclusion

We found that in the absence of distance-cues for the standard object only a minority of *O*s produced matches in which retinal images were equated. The previous result, that such matches occur regularly when both the standard and the comparison-object are given without distance-cues, thus becomes a fact of minor importance. Evidence for this view is to be found in the nature of those matches which, in the case of a majority of our *O*s, replace the equation of retinal images. They make large matches when the comparison-objects, whose sizes can be readily perceived, are large, and small matches when comparison-objects are small. This inconsistent type of responding shows clearly that the standard object in reduced conditions does not elicit unambiguous size. That image-size in the absence of distance-cues has the power to determine size-perception directly is no longer a feasible assumption.

How, then, can one account for those matches in which image-sizes are equated? It does not seem particularly important to find an answer to this question, since it has been shown that these matches are readily replaced by an inconsistent way of responding, but we believe that the equation of image-sizes results from an implicit assumption of equal distance of the standard and the comparison-object.

2. The Role of Slant in the Perception of Shape

When a figure or the plane surface of an object is oriented obliquely to the line of sight, the shape of its retinal image differs from its real shape; if the perceived shape nevertheless approximates the objective shape, we call this an example of "shape-constancy." The traditional explanation of shape-constancy assumes that the orientation of the figure or surface is registered, and its slant relative to the line of sight taken into account, as the shape is perceived. This explanation is derived by analogy to other constancies, as, for example, size-constancy, where distance is taken into account. There is, however, no empirical evidence in the literature that the perceptual process follows such a course. Experiments in the area hardly go beyond the demonstration of shape-constancy. As a matter of fact, that the perception of shape depends on cues for slant is not even a logically necessary assumption.

To talk separately of slant and shape makes little sense where, with monocular observation, only perspective cues for slant are given. Such perspective cues consist in the deformation of the retinal images of familiar shapes and they imply "assumptions" about the true shapes. Only when these assumptions are correct, that is, when the shapes viewed are in fact the familiar ones, will adequate cues for slant exist, but in that case, cues for slant are no longer needed; the "assumptions" themselves can account for the perception of familiar shape.

When a slanted surface is binocularly observed and stereoscopic

Written in collaboration with Mary E. Moore. Reprinted from *The American Journal of Psychology*, 1962, 75, 289–293.

vision operates, the notion that both shape and slant result directly from the given disparities is quite feasible. Those who think in terms of an inherently three-dimensional perceived space with an inherent geometry would take such an assumption for granted. When, for example, the two oblongs of Figure 1 are stereoscopically combined, the given disparity causes the right vertical edge of the perceived rectangle to be located in a frontal plane a certain distance behind the frontal plane of the left edge. Hand in hand with this oblique position goes a greater width of the perceived oblong. When the existence of a perceptual space is assumed in which the primary stereoscopic effect takes place, the geometry of the space, whether it be innate or established by learning, will determine the greater distance between the vertical edges of the obliquely oriented oblong. Slant and shape will be equally direct results of the stereoscopically caused depth between the oblong's vertical edges.[1]

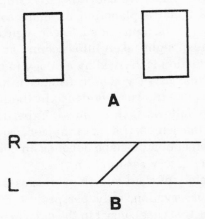

Fig. 1. Diagrams showing (A) stereogram of an oblong standing obliquely in space and (B) ground plan of the perceived arrangement in depth. L is the frontal parallel plane of left edge, R the frontal parallel plane of right edge.

These considerations, of course, show merely that the postulate of a process which takes tilt into account may be unnecessary; they do not preclude the existence of such a process. We can, therefore, be sure of the facts only by setting up an experiment in which such

[1]For different reasons, Gibson, too, would hold this view. He would expect "shape-at-a-slant" to be the simple and immediate result of stimulation.

a process, if it existed, could assert itself. This can be done by creating conditions under which cues for slant are more adequate than cues for shape. If these conditions yield constancy commensurate with the cues for slant, the potential of such cues would be demonstrated.[2]

Such an experiment was performed with black isosceles triangles as the slanted figures. A triangle was chosen as the stimulus because it does not convey any perspective cues for slant when the tip is tilted back from the frontal parallel plane. The triangles were fastened to a slanting white surface of oblong shape whose edges were clearly visible against a black table top. An arrangement was used which permitted *O* to see the edges of the oblong surface with both eyes but restricted his view of the triangle to one eye only. The slant of the oblong background, then, was represented by stereoscopic as well as perspective cues, while the figure itself was stripped of both of these, the major cues for shape and slant. Inasmuch as the triangle usually is seen to lie in the plane of the white surface, the cues for slant of the oblong background also could serve as cues for the slant of the triangle. The results to be reported below show that this was indeed the case.

Method

Triangles, with a base of 2.5 in., were presented on two slopes. Under Condition 1, a 4-in. high triangle rested on the oblong surface when its slant was 59.5°, that is, when it formed an angle of 59.5° with the frontal plane of *O*. Under Condition 2, this tilt was 46.5° and the triangle had an altitude of 2.95 in. The two conditions were so chosen that the triangles produced retinal images of identical shape. The perceived shape of the triangles was measured by a matching procedure. A series of comparison-triangles was used ranging from 1.6–4.4 in. in altitude in steps of 0.1 in. Like the two standard triangles, they were made of black cardboard, were isosceles, and had a base of 2.5 in. Each was fastened to a white cardboard 10 X 10 in., which could be inserted in a wooden frame standing in frontal parallel position

[2]This plan differs from that of B. K. Stavrianos (*Archives de Psychologie*, 1945, 49, no. 296, 1–94) and of Jacob Beck and J. J. Gibson (*Journal of Experimental Psychology*, 1955, 50, 125–133). These authors were concerned with the question whether apparent shape and apparent slant are linked. We are asking whether *cues* for slant can have an effect on apparent shape.

12 in. from O's eyes. Beyond the frame was the slanting white surface on which the standard triangle was presented, its center 31 in. from O's eyes. By pushing a cardboard with a comparison triangle into the frame and pulling it halfway out, E could give O alternate views of the standard triangle and of a comparison-triangle. The position of the comparison-triangle, when fully inserted in the frame, was such that it was visible binocularly to O, while the small obstruction in front of O's left eye blocked out the standard triangle for this eye, but not the edge of the white surface on which it rested. A head-rest served to maintain these relations throughout the experiment. An abbreviated method of limits was used for the matching, with two ascending and two descending series presented in alternation. To give Os practice in matching, a third standard triangle, smaller than either of the experimental triangles, was matched initially, using one ascending and one descending series. Sixteen Os were studied in this experiment.

In addition to the main experiment, two control experiments were performed. In both, cues for the slant of the background surface on which the standard triangle rested were eliminated by inserting a screen with a circular hole between the frame for the comparison-triangles and the display for the standard figure. The size of the hole was so chosen that only the triangle and part of the homogeneous white surface on which it rested were visible, but not the edge of this surface. In the first of the control experiments, O wore an eye-patch and had to observe monocularly; in the second, he was allowed to see the triangles with both eyes. Eight Os participated in the monocular and 16 in the binocular control experiment. The measuring procedure was the same as in the main experiment.

Results

The matches in the main experiment show a high degree of constancy. The mean perceived altitude for the 4-in. triangle was 3.4 in. when this triangle was slanted to produce a projection on the frontal plane of 2.03 in. in height. For the other standard, whose altitude was 2.95 in., and which, because of smaller slant, produced the same projection, the mean altitude match was 2.71 in. The difference between these means is highly reliable ($t = 12.62$, $p < 0.001$). Since the triangles produce identical retinal images, the only difference in stimulation which can account for the difference in the perceived altitude of the triangles is in the cues for their slant.

TABLE 1
Mean Perceived Altitude of Triangles (in In.)

Objective altitude	Projective altitude	Main experiment	First control	Second control
4.00	2.03	3.40	2.41	3.58
2.95	2.03	2.71	2.28	2.83

In the first control experiment, the monocular view through the screen was supposed to represent reduction-conditions. Thus, by comparing the results of this experiment with those of the main experiment, we can obtain the traditional proof of constancy, a difference between matches under reduction- and under constancy-conditions. In the first control experiment, the mean perceived altitude of the two standard triangles was small and nearly the same; namely, 2.41 and 2.28.[3] The differences between these values and the means of the altitudes perceived in the main experiments reported above were highly significant as the difference for the 4-in. triangle showed a t of 15.12 ($p < 0.001$) and, for the 2.95-in. triangle, t equaled 8.52 ($p < 0.001$). For both standard triangles, the matches obtained in the main experiment were close to the true shapes of the triangles and those obtained in the monocular control experiment were close to the shape of their projection on the frontal plane (Table 1). In the main experiment, therefore, the slant-cues for the surface on which the monocularly viewed standard triangles rested produced a strong constancy-effect, and there can be no doubt that cues for slant influence perceived shape.

Just how complete is the shape-constancy thus achieved? The answer comes from a comparison between the matches obtained in the main experiment with those of the second (binocular) control experiment where conditions for shape-constancy are optimal. As Table 1 shows, the binocular matches are not very different from those obtained in the main experiment. This difference is barely significant for the 4-in. triangle ($t = 2.41$; $p < 0.05$), but not for the

[3]The difference of 0.13 in. proved, however, to be significant. No attempt was made to find the reason for the difference.

2.95-in. triangle ($t = 1.98$; p. > 0.05). The binocular match of 3.58
in. for the 4-in. triangle whose slant was almost 60° implies a sizeable lag in constancy, which is in keeping with the results usually
obtained for large slants.

Conclusion

In this investigation, good shape-constancy for a figure was obtained
solely from cues to the slant of its background. To be sure, the
investigation dealt with an entirely artificial situation. Its significance lies in the fact that it provides a clear instance where, in the
perception of shape, slant *per se* is taken into account, and that the
existence of a process in which perception of shape takes this route
is thus demonstrated. No definite claim can be made for the importance of this kind of process in everyday perceptual functioning. As
was shown above, there are no compelling reasons for postulating
the occurrence of such a process under ordinary conditions. On the
other hand, this does not mean that, once the existence of such a
process is demonstrated, it is unlikely to participate in ordinary
perception of the shape of slanting surfaces. In three-dimensional
form-perception, duplication of function is the rule rather than the
exception. The importance of the demonstration lies in its theoretical implications. One may now, for instance, take the view that
stereoscopic perception directly determines only depth and slant,
but that the shape of the slanted surface is the product of a process
by which slant is taken into account.

3. The Constancy of Stereoscopic Depth

It is one of the elementary facts of stereoscopic vision that retinal disparity represents depth quantitatively. The greater the distance in depth between two points on an object, the greater will be the disparity with which their images are given in the two eyes, and, up to a point, the greater will be the perceived depth-interval between them. Nevertheless, just as the size of a retinal image does not depend alone on the size of the corresponding object, the amount of retinal disparity between two points does not depend exclusively on their distance in depth; in both cases, the distance of the object from the eyes is important. There should therefore be a constancy-problem in stereoscopically perceived depth which corresponds to the problem of size-constancy: If the perceived-depth between two points on an object is to correspond to the distance in depth between the two points on the physical object, the distance of the physical object from the eyes must, in some fashion, be taken into account.

The problem of the relation between perceived depth and the distance of the depth-interval from the eyes has attracted surprisingly little attention in the last half century, considering the great interest that exists in stereoscopic vision. Older experiments, to which references may be found in Linschoten,[1] did demonstrate a considerable degree of stereoscopic depth-constancy. In this paper, we explore some of its properties and attempt to show how they serve to explain some familiar phenomena.

Written in collaboration with Carl Zuckerman. Reprinted from *The American Journal of Psychology*, 1963, 76, 404–412.

[1] J. Linschoten, *Structuranalyse der binocularen Tiefenwahrnehung*, 1956, 180.

Although the problem of stereoscopic depth-constancy and the problem of size-constancy owe their existence to the same variable, namely, the distance of the object from the eyes, they differ in quantitative terms. Whereas the size of the retinal image decreases directly with the distance of the corresponding object from the eyes, the amount of retinal disparity is inversely proportional to the square of the distance.[2] It follows that different mechanisms must underlie the two constancies, if the perception of stereoscopic depth operates more or less adequately.

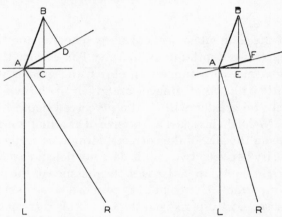

Fig. 1. Retinal disparity as a function of distance. *A* and *B* are two points in the horizontal plane which are arranged in depth in relation to *O*. *AL* is the direction from *A* to the left eye and *AR* the direction to the right eye. On the left, *AC* is the projection of *AB* on the frontal plane through *A* of the left eye, *AD* its projection on the frontal plane of the right eye. The difference in length of these two projections is the immediate cause of the disparity when *AB* is given. On the right, the distance of *AB* from the eyes is assumed to be doubled, which diminishes the difference in the directions from which the two eyes view *AB* to one half (compare the angles *LAR*). As a consequence, the projections of *AB* on the frontal planes of the two eyes, *AE* and *AF,* are more nearly equal; they differ in length only half as much as do *AC* and *AD*. This change in the relative width of projections of depth-intervals with changing viewing direction is one of the causes for the dependence of disparity on distance.

That disparity should be inversely proportional to the square of the distance of the depth-interval from the eyes can easily be made clear. There are two reasons why disparity should vary with distance: (1) Inasmuch as disparity consists in small differences in the

[2]C. H. Graham, Visual perception, in S. S. Stevens (ed), *Handbook of Experimental Psychology,* 1951, 888; K. N. Ogle, *Researches in Binocular Vision,* 1950, 136.

width of the retinal images in the two eyes, it must decrease in proportion to the distance of the object from the eyes as do retinal images themselves. (2) Disparity comes about because the two eyes view an object from slightly different directions. The greater this difference in viewing direction, the greater will be the disparity that results from a given depth-interval (Figure 1). The farther the object is from the eyes, the less the two directions differ from each other, and the smaller should be the disparity that a depth-interval of a given amount will cause; in fact, disparity should decrease, for this reason, in proportion to the distance of the object from the eyes. Since these two factors are independent of each other, disparity should decline with the square of the distance.

Let us briefly compare stereoscopic depth-constancy with size-constancy. The size of an object's retinal image decreases in proportion to its distance from the eyes, and the perceptual process, compensating for this size-loss in the stimulus-situation, operates more or less according to Emmert's law: The perceived size is equivalent to the size of the image multiplied by the registered distance. The disparity that corresponds to a given depth-interval decreases in proportion to the square of the distance from the eyes of that depth-interval, and a compensating mechanism that leads to complete constancy would therefore have the perceived depth be dependent on the given disparity multiplied by the square of the distance.

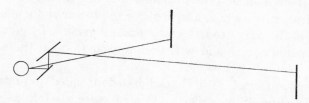

Fig. 2. Lateral view of the arrangement. Only the right eye and one set of mirrors are shown. Convergence is changed by so turning the upper mirror (about a shaft that is parallel to that mirror and to the plane of the drawing) that it is on a slant relative to that plane. The vertical rods are shown as they are used for adjusting convergence to half the object's distance.

Probably the clearest demonstration of the compensating process underlying stereoscopic depth-constancy can be obtained through an arrangement that permits manipulation of the cues for distance of an object from the eyes while keeping its actual distance, and therefore the disparity, constant; this should, of course, result in changes of perceived depth. In such an experiment, three-dimensional wire forms were observed either directly or through lenses and a mirror-arrangement which changed accommodation and convergence. The effect of the artificial alteration of these distance-cues on the apparent depth of the wire form could be gauged by comparing depth-estimates made under the two conditions of observation.

A sketch of the mirror-arrangement used to manipulate convergence is shown in Figure 2. The ocular mirrors are so fixed in a 45° slant in O's sagittal plane that they reflect vertical beams into O's eyes. The objective mirrors are suspended by two joints. One joint lets the mirror turn about a horizontal frontal-parallel shaft and makes tilting it in O's vertical sagittal plane possible; it is used to make the viewed object appear at its true elevation above the table. The shaft of the other joint is parallel to the mirror-surface and lies in the vertical sagittal plane; these latter joints are used to make the object appear straight in front and to manipulate the convergence with which it is viewed. To adjust this convergence, a thin vertical rod is set on the table in the place where the experimental object will eventually be; this rod is seen only through the mirror-arrangement. Another vertical rod is so suspended from above that it is visible through the gap between the ocular and the objective mirror; it is placed at the distance of the intended convergence. By so adjusting the objective mirrors that for each eye the lower rod appears as an extension of the upper rod, the two rods are made to be viewed with the same convergence and will then appear to be at the same distance.

Two wire-forms, both shaped like four-sided pyramids with nearly square bases but differing in size, were used. Each was supported by a shaft attached to one edge of the base. When these objects were presented, the base was always in frontal orientation and the apex pointed toward O. The critical object was placed on the table and was viewed through the mirror-arrangement. Its base had an edge of 12.5 cm., and the distance from apex to base was 12.4 cm. The other wire-pyramid was half as large in all dimensions and served as control object. It was suspended from its shaft above the larger pyramid and was viewed directly through the gap between the ocular and the objective mirror.

The *O*s gave depth-estimates by adjusting the variable length of a thin brass rod they held in their hands to the apparent distance between apex and base of a pyramid. This procedure of obtaining judgments of depth had previously been used successfully.[3] Perceived size also can be expected to be altered when cues for distance are changed, and size-estimates, using the length of a diagonal of the base, were obtained along with the depth-estimates. This made it possible to compare stereoscopic depth-constancy with size-constancy under identical conditions.

The critical wire pyramid was placed 133 cm. from *O*'s eyes, with the detour by way of the objective mirrors taken into account. The mirrors were so adjusted that *O* viewed the wire-form with a convergence for half the real distance (66.5 cm.), and he wore −0.75-diopters lenses, enabling him to see the wire form with the eyes accommodated for the same half-distance.[4] Under the assumption of complete constancy in accordance with the altered distance-cues, *O* should perceive the large pyramid under these critical conditions with half the normal size and with 25% of the normal depth. Since retinal image-size and disparity remained unchanged, and convergence and accommodation represented half the real distance, perceived size should be expected to become reduced by a factor of two and perceived depth by a factor of two squared. These expectations could be tested by comparing the size- and depth-estimates obtained for the critical pyramid with estimates obtained for the control pyramid which was also placed 133 cm. from *O*'s eyes and was viewed directly and without the lenses, *i.e.* with veridical convergence and accommodation. Since the control pyramid was half as large as the critical one, complete constancy under both conditions of viewing would cause the bases of the two pyramids to appear equal in size, and apparent depth should be half as great for the critical as for the control pyramid (Table 1, column 4).

The 18 *O*s who were studied here first viewed the larger pyramid and gave an estimate of depth and one of size, while the smaller

[3]Hans Wallach, M. E. Moore, and Linda Davidson, Modification of stereoscopic depth perception. *American Journal of Psychology*, 76, 1963, 191–204. In the present volume, Chapter X, selection 2.

[4]When a real object is moved from a distance of 133 cm. to a distance of 66.5 cm., accommodation should increase by 0.75 diopters. The same change should take place when an object that stays at a distance of 133 cm. is viewed through a — 0.75 diopter lens for which accommodation has to compensate.

pyramid was hidden by a screen, then the larger pyramid was covered and they made corresponding estimates for the smaller pyramid.

TABLE 1

Results of the Experiment with Wire-Forms

	Mean estimates and confidence-limits at the 1% level		Ratio (critical/control)		
	Critical condition	Control condition	Experi-mental	Complete constancy	No constancy
Size	8.88 ± 0.82	7.13 ± 0.59	1.245	1.0	2.0
Depth	4.07 ± 0.40	6.43 ± 0.82	0.633	0.5	2.0

Results

The first and third columns of Table 1 give the results. They show that manipulation of convergence and accommodation alone produce a fair degree of size-constancy as well as of stereoscopic depth-constancy. Note in this connection the small confidence-limits, which nowhere exceed 15%. A comparison of the ratios formed by the critical and the control-estimates with the expected ratios shows that the deviation from ideal constancy was about the same for size and for depth, and amounted to about 25%. No generalization should be made, however, from this approximately equal lag in constancy. The deviation from ideal size-constancy is ordinarily much smaller. Ours is undoubtedly due to the fact that convergence and accommodation were the only distance-cues available. The parallel between the two constancies may well cease when further distance-cues are introduced. The results are, nevertheless, impressive when the effectiveness of convergence and accommodation is considered. They contradict the widely held view that accommodation and convergence do not serve as reliable cues for distance.[5]

(1) BEHAVIOR OF THE ANAGLYPH

A simple and interesting method of demonstrating stereoscopic depth-constancy involves the use of anaglyphs, in which the left-eye and the right-eye view of an object or a scene are printed in different

[5]See E. G. Heinemann, Endel Tulving, and Jacob Nachmias, The effect of oculo-motor adjustments on apparent size. *American Journal of Psychology*, 72, 1959, 32–45.

colors, one superimposed on the other. Viewed through colored spectacles so chosen that the right eye sees only the right-eye view and the left eye only the left-eye view, the anaglyph produces the stereoscopic effect. An anaglyph has useful properties: It is, as it were, an outward projection of the given retinal disparities, for the horizontal distances between corresponding left-eye and right-eye contours represent those disparities.

We found that when the distance of an anaglyph from the eyes is changed, stereoscopic depth is altered—increasing this distance will enhance perceived depth—and this is a manifestation of stereoscopic depth-constancy. To understand this we have to recall the two reasons for the decline of disparity with the square of an object's distance from the eyes. The first one, that disparity, which consists in differences in width of the retinal images of an object in the two eyes, must decrease with the distance of the object as do the images themselves, applies to the anaglyph also. As its distance from the eyes increases, its retinal image decreases in size and so also do the projections of the distances between left-eye and right-eye contours. The second reason for a decline of disparity with distance under normal conditions has to do with the way surfaces or pairs of points that occupy depth project on the frontal plane of each eye when distance is varied (Figure 1). For a given depth-interval, the difference in the width of the projection, which, in turn, causes the disparity, varies inversely with distance. In the anaglyph, it is these projections that are given rather than the depth-intervals as such, and there is no reason for these projections to vary when the distance between the anaglyph and the eyes is changed. With only one of the two reasons for the change of disparity with distance operating, the disparity caused by an anaglyph varies in proportion to the distance only.

We have already stated that, inasmuch as disparity is inversely proportional to the square of a depth-interval's distance from the eyes, a compensating perceptual process must enhance perceived depth in proportion to the square of the distance, if that depth is to remain completely constant. Since, in the case of the anaglyph, disparity decreases in proportion to the distance only, a perceptual process that enhances perceived depth in proportion to the square of the distance does more than make up for the "distance loss": While disparity declines in proportion to the distance only, the perceptual process enhances depth in proportion to the square of the distance. The net result is that perceived depth in the anaglyph should increase ideally in proportion to an increase in distance.

A measurement of the actual effect of distance-change on anaglyph-depth was taken. The Os were asked to reproduce the apparent depth-interval between two particular contours in an anaglyph with a caliper. Each one of 39 Os reproduced the same depth-interval twice, once when the anaglyph was 18 in. from the eyes and again when that distance was doubled. For the 18-in. distance, the mean of the caliper-settings was 2.07 cm. and for the 36-in. distance it was 3.45 cm. The ratio of 0.6 between these means is to be compared with the ratio of 0.5 which would denote complete constancy. Though small, this deviation from ideal constancy turns out to be highly reliable ($p < 0.001$).

The dependence of the depth perceived in an anaglyph on the distance of the anaglyph from the eyes was also observable in three-dimensional motion pictures, for the stereoscopic effect here was produced by an anaglyph technique. Variations in apparent depth with a change in O's distance from the screen were here quite startling, because of the great range over which distance could be varied.

(2) PERSPECTIVE-CUES IN STEREOSCOPIC DEPTH-CONSTANCY

With the help of the anaglyph technique, we were able to show that not only oculomotor cues for distance operate in stereoscopic depth-perception, but perspective cues also, as is the case in size-perception. Proving this is difficult because with stereoscopic depth the main issue, binocular regard as such cannot be avoided. The demonstration made use of a pseudoscope, an instrument that reverses stereoscopic depth, to create a discrepancy between binocular and perspective distance-cues. Four identical anaglyphs were prepared. Two of them were suspended in the upper part of the pseudoscope's field, one of these at a 3- and the other at a 5-ft. distance from O's eyes. The other two were placed on the table below which was covered with a plaid tablecloth to strengthen perspective-cues. They also were 3 and 5 ft. from O's eyes. Viewed through the pseudoscope, all four anaglyphs showed the expected reversal of depth. In the case of the suspended anaglyphs, the distances at which they were perceived were also reversed; the nearer one appeared to be more distant than the objectively farther one. Now we come to the first essential point: The nearer anaglyph which, due to the pseudoscopic distance-cues, appeared to be farther away, showed a greater depth. Although the same pseudoscopic distance-cues were present for the anaglyphs that rested on the tablecloth, their apparent distances from *O* were not reversed. As is normal for this particular contradictory arrangement of cues, the perspective-cues for distance prevailed over the binocular ones, and the objectively more distant anaglyph appeared to be farther away.There was again a difference in depth displayed by the two anaglyphs, but here the objectively farther anaglyph showed the greater depth. Perceived depth varied in accordance with the prevailing distance-cues, the perspective ones, which thus proved to operate in stereoscopic depth-constancy.

(3) EFFECT OF OPTICAL MAGNIFICATION

The dependence of stereoscopic depth on distance also largely explains the familiar fact that a scene viewed through binoculars appears to have reduced depth.[6] Binoculars, like other telescopes, magnify the retinal image of a viewed object. For various reasons, this magnification results in a shortening of the perceived distance rather than enhanced perceptual size. Familiar size undoubtedly

[6]Among previous interpretations of reduced depth due to magnification, J. M. Vanderplas (On the flattening-effect of optical magnification. *American Journal of Psychology,* 73, 1960, 473–478) proposed to explain the effect in purely optical terms. He claimed that an object's final image formed by a telescope has a location "in optical space" which, in relation to the size of that image, might account for the effect. However that may be, Vanderplas failed to explain how the location of an image "in optical space" can be given to the eye.

S. Howard Bartley pointed out (*Beginning Experimental Psychology,* 1950, Chapter 15) that the retinal images of a near and a far surface of a solid object do not only increase in size when the object is brought nearer to the eye, but also change the *ratio* of their sizes. Optical magnification also increases image-sizes but does not change that ratio. If the size-ratio of the surfaces themselves were given, the image-size ratio produced by magnification could indeed lead to the flattening effect, but Bartley does not explain how that objective ratio is given. It is conceivable that, in the case of an orthogonal object and with an implicit assumption of orthogonality operating in perception, the ratio of image-sizes might, in fact, be the basis for the perception of depth, and therefore cause the flattening effect. If this were the explanation, the flattening effect should be restricted to orthogonal objects, but that is not the case. We were able to demonstrate with depth-estimates a strong reduction in depth when the wire pyramid described in this article was viewed through two-power binoculars.

plays a role here, particularly when one looks directly at the scene before viewing it through the glasses; but convergence also probably is responsible for the diminished apparent distance, for, with binoculars, magnification increases the angle of convergence with which an object is viewed, as well as its retinal image (Figure 3).

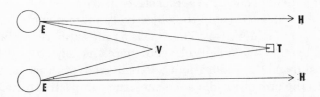

Fig. 3. Effect of magnification on convergence. *EH* are the lines of sight when the eyes are converged for infinity. The angles *TEH* are the convergence-angles for an object *T*. Binoculars will magnify the angles *TEH* in proportion to their power, producing new convergence-angles *VEH*, which serve as cues for a diminished distance of the object. In every convergence-angle, one leg must coincide with *EH*.

It is this reduced distance that goes hand in hand with reduced depth. As in the case of the anaglyph, magnification increases retinal disparities only in proportion to the distance-reduction, not to its square. This is so because disparities increase only due to the image size enhancement. Since the object remains at its actual distance, there is no change in the directions from which the eyes view the object, and the shapes of the projections of the depth-intervals are not altered. Were the distance to the object actually shortened, disparities would increase with the square of the distance-reduction. Stereoscopic depth-constancy largely compensates for this increase in disparity by causing the perceived depth that corresponds to a given disparity to increase nearly with the square of the distance. Inasmuch as the same compensation takes place when magnification increases disparity only in proportion to the distance reduction itself, perceived objects should lose depth under magnification. Ideally, the contraction of perceived depth should be proportional to the reduction in distance.

4. On Constancy of Visual Speed[1]

When investigating the constancy of visual speed J. F. Brown[2] discovered what he called the transposition principle of velocity. In his account the constancy of visual speed and the principle of transposition occur as unrelated facts. This paper attempts to show that constancy of visual speed can be understood as a consequence of the transposition principle.

When objects which move with the same objective velocity are presented to the resting eye at different distances one perceives them as moving with approximately equal speed, although the displacements of their retinal images per unit of time vary in inverse proportion to the distance. This is what we call the constancy of visual speed. Its formal similarity to the constancy of size is obvious. Two identical objects presented at different but moderate distances from the eye have almost equal phenomenal sizes, although the linear extensions of the corresponding images are inversely proportional to the distances at which the two objects are presented to the eye. It seems plausible to assume that constancy of visual speed is simply a consequence of size constancy. One might argue that visual speed depends not on the length through which an image passes on the retina per unit of time but on the visual extension through which the object moves. Since the latter extension remains approximately constant even if its objective size is projected from different distances and therefore with varying retinal size, the constancy of

Reprinted from *Psychological Review,* 1939, 46, 541–552.

[1]The writer wishes to express his appreciation to Professor Wolfgang Köhler and also to Dr. Richard S. Crutchfield for their aid in preparation of this paper.

[2]J. F. Brown, Ueber gesehene Geschwindigkeiten. *Psychologische Forschung* 1927, 10, 84–101. Also J. F. Brown, The visual perception of velocity. *Psychologische Forschung,* 1931, 14, 199–232.

visual speed seems to follow without any further assumptions.

This was indeed the reasoning which led J. F. Brown to his investigation of the constancy of speed. His actual observations, however, did not entirely confirm this view. While with moderate distances and under otherwise favorable conditions size constancy is almost absolute, constancy of speed proved to be considerably less perfect. When two objects moved at different distances from the eye, the objective velocity of the more distant object had to be distinctly greater, if the two phenomenal speeds were to appear as equal. Brown concluded that the constancy of speed cannot simply be deduced from the constancy of size. He therefore began a thorough investigation of "the factors that condition phenomenal velocity."

In his experiments Brown had his observers compare the speeds in two movement-fields which from experiment to experiment differed in various respects. Probably his most important finding is the transposition principle, which he established in experiments in which the two movement-fields differed only with respect to their size, being transposed in all their linear dimensions in a certain proportion. A movement-field consisted of an opening in a black cardboard screen and black dots of equal size moving through this opening on a white background. The dots were pasted on a roll of white paper running over two moving drums which were hidden by the screen. The drums were far enough apart so that only a flat surface was visible through the opening. The field in the opening was uniformly illuminated. The surface of the paper was smooth so that no cues of its motion could be obtained, except from the dots. The observer was to compare successively the speed with which the dots in two such movement-fields passed through their respective openings. In one of the fields the velocity was variable and could be stepped upwards or downwards under the direction of the observer until the speed in the two movement-fields appeared to be the same. Then the velocities were measured and their quotient was computed. The movement-fields were placed far enough apart so that only one could be seen at a time.

In one of these experiments, for instance, the movement-fields were transposed in a ratio 2:1, i.e. all the linear measures in one of the moving fields, namely the size of the opening, the diameter of the dots and their distance from one another, were twice as as large as the same measures in the other moving field. After the objective velocities were so adjusted that the phenomenal speed in the two movement-fields was the same, the objective velocity in the larger field (A) was found to be almost twice as great as in the smaller field (B). Where V_A is the velocity in A and V_B the velocity in B when phenomenal equality is attained, V_A / V_B was found to be 1.94 (average for 7 observers).[3] When the spatial transposition of the two movement-fields was 4:1, the speeds in the two fields were judged to be equal when the ratio of the objective velocities was 3.7 (average for 5 observers).[4] Thus the objective velocity in the 4 times larger field A was approximately 4 times as great as was that in the smaller field B, when visually both movements seemed to have the same speed. On the basis of these results Brown formulated the principle of velocity transposition: If a movement-field in a homogeneous surrounding field is transposed in its linear dimensions in a certain proportion, the stimulus velocity must be transposed in the same proportion in order that the phenomenal speed in both cases be identical.

The velocity ratios actually measured by Brown departed significantly from the figures called for by this principle, particularly when the difference in the dimensions of the two movement fields was still larger. When the transposition was in the proportion 10:1, the ratio of the velocities was 8.22[5] (average for 4 observers; cf. below for additional results). Still these various departures from the theoretically expected values seem very small when we compare them with the enormous effects of the transposition phenomenon which were actually found. In the last mentioned case with a transposition of 10:1 where the departure from the expected value was 18%, the actually measured effect of the transposition phenomenon was as high as 722%.

In a quite similar way Brown had previously determined to what degree constancy of speed is actually realized. Two identical movement-fields were placed at different distances from the observer and the ratio of their velocities was varied until the speeds

[3] J. F. Brown, Ueber gesehene Geschwindigkeiten. *Psychologische Forschung*, 1927, 10, 91, Table 5.

[4] *Ibid.*, p. 92, Table 8; also Brown, J. F., The visual perception of velocity. *Psychologische Forschung* 1931, 14, 216.

[5] J. F. Brown, The visual perception of velocity. *Psychologische Forschung*, 1931, 14, 216.

in the two fields seemed to be equal. The movement in the more distance field was then 1.12, 1.15, and 1.21 times faster than the other, where the ratio of the distances from the observer was 1:3.3, 1:6.6 and 1:10 respectively.[6] Perfect constancy, of course, would have yielded in each case the ratio 1 instead of the listed quotients. Again, the actually found figures depart only little from the values to be expected for perfect constancy, when we compare them with the values which we should find if phenomenal speed were proportional to the velocities on the retina. On the other hand the departure from ideal constancy is here significantly larger than the departure which size constancy shows, a difference great enough to justify Brown's conclusion that constancy of speed cannot be deduced from size constancy.

We are thus facing an apparently paradoxical state of affairs. On the one hand we find a speed constancy of high degree, when speeds in movement-fields at different distances from the eye are compared; on the other hand the transposition experiments show that at a constant distance objective velocities may appear equal when one is as much as 8 times faster than the other. The fact that the reported transposition experiments were done under unnatural dark-room conditions affords no comfort. When Brown repeated the experiments with daylight illumination so that the continuity of the spatial framework was plainly given, he obtained for the same ratios of transposition, namely 2:1, 4:1 and 10:1, the velocity ratios 1.57, 2.71 and 6.17.[7] Even under these conditions of adequately structured visual field the transposition phenomenon remains striking.

In an intricate state of affairs like this the first thing to do is to examine closely the immediate stimulus situation. It is in the present case represented by the retinal images of the movement-fields. In a transposition experiment the retinal images of the two movement-fields bear to each other the same proportion as the objective movement-fields themselves, and the rates of the shifting dots on the retina are also proportional to the objective velocities. In the constancy experiment the situation is different in that here the movement-fields are presented at different distances from the eye, and the retinal images have different sizes, although they correspond to objectively identical fields. More specifically, their dimen-

[6] *Ibid.*, p. 208, Table 1.

[7] *Ibid.*, p. 215, Table 7.

sions are inversely proportional to the distances at which the corresponding movement-fields are presented. When, for instance, of two identical movement-fields, A is presented at 2 m. distance and B at 4 m. distance, the image of A is linearly twice as large as the image of B. Let us assume for the moment that constancy of speed is perfect, so that the speed in the fields A and B would seem to be the same when the objective velocities are equal. Since displacements in A and B produce retinal displacements which are twice as large in the case of A as they are in the case of B, phenomenal speeds are equal when the *retinal velocity in A is twice as great as that in B.* Let us now consider a case of the transposition phenomenon under the assumption that the principle of transposition also holds perfectly. If A' be a movement-field twice as large in all dimensions as B' and if both be presented at the same distance from the eye, the retinal image of A' is twice as large as that of B'. According to the transposition principle, the phenomenal speed in both fields is the same when the objective velocity in A' is twice as great as in B'. This being the case, *the velocity in the retinal image of field A' is also twice as great as is that in the retinal image of B'.* We thus find that the two different experimental situations yield essentially the same processes *on the retina*. The constellations of phenomenal equality in the constancy experiment on the one hand and in a transposition experiment on the other hand, both referred to the retina, are exactly alike. Thus, if we apply the principle of transposition *to the retinal images* of the two movement-fields in a constancy experiment, this principle leads to equality of phenomenal speed, *i.e.,* to just the fact which is commonly called constancy of speed. In this manner constancy of speed can be explained without any further hypothesis. Incidentally, in this explanation there is no reference to constancy of size. *The transposition principle alone, if applied to retinal images and retinal displacements, yields constancy of visual speed.*

In this connection, it may be useful to give the transposition principle another formulation. Velocity is usually measured as displacement per unit of time. We then may say: In movement-fields of identical shape and different dimensions the phenomenal speed is the same when the displacements per unit of time are equal fractions of the respective openings. Or simply: In transposed movement-fields, the perceived speeds are the same when the *relative* displacements are equal. Since in a transposition experiment the retinal

images of the movement-fields have the same size proportions as the
actually presented movement-fields, the principle applies directly to
the retinal images. On the other hand, if in a constancy experiment
the distance of a field A from the eye is half that of an identical field
B, the retinal image of A is linearly twice as large as that of B.
According to our principle, the two images will again yield the same
phenomenal speed when the retinal displacements per unit of time
cover equal fractions of their respective movement-fields on the
retina. What does this mean in objective physical terms? The very
problem of constancy of speed arises from the fact that the same
physical displacement causes different retinal displacements, depending upon the objective distance of the movement-field. More
concretely, the retinal displacements are inversely proportional to
the distance of the field. But, as I just mentioned, the retinal image
of the field itself is also linearly in inverse proportion to the distance.
Consequently the retinal displacement per unit of time remains a
constant fraction of the retinal movement-field when in objectively
identical fields the same objective velocity is given at varying distances. Thus, from the point of view of the transposition principle,
the condition for constant phenomenal speed is fulfilled precisely
when objective circumstances are those of constancy of speed.

Actually, constancy of speed is not perfect. But the results of
transposition experiments, too, fall somewhat short of exact proportionality as shown by the figures that have been quoted. In the case
of the transposition phenomenon, Brown attributes the departures
from the ideal values to defective homogeneity of the surrounding
fields. Although as a rule the transposition experiments are performed under darkroom conditions, the illumination of the movement-fields themselves somewhat lightens the surroundings. That
inhomogeneity of the surrounding fields reduces the transposition
phenomenon is one of Brown's well-established results. He reports
3 series of transposition experiments under different conditions of
illumination. We shall quote here only the results which he obtained with a transposition ratio of 10:1. They are representative for
the trend in the 3 series. One experiment was made in daylight
illumination, and gave the velocity ratio V_A / V_B 6.17, where V_A
refers to the 10 times larger field. Another experiment was done in
a dark room, but the illumination of the movement-fields somewhat
lightened the surroundings of the fields. This had a definite effect on

the result, as Brown points out conclusively.[8] V_A / V_B was here 6.83. In the third series the illumination of the movement-fields "was cut down considerably so that the surrounding fields approached homogeneity." The ratio here obtained was as high as 8.22. Indeed the departure from the ideal ratio (which would here be 10) is doubled when the observation is made with daylight illumination (6.17 as against 8.22). Brown was able to obtain a further decrease in proportionality. He covered the two cardboards in which the openings of the movement-fields were cut with a wallpaper which showed a regular geometric pattern. He then repeated the experiment, using an objective transposition ratio of 4:1, and of course daylight illumination. The resulting velocity ratio now was approximately 2, whereas the same pair of movement-fields gave a ratio of 2.7 when, again in daylight, a homogeneous black cardboard surrounded the movement-fields.[9]

This experiment clearly demonstrates the manner in which an inhomogeneous environment influences the velocity ratio. Such an environment disturbs the simple proportionality of the movement-fields. Phenomenal speeds are equal when the displacements per unit of time are the same in proportion to the dimensions of their respective fields. If both fields are surrounded by the same pattern, a common framework is introduced which will tend to equalize conditions and thus to reduce the influence of transposition. In the case of the ordinary daylight experiment the outer edge of the two equal cardboards is introduced as such a common framework.

The departure from perfect constancy of speed is not much discussed in Brown's paper. Constancies are rarely quite complete. Some authors attribute almost explanatory significance to the fact that actually visual size, brightness and shape lie somewhere between the properties of the "real" objects and properties corresponding to the retinal situation. According to our discussion, contancy of speed is no longer an independent fact but rather a by-product of the transposition phenomenon. It is in this light that we have to discuss the departure from perfect constancy of speed.

Generally, constancy of size and of shape are enhanced when

[8]*Ibid.*, p. 216, discussion of curve *b*.

[9]*Ibid.*, p. 218.

one changes from darkroom conditions to daylight illumination. For
the transposition phenomenon the opposite is true. It decreases upon
such a change. It should be interesting to note in what way constancy of speed reacts to changes of illumination. The figures quoted
by Brown for speed constancy under the two different conditions
show *no* significant difference.[10] At the first glance, it may seem
surprising that daylight illumination has not the same unfavorable
effect on speed constancy as it has on the transposition phenomenon,
when the two facts are interpreted as being fundamentally the same
thing. But when we consider the matter again in terms of retinal
images, and recall the way in which daylight conditions influence
the transposition phenomenon, we find this result of Brown in line
with our notions. Daylight conditions disturb the transposition phenomenon by introducing unproportional (equal) elements in the environment of the movement-fields. There should be no such
unfavorable effect when strictly *transposed* surroundings are added
to the transposed movement-fields proper. And this is what daylight
illumination actually does in a constancy experiment. Here the
movement-fields are objectively identical, and the transposed sizes
of the retinal images are due to the fact that they are projected from
different distances. But the same holds for the objectively identical
forms in the immediate surroundings of the movement-fields, as, for
instance, the edges of the cardboard screens and the supporting tables. Their retinal images are transposed in the same ratio as are the
movement-fields themselves. In this way only proportional elements are added to the transposed movement-fields, and these cannot impair the effect of the transposition principle. On the other
hand, they do not seem to improve it either. Brown's results, according to which the departure from ideal constancy is about the same
for daylight illumination as for darkroom conditions, indicate that
the addition of proportional elements does not serve to increase the
effect of the transposition principle. Obviously, the movement-fields
as such furnish a framework which guarantees this effect, and not
much is changed when further proportional structures are added on
the retina.

On the other hand it remains true that neither constancy of

[10] *Ibid.,* p. 208 f., Tables 1 and 2.

speed nor the transposition principle is completely realized. We have seen that in the case of speed constancy the deviations are not due to additional structures in the environment. We may therefore doubt whether in the case of transposition unproportional elements are *entirely* responsible for the deviations.

Incidentally, when we compare the departure from perfect constancy with the departure from complete transposition in the results of Brown's transposition experiments, we find that one of Brown's darkroom series yields about the same departure from the ideal transposition values as was found in corresponding constancy experiments.

For the purpose of such a comparison we consider again the velocities on the retina. Unfortunately, there is only one case in which transposition in the dark room and an experiment on constancy can be strictly compared; a constancy experiment in which the ratio of the distances of the movement-fields from the observer was 1:10, and a transposition experiment in which the movement-fields were transposed in the ratio 10:1. In both cases the retinal images of the movement-fields bear the same size proportions. In the constancy experiment equality of speed was attained when the velocity in the more distant field was 1.21 of that in the nearer (average of five observers, Table 1).[11] This means that the retinal velocity corresponding to the more distant field was .121 of that corresponding to the other; for, the image of the more distant field was one-tenth of the size of the other field, and the same, of course, was true of the retinal displacements. With this figure we have to compare the result for the size ratio 10:1 when transposition was measured in a dark and nearly homogeneous room. The velocity ratio here obtained was 8.22 (average of four observers). The ratio of the retinal velocities which we computed for the corresponding constancy experiment was .121. This is the quotient of the velocity in the smaller retinal movement field and the velocity in the larger one. Since Brown presents the velocity ratios for transposition experiments in the converse fashion (velocity in the larger field divided by that in the smaller field), we have to express the result of the constancy experiment as 1/.121 instead of .121. If this is done the figures become comparable. The value of 1/.121 is 8.26, in notable

[11] *Ibid.,* p. 208.

agreement with 8.22, the result of the transposition experiment.

In a constancy experiment with the distance ratio 1:5 the ratio of the objective velocities was 1.14 when phenomenal equality was attained (average of four observers, Table 2).[12] For the corresponding transposition ratio, 5:1 no data are available from the darkroom series in question. But the velocity ratio 3.7 for the transposition ratio 4:1, which is rather close to 5:1, taken together with the ratio 8.22 for 10:1,[13] permits by interpolation the computation of the value for the ratio 5:1, which is 4.45. In order to make the result of the constancy experiment, namely 1.14, comparable to this figure, we reduce this to retinal velocities and take again the reciprocal value (cf. above). The result is 4.39, again a close agreement.

We may conclude from these cases of agreement, that the transposition experiments to which they refer were done under optimal conditions; i.e., that a further decrease in the illumination would not improve the transposition of velocities in movement-fields of different sizes. For, the results of these transposition experiments correspond exactly to those of the constancy experiments with which they were compared. And in these, we have seen, results were optimal because all additional structures were properly transposed on the retina by virtue of the essential experimental conditions.

We now have to ask ourselves what factors limit the exact validity of the transposition principle. Recently D. Cartwright[14] was able to show that the difference threshold for the position of a point within an opening exhibits the same dependence on the properties of the opening as does phenomenal speed. In a three times larger opening the threshold for changes of position of a point was found to be 2.7 times larger than that in a smaller opening. Approximately the same ratio was obtained by Brown, when he determined the physical velocities which gave equal phenomenal speeds in openings of the relative sizes 3 and 1. In a second instance a similar agreement was found between the ratio of velocities which yielded equal phenomenal speeds, and the ratio of the threshold of position measured under comparable conditions. This parallelism suggests a close relationship between visual speed and the threshold for

[12] *Ibid.,* p. 209.

[13] *Cf.* above.

[14] D. Cartwright, On visual speed. *Psychologische Forschung,* 1938, 22, 320–342.

changes of position. Actually, several phenomena in the field of visual speed can be explained, if we realize that our sensitivity for changes of position depends on a great many factors. Here it seems relevant that this sensitivity follows Weber's law within certain limits. Strict validity of Weber's law for spatial changes would mean that the threshold for changes of position is proportional to the size of the openings in which the threshold is measured. From this point of view one might expect the transposition principle of velocities to be fully realized. Actually, Weber's law does not strictly hold in this field. This follows clearly from Cartwright's experiments. But the departure from Weber's law seems to be of about the same magnitude as the departure from ideal transposition of velocity. Thus the departure from ideal transposition of velocity may be attributed to the fact that Weber's law does not strictly hold in the case of spatial changes.

Postscript

Recently, I. Rock, L. A. Hill, and M. Fineman (Speed constancy as a function of size constancy. *Perception and Psychophysics,* 1968, 4, 37–40) demonstrated that there is also a constancy of visual speed that operates as an analogue to size constancy. They found that the rate of subject-relative displacement of a single luminous object in the dark is evaluated by taking distance into account. Speed matches approaching veridicality between objects at different distances were obtained only when distance cues were allowed to operate. The authors do not propose that their discovery provides an alternative to the explanation of speed constancy given above. They write: "Since speed constancy can also be explained in terms of the transposition principle—an explanation which requires no assumption about taking distance into account—it appears to be the case that there are two bases for speed constancy in daily life."

Evidence for the effectiveness of the transposition principle is found in one of Brown's experiments, where, by coincidence, the transposition principle operates in conflict with distance cues (J. F. Brown, The visual perception of velocity. *Psychologische Forschung,* 1931, 14, 209). When of two movement fields, one 2 m. and the other 4 m. from *S*, the more distant field was twice as large in every way, speeds appeared to be the same time when the velocity in the 4 m. distant field was twice as large as that in the field at 2 m. Although observation was binocular, no speed constancy was obtained; the results, however, conformed to the transposition principle. This is another example that shows object-relative displacement to be more effective in motion perception than subject-relative displacement.

The role of memory in visual perception

1. Some Considerations Concerning the Relation Between Perception and Cognition

A look around in a familiar environment and find that nearly every object has meaning. This meaning I experience as an objective fact, and I perceive it out there in the thing. A hammer looks like something with which to drive a nail into a wall or something with which to smash a vase. I have the impression that I perceive these meanings in the object even while I realize that they do not come to me through my eyes at the moment of perceiving them but must be furnished by a memory function, for they were given by previous experience with the object.

I suspect that this discrepancy between experience and function is responsible for some of the vagueness of conception in this part

Reprinted from *Journal of Personality,* 1949, 18, 6–13.

of psychology. The remedy seems to be to acknowledge it explicitly: The meaning which the hammer has for me is, *functionally* speaking, the effect of past commerce with that object, but it is experienced as being seen in the object of equal status with color and form. We have here the effect of a recall process in which recall is not experienced as such. Instead the contribution of memory appears as part of a percept.

There is no reason why this recall process should be essentially different from other recall processes as, for instance, recognition and recall by association. As Köhler reviving an old argument of Hoeffding's has pointed out (5; 3, 126–144), any recall which is occasioned by a perceptual experience involves a process in which such an experience brings into function a memory trace of a similar experience of the past. This is true also where the subject recalls an associated content. When I pass a man on the street whom I have met before, I may, for instance, recall his name. This recall presupposes an association between a visual trace, say of the man's face, and a trace of his name. But the association alone does not explain recall of the name on this occasion. Face and name left associated traces when I was introduced to the man in the past. When I meet the man again, he is, of course, on the whole the same physical object, and I may immediately experience him as the same person I met before; but *functionally* speaking there are two separate psychological events involved, the perception of the face on the occasion of the first meeting and a present perceptual process of the "same" face. The former is now represented by a memory trace, and it is this trace which provides the access to the trace of the name. Yet it is one of many traces of faces which I might recognize, and so the question arises how the appropriate one is brought into function. As Köhler has argued, the only possible answer is that the similarity between the original process of seeing the face, now represented by its trace, and the present process is responsible for the proper selection of this trace. Recall by association, then, consists of two steps: A process of recall by similarity by which the present perceptual process makes contact with the trace of a similar process of the past, and secondly, recall of a content associated with this trace.

The necessity for such an assumption is not avoided by thinking in terms of responses instead of associated contents. One speaks of the same stimulus when the same combination of physical processes affect the sense organs of the subject or, more loosely, when these combinations appear to the experimenter as the same. Yet, when the same stimulus occurs repeatedly to produce a particular response, we deal, of course, with different, initially unconnected psychological events, and they must in some fashion manifest their identity in the nervous system of the subject before that particular response can be aroused. In a relatively small number of cases the assumption might possibly be made that afferent processes produced by different stimuli will arrive at different places in the nervous system and manifest the identity of the respective stimuli by their locale. But where the stimulus is characterized only by its spatially or temporally extended pattern as, for instance, in the case of visual forms, of speech sounds, and of noises, this assumption cannot be made. Similarity between the processes produced by different occurrences of the "same" stimulus must account for its identification.

Recall by similarity may occur without recall of an associated content, namely, in pure recognition where it merely produces a feeling of familiarity.

The same process of recall by similarity must be involved when meaning is perceived, unless a set is operating. No matter what the nature of meaning may be, as long as a meaning content was acquired in the past it is necessary to postulate the same sequence of recall processes in order to explain how meaning comes to appear in perceptual experience: first, a step of recall by similarity between the sensorily determined perceptual process and a trace complex with which the meaning content is connected, and secondly, the coming into function of the connected meaning. Since in a familiar environment most perceptual objects appear meaningful, such recall processes must readily take place all the time, and because they do, their mediation usually goes unrecognized.

I have just used the term trace complex, because often what appears as a familiar or meaningful object has occurred in the past not only once but at several different times. Frequently a number of these occurrences have contributed in different ways to the meaning content. When recall takes place, the total meaning seems to be given. This indicates that the recall process established contact, not with a trace of any one of these occurrences, but with a trace complex which represents features of a number of them. In short, the various occurrences must have previously become connected so that they could contribute to the total meaning content and later, in a recall process, function together. These connections are themselves the effects of recall processes which took place in the past, when at the second occurrence of the object contact was made with the trace of the first one, and later, when the third occurrence brought into function the trace complex of the first two, and so on. In this fashion, recall by similarity accounts for a cognitive product of temporally separated events and, in many cases, makes learning by repetition possible.

Often the function of a memory trace which participates in a perceptual process is not merely to add its content to the sensorily determined qualities of color and shape. It may change the organization of the primary process by imposing a different internal grouping as in the case of the Street Figures. Or new perceptual qualities may emerge after a trace reference has been established, as, for instance, physiognomic qualities. They are seen only when the primary form pattern has been recognized as a face. But when that has happened, the seen physiognomic qualities depend mainly on the sensory conditions.

Yet no matter how intimate and varied in function the interplay of a primary process and an aroused trace may be, it must be preceded by a process of trace selection. Where no set is operating, this selection process consists of recall by similarity and is therefore initiated by the primary perceptual process and highly dependent on its characteristics. The selection process must be distinguished from the interplay between trace and primary process, for it is prerequisite for this interplay.

The intervening of this selection process before a pertinent memory trace can influence a perceptual process introduces an element of fortuity into experiments on the effect of central factors on perception, or, rather, what amounts to fortuity from the viewpoint of such studies. We are all aware of the difficulties which the incomplete knowledge of the subject's past means for experimentation and its evaluation. But even if we had a complete inventory of the subject's previous experience, we would not be much better off because it would still be to a degree fortuitous whether a psychologically pertinent trace content actually comes to participate in the present process. Köhler and Restorff have demonstrated that whether or not an experience of the past through recall by similarity gains an influence on a present process depends on the content and structure of the time interval between that experience and the present (1; 5; 3, pp. 126–144). Frequency and recency of the mental event which the pertinent trace represents undoubtedly also plays a role in whether or not contact is made with the trace (1, 5). Therefore, where trace selection is left to spontaneous recall, the influence of a need or of another central factor on perception is not altogether a dynamic matter. This must be borne in mind when quantitative results are interpreted. They represent not only the strength of the central factor in the perceptual process but also the probability of the occurrence of the contact with the pertinent trace.

This last consideration presupposes, of course, that, as in the case of meaning, central factors gain whatever influence they may have on perception through mediation of a more or less specific memory trace. This is certainly true of values which with few exceptions are themselves mediated by meaning. This is also true of needs. On the whole, particularly in a mentally healthy individual, a need becomes operative only in specific situations. A given situation must be recognized as belonging to a certain kind which is specific for the operation of a particular need. It is even true of drives when they are aroused by their drive objects. Except for the relatively rare cases where cathexis of a novel drive object occurs in the perceptual situation, the capacity of an object or situation to arouse a drive was acquired in the past, and this product of previous cathexis is brought into function through a recognition process.

That the arousal of a pertinent memory trace must precede the influence of central factors on perception is particularly important where these factors are supposed to affect recognition, as in the case of tachistoscopic studies (6). It seems very likely that the arousal of a pertinent trace amounts to recognition. But the assumption that values and needs affect recognition seems to contradict this simple conception. For these central factors which supposedly have an influence on whether or not recognition occurs come into play through the arousal of pertinent traces. This makes no sense if recognition is equivalent to trace arousal. A solution to this dilemma will have to be found in a closer analysis of the psychological processes which go on in such experiments.

Up to the present the main interest of the studies on the influence of central factors on perception has been in demonstrating such effects. Such demonstrations show to what extent the organization of perceptual processes can be influenced by contents and conditions of central origin. But this is not the only way in which studies of this kind may contribute to the investigation of perceptual functions. They may be helpful in answering the following question: To what stage of organization must a visual process develop before it can arouse a memory trace? Since, in the absence of a "set," central factors gain an influence only *after* pertinent traces have been aroused, properly designed experiments which attempt to produce such an influence may be a way to answer this question.

I should like to clarify this question briefly: A number of perceptual functions besides the strictly sensory processes have to take effect to bring about visual percepts as we experience them. They are, to name only those which are of interest in this context, the interaction process on which the formation of dense surface colors depends, organization due to grouping factors, and the formation of "figure and ground." The question is whether they must also take effect before a pertinent memory trace can be aroused.

The answer to this question has certainly to be affirmative in so far as the colors of the achromatic scale are concerned. The gray color seen in a certain region of the visual field depends on the relation of the intensity of stimulation received from this region and the stimulus intensity of the surrounding region (9). An interaction between the local processes must be responsible for the gray color. A light gray can be changed into a dark gray either by lowering the stimulus intensity in the region in which the gray is seen or by raising the intensity in the surroundings. The end results of these changes cannot be told apart, although in one case stimulation in the gray region changes and in the other it does not. This shows that no sensory process which corresponds to the intensity of local stimulation has trace representation; only the product of the interaction process plays a role in recognition.

The evidence concerning grouping pertains only to line figures. Demonstrations of Köhler's (4) and the work of Gottschaldt (2) have made it clear that figures with which the subject is well acquainted will not be spontaneously recognized when lines are added which prevent these figures from appearing as separate units. I think it is easy to rule out the possibility that the comprehensive figure which comes about through such addition prevents recognition of the "hidden" figure by initiating its own recall process in competition with the "hidden" figure. Rather, "hidden" figures fail to be recognized because they do not appear as separate units and are therefore unable to make trace contacts. Since in the case of line figures the formation of units is ruled by grouping principles, organization due to grouping factors should precede trace arousal. There is certainly need for direct evidence to support this reasoning.

The evidence concerning "figure and ground" is at present contradictory. The essence of the distinction of figure and ground is that only the area designated as figure has form. Rubin has demonstrated that an area will be recognized by its shape only if it is seen as figure (7). This means that the sensory pattern must first be organized in terms of figure and ground, before the figure areas establish contact with specific memory traces.

This seems to be irreconcilable with the result of the brilliant experiment of Shafer and Murphy (8). It demonstrated an influence of previous reward and punishment on the perception of figure and ground in an ambiguous design. An outline circle was divided by an irregular vertical line of such a shape that each half of the circle could be seen as a profile of a face of half-moon shape. Prior to the test in which two such ambiguous figures were used each half-moon shape was presented singly, and each presentation was always accompanied by a reward or a punishment. In the test, the previously rewarded half-moon shapes were predominantly recognized, that is, seen as a figure.

There can be no doubt that in this experiment the aftereffect of previous reward and punishment was connected with the traces of the forms of the training series and could become effective only through the arousal of these traces. Thus, figure-ground distribution is influenced by factors which can only come into play *after* the pertinent trace has been aroused. This seems to contradict the conclusion drawn from Rubin's result that formation of figure and ground must precede trace arousal.

This contradiction disappears only when one takes into account that Rubin worked with solid figures, that is, pattern where the contour between figure and ground is formed by the borderline between different colors, whereas Shafer and Murphy used outline figures. The black line on white which here forms the contour between figure and ground also has form in its own right and can therefore make trace contact. A repetition of Shafer and Murphy's experiment with solid figures would really go to the heart of the matter. My hunch is that it would fail to demonstrate any influence of reward and punishment on figure-ground distribution.

I have recently become impressed with the extent to which memory traces participate in simple perceptual processes. They not only impart meaning or impose grouping as previously mentioned; they also seem to be responsible for the perception of three-dimensional form where perceptual conditions for primary organization in depth are absent or weak.

In this situation the full answer to the question, at what stage of perceptual organization pertinent traces can be aroused, seems to be very much needed. As matters stand I would say that the interaction process on which the formation of dense surfaces depends, the formation of figure and ground, and in some cases, organization due to the grouping factors must develop before traces can be aroused through similarity of form. That such processes must occur before traces can be aroused may possibly be one of the reasons for the great stability of simple perceptual processes and the high degree of independence from other psychological functions which they exhibit. One may say that, up to a certain point, the development of percepts is protected against interference by central factors, because the developing percepts are inaccessible before trace contact has been made.

References

1. Bartel, H. Ueber die Abhängigkeit spontaner Reproduktionen von Feldbedingungen. *Psychologische Forschung,* 1937, 22, 1–25.
2. Gottschaldt, K. Ueber den Einfluss der Erfahrung auf die Wahrnehmung von Figuren I. *Psychologische Forschung,* 1926, 8, 261–317.
3. Köhler, W. *Dynamics in psychology.* New York: Liveright, 1940.
4. Köhler, W. *Gestalt psychology.* New York: Liveright, 1929, Chapter VI.
5. Köhler, W., and von Restorff, H. Zur Theorie der Reproduktion. *Psychologische Forschung,* 1935, 21, 56–112.
6. Postman, L., Bruner, J. F., and McGinnies, E. Personal values as selective factors in perception. *Journal of Abnormal Social Psychology,* 1948, 43, 142–154.
7. Rubin, E. *Visuell wahrgenommene Figuren.* Berlin, 1921.

8. Shafer, R., and Murphy, G. The role of autism in a visual figure-ground relationship. *Journal of Experimental Psychology,* 1943, 32, 335–343.
9. Wallach, H. Brightness constancy and the nature of achromatic colors. *Journal of Experimental Psychology,* 1948, 38, 310–324.

2. The Memory Effect of Visual
Perception of Three-Dimensional Form

The kinetic depth effect that has been discussed in a preceding paper (2) enables monocular Ss to perceive three-dimensional form as directly as do persons with serviceable binocular vision by means of retinal disparity. Yet this effect alone does not, of course, solve the entire problem of the perception of solid form. Three-dimensional form is seen monocularly also when the observer does not move in relation to the object and it is also perceived in photographs and drawings. It has been mentioned in the preceding paper that an empiristic explanation of these cases of three-dimensional form perception becomes more feasible through the demonstration of the kinetic depth effect. This is so because no empiristic explanation can be termed successful until it is made clear how the original process or experience is brought about under whose influence current experience is supposed to occur. Prior to the demonstration of the kinetic depth effect (*KDE*) no process was known which could account in a satisfactory way for the "original" perception of three-dimensional form in monocular Ss.

Two different approaches have been made to explain the perception of three-dimensional form that occurs in the absence of retinal disparity or of other specific cues for visual depth. It has been proposed that three-dimensional forms are seen under these circumstances because the corresponding retinal patterns have the power to evoke them directly. Gibson (1), who holds such a view, believes that such retinal patterns have geometric characteristics which are

Written in collaboration with D. N. O'Connell and Ulric Neisser. Reprinted from *Journal of Experimental Psychology*, 1953, 45, 360–368.

specific stimuli for depth just as there are specific stimuli for color, pitch, etc. Many Gestalt psychologists believe that visual processes are spontaneously organized so that certain patterns of stimulation lead to three-dimensional forms and others to plane forms in perception and they have tried to formulate the principles which underlie such organization. When three-dimensional objects are seen as three-dimensional forms, it is due to the fact that their retinal projections have properties which favor organization as three-dimensional forms. The other approach is, of course, the empiristic one. It is believed that previous experiences can cause a present perception in three dimensions.

For a number of reasons, one of which—the nature of the *KDE* itself—will be discussed below, we came to believe that an influence of past experience plays an important role in the perception of three-dimensional form and set out to demonstrate such an effect in a stringent way. Such a demonstration requires that a retinal pattern, which at the outset is seen as a plane figure, gives rise under identical external conditions to the perception of a three-dimensional form after an intervening exposure of the same pattern given under conditions which cause it to be seen as three-dimensional.

Method

There are several ways in which a pattern can be made to appear as a three-dimensional form in the intervening exposure. We found it most appropriate to use the *KDE* for this purpose, and experiments were done with a shadow technique (2). A three-dimensional wire figure was placed behind the translucent screen which was so chosen that its shadow visible on the other side of the screen looked two-dimensional to all *S*s in a stationary exposure. In the intervening exposure, the wire figure was turned back and forth so that a deforming shadow was cast which *S* eventually perceived as a three-dimensional form due to the operation of the *KDE*. This was followed sooner or later by the test exposure in which the same stationary shadow was presented which had been shown in the first exposure. The critical question of the experiment was whether or not it would now appear three-dimensional.

The same wire figures were employed as in the experiments of the preceding paper (2). They were the "helix," the "parallelogram," and the "110° corner." Three experimental series will be reported and in each all three figures were presented. However, the purpose of experimenting with the 110° corner was different from the purpose of experimentation with the other two figures. Merely for technical reasons were all three figures presented in the same series. The results for the 110° corner will therefore be discussed separately at the end of this article. We begin with a description of the three series. Since each of the series, insofar as the helix and the parallelogram were concerned, was designed to answer a different question, the results of the different series will be separately presented and discussed.

The experimental series were composed of moving exposures and of stationary presentations of the various figures shown individually. In the moving exposure the wire figure behind the screen rotated back and forth through an angle of 42° at the rate of one cycle in 1.5 sec. The shadow was shown for 10 sec. by turning the lamp in whose light the shadow was visible on and off, and then S was asked for a report on what he had seen. The 10-sec. exposure was repeated until the report clearly indicated that S had seen the correct three-dimensional form. If this did not happen within 12 such exposures, the moving presentation was listed as having failed.

The shadow for the stationary presentation was cast by the wire figure in a position within the range of the rotation of 42°. Figures 2, 3A, and 4 of the previous article (2) show the shadows employed in the stationary presentations. All stationary presentations employed the same shadow of each wire figure and lasted for 5 sec. Our Ss were undergraduates of Swarthmore College.

SERIES I

There was first a stationary exposure of the 110° corner. Then, moving exposures of the helix, the 110° corner, and the parallelogram were given. Stationary test exposures of the three figures in the same order followed. Thus, the moving exposure and the test exposure of a given figure occurred a few minutes apart. For the helix, the moving exposure of the 110° corner and of the parallelogram intervened, and, in the case of the parallelogram, the stationary exposures of the helix and of the 110° corner came between the moving and the test exposure of that figure. This series was presented to 33 Ss.

Since no stationary exposure of the helix and the parallelogram was made in this series prior to the moving exposure, stationary presentations of these figures were given to a control group of 16 *S*s to find out what percentage of *S*s would see the figures two-dimensional at the outset.

SERIES II

Here two groups of 20 *S*s were employed. Only the 110° corner and *one* of the other two figures were presented in moving exposure. The remaining figure served as a control and was given only in the final stationary exposure together with the two experimental figures. Thus, for an *S* of the helix group the sequence of presentation was the following: First came a stationary exposure of the helix followed by one of the 110° corner. Thereupon, the moving presentations of the helix and of the 110° corner were made in that order. These were followed by stationary exposures of the helix, of the 110° corner, and finally of the parallelogram which had not been seen by these *S*s before. For *S*s of the other group, the parallelogram was given in place of the helix and vice versa.

SERIES III

This series differed from Series I only in two points. The sequence in which the figures were presented both in the moving and in the stationary test exposure was parallelogram, helix, and 110° corner. Also, a large time interval was introduced between the moving and the test exposures. For 12 *S*s this interval was 24 hr. and for 11 *S*s seven days.

Results for "Helix" and "Parallelogram"

The purpose of Series I was simply to demonstrate that the perception of a three-dimensional form in the moving exposure would tend to make the figure appear three-dimensional in the stationary test exposure also. Evidence that prior to a moving exposure our two figures appear two-dimensional in stationary presentation comes here from a control group of 16 *S*s. Both figures were seen plane by all of them. The results for the moving and for the test exposure are simple in the case of the parallelogram. All 33 *S*s saw this figure three-dimensional in the moving exposure and all of them reported the same three-dimensional form in the stationary test exposure. In the case of the helix, 31 of the 33 *S*s reported this figure as three-dimensional in the moving presentation after various exposure times; the remaining 2 saw it as a plane deforming figure and saw it two-dimensional in the test exposure also. Of the critical 31 *S*s who had seen the helix three-dimensional in the moving presentation a majority of 26 reported seeing the three-dimensional form when the stationary shadow of the figure was presented in the test exposure; the remaining 5 *S*s saw a plane figure.

These results demonstrate a strong influence of an earlier experience in the perception of three-dimensional form. What is the nature of this influence? Does it consist in a tendency to see further figures three-dimensional after some have been perceived in this fashion under the same circumstances, or is it an influence of an earlier perception of a particular figure on the perceptual process which takes place when this particular figure is given again? Series II was designed to answer this question. It will be remembered that only one of the two figures was presented to a given *S* in moving exposure, but both figures were presented in the test exposure. If we are dealing with a general tendency, both figures should be seen three-dimensional in the test exposure by a majority of the *S*s. If the influence is in the nature of an individual figure causing a later exposure of that figure to be seen in the same three-dimensional way, only the figure previously given in moving exposure should appear three-dimensional.

In this series a stationary control exposure of the figure for which an aftereffect was to be established was given to the experimental *S*s prior to the moving presentations. All 40 *S*s saw the figure that was presented to them as being two-dimensional and this confirmed the results of 16 control *S*s of Series I.

In the moving exposure, 18 out of 20 *S*s saw the helix three-dimensional and all *S*s perceived the parallelogram in this fashion. In the stationary test presentation, 13 out of the 18 *S*s who had been given a moving exposure of the helix and had then seen a three-dimensional form saw this figure again three-dimensional, and 5 reported a plane figure. The parallelogram was seen three-dimensional by 17 of the 20 "parallelogram *S*s." These data agree well with those obtained in Series I and show a strong influence of the perception of three-dimensional form in the moving presentation on the reports in the test exposure. The new information to be gained from the present series comes from the test exposures of the figures which had *not* been previously presented to the respective *S*. Of the 20 *S*s who had been given the parallelogram in moving exposure and had seen it three-dimensionally, only one perceived the helix in three dimensions. The results are somewhat different for the parallelogram in this situation. As many as 7 of the 20 *S*s to whom it had not been presented in moving exposure reported seeing it in three dimensions (19 of them had seen at least the 110° corner three-dimensional).

For the helix, these results are quite unequivocal. Whereas 13 out of 18 *S*s who had seen this figure three-dimensional before saw it so in the text exposure, this was the case with only 1 out of the 20 *S*s who had seen only the other figures in this fashion. The influence which causes the perception of three-dimensional form in the stationary test exposure appears to come from a previous three-dimensional perception of the *same* figure only. For the parallelogram we have to compare the result 17 out of 20 *S*s who had seen the same figure three-dimensional with 7 out of 19 *S*s who had seen only either one or two other figures in this fashion. Although there is for this figure an influence of a general kind, the specific influence which comes from a previous three-dimensional perception of the same figure is much stronger. It should be mentioned that the shadow of the parallelogram is more easily seen in three dimensions than that of the helix. Often a mere suggestion like "could this be a tetrahedron" suffices to make this figure appear three-dimensional. When the results for the helix and the parallelogram are taken together, the difference between the cases due to a general effect (8 out of 40) and those cases where the same figure had been seen three-dimensional before (30 out of 38) is reliable at better than the .01 level of confidence. It seems safe to conclude that our aftereffect consists in an influence of the perception of a figure upon a subsequent perceptual process which takes place when the same figure is given again, and that, in the case of some figures, previous exposures of different figures may exert a similar influence as if by suggestion. (Further evidence on this point comes from the experiments with the 110° corner reported below.)

Some readers may find difficulty with this formulation. How do we know, they may ask, that we have here really an effect on perception, that *S*s actually *saw* a three-dimensional form? It could be that *S*s reported a three-dimensional form because they had previously seen the same pattern on the screen as three-dimensional and knew that the pattern represented such a form. The evidence on this point is clear and simple. When directly after the test exposure *S*s were allowed to inspect the stationary shadow for a longer period, a large percentage of them reported Necker cube-like reversals of the figures that they had described. Everybody who has seen a drawing of a three-dimensional figure reverse will agree that only an actually perceived three-dimensional form will exhibit these changes. Where these reversals occur, coming on unexpectedly and initially appearing to be objective, three-dimensional forms are seen with all concreteness. Many *S*s of Series II who had reported seeing three-dimensional forms on the test presentation were given prolonged exposures of the stationary figures. For the helix, 13 out of 14, and for the parallelogram, 20 out of 24 *S*s reported reversals spontaneously.

In Series I and II, the time interval between the perception of a figure as a three-dimensional form and the test presentation amounted to a few minutes. In Series III this time interval was much longer. Twelve *S*s were tested after 24 hr. and 11 after seven days. All *S*s perceived a three-dimensional form in the moving exposure of both figures. In the 24-hr. group, all *S*s saw the parallelogram three-dimensionally in the test exposure and 11 out of 12 did so in case of the helix. In the seven-day group these numbers are 10 out of 11 for both figures.

In this series the test for the parallelogram always preceded that of the helix, and this may have favored a three-dimensional appearance of the helix. We therefore report data from another similar experiment where, after a 24-hr. interval, the helix was the first figure tested. Of nine *S*s who had seen the helix three-dimensional in the moving exposure, seven saw it three-dimensional in the test presentation.

It appears from these data that the aftereffect can be obtained virtually undiminished after longer time intervals, and that it should be termed a memory effect. Moreover, the results of Series

II indicated that we were dealing largely with the effect of individual memory traces.

How does a memory trace produce its effect on the perception in a test exposure? Does it merely give an indication that the pattern concerned must be perceived as three-dimensional or has a trace the capacity to determine a specific three-dimensional form for the new perception? So far, the answer to this question comes only from a consideration of the kinetic depth effect (*KDE*) which was described in the previous paper (2). The very nature of this process makes it necessary to ascribe to a memory trace the power to determine the organization of a visual form process. Stimulation for the *KDE* consists in a deforming retinal projection which is produced when a three-dimensional object changes its orientation to *S*. At any moment the retinal projection assumes a slightly different shape and every one of these momentary images can have a form such that it would produce a perception of a two-dimensional figure, if it were presented by itself, that is, not in the context of the deforming projection. However, within the context, that is, when it is given in continuous sequence with all the other momentary images which make up the deforming projection, it produces the perception of a three-dimensional object which changes its apparent orientation to *S*. The apparent momentary aspect of the perceived object corresponds to the particular retinal image which is given at that moment. This makes it clear that any one of the momentary retinal images gives rise to a perceived three-dimensional form only because it was preceded by a number of different images of the object. At the moment when it is given on the retina the preceding images are matters of the past. Pertinent stimulation is given in temporal sequence and the perceived form is its cumulative result. From the moment at which three-dimensional form is first perceived, a complex memory trace which represents this result of the preceding stimulation must be assumed to participate in the perceptual process. To be sure, this trace alone is not the correlate of perceptual experience; stimulation by one of the momentary retinal images is also necessary to bring about the three-dimensional percept. But it is obvious that the perceptual process to which a momentary image gives rise must attain its form in three-dimensional space due to such a trace.

If perceived three-dimensional form must be ascribed to the organizing power of a trace in the case of the *KDE,* it seems justifiable to assume that the effect of a trace in our test exposure is of the same nature. The motion of any one of our wire figures in kinetic presentation can be stopped and *S* will continue to see the stationary shadow as the three-dimensional form that he had seen during the moving presentation. There appears to be no reason to assume that at this point, a trace action of a different nature takes place. One should rather think that here, too, the trace causes perception of a specific three-dimensional form. It may be mentioned that such consideration of the nature of the *KDE* was one of the reasons why we expected to find a wide influence of past experience on form perception.

Results for "110° Corner"

We have shown that a memory effect on form perception is easily demonstrated and that it readily bridges large time intervals. We are inclined to believe that this effect plays a large role in ordinary perception of space and of solid form. We think that, at least in the adult, memory effects are responsible for the majority of instances of perception of solid form and of the spatial arrangement of the objects in the visual field.

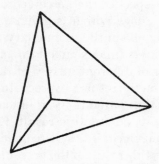

Fig. 1. Figure always seen as three-dimensional

If this is so, why did we demonstrate the effect only with two different figures? The answer is that suitable wire figures are hard to find because the shadows of most of them look three-dimensional from the outset. We believe that this is so because of the great wealth of previous experience with three-dimensional form. A pattern, like Figure 1, that can be interpreted as representing three surfaces meeting to form a spatial corner, will always be seen in that fashion. This is true even in cases where such a pattern is part of a large one as in Figure 2. Although this figure as a whole makes no sense as a three-dimensional form to most Ss, three-dimensionality is seen at the two places where three lines meet to form a Y, most convincingly so at the lower one. Such a Y-shaped pattern is very frequently present in the projections of solid objects, as, for instance, in the projections of corners of boxes and of rooms, and there is much occasion to establish previous experience of three-dimensionality in connection with it. Wire figures which contain it are not suitable for our experiments where the given shadow pattern ought to appear two-dimensional in the control exposure.

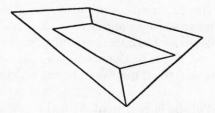

Fig. 2. Figure that makes no sense as a three-dimensional form

Yet, there is nevertheless a way to make use of such a pattern for the demonstration of a memory effect, namely, if we are satisfied with establishing a modified three-dimensional form in the moving exposure. A Y pattern will look like the edges of a corner to many Ss, but that corner will frequently appear rectangular, presumably because in the great majority of previous encounters the Y pattern has been produced by a rectangular corner and has been seen as one. If, in the moving exposure, the Y pattern can be made to appear, say, as an obtuse corner, there is then the question of how it will look in the test exposure. If it is again seen as an obtuse corner, an aftereffect of previous experience has been established within our experiment.

Such an experiment was performed with the 110° corner. As mentioned above, this figure was presented in all three experimental series and in every one the control exposure was given to the experimental Ss. Thus, all Ss were given first a stationary control exposure, then a moving presentation, and finally a stationary test exposure of this figure. Fortunately, this particular Y pattern was seen as a two-dimensional figure in the control exposure by as many as 56 of the 96 Ss who participated in the three series, a number much higher than we had hoped for when the experiment had been planned; their results will be reported later. Of the remaining 40 Ss, 17 saw an obtuse corner in the control exposure and 23 saw a rectangular one. With regard to the question just raised, we are concerned with this latter group. In the case of 2 Ss of this group, the moving exposure failed to produce a perception of an obtuse corner, which reduces the number of Ss in this pertinent group to 21. Of these 21 Ss who did see a rectangular corner in the control exposure and an obtuse corner in the moving exposure, 8 reported a rectangular corner in the test presentation and 13 an obtuse corner. While the former did not display an aftereffect of perception in the moving exposure, the 13 Ss who saw an obtuse corner in the test presentation saw the shadow as one three-dimensional form at the outset and later, presumably as a memory effect of the moving exposure, as a different one. It means that a single experience can modify a form perception which itself may well be the outcome of previous experiences.

The total result of the experiment with the 110° corner is given in Table 1. It lists the results of all three experimental series and is arranged in the following manner: Above the center line there are listed the 11 occurring combinations of Ss' reports in the three exposures. They play the role of headings for the 11 columns of data below and they are grouped under 5 capital letters in a manner which will be explained later on. The first horizontal row refers to the first stationary or control exposure; the second to the moving exposure; and the third row to the second stationary or test exposure. For instance, an S who sees the corner as a two-dimensional figure in the control exposure, as an obtuse corner in the moving exposure, and as a rectangular corner in the test exposure falls under the combination heading below the letter C (2D, Obt., Rect.), and the number of Ss who gave this particular sequence of reports in each series is given under this heading. The first three horizontal rows of numbers give the results for the three series separately and the fourth row the totals.

All three combination headings under A show no change from one exposure to another and the 14 Ss who gave these report sequences did not contribute in any way to the outcome of the experi-

TABLE 1
Number of Ss Giving Various Response Sequences to 110° Corner

	A No Change			B Full Aftereffect			C Partial Aftereffect	D No Aftereffect		E Random Result	
Control	2D	Rect.	Obt.	2D	2D	Rect.	2D	2D	Rect.	Obt.	Obt.
Moving	2D	Rect.	Obt.	Rect.	Obt.	Obt.	Obt.	Obt.	Obt.	Obt.	Obt.
Test	2D	Rect.	Obt.	Rect.	Obt.	Obt.	Rect.	2D	Rect.	2D	Rect.
Series I	0	0	5	1	8	4	7	1	3	2	2
Series II	1	1	4	1	19	4	3	5	1	0	1
Series III	0	1	2	0	9	5	0	1	4	0	1
Total	1	2	11	2	36	13	10	7	8	2	4
Grand Total		14			51		10		15		6

ment. This reduces the total number of Ss to be considered to 82.

The headings under B have two features in common: the reports for the moving exposure differ from those for the control exposures in the direction of a more adequate perception of the spatial form of the corner, and the reports for the moving and the test exposure are the same. Thus, these three headings represent three report sequences which denote a memory effect of the experience in the moving exposure on perception in the test exposure. However, to the 51 Ss who gave one of these report sequences should be added the 10 Ss under C who, although they did not give the same report in the test exposure that they gave in the moving exposure, nevertheless showed a change in the proper direction, if the control and the test reports are compared; they reported a plane figure in the former and a rectangular corner in the latter.

The two report sequences under D represent those cases that could have shown a memory effect of the perception in the moving exposure but did not; that is, the reports in the test exposure were the same as the reports in the control exposure. Under E two report sequences are listed which make no sense, and the total of six Ss listed here gives an idea to what degree randomness figures in our results.

It should be pointed out that the data in the third horizontal row (Series III) were obtained with intervals of 24 hours or seven days between the moving and the test exposures. The results for this group of 23 Ss do not differ significantly from those obtained after brief intervals (Series I and II).

To summarize: Of 82 Ss, 61 gave reports indicating a memory effect operating between perception in the moving and perception in the test exposure, 15 showed no such effect, and 6 gave results which denote independence of the perception in the test exposure of both preceding exposures. With three-quarters of the Ss yielding positive results, this experiment represents another demonstration of a memory effect on form perception.

The data given in Table 1 also throw light on an issue that has already been raised with regard to the two other wire figures, namely whether the aftereffect is caused by a previous three-dimensional perception of the *same* figure, or whether the figure is seen three-dimensional because of a general tendency arising in the experimental situation to see further figures three-dimensional. If the latter were true, one might expect that those Ss who see the corner three-dimensional in the test presentation as the result of an aftereffect will report a rectangular or an obtuse corner in about the same proportion as do Ss who see this figure three-dimensional at the outset. Among the 96 Ss , 40 saw the corner three-dimensional in the control exposure and of these 23 reported a rectangular and 17 an obtuse corner. On the other hand, a total of 48 Ss saw this figure three-dimensional in the test presentation as an aftereffect of the moving exposure; they are listed under the following three headings: 2D, Rect., Rect.; 2D, Obt., Obt.; and 2D, Obt. Rect. If the aftereffect consists in a general tendency to see the figure three-dimensional, one should expect these Ss to report a rectangular or an obtuse corner in about the same ratio as the previously mentioned 40 Ss, that is, in a proportion of about 23 to 17. This was not the case; only 12 Ss reported a rectangular corner and 36 an obtuse corner. The difference between 12 and 36 is reliably different from the difference between 23 and 17 at the .01 level of confidence.

If, on the other hand, the appearance of the corner in the test presentation largely depends on the perception of the corner in the moving exposure, we should expect to find a preponderance of Ss reporting an obtuse corner in the test, because 46 of the 48 Ss saw an obtuse corner in the moving exposure. This was indeed the case; 36 of the 46 Ss reported an obtuse corner again in the test presentation and the hypothesis that these two results are related is confirmed at the .01 level of confidence. In other words, these results can be ascribed, at least in part, to an influence of a specific perceptual experience upon a later perceptual process.

Summary

The shadows of three different three-dimensional wire figures were shown on a translucent screen. These figures were so chosen that their shadows appeared two-dimensional to the majority of *S*s. By use of the kinetic depth effect, that is, by turning the wire figures back and forth, the shadows were then made to appear three-dimensional. After intervals which ranged from minutes to a week, the stationary shadows were presented again in the same fashion in which they had been exposed originally and were then reported to appear three-dimensional by a large number of *S*s. In order to make certain that these reports were based on three-dimensional percepts, rather than on inferences concerning the perceptual objects, a number of *S*s were given prolonged test exposures and nearly all of them reported spontaneously reversals of the kind which are usually demonstrated with a Necker cube. Thus it was demonstrated that a previous perceptual experience can cause a later form perception to be three-dimensional. Evidence was presented that general set played only a minor role in the reported experiments and that the aftereffects obtained were to a large part due to the influence of the memory of individual figures.

References

1. Gibson, J. J. *The perception of the visual world.* Boston: Houghton Mifflin, 1950.
2. Wallach, H., & O'Connell, D. N. The kinetic depth effect. *Journal of Experimental Psychology,* 1953, 45, 205–217. In the present volume, Chapter II.

Postscript

It should be emphasized that, in the experiments reported above, the kinetic depth effect was used only to produce primary perception of three-dimensionality. Any other depth cue could have served this purpose. Later, I repeated the experiment using binocular vision, that is, stereoscopic depth perception, to cause the critical shapes to be seen in three dimensions. Essentially the same results were obtained as before.

3. Recognition and the Localization of
Visual Traces

If an unknown figure is shown in one retinal position, will this figure be recognized later when it is shown in another retinal position? This question was answered in the affirmative more than fifty years ago by J. von Kries and the experiments of Becher confirmed Von Kries' position,[1] but psychologists have continued to seek some effect of retinal position on recognition. Stimulation of the left half of the retina activates the striate area of the left hemisphere and stimulation of the right side of the retina activates the right hemisphere. If a figure is first presented in such a way that its image falls on the left half of the retina and later is projected on the right half of the retina, the path of neural excitation to the cortical locus of the first process certainly is different from what it would be if the second presentation were made in the same retinal location as the first one. If memory traces are localized at the cortical place of the primary process which they represent, or if that place is in some other fashion involved in their arousal, such differences in the path of neural excitation should indeed exist. There is, of course, still the question whether such a difference, if it exists, can be detected. We know of four attempts to show an effect of retinal position on recognition. They all failed and the results of the work therefore remained unpublished. Our own attempt which is here reported was made because we felt that we could employ an unusually sensitive method.

Written in collaboration with Pauline Austin Adams. Reprinted from *American Journal of Psychology,* 1954, 67, 338–340.

[1]Wolfgang Köhler, *Dynamics in Psychology,* 1940, 128–129.

We used the silhouette of an ambiguous figure which was first used by Irvin Rock in as yet unpublished research on spatial orientation. This figure is usually recognized as a dog when it is presented

Fig. 1. The ambiguous figure

with the long axis in horizontal orientation, and as a chef when that axis is vertical. Tilted 45° as in Figure 1 it is a fairly balanced ambiguous figure. Our experiment consisted in presenting the dog-version in one retinal position and the chef-version in another one. Finally, the figure was presented in its ambiguous orientation in either one of these positions. It would then presumably be recognized either as a dog or as a chef. An effect of position would be demonstrated if the ambiguous version were recognized predominately as that figure which had previously been given in the same retinal position.

In an experiment of this kind, the critical figure must be presented in such a way that only spontaneous recognition occurs, and no expectation on the part of *O* related to the purpose of the experiment can be allowed to develop. We therefore cast our problem in the form of an experiment on peripheral recognition of familiar forms. Nine silhouettes of familiar forms were presented singly in four different positions a short distance from a fixation mark. Among these were the dog-version and the chef-version of the critical figure. The tenth figure presented was the critical figure in its ambiguous orientation. With ten figures presented for recognition, there was little danger that *O* would concern himself specially with one of the critical figures.

Procedure

Each figure was flashed on a screen by an opaque projector for 0.4 sec. The size of the figures on the screen varied from 3.0 in. to 4.5 in. for the larger dimension. The fixation-mark consisted of a light spot of ¼-in. diameter (projected on the screen by another lantern) which was 53 in. above the floor and remained visible throughout the experiment. Each figure was centered about a point 2.5 in. from the fixation-mark at an angle of 35° above or below the horizontal. It was always presented in one of the four positions, upper left, lower left, upper right, or lower right, except for the critical figures whose position varied. The *O* was seated at a distance of 53 in. from the screen directly in front of the fixation-mark. The room was dimly illuminated by a table lamp placed at the far end behind *O.*

The following instructions were given: "This is an experiment on how people recognize things. I will flash some pictures on the screen very quickly. Looking directly at the point of light, will you name the object which you see? Remember, always look directly at the point of light during the exposures. I will give you a ready signal before each picture."

The non-critical figures used represented the following things: whale, tree, car, duck, house, pitcher, and boat. The critical figures were presented in the second and sixth places in the sequence—after the whale and after the duck—and in the tenth place. They were given only in the upper positions. When the chef-version was given on the left, the dog-version was given on the right, and *vice versa.* The presentation of the critical figures varied in three ways. The dog-version was given either on the left or on the right, and it was given either in the second or the sixth place in the sequence; the ambiguous version was given either on the left or on the right. We used all combinations of these variations in a balanced design which thus involved eight different presentation-sequences.

Altogether 87 *O*s, undergraduates of Swarthmore College, were used. To 39 of them, however, the ambiguous figure was not presented, either because they had not recognized one of the versions of the critical figure (18 *O*s), or they had incorrectly recognized it (4 *O*s), or they had seen it as the other version of the critical figure (17 *O*s). Apparently the dog-version was easier to recognize than the chef-version, because 37 of the 39 failures of recognition occurred when the latter was presented. When an *O* failed to recognize one of the critical figures, the presentation sequence employed was given to another *O.* This procedure was continued until each of the eight presentation-sequences had been completed six times and 48 *O*s had completed the whole experiment.

Results

All 48 *O*s saw the ambiguous form of the critical figure either as a dog or as a chef, and as one of them only. Of the 24 *O*s to whom the ambiguous figure was presented in the retinal position in which the dog-version had previously been given, 16 recognized the ambiguous figure as a dog and 8 as a chef. Of the remaining 24 *O*s, to whom the ambiguous figure was presented in the position in which the chef-version had previously been given, 20 recognized the ambiguous figure as a chef and 4 as a dog. Thus, 36 of the 48 *O*s recognized the ambiguous figure as the version which had previously been presented in the same retinal position (*near-plant*), and 12 *O*s recognized the ambiguous figure as the version which had been presented on the other side of the fixation-mark (*far-plant*). The difference is significant beyond the 0.2-% level.

Before we draw the conclusion that retinal position of stimulation affects the recognition of a figure, an alternative interpretation must be discussed. When the 12 cases in which recognition had apparently been in terms of the far-plant were inspected, it was found that in 9 of them the ambiguous figure had been presented on the left of the fixation-mark. In the majority of these cases, then, the version in terms of which the ambiguous figure was recognized (the effective plant) had been presented on the right of the fixation-mark and thus had caused a primary cortical process in the left hemisphere. Although the difference between 9 and 3 does not represent a reliable trend, the possibility that a plant in the right half of the visual field proves more effective than a plant in the left half must be seriously considered.

Among the results for all 48 *O*s there were 30 cases in which what turned out to be the effective plant had been presented in the right half of the visual field. The question arises as to whether our main result can be explained on the assumption that a right-field plant dominates recognition. To answer this question we must consider the 18 cases in which, because the effective plant had been on the left side of the fixation-mark, the results could not possibly be ascribed to left hemispheric dominance. Of these 18 *O*s, 15 recognized the ambiguous figure in terms of the near-plant and this preponderance is statistically reliable at the 1-% level. Our results thus show an effect of position even if all cases of effective plant in the right half of the visual field are assumed to be the consequence of left hemispheric dominance. Whether such dominance does play a role in our experiment remains to be seen; our results do not as yet demonstrate it reliably.

4. On Memory Modalities

When one carefully observes how his memory contents come to him in recall, he is led to the conclusion that there are memory modalities just as there are sense modalities. Such observations can be discussed with psychologically unsophisticated people. When the question is raised with such a group how one recalls telephone numbers, there will be many who say they recall them "by the sound." A few will dissent; they recall them in script or print. Some will be uncertain or even incredulous when they hear these claims. Neither description seems to fit in their cases. They recall numbers as such, devoid of sound or shape. It is hard to say whether they use a conceptual memory which delivers numbers in abstract form for which verbal expression is sought only when the need arises (corresponding to the process by which one fits verbal expression to a thought, a necessity which leads to explicit searching when an original thought must be expressed) or whether they recall them in a verbal form that stems from memory associated with some motor center for speech.

We are not at all sure whether this exhausts the possibilities or characterizes correctly the non-sensory modalities used in the recall of numbers. It is also possible that in many people different modalities function in such close association with each other that a given content emerges at once in two modes. Yet, with regard to the existence of separate auditory and visual memory modalities we feel sure of our ground.

Different memory modalities may even harbor different products of learning related to the same performance. When the senior author adds numbers he ordinarily uses an abstract memory. New numbers, i.e., the results of individual additions, come to mind as entities that represent their arithmetical characteristics. When

Written in collaboration with Emanuel Averbach. Reprinted from *American Journal of Psychology,* 1955, 68, 249–257.

numbers are sub-vocally pronounced they are pronounced in English. If, however, long columns of figures have to be added, a shift to a different method will soon occur. Numbers are now read in German and the result of an addition is held in mind in German for the addition of the next number. His performance becomes effortless and seems to run off automatically like the recall or recitation of a well-memorized poem where the words are first recalled and then understood. He has had much practice with long addition in his youth in Germany. Associations then acquired apparently become available as the shift into German occurs. What interests us here is that the result of each succeeding addition is "heard" or sub-vocally pronounced, he is not sure which. The process appears to be based entirely on verbal associations, whereas in the method now ordinarily employed numbers come to mind as mere numerical entities. The new method apparently evolved as German verbiage disappeared from all thought processes.

There is not much hope that the questions about the nature of different modalities of memory and their association can be answered by observations like those here reported. Clearly, experimental research is needed, but so far such observations have not influenced experimental work on memory. Yet, even if memory modalities were not interesting in their own right, there are good reasons why it is necessary to deal with them now. In the first place, certain experimental results can be interpreted when one assumes that multiple memory for a given content can occur when several modalities are involved. Secondly, we believe that the conception of memory modality is essential in the study of recognition. We begin by discussing this latter point.

It is a basic assumption in our thinking about simple recognition that a given perceptual experience arouses directly only a memory laid down in the corresponding memory modality, i.e., that memory modality which belongs with the same sensory modality which gave rise to the perceptual experience. With Köhler we believe that simple recognition is based on the similarity between the perceptual experience that gives rise to recognition and a more or less identical previous experience currently represented by a memory trace.[1]

[1]Hans Wallach, Some considerations concerning the relation between perception and cognition. *Journal of Personality*, 1949, 18, 6–13. In the present volume, Chapter VIII, selection 1.

Such similarity can obviously manifest itself only if the memory trace is of the same modality as the perceptual experience. Thus, a novel verbal item that has been presented auditorily should not be recognized directly when the second presentation is a visual one. Only if the nonsense word is now "read," that is, if the visual experience is translated into some verbal mode, may the trace of the original auditory experience be aroused. It must similarly be assumed that a conceptual memory, e.g., the meaning of a word, can be aroused by, say, an auditory experience only indirectly; namely, through the arousal of the trace of a previous similar auditory experience and from there by way of a previously established connection to the conceptual memory item.

Results of a recent experiment on the effect of verbalization by Kurtz and Hovland can be interpreted in the light of this discussion.[2] Children were shown familiar objects and were asked to find and encircle the names of these objects on sheets on which they were listed and to pronounce them; or, in the case of the control group, to encircle the photographs on sheets that showed only photographs. A week later, tests of recall or recognition were unexpectedly given.

On the recall-test, *S*s of the experimental group who had marked the names of the objects did better than the *S*s of the control group who had marked the photographs. We agree with the authors that this is due to verbalization forced upon all experimental *S*s when they had to mark the names of the objects and had to pronounce them aloud, while the control *S*s would verbalize only spontaneously and probably did so infrequently. We believe, however, that this verbalization effect depends on the formation of multiple traces for a given item. To an experimental *S* each item is, in effect, presented as a visual object and as a mimeographed word which is seen and pronounced. Thus, apart from the formation of conceptual memories which does not necessarily depend on verbalization, each presentation can give rise to two visual memories; namely, of the object and of the word, an auditory memory of the word pronounced, and perhaps a memory of still another modality left by the act of pronouncing. The last three would not arise in the control experiment unless *S* had spontaneously verbalized. There are a number of

[2]K. H. Kurtz and C. I. Hovland, The effect of verbalization during observation of stimulus-objects upon accuracy of recognition and recall. *Journal of Experimental Psychology*, 1953, 45, 157–163.

ways in which multiplication of traces for a given content could conceivably favor recall.

The results of the recognition-test require a more detailed discussion. In both groups recognition was tested for half the items with photographs and for the other half with mimeographed words. Thus, there were four different results arising from the four combinations of two learning- and two test-conditions. Visually learned material was tested with visual items or with verbal items, and visually *and* verbally learned material was tested with visual or verbal items. In three of the four combinations could direct recognition regularly operate in the test, because the items presented in the test-situation had occurred identically in the learning-situation. Only when merely visually learned material was tested with verbal items was this not the case. It is for this last combination that Kurtz and Hovland obtained by far the lowest mean recognition-score; namely, 5.46 as against 6.38, 6.58, and 6.71 for the other three combinations where direct recognition could operate.

Yet, on the average more than five correct recognitions out of a total of eight possibilities were made in this combination where presumably direct recognition would not take place. It must be assumed either that, with visual presentation, spontaneous verbalization was very frequent or, more likely, that indirect recognition played a major role in the test. Indirect recognition could take place in the following manner. S could not fail to be aware of the meanings of the familiar objects that were presented to him (although the task of finding and marking them on the sheet did not require it) and this awareness should leave a memory in some trans-sensory modality. When the verbal items were presented in the test, awareness of their meaning could lead to recognition in this mode. Whatever the nature of indirect recognition may be, it has equal possibilities in all four experimental combinations. That the combination of visual learning with verbal test gave a markedly lower score than the other three combinations should therefore be attributed to the failure to permit operation of direct recognition, which singles out this combination.

Kurtz and Hovland gave a different interpretation to the results of the recognition-tests. They see in them a confirmation of the hypothesis that "the accuracy of retention would be increased by verbalization at the time of stimulus-observation."[3] This hypothesis predicts a difference between the score for the combination of visual learning with verbal test (5.46) and the score for combination of visual and verbal learning with verbal test (6.38), and this difference was obtained. It also predicts, however, a difference between the score for the combination of visual learning with visual test (6.71) and the score for the combination of visual and verbal learning with visual test (6.58) in favor of the latter, and this difference was not obtained. The authors propose additional hypotheses to account for this finding. The largest of all differences—namely, the one between the score for the combination of visual learning with verbal test (5.46) and the score for the combination of visual learning with visual test (6.71)—cannot be predicted from a verbalization hypothesis alone. The outcome of the three comparisons is, of course, in agreement with our own approach which simply predicts a lower score for the combination of visual learning with verbal test, because it does not permit direct recognition to operate.

Our own experiment was an attempt to demonstrate the existence of memory modalities in a manner that involved some confirmation of our basic assumption; namely, that direct recognition requires the perceptual event which evokes the recognitive process and the trace which is aroused to be of the same modality.

Our interpretation of Kurtz and Hovland's results was based on two assumptions: (1) Memory modalities make possible the formation of multiple memory traces for a given content, and an ensuing duplication may favor retention or recall or both.[4] (2) Direct recognition can take place only if the test-item is perceptually similar to the event that left the pertinent trace, i.e., is of the same modality. The result of the present experiments can be understood from these two premises. The learning situation was such that the material was acquired in at least two modalities, and the test of recognition was varied in such a manner that either both modalities could come into play or only one. A higher recognition-score was expected in the

---

[3] *Op. cit.,* 162.

[4] The term memory-trace is not meant to suggest a particular theoretical position. It is merely a convenient way to refer to the memory of an individual psychological event.

former case. The particular form of the test situation depended on our notion of direct recognition.

Nonsense words were presented on a memory drum and S was asked to read them alternately forward and backward. After that S was unexpectedly tested for recognition of the words. The test-series was also presented on a memory drum, though at a faster rate, and S was asked to state promptly, before the next word appeared, whether the given word had occurred before or was new. Inasmuch as in the learning situation the words had to be read aloud, there was for S an occasion to form multiple traces for all words, visual traces from seeing the words on the drum, auditory traces from hearing them pronounced, and perhaps traces left by the act of pronouncing. In the test, the words were again presented visually and this made direct arousal of the visual traces possible. Beyond that, however, we expected S to "read" the words, i.e., to translate the visual experience into some verbal mode. The resultant mental process could then arouse traces left by the reading of the words in the learning situation.

This is where the fact becomes important that in the learning situation half the words were read forward and half backward. We assume that S "read" the words forward in the test (if he read them at all) and, therefore, that the mental process of reading could lead to the arousal of original reading traces only in the case of those words which originally had been read forward. On the verbal level, a word read forward and a word read backward are very different entities, and the experience of reading a word forward in the test is so different from the previous experience of reading it backward that it cannot be expected that the trace of the latter becomes aroused when the former occurs. Thus, only visual traces could serve in the recognition of words originally read backward, whereas multiple traces were available for the recognition of words read forward. We could, therefore, expect a higher recognition for the words that were originally read forward, provided that the assumption was correct that S "read" the words only forward in the test-situation.

We base this assumption on the fact that the rate of exposure on the test was far too high for reading each word twice, once forward and once backward. Thus, only if S knew at the moment when each word appeared whether it had been read forward or backward in the learning situation could he read the words in the right direction. To know this, however, the visual trace of the word would have to be aroused first, because without such an arousal memory mediating this knowledge could not come into play. Yet, the arousal of the visual trace would be equivalent to recognition. Thus, recognition in some verbal mode achieved by this route should be unnecessary and should not influence the recognition score. To repeat, the expected result was a higher recognitive score for forward read words. If such a result were obtained it might be open, however, to a different interpretation. Since it is harder to read words backwards than it is to read them normally, it might be argued that conditions in the learning situation favored the words read forward and thereby caused the result.

The interpretation given above can be checked with the control *S*s who learned by reading *all* of the words backward. Our interpretation of the expected result for the main experiment depends on the fact that in the test *S*s who had learned by reading the words alternately backward and forward would not know which words had originally been read backward. This would not be true for *S*s of the control group who would have read all words backward. In the test, they may attempt to read the words backward and have a relatively high score in recognition, since both visual traces and memories in the verbal mode would become available. If such a result were obtained the alternate interpretation would have to be rejected.

Experiment I

PROCEDURE

Sixteen two-syllable nonsense words each consisting of six letters were presented to the subject one by one on a memory drum at a rate of a word every three seconds. Fifty-two *S*s, undergraduate students at Swarthmore and Bryn Mawr Colleges, participated. They were divided into three approximately equal groups. The *S*s of Group A (18) were asked to read the first word forward, the second word backward, and so on; the *S*s of Group B (17) had to do the same alternately forward and backward reading but started by reading the first word backward. The *S*s of Group C (17) were asked to read all words backward. The task was presented to the *S*s as an experiment in reading. None of them expected that a test would follow the reading.

In the recognition-test which followed the rate of presentation was stepped up so that each word was presented only for 1.5 sec. To prepare S for the high speed of the test, he was first presented with a short trial, which consisted of the first and last words of the original list and of three novel words. Thereafter he was given the recognition-test proper. The list started out with two novel words followed by the remaining 14 words of the original list arranged in a new sequence. These two presentations were introduced by appropriate instructions which included a statement that the lists would contain words that had not appeared before. S was urged to respond quickly to every word as soon as it appeared. For some Ss—two from each of Groups A and B and one from Group C—the speed was too high; they became flustered and stopped responding. These cases were dropped from the study and were not included among the Ss reported as participating.

TABLE 1
Mean Number of Recognitions for Seven Words

Recognition for	Group A	Group B	Group C: Words read backwards by	
			Group A	Group B
Words read forward	4.71 (67%)	5.25 (75%)		
Words read backward	3.12 (45%)	3.00 (43%)	5.36 (77%)	4.88 (70%)

RESULTS

The results for the 14 words which had appeared both in the learning list and in the main list are given in Table 1. For Groups A and B separate scores are given for the words that were read forward in the learning situation and those that were read backward. Inasmuch as different words were read backward by Ss of Group A and Ss of Group B, the results for Group C, where all words had been read backward, are also divided into sets of seven words dependent on whether the particular words had been read backward by Group A or by Group B. Thus all results in the table are given as mean numbers of recognition of seven words.

The difference between the mean scores of words read forward and backward is reliable in the case of each group (Groups A and B) at the 0.01-level ($t = 4.18$ and 8.65). When the results for Groups A and B are combined mean recognition for words read forward amounts to 71% and for words read backward to 44%. This is the difference we expected.

The result for Group C, where Ss read all words backward, is to be compared with the scores for words read backward obtained with Groups A and B. Group C shows the higher amount of recognition and this difference is reliable in the case of each set of seven words at the 0.01-level ($t = 6.22$ and 4.48). In fact, recognition in Group C is as high as recognition for words read forward in Groups A and B, with the mean recognition for all words in Group C at 73%. This makes it possible to reject the alternate interpretation of the main result of the experiment which ascribes the lower recognition for words read backwards to the learning conditions.

Experiment I still has one essential shortcoming: We do not know how much genuine recognition the score of 44% obtained for the words read backward in Groups A and B actually represents. There are only two ways in which an S can respond in such a test and the chance level for a recognitive response is 50%. Thus, if we wish to know to what degree visual memory contributed to recognition, or whether it did so at all, we have to find out how frequently novel words introduced into the test-list are mistakenly recognized.

To do so, part of Experiment I was repeated and novel words were introduced in the test. Groups D and E of 15 Ss each followed the procedure employed for Groups A and B, except that the test was somewhat changed. It consisted here of five of the words read forward, five of the words read backward, and five novel words arranged in random order. Only 10 words from the learning-list instead of 14 were included in the test-list in order to make the latter comparable in length to the test-list of 16 words which had been given to Groups A and B.

The combined results for Groups D and E showed a mean recognition score of 78% for words read forward and of 56% for words read backward. The number of judgments indicating mistaken recognition of novel words amounted to 25%. The difference between recognition of words read forward and words read backward is reliable at the 0.001-level, as is the difference between recognition of words read backward and mistaken recognition of novel words. This latter difference, that is, the extent to which recognition of words read backward exceeds the score for mistaken recognition of novel words represents the genuine recognition of words read backward.

Experiment II

This experiment was meant to serve a double purpose. In the first place we wished to repeat the essential parts of Experiment I with different word-material. In the second place we wished to explore another way of using the technique of alternately reading forward and backward in making part of the memory of a given item unavailable for recognition. Some words read backward were presented in the test in reverse spelling and therefore could not be recognized visually. If they were read forward, however, they would verbally be the same as in the original presentation where they had been read backward. Thus recognition would be due to verbal rather than to visual memory.

PROCEDURE

The reading list consisted of 22 nonsense words of five letters, one letter less than the words used in Experiment I. Again the first and last words of the list were used in the trial-test and did not appear in the test proper. Twelve words were used for a repetition of Experiment I and the remaining eight were used for experimentation with reverse spelling.

Two groups of 15 Ss each (Groups A and B) had to read the words alternately forward and backward, and a third group (Group C, also 15 Ss) read all words backward. Again, words read forward by Group A were read backward by Group B, and vice versa, except for the eight words devoted to experimentation with reverse spelling. They occupied slightly different positions on the lists that were read by Group A and by Group B, such that four of them were read forward by *both* groups and the remaining four were always read backward. The four words read forward were used only to equalize the total number of words available for forward and for backward reading, and their recognition was not included in any of the results. The four words read backward appeared in the test-list for Group A with normal spelling, but for Group B they were spelled in reverse. This made it possible to compare recognition based on verbal memory with recognition based on visual memory for the same individual words.

RESULTS

The part of Experiment II that was devoted to a repetition of the procedure of Experiment I confirmed the results obtained there. The scores of Groups A and B combined yielded a level of recognition of 78% for words read forward and of 62% for words read backward. The difference was reliable at the 0.001-level. As in the previous experiment recognition by the Ss of Group C who had read *all* words backward was as high as recognition of words read forward; namely 76%. This score was also reliably different from the score for words that had been read backward by the Ss of Groups A and B. Thus all essential results of Experiment I were obtained again.

Recognition of the words read backward that were presented in the test spelled in reverse was as high as 60% and was not essentially different from recognition of the same words when they were tested in normal spelling (64%). Such scores should represent genuine recognition by a reliable margin. That there was an appreciable recognition of words read backward and tested in reverse confirms once more our contention that separately usable traces were left in our learning presentation.

Conclusions

Contents of memory are usually defined in terms of the external events to which they refer. It seems, however, to be more adequate to consider instead the psychological processes that occur when the external events are perceived. This becomes important when a given external event leads to a number of different psychological processes each of which may leave its own memory trace. For instance, when nonsense syllables are visually presented S will not only see each syllable, he will also silently pronounce it and two psychological processes will then result from one objective event, each of which may leave its trace. If instead of nonsense syllables, meaningful words are presented and S is also aware of the words' meanings, there may be for each item still another trace which is left by the process of being aware of the meaning. Evidence has been presented which shows that such multiple traces for a given external event enhance scores in tests of recall and recognition.

More important, however, than the influence of multiple traces as such is an issue which is related to the nature of recognition. In the absence of a set, recognition is based on the similarity between the perceptual process which gives rise to recognition and the memory of the pertinent previous experience. Here it becomes important that different traces pertaining to an external event stem from psychological processes which are of different modality and thus dissimilar to each other. No direct recognition should, therefore, occur between a process and a trace of different modality, although the two pertain to identical external events. Predictions derived from this premise were confirmed.

On perceived identity

1. The Direction of Motion of Straight Lines

Perceived motion has two properties, speed and direction. Ordinarily direction is simply the direction of the path that the moving object traverses. To be sure, the question arises whether it is the path of the moving object relative to O that is decisive for the perceived direction of motion or its path in relation to the objects surrounding it. If direction of motion functions analogous to speed (see Chapter V), it should be expected to depend more on the displacement of the moving object in relation to other objects than on its displacement in relation to O. That this is true is demonstrated by experiments on induced motion. Take the case of an oblong which is being displaced horizontally to the right and is surrounded by a circle moving vertically downward. The oblong will then move horizontally relative to O, and when he fixates a stationary point, the image of the oblong

will move on the retina horizontally, but he will see it move
obliquely, in the direction of its displacement with respect to the
surrounding circle.

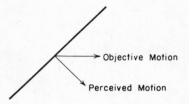

Fig. 1.

Perceived direction of motion becomes particularly interesting
when it has no counterpart in the stimulus conditions. This is the
case when homogeneous straight lines are observed whose ends are
in one way or another hidden. A long straight line tilted clockwise
by 45 degrees may serve as an example (Figure 1). It is projected on
a large screen and is viewed from a point so close to the screen that
the observer does not notice its ends because of their peripheral
location. Objective motion of the line in a horizontal direction will
be perceived as motion in an oblique direction. When the line is
moved horizontally to the right it will be seen to move obliquely
down to the right.

There are two questions connected with this observation: Why
is the line free to move perceptually in a direction that differs from
its objective motion direction, and how is the particular direction in
which it is seen to move determined? The answer to the first question is related to the fact that the line is straight, homogeneous and
without visible ends. Because of these characteristics the line does
not present the eye with identifiable points or parts. Not only absence of microstructure is important here. That a straight line, like
a circle and a helix, has a constant curvature and therefore no identifiable form features is also a factor. Only if the line showed some
irregularities or identifiable form features whose paths could be
observed, would its real movement direction be given. That a tilted
line like that in Figure 1 moves objectively on a horizontal to the
right or vertically down would be noticeable because the irregularities would be seen to move either horizontally or downward. But in

the absence of such identifiable parts no clues as to the line's objective displacement are transmitted to the eye. Whether it moves downward or horizontally to the right or in any other direction within the right or the lower quadrant remains undetermined by the given stimulus conditions. Only to which one of its two sides the line is shifting is given to the eye. If its objective motion is horizontal to the right, a shift to the lower and right side is given to the eye and this naturally excludes perceived motion in any direction on the other side. But beyond this, no clues for the objective movement direction reach the observer and, should he see the line move in a specific direction, no agreement between the perceived direction with the objective motion should be expected, except by coincidence. In fact, if perceptual experience were here commensurate with the given conditions of stimulation, the line should not be seen to move in a specific direction at all, for, though as a physical object it moves in a definite direction, as a stimulus entity its motion is without a specific direction. What such a motion would be like if it did occur in experience cannot be visualized, for imagination does not serve us here. It is certainly never perceived; the line always appears to move in a specific direction.

What is this direction? When the line is shown in a completely homogeneous field, it is always seen to move in a direction perpendicular to the line itself. This rule is easily demonstrated: a line in a vertical orientation, for example, may be moved in any direction, but it will always appear to move horizontally. (An exception is, of course, a vertical motion of the line, which produces no visible change at all.) If, on the other hand, lines of various orientations are all moved in the same direction objectively, each one will be seen to move in a different direction, that is, perpendicular to its own orientation.

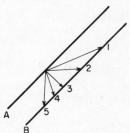

Fig. 2.

I have no definite answer to the question why this particular direction always results and can offer only speculations. Motion in a direction perpendicular to the line distinguishes itself in two ways. In the first place, this direction is the resultant of all those directions in which the line is free to move. Secondly, movement in the perpendicular direction is distinguished by its velocity; motion in any other direction would have to be faster. Figure 2 makes this clear. It shows two successive positions of a moving straight line and a number of arrows indicating various directions in which the line might be seen to move to reach position B from position A. The perpendicular direction (3) represents, of course, the shortest path between the two positions. Inasmuch as the time that it takes the line to shift from position A to position B is given and therefore the same no matter which path the motion appears to take, the line covers the interval between the two positions at the lowest possible velocity when it takes the shortest path. We shall later on report observations that show that this consideration is relevant: when the line is forced to move in an oblique direction, which amounts to a longer path, it is indeed seen to move with higher speed.

Straight Lines in Apertures

There is another way in which the ends of our line can be hidden. One can let it be seen moving behind an aperture in a screen. The line may be drawn on a wide paper belt which runs over two rollers placed behind and parallel to the screen. When the edge of the paper belt is vertical so that it can move either up or down and when the line is on a 45-degree tilt, visible in a circular aperture, it appears to move again in a direction perpendicular to itself, that is, obliquely, and this happens even when the grain of the paper is noticeable and is seen to move in a vertical direction.

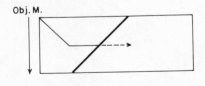

Fig. 3.

When the circular aperture is replaced by one in the shape of an oblong, say 1.5 in. high and 4 in. long, the line changes direction during its passage through the aperture (Figure 3). When it becomes visible in the upper left corner, it moves in oblique direction, but as its lower end passes the lower left corner it appears to turn and move in a horizontal direction. At the end of its passage, as it moves by the upper right corner, it is sometimes seen to turn into the oblique direction, or it may continue along its horizontal path. The first change in direction, however, always takes place, and when that has happened, the line is seen to move parallel to the upper and lower edge of the aperture, to which it is now adjacent. This direction of motion parallel to adjacent parallel aperture edges is distinguished from all other directions in which the line could be seen to move by the simplicity of that motion process. Let us assume for the moment that the line is seen to continue in its oblique direction after it has passed the lower left corner and has started to pass between the upper and the lower edge of the aperture. In that case, new parts of the line would keep becoming visible at the upper edge while other parts would keep disappearing at the lower edge. When the perceived motion is parallel to these edges, this constant changing of the line is avoided and all parts of the visible line remain the same. Any other direction of motion would involve such changes.

This consideration presupposes that the perceived line and its parts have identity, although it is precisely the absence of any features identifying the parts of the line which distinguishes it as a stimulus object. This difference between the experienced line and the properties of line as a stimulus object seems to be of critical importance. In experience, the line moving between parallel edges does not have the indefinite character that would be commensurate with the character of the line as a stimulus object. When it moves between parallel edges, the line is experienced as a self-contained unit, not different from a short line of finite length that is visible in a homogeneous field. It has terminal points and a center, parts which have their identity by virtue of their role in the whole. This identity of the parts of the line has the same effect as given inhomogeneities; observations with a pair of lines that cross each other show this (Figure 4). A second line is added so that the two lines form an X and the screen is put in such a position that the point where the lines interact passes through the center of the aperture. When the lines move downward, they enter the aperture at the upper left and the upper right corner respectively, and, after passing the two lower corners, will appear to move horizontally toward each other (Figure 4, a and b). When the point where the lines intersect enters the aperture, the horizontal motion of the lines will usually remain undistrubed (Figure 4, c and d); one line will be seen to slide over the other as if they crossed only incidentally. The downward movement of the crossing point does not affect the motion of the lines. When attention is paid to it, it actually appears to slide down along one of the lines. This is the decisive observation; it implies that, in experience, the line has identical parts in relation to which the crossing point is seen to shift.

A tendency of the line to appear to move parallel to an adjacent aperture edge may also prevail when the line passes between edges that form an angle. If, for instance, the observer fixates the vertical edge of an oblong aperture on the side where the line first becomes visible, he very frequently sees the line move in a vertical direction, that is, parallel to that edge. Here, the parts of the line near the fixated edge are perceived as identical and determine the motion direction. Such perceived identity accounts for the tendency of the line to move parallel to the adjacent aperture edge. This tendency completely dominates the line's motion when it passes between parallel edges, as the following experiment shows. The paper belt on which the line is drawn is here not homogeneous but consists of a conspicuous wallpaper pattern. When the line and the aperture are arranged as in Figure 3, with line and pattern moving objectively downward, the line is first seen moving downward with the pattern. But when it has passed the lower left corner and is adjacent to the two horizontal edges, it turns into a horizontal direction. Since the motion of the pattern remains, of course, unchanged, line and pattern no longer move together; the line is sliding to the right while the pattern moves down.

Patterns of Straight Lines

A new factor enters the picture when instead of a single line a number of evenly spaced parallel lines move in an aperture. There is a tendency here for the lines to form a rigid pattern with all lines moving in the same direction at a given moment. In an oblong

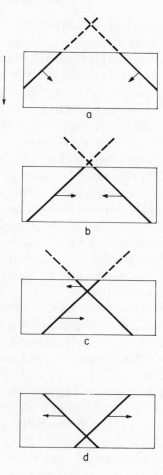

Fig. 4.

Fig. 5.

aperture (Figure 5) all lines move initially in a horizontal direction. The oblique motion that is displayed by a single line when it passes through the upper left corner does not take place. The pattern is seen to move as a whole; it appears to enter the aperture on the left, move between the horizontal edges, and leave the aperture on the right. Thus, the pattern is limited only at the horizontal edges and enters and leaves the aperture like an endless stream at the sides. When this motion has been observed for ten or twenty seconds a most unexpected change occurs. The whole pattern suddenly appears to move vertically downward. In this phase it seems to enter the aperture at the upper edge and leave it at the lower. (This happens whether the objective movement of the lines is vertical or not; if, e.g., the objective movement is obliquely down to the right, the same change occurs.) The vertical motion lasts for a brief time and is, unaccountably, replaced by the horizontal motion, which, lasting somewhat longer, again changes to the vertical motion, and the two motions keep alternating in this manner.

The same motions alternate when the pattern is given in a square aperture, though here the periods of horizontal and vertical motion are more nearly equal in length. At the beginning of the observation, the lines often move in an oblique direction as would a single line of the same tilt, but soon regular alternation between horizontal and vertical motions begins. For some observers the change from one direction to the other does not occur abruptly, but consists each time in a shifting through the intermediary oblique direction.

These changes have an entirely objective character. Naive subjects are, as a rule, not aware that the observed motion changes are "subjective" and do not correspond to changes in the objective movement. In an experiment shortly to be reported, Redslob had more than twenty subjects observe and report these changes repeatedly. Specific interrogation showed that only one subject suspected that he was not observing real switches in direction.

It frequently happens that, where the given conditions of stimulation allow for two distinctly different perceptual experience, these experiences spontaneously alternate. Patterns in which Figure and Ground reverses, spontaneous inversions of depth seen in drawings of geometric solids executed in isometric perspective, and the apparent reversals of rotation direction of monocularly observed turning objects are examples. If it is taken for granted that our line pattern has the tendency to move in the direction of parallel aperture edges, the given stimulus conditions are capable of giving rise to two different perceptual processes, namely, motion parallel to the vertical edges and motion parallel to the horizontal ones. In this case, too, it so happens that the two possibilities become alternately manifest.

The Cause for Changes in Direction of Motion

Each change in the direction of motion is apparently caused by the motion process that precedes the change. When, for instance, vertical motion changes into horizontal motion, it is the vertical motion which produces the conditions that bring the change about. This can be inferred from the experiments by Redslob (1938) in which one of the two possible movements was prolonged beyond its normal time period and the temporal pattern of the subsequent changes were recorded. Redslob used, among others, a pattern of horizontal stripes alternating black and white and had it move vertically through a square aperture. Because the stripes were parallel to the horizontal pair of aperture edges, they could be seen only in vertical motion. After this motion had been observed for 35 sec., the horizontal stripe pattern was replaced by a pattern of oblique lines in a square aperture somewhat smaller than the aperture in which the stripes were given, and the subject was asked to report each change as it occurred. The record so obtained was compared with three records of motion changes observed when *no* vertical motion preceded the presentation of the ambiguous field of oblique lines. It was found that a preceding observation of vertical movement in most cases tended to favor horizontal motion early during the observation of the ambiguous field. Subjects who originally start out by seeing vertical motion reported horizontal motion as the first phase and those who ordinarily report horizontal motion at the start, saw that motion for a prolonged period. A measure of this increase in the duration of the horizontal motion phase was designed which also took account of those cases where initially horizontal motion replaced vertical movement. An average measured effect of 6.8 sec. was found which proved highly reliable. Also in 69 out of 85 individual experiments an increase of 3 sec. or more in the duration of the horizontal motion was obtained. This effect[1] is brought about by conditions unfavorable to continuation of a prolonged motion process, i.e., horizontal motion in the ambiguous field is favored only becasue prolonged vertical motion had produced conditions unfavorable to further vertical motion. Redslob demonstrated this with an experiment in which the horizontal stripes move vertically *upward* while the possible motions in the ambiguous field were horizontal and vertically *downward*. No effect was obtained; for 24 subjects here employed the average increase in the duration of horizontal motion was practically zero (.3 sec.). Neither horizontal nor vertical movement was favored. It seems that an effect is obtained only when one of the movement directions possible on the ambiguous field coincides with the direction of the prolonged motion.

Redslob found that the condition unfavorable to the continuation of a prolonged movement process dissipates quickly. Seven interruptions of the observation of the moving stripes for 1 sec. only (with the total presentation period increased from 35 sec. to 42 sec. to make up for the interruptions) reduced the average increase in the duration of horizontal motion from 6.8 sec. to 3 sec., and instead of 69 out of 85 only 10 out of 22 individual observers showed an effect, a change that was significant at the .01 level.

The moving pattern that produces Redslob's effect and the ambiguous field must be projected on the same retinal area; perceived localization is not relevant. Redslob obtained a full effect when the moving stripes and the ambiguous field were located in different directions from the observer, provided both were projected on the same retinal region; and the same result was obtained when the moving stripes and the ambiguous field were presented at different distances from the observer, provided that the retinal image of the ambiguous field was not larger than that of the aftereffect producing pattern. A full effect was obtained for instance, when the stripes were presented at a distance of 1.5 m. from the observer and a four times enlarged ambiguous field at a distance of 6 m. The latter looked much larger than the aftereffect producing pattern of stripes, but the retinal projections of the two fields were approximately the same. When, on the other hand, the aftereffect producing field was at a

---

[1]This effect should not be confused with the so-called aftereffect of motion which is observed when, after prolonged inspection of a moving pattern, one looks at a stationary pattern and observes an illusory motion in the opposite direction.

distance of 6 m. and the ambiguous field at 1.5 m. and both were of normal size so that the latter's retinal image was much larger than that of the former, the effect was significantly diminished.

Direction of motion also is effective in terms of the retina rather than in terms of experienced space. Redslob had her subjects observe the stripes in vertical downward motion with the head in upright position, but the ambiguous field was observed with the head tilted by 90 degrees to the left. The ambiguous field was so arranged that horizontal movement to the right and motion vertically downward were possible. The latter coincided with the direction in experienced space of the motion of the stripes, while the horizontal movement coincided with the direction of that motion *on the retina*—this, because the head was tilted before the ambiguous field was presented. It was found that the vertical direction was significantly favored, which means that the Redslob effect is unfavorable to the horizontal movement, i.e., the direction *on the retina* of the vertically moving stripes prior to the tilting of the head.

Line Pattern in a Triangular Aperture

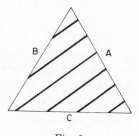

Fig. 6.

When a pattern of lines is shown in a triangular aperture as indicated in Figure 6, several motion process can be observed. In one of them different parts of the pattern appear to move simultaneously in different directions. At the start of the observation period, the lines usually appear to move parallel to edge *A*. After a little while, they seem to turn and move parallel to edge *B*. Eventually, the pattern seems to be split in two. The lines adjacent to edge *B* continue to move in the direction of that edge, whereas the lines that

end at edge *C* seem to move parallel to *C.* The observer has the
impression that there are now two different line patterns, one moving downward and the other obliquely upward to the right. That
each individual line as it passes the lower left corner changes over
from being part of one pattern to being part of the other pattern
remains virtually unnoticed. Where the two patterns border on each
other and neighboring lines belong to patterns whose direction of
motion differs by 120 degrees, one sees the lines gliding past each
other. This is a significant observation, for it implies that, in experience, the lines have an identity which, as stimulus objects, they do
not possess. This identity results from the lines' membership in the
patterns to which they belong.

Complex Line Patterns

Fig. 7.

A pattern of crossed lines which is moved downward behind a
square or oblong aperture (Figure 7) will be seen to move for a long
time in the direction of its objective movement. With prolonged
inspection, however, this motion will break up. Instead of the pattern of diamonds, two series of oblique lines are seen to move in
opposite directions, one in front of the other. The lines tilted clockwise are then moving to the right and the other lines to the left. This
divided motion lasts only briefly and downward motion of the unified pattern returns. Now it is replaced more quickly by the horizontal motion phase. The two phases continue to alternate, with the
phase of unified motion generally lasting longer than the phase in
which two patterns move in opposite directions. After long observation of these changes, it may happen also that, while one series of
oblique lines moves horizontally, the other is seen in vertical motion.

Fig. 8.

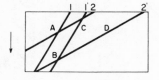

Fig. 9.

A significant observation is made with a double pattern like that shown in Figure 8 where both series of lines are tilted to the same side. When such a lattice work pattern is seen in horizontal instead of the objective vertical motion, the two series of lines also separate. A consideration of Figure 9 makes it clear why. It shows one line of each series (1 and 2) in two positions—an earlier position where their crossing point is in *A* and a later position, 1' and 2', where it is in *B*. When the lines are assumed to be in horizontal rather than in vertical motion, the point on the line 1 that was the crossing point *A* in the earlier position is in the later position in *C* and the same point on line 2 is in *D*. The lines make their horizontal motion independently of each other, with line 2 running ahead of line 1. The crossing point itself is no longer anchored in the lines but slides downward as the lines move to the right.

As predicted by these considerations, two series of lines are seen to move independently, one in front of the other when horizontal motion sets in, and since horizontal motion involves such a breaking up of the lattice work pattern, it occurs only after prolonged observation. The important point here is that the two independent series of lines appear to move with markedly different speeds. The more tilted lines seem to move much faster than the other series. This is consistent with the fact that during a given time interval the former appear to travel a larger distance than the latter, as Figure 9 shows. During the time interval in which the lines in their objective vertical movement proceed from *A* to *B,* the more tilted line (2) appears to travel from *A* to *D,* whereas the other line (1) appears to move from *A* to *C.*

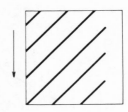

Fig. 10.   Fig. 11.

When a pattern of oblique lines that shows a vertical gap, as indicated in Figure 10, is used and is moved downward through a square aperture, the onset of horizontal motion is also delayed. When it takes place, the gap is seen as a detached strip and the lines form a uniform pattern which appears to move behind the strip. When the motion becomes again vertical, the strip disappears and the lines, as before, appear to end at the gap.

When the line pattern ends laterally as shown in Figure 11, horizontal motion is very much delayed. Prolonged observation often produces first divided motion similar to that which develops in a triangular aperture; lines that end at the upper edge of the aperture move horizontally and lines whose ends are visible on the right side of the pattern move downward. Eventually, nearly all observers see uniform horizontal motion. For most observers the area on the right that is free of lines becomes a strip behind whose edge the lines disappear, exactly as they would disappear behind the aperture edge, if the pattern filled the aperture completely. However, this does not always occur immediately when unified horizontal motion first takes place. For many observers several periods of horizontal motion are required before they "see clearly" what happens at the right side of the pattern. Prior to the formation of the strip, the lines seem to vanish unaccountably. Although the emergence of the strip has characteristics of a thought process—the edge behind which the lines disappear is formed in correspondence to the left aperture edge, from behind which the lines appear to enter the aperture, and the emergence of the strip serves to clarify an otherwise obscure event —the strip has in every way the reality of a perceptual experience.

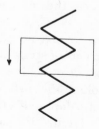

Fig. 12.

When a zig-zag line is observed moving downward through an oblong aperture (Figure 12) an even more complex sequence of spontaneous changes in the perceptual process takes place. At first, the line is seen, of course, in simple downward motion. But as a condition unfavorable to this motion process develops with prolonged observation, short horizontal motions become noticeable at the upper edge of the aperture. As each one of the short tilted lines that make up the zig-zag pattern enters the aperture at its upper edge, it seems to move sideways, each clockwise tilted line to the right and the next line to the left. This alternate motion to the right and to the left becomes gradually more conspicuous, and the downward motion becomes less and less noticeable and finally stops altogether. No longer does the zig-zag line enter and leave the aperture. It has also lost all rigidity, and its sole motion is a snakelike deformation within the confines of the upper and lower aperture edges. Suddenly this rather violent motion stops, and a rigid zig-zag line is again seen to move through the aperture. Soon alternate motion to the left and to the right begins again at the upper edge, becomes gradually stronger until the whole line wiggles wildly only to change again suddenly into a quiet downward motion. This sequence is repeated a few times until, again entirely unexpectedly, a still different process occurs. At the height of the deformation phase the aperture seems to become a three-dimensional space in which a three-dimensional form like a bent wire serenely rotates about a vertical axis. This lasts only a few

seconds and also gives way to the plane zig-zag line moving downward. But from now on this rotation phase returns again and again
soon after the start of the deformation phase. We have here a sequen-
tial arrangement of different perceptual processes that are all based
on the same sensory input, the downward motion of the zig-zag line,
and where one process produces the neural conditions that cause the
subsequent one.

Some observers describe the three-dimensional form as rounded
like a helix; for others it consists of straight lines and sharp corners.
I believe that it is the product of a kinetic depth effect, with the
deformation phase in the role of the distorting plane figure that, in
an ordinary case of the kinetic depth effect, causes the perception of
a three-dimensional form. To be sure, the rotating three-dimensional
form that is here perceived does not correspond to a changing projection exactly of the form of the given motion of the zig-zag line. But
that need not be because the kinetic depth effect functions inaccu-
rately. Our three-dimensional form results from the deformation
phase, which is the product of a deteriorated perceptual process.
Hence, the relation between the given retinal process and the three-
dimensional form is not a direct one as is the case in an ordinary
kinetic depth effect. (See Chapter II for the kinetic depth effect.)

Reference

Redslob, O., Ueber Sättigung gesehener Bewegungsrichtung. *Psychologische Forschung,* 1938, 22, 211–237.

2. Circles and Derived Figures

in Rotation

I t is a well-known fact that figures change their appearance with a change in their spatial orientation. "Many years ago, E. Mach pointed out that if we turn a square on an edge its appearance differs strikingly from the same objective square when it rests on a side."[1] Orientation alone makes it possible to differentiate between a "p" and a "q" in print where they have congruent shapes, and in printing types without serifs the forms of the letters, b, d, p, and q, differ from each other only by virtue of their orientation, all four shapes being congruent. Thus, in the perception of adults, orientation produces properties of form that do not originate in the given shape but that are, nevertheless, indistinguishable from the shape-dependent properties. Spatial orientation of a figure and the resultant form are, of course, dependent on a framework to which this orientation is related. Thus, we may speak of form-properties dependent on framework. In this paper, a different but equally impressive effect of such a framework will be reported.

When a homogeneous circle is drawn or pasted on a background of different color and this pattern is viewed while it is rotated on a turntable at moderate speed, the circle does not seem to turn. This is the case even when the rotation of the background is clearly visible. That under certain conditions a homogeneous circle which

Written in collaboration with Alexander Weisz and Pauline Austin Adams. Reprinted from *American Journal of Psychology* 1956, 69, 48–59.

[1]Wolfgang Köhler, *Dynamics in Psychology*, 1940, 22.

rotates about its center may not seem to turn is easily understood. When it is rotated about its center no visible change takes place. This is because any part of the circle can be superimposed on any other part; the circle shares this property with the straight line and the helix. No cues are conveyed to the eye that would indicate whether the homogeneous circle turns or does not turn. Where the surroundings of the circle are visibly stationary, a rotating circle might be expected to appear standing still. As already mentioned, however, the circle seems to stand still even when its background is seen to turn, and this cannot be understood merely from the fact that no sensory data convey the state of motion of the circle. If this were the only factor in the situation the circle would rather be expected to appear to be turning together with its background. It seems that there is a positive factor operating that causes the perceived circle not to turn. That this is the case is demonstrated by the following observation.

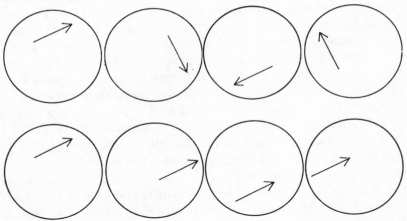

Fig. 1. Four positions of arrow revolving clockwise on turntable. Top row: when arrow is attached to table and turns with it. Bottom row: when arrow is rigged to maintain its direction during rotation.

When a circle is placed eccentrically on a turntable, its perceived motion again differs from the objective condition. Its objective motion can be considered as consisting of two concurrent movements. It has a *revolving*, translatory motion, i.e., a movement of the circle as a whole around the center of the turntable. It also *rotates* once about its own center during one revolution of the turntable. What happens here is readily seen if one substitutes another figure for the circle. If, for instance, an arrow is fastened eccentrically to the turntable, it will point successively in all directions of the compass as the turntable turns through a full rotation (Figure 1, first row). It thus turns once about itself during such a rotation. This is exactly what the circle does, except that this rotation of the circle is not conveyed to the eye. Its revolving motion, that is, the movement of the circle as a whole about the center of the turntable, is, of course, clearly visible; but the turning of the circle about its center is not seen. As a result the surface of the turntable appears to move in relation to the edge of the circle. To have the arrow move analogous to the experienced motion of the circle, we would have to install a mechanism that would permit the arrow to remain pointed in a constant direction, that is, *not* to rotate, while it is revolving with the turntable (Figure 1, second row). In the *O*'s experience, the eccentrically placed circle behaves exactly as the arrow does when it is rigged in this manner. Under these conditions, the arrow would rotate relative to the surface of the turntable, since it maintains a constant orientation while that surface turns about its center. Similarly, the edge of the circle should appear to slide relative to the rotating surface of the turntable, and this is actually observed.

We have pointed out that a homogeneous circle does not convey cues to the eye as to whether it turns about its center. Thus, insofar as conditions of stimulation are concerned, it does not matter whether a circle is fastened to the turntable and turns with it, or whether, like the arrow, it is rigged so as not to rotate when it is going around with the turntable. Briefly expressed: with regard to rotation, the conditions of stimulation are indeterminate. Why, then, is it that except for its revolution, the circle so clearly seems to stand still? If perceptual experience here depended merely on conditions of stimulation, the state of rotation of the circle should remain vague or it should be seen to rotate together with its background. Conditions originating within the perceptual process must be responsible. Seeing the circle stand still as it revolves with the turntable means that its various parts, indistinguishable in shape from one another, remain in some fashion identified. They are identified in relation to the directions of the visual field. The top part of the circle remains top part throughout a revolution, and its left horizontal pole retains the property of being the left horizontal pole, etc. A framework in relation to which the directions of the visual field are defined must be in play.

The framework, however, enters here into a unique function. The framework-dependent properties mentioned in the beginning are a result of "orientation" of a figure with respect to the framework; the figure has features of shape, identifiable in their own right, that stand in clear relations to the directions of the visual field.[2] Such identifiable features are lacking in the shape of the circle. Instead, identical parts or points are *created* in the perceptual process in dependence on the framework. Identity is imparted to aspects of the circle.[3]

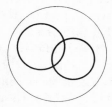

Fig. 2. Two homogeneous rings on turntable

The notion that the various parts of a circle remain identified as it revolves around the turntable is supported by concrete observations. When two homogeneous rings are so placed on the turntable that they are crossed (Figure 2) and are turned at a moderate speed, they will first be seen to turn as a unit. Sooner or later, however, they will appear to move independently of each other, each ring having ceased to turn as it revolves with the turntable. In this stage one ring always seems to slide over the other. When one pays attention to one of the points where they cross, one clearly sees one ring move across the other ring. In experience, the ring consists of definite parts

[2]Actually the facts are somewhat more complex. See Kurt Koffka, *Principles of Gestalt Psychology*, 1935, 184.

[3]As mentioned above, the straight line shares with the circle the peculiarity that any part of such a curve can be superimposed on any other part. Barring visibility of its ends, no parts or points along a straight line are identifiable on their own. It is interesting that the movement of straight lines also shows peculiarities that imply an imparting of identity to points or parts along that curve, although here the imparted identity derives from other conditions. See Hans Wallach, Ueber visuell wahrgenommene Bewegungsrichtung. *Psychologische Forschung.*, 20, 1935, 325–380. Also see in the present volume Chapter IX, selection 1.

which move in relation to the other ring. As stated, these parts
originate in the perceptual process being an imparted identity.

At this stage, the rings are seen to move exactly as two figures
which, by virtue of their shape, have a definite orientation and, like
the arrow of the earlier example, are rigged so as to maintain a
constant orientation. The triangles of Figure 3 may serve as an example. As they revolve with the turntable they continuously change
their position with respect to each other and cross each other at
different points. Whereas they perform this motion owing to a mechanical arrangement, the circles do it owing to our perceptual
effect.

Fig. 3. Three arrangements of two triangles on turntable. Rotation clockwise

An impressive demonstration of the power of this effect can be
made with a figure which looks like two incomplete disks attached
to each other (Figure 4). When this figure is first rotated on a turntable it is, as a rule, simply seen to turn. When, however, it is observed
for a little while, a change takes place. Two complete disks seem to
revolve about each other but seem not to rotate. Where they overlap,
one of them clearly appears to be on top of the other one and to slide
over it. Some *O*s even "see" the contour of the upper disk in the
region of overlap. (To understand this latter observation it must be
kept in mind that the disks appear to change their position with
regard to each other as they revolve, such that continuously different
parts of a disk move into the region of overlap. Thus, the part of the
disk which seems to be on top of the other one at one moment was
seen just before bordering on the turntable surface where its contour
was seen against a ground of different color.) The whole process is
essentially the same as that observed with the two rings. In the
present case, however, our effect also causes two figures to appear

instead of one and, for some *O*s, causes a contour to appear on an
objectively homogeneous surface.

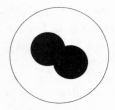

Fig. 4. Two incomplete disks attached to each other

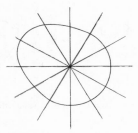

Fig. 5. A deformed circle covered by a pattern of radial lines

Another demonstration of the strong tendency of a circle to
appear stationery can be given with a wide ring (about 2 in. wide
when its diameter is 8 in.) whose outer edge is smooth and whose
inner edge is scalloped. When such a figure is slowly turned about
its center, the scalloped edge is, of course, seen to revolve, but the
smooth outer edge appears to stand still. While a certain part of the
circular outer edge is seen to remain in its place, the part of the inner
scalloped edge right across from it seems to move on. This gives rise
to the odd impression of a continuous shearing in the surface of the
ring. Again, the merely imparted identities of the parts along a
circular edge function with all concreteness.

It is interesting that this imparting of identity may also take
effect with figures which to some degree depart from circular form
and have an orientation by virtue of their shape. A deformed disk

whose shape is shown in the oval outline of Figure 5 may serve as an example. When it is rotated about its center it seems to stand still, although it has a distinct orientation when it is seen at rest. Instead of a rotation of the whole figure, a continuous deformation seems to take place; a bulge is seen moving around and around like a wave. This peculiar experience is itself the result of the imparted identity. The schema according to which identity is imparted can be visualized as a pattern of radial lines that lies over our figure such that its center coincides with the center of the figure. An intersection of a radial line with the contour of the figure represents a point perceived as identical. Such an intersection would remain approximately in place if our figure were turned under the stationary pattern of radial lines, and the same would be true of points perceived as identical on the contour of the turning figure. When the bulging part of the contour passes by, such an identical point first moves outward and then inward just as an intersection between the contour and a radial line would do. Thus, the passing of the bulging part causes motion primarily in the radial direction. The radial motions of the various points add up to the impression of a traveling deformation.

The well-known expanding or contracting of a rotating spiral is another example of the effect of imparted identity. An Archimedean spiral of moderate pitch, presented concentrically in the circular aperture of a screen that conceals its external end, will show no turning motion at all when it is rotated about its center; it will only seem to expand or contract. A part of the spiral that lies in a certain direction from its center is seen to remain in that position, while objectively it moves to one side and is replaced by an adjacent section where the curve has, say, a larger radius. This happens simultaneously to all parts. From moment to moment, objective sections having a greater distance from the center come to be located in certain radial directions. And, since it is to these locations that identity is imparted, every part is seen to move in a radial direction and the whole curve is seen to expand.

Deformations displayed by a rotating ellipse that is not much different from a circle can be explained in a similar way. When an ellipse whose axes measure 25 and 23.5 cm. is placed on a contrasting background and rotated about its center, it appears to stand still while its contour seems to pulsate. A perceptually identical part of the contour moves alternately inward and outward in a radial direction.

Deformations much stronger than the ones just reported can be observed when an ellipse is used that departs more from the circular form. They have been described by Musatti,[4] who from such observations went on to investigate the three-dimensional effect that can occur with such ellipses; the latter will be discussed below. We found that the largest effects could be observed with an ellipse in which the lengths of the major and minor axes were approximately in a ratio of 3 to 2. In that case the deformations were so strong that the whole figure appeared to be fluid. Its motion is hard to describe. It is by no means deformation of a stationary form alone; the figure also turns. Probably its deviation from circular shape is so strong that the change in orientation makes itself felt. Identity is also imparted to locations along the ellipse and this produces its deformation. As turning and deformation occur together a peculiar amoeba-like motion results. It should be added that for some of our Os the deformation was somewhat restricted and did not affect the region in the immediate neighborhood of the poles of the major axis. For these Os the figure was perhaps too strongly elliptical. A still narrower ellipse is seen to revolve as a rigid form by all Os.

The motion of the ellipse is the same, no matter whether it is rotated about its center or whether it is placed eccentrically and revolves on the turntable. Fixation does not affect it. For instance, when it is placed eccentrically it does not matter whether the center of the figure or the center of the turntable is fixated. The same holds for observation of circles and other figures. Thus, eye-movements are presumably not the cause of our effects. As is to be expected no deformations occur when the ellipse revolves on the turntable but does not rotate, that is, when it is eccentrically attached to the turntable and, owing to a suitable mechanism, is kept constant in orientation throughout.

It should also be mentioned that the deformations of the ellipse did not appear immediately when the turntable was set in motion. It took from 5 sec. to 1 min. before a naive but properly instructed O reported that the figure looked fluid. This delay can be avoided, however, if O is not permitted to see the ellipse at rest. All of 10

[4]C. L. Musatti, Sui fenomeni stereocinetici, *Arch. Ital. Psicol.*, 3, 1924, 105–120.

naive *O*s saw the figure immediately as fluid when the turntable was already turning at the start of the observation period. On the average, they reported this 4 sec. after the start of the observation, whereas 10 other *O*s who were allowed to see the figure first at rest reported that the figure had become fluid on the average 11.5 sec. after the turntable was set in motion, a difference reliable at the 5% level of confidence. The reason for the delay under the latter conditions is still obscure.

The Stereo-Kinetic Phenomenon

When one observes the deforming motion of the ellipse lying in a plane for sometime with one eye, a further change may occur. The figure appears to rise out of the plane of the turntable as a circular disk. For instance, when a pattern like the one shown in Figure 6 is slowly turned, an *O* viewing it monocularly may experience two changes in the perceived process, only the first of which has so far been discussed. At the outset he sees a rigid figure revolving about the center of the turntable much like the white ellipse when it is seen at rest. Next the ellipse seems to be fluid and moves around in wallowing amoeba-like motion. Finally, this ever-changing form may turn into a rigid circular disk which rises out of the plane of the turntable at an angle of about 45° and seems to roll around its center in this slanted position. That such a three-dimensional effect can be obtained with a rotating ellipse was apparently first discovered by Musatti who described this effect in the paper previously mentioned. In the same paper Musatti deals with still another depth effect which also emerges when a rotating plane pattern appears to distort. Inasmuch as it occurs with rotating patterns of circles, it, too, must here be discussed. This effect, which, according to Musatti, was discovered by Benussi in 1921, will be described later. Musatti refers to both these effects as "stereo-kinetic" phenomena. They bear resemblance to the kinetic depth-effect, whose properties have more recently been investigated, and the question arises whether they can be considered as instances of this effect.[5]

[5]Hans Wallach and D. N. O'Connell, The kinetic depth effect. *Journal of Experimental Psychology*, 45, 1953, 205–217. In the present volume, Chapter II.

Fig. 6. An ellipse on turntable

In brief, the kinetic depth-effect (*KDE*) can be obtained when the shadow of a solid object in rotation is observed. Under these circumstances usually a solid form is perceived similar to that which casts the shadow. This happens even if that form is so chosen that, when it is presented stationary, its shadow is seen as a plane figure. The shadow of the turning object changes its shape continuously and this deformation is the cause for the three-dimensional appearance of the shadow. A rigid three-dimensional form is seen instead of the continuously distorted plane figure that is actually given. Only a turning motion of the perceived rigid form reflects the given distortions. This motion usually will closely resemble the rotation of the object that casts the shadow, although its direction may be reversed. The *KDE* can also be obtained with the shadow of a plane figure that turns in space. The effect here is to cause a rigid plane figure, turning in depth, to appear in place of the distorting shadow.

There is, of course, an important difference between the "stereo-kinetic" phenomena and the *KDE*; namely, that in the case of the former no deforming patterns are objectively given. Rather, the deformations that are the antecedent of a depth-effect are perceived merely as a result of another perceptual effect which causes the given rotating patterns to distort. Yet, it is possible that the transformation from a percept consisting of a deforming figure located in the plane of the turntable into one consisting of a form arranged in depth is an instance of a *KDE*.

To test the possibility that the stereo-kinetic phenomena are instances of the *KDE* we have to ask whether they conform to the characteristics of this effect. If stimulus conditions are adequate, the *KDE* will occur without suggestion and irrespective of set. This criterion emerged in previous research on the *KDE*.[6] It was found that a three-dimensional effect will occur regularly and spontane-

[6]Wallach and O'Connell, *op. cit.*, 209–211.

ously when the shadow or the retinal image of a turning object shows contours or lines that change simultaneously in direction and length. On the other hand, forms whose deformations consist merely in a lengthening and shortening of contours will not regularly produce depth-effects. For instance, the shadow of a T-shaped wire figure that turns back and forth about its vertical axis will be seen turning as a rigid form only by one out of three naive Os; the others will see the horizontal line expand and contract in the plane of the screen. An appropriate suggestion or prior presentation of a pattern that does produce a *KDE,* however, will cause almost all Os to see a turning T-figure.

The following experiment is an attempt to test in similar fashion whether Musatti's effect occurs regularly and spontaneously.

PROCEDURE

A black cardboard disk 20 in. in diameter on which a white ellipse was pasted (Figure 6) was turned about its center at a rate of about 20 r.p.m. The turntable stood on the floor and the disk revolved in a horizontal plane about 6 in. above the floor. O was directed to stand next to the turntable and to look straight down on it. The illumination was indirect and of moderate brightness, a condition favorable to the emergence of the effects to be observed. Forty-seven Os participated. They were students and some staff members of Swarthmore College. None was familiar with the effects to be observed.

O began his observation with both eyes open and was told to describe the way the white figure looks as it moves around the disk —and to report any changes in its appearance as they occur. After 30 sec. O was asked to cover one eye with his hand and to continue to describe the way the figure looked to him. When O failed to describe the ellipse as a disk rising out of the plane of the turntable at a tilt, E asked the following question: "Can the figure be seen as a disk rolling around on its edge?"

The Os failing to observe the Musatti effect spontaneously were divided into three groups. One group (17 Os) was asked the question after 10 sec. of monocular observation; a second group (17 Os) was asked the question after 30 sec.; and the third group (13 Os), after 60 sec. After the question was asked the observation-time was extended 45 sec.

RESULTS

Sooner or later during the binocular observation period all 47 *O*s saw the ellipse deforming, but none of them saw it as a disk rising out of the plane of the turntable. Inasmuch as a *KDE* can be obtained regularly with binocular observation of a deforming shadow, this in itself is an important result; it differentiates between Musatti's effect and the *KDE*. During monocular observation only 6 *O*s reported seeing the tilting disk prior to the suggestion and 7 *O*s never saw it. This leaves 34 *O*s who saw the tilting disk only after the suggestion had been given. Of the 30 *O*s for whom the suggestion was to be delayed until 30 or 60 sec. of monocular observation had passed, 5 saw the tilting disk prior to the suggestion, 5 never saw it and 20 saw it only after the suggestion had been given. The fact that 17 of these 20 *O*s reported seeing the tilted disk within 5 sec. after the suggestion had been made further argues that these reports are connected with the suggestion.

Some reader may wish to question whether *O*s who reported a tilting disk only after the suggestion was given actually perceived it. The *E* who received these reports believed that *O* described a real perceptual experience. The descriptions usually included features that were not given or were not logically implied in the suggestion. After *O* had reported a tilting disk he was asked to move back 2 ft. from the turntable and look obliquely down on it. When the turning pattern is viewed from such an angle, the disk may change its slant as it seems to roll around the turntable, and such an experience is in agreement with conditions of stimulation.[7] *O* was asked, "Does the disk appear to stand up more vertically when it is nearest to you or when it is opposite you?" Of the 34 *O*s who saw the tilting disk only after the suggestion had been given, two did not notice changes in slant, 30 reported those changes that should be seen if the per-

[7]Assume a real disk is rolling about the turntable leaning toward its center. (All our *O*s saw the disk tilted in this direction.) If the disk were maintaining a constant angle of slant, say of 45°, it would intercept the line of regard more nearly at a right angle when it is in the near position where its slant is away from *O* than when it is in the far position where it leans toward *O*. The shape of its elliptic retinal projection would therefore change; the retinal image would be more circular when the disk is in the near position. Actually, however, the retinal image hardly changes, because an ellipse in the plane of the turntable is objectively given. Such an unchanging retinal image can be produced by a real disk only when its slant is steeper in the near position and more nearly horizontal in the far position.

ceived slant fitted conditions of stimulation and two *O*s reported the opposite changes. Thus the great majority of *O*s noticed features of the perceptual process that were not contained in the suggestion or deducible from it without an intimate knowledge of the complex geometrical situation; they could only be "perceived." (Failure to report the correct changes does not imply that *O* did not actually see the tilted disk; it merely means that the oblique direction of viewing the turntable failed to have its effect on the slant of the disk.)

Thus it seems safe to conclude that the majority of naive *O*s see the tilted disk only when an appropriate suggestion is given. By no means can it be claimed that Musatti's effect occurs regularly and spontaneously. It is in this respect strikingly different from the *KDE*.

Benussi's Effect

Benussi's effect can easily be obtained when a pattern like Figure 7 is turned about its center and is observed monocularly. Quite soon the rings will appear to be arranged in depth. Usually they seem to form a cone rising out of the plane of the turntable. The top of the cone performs a slight circular motion, but apart from this a rigid solid form is seen.

Here, too, the three-dimensional stage is preceded by another illusory perception: The ring pattern, still in one plane, fails to rotate as a whole. Instead the pattern is in continuous deformation. Although none of the rings appears to turn, the inner ones circle about in relation to the outer ring and the extent of this motion is different for each, with the innermost ring moving most. This peculiar experience again finds its explanation in the tendency of a rotating circle to appear to stand still, which was discussed above. If rotation is eliminated from their motion, only the slight revolution of the inner rings will be visible, which is the result of their eccentric location on the turntable. Since their eccentric locations differ in degree and therefore their revolving motions differ in extent, they perform this motion independently of each other, and the pattern appears to undergo distortion.

In the three-dimensional stage an almost rigid solid, a truncated cone, replaces the deforming plane pattern. Again the question arises whether this is the result of a *KDE*. An experiment was performed to test whether Benussi's effect occurs regularly and spontaneously. Since, however, Figure 7 is sometimes seen in three dimensions when given at rest, a different pattern of circles was designed which, when stationary, remains in a plane for most *O*s and this pattern was used in our experiment.

Fig. 7. Four rings on turntable   Fig. 8. Six overlapping rings

PROCEDURE

The pattern of Figure 8 was fastened to the turntable and presented under three different conditions: *O* first described it at rest; then it was rotated at 20 r.p.m. and observed binocularly, *O* being asked to describe what he saw and report any changes that might occur; then, if he failed to report a three-dimensional form within 30 sec., he was asked to cover one eye. After 30 sec. of monocular observation he was asked whether the figure could be seen as three-dimensional. Twelve naive *O*s participated.

RESULTS

All *O*s described the stationary pattern as a plane figure. During monocular observation of the rotating pattern 11 *O*s reported the three-dimensional form, which in the case of Figure 8 resembled a bedspring, spontaneously and only one needed the suggestion. Even more strikingly 10 of the 11 *O*s saw it during binocular observation. Thus the result for the pattern that produces Benussi's effect is strikingly different from our results for the ellipse. Benussi's effect was almost always spontaneously obtained whereas, in the case of the ellipse, of a comparable group of 25 *O*s who ultimately saw the tilting disk, 20 needed a suggestion to do so. Moreover, 10 out of 12 *O*s obtained Benussi's effect with binocular observation, whereas the tilting disk was never seen under this condition.

Our results show that Benussi's effect occurs regularly and spontaneously. It resembles in this respect the *KDE*. The question arises whether other criteria of the *KDE* fit Benussi's effect. It has been mentioned that the *KDE* occurs where contours change simultaneously in direction and length. It should be added that this also applies to intervals between objects or points: if an imaginary line connecting them undergoes these changes simultaneously they will appear to move at different depth.[8] To be sure, the rings and circles of the Benussi patterns do not present the eye with distinct parts. Nevertheless, such parts are perceived. In spite of the rotation of the whole pattern each circle is clearly seen to be at rest, that is, to maintain its orientation, again as the result of an imparting of identity. In the present case, this effect accounts for seeing a part of one circle move in relation to a part of another circle. Imaginary lines connecting such parts change in length and direction (Figure 9) and thus the deformations meet the conditions of the *KDE*.

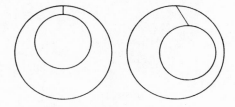

Fig. 9. Two circles before and after clockwise rotation of 90°. The line that connects the top points of the circles changes both in length and direction.

It has been stated above that in the case of the ellipse, too, the deformations are the result of an imparting of identity. Here, however, the result is usually incomplete; the figure, though deforming, is also seen to turn as it revolves about the center of the turntable. Whether this is the reason for the failure of the depth effect to occur spontaneously in the case of the ellipse remains to be seen.

Summary

A rotating circle seems to stand still, a rotating spiral seems to expand or contract, and an ellipse displays flowing deformations

[8]Wallach and O'Connell, *op. cit.,* 214.

when it is turned. All these observations were found to be related. They were explained as the result of subjectively identical points along the contours of these figures that arise in relation to the absolute directions of visual space.

When such illusory deformations are observed monocularly, a change may take place and so-called stereo-kinetic phenomena may be observed. Instead of the deforming patterns, a solid form or a rigid plane figure moving in depth may be seen. These phenomena were compared with the kinetic depth-effect. It was found that one of these phenomena (Benussi's effect) can indeed be regarded as a case of the kinetic depth-effect, whereas one obtained with an ellipse is of a more complex nature.

Perceptual learning

Adaptation based on cue discrepancy

1. Informational Discrepancy as a Basis
of Perceptual Adaptation

When sensory contact with the physical environment is altered
by interposing optical or acoustical devices such as wedge prisms,
reversing prisms, inverting lenses, magnifying lenses, telestereo-
scopes, or pseudophones, a modification of the perceptual processes
can sometimes be demonstrated such that veridicality of perception
is partially or totally restored. This modification, then, serves to
compensate for the misinformation reaching the eye or ear owing to
the interposed device. There are two types of explanation that may
account for such corrective modification of the perceptual processes:
    1. Some sensory indication of the misinformation provided by

Reprinted from S. J. Freedman, ed., *The neuropsychology of spatially
oriented behavior.* Homewood, Ill.: The Dorsey Press, 1968.

the interposed device must be available to the subject, or

2. The misinformation must concern sensory data that are connected with a normative perceptual process, i.e., one that tends toward some distinct state, such as immobility, invariance, or rigidity; and this process must still be modifiable. When this condition is met, a process modification can take place that tends to reestablish the distinct state and, in effect, compensates for the misinformation.

These two types of explanation may take the following forms.

I. Adaptation Based on Veridical Information

Where adaptation presupposes indication of misinformation, three ways seem conceivable by which such indication may be obtained:

a) Perceptions resulting from the altered stimulation may differ from memories of corresponding perceptions that occurred prior to the period of exposure to the interposed devices. There is now no evidence that discrepancy between perception and relevant memories leads to adaptation.

b) Sensory information unaffected by the interposed device may be available which leads to veridical perception of the affected perceptual property. This explanation is based on the fact that a number of perceptual parameters depend on two or more different types of sensory cues (Wallach & Karsh, 1963). Visual depth perception, which may depend either on retinal disparity in the case of stereoscopic vision, or on the kinetic depth effect (Wallach & O'Connell, 1953; Green, 1961), or on perspective depth cues (Gibson, 1950), is one example. The perception of the visual vertical, which depends on sensory effects of the direction of gravitation as well as on the orientation of patterns in the visual field usually indicative of the vertical direction (Asch & Witkin, 1948), and the perception of visual motion, to be discussed later, are further examples. We shall call different kinds of cues determining the same perceptual parameter "paired cues." When one of a pair of cues is affected by the interposed device, the other cue may provide the information necessary to assess the effect of the device on the affected cue and hence on the subsequent perceptual process. A discrepancy between paired cues would be the basis of adaptation.

c) The subject may manipulate his environment and encounter

discrepancies between his perceptions and the mechanical properties of the environment. Whether discrepancy between perception
and the properties of the physical environment as encountered by
action is a condition of adaptation in its own right or whether all
such cases fall under cue discrepancy remains to be seen.

How does cue discrepancy lead to adaptation? When a pair of
cues determine a perceptual parameter, two separate perceptual processes ensue which have only their result in common: the particular
parameter for which they are responsible. If each of these perceptual
processes produces veridical perception, the parameter value determined by one will, of course, be in agreement with the parameter
value determined by the other. But when one of the cues is altered
by an interposed device, this agreement will be lost and the two
converging perceptual processes will then produce different values
for their common parameter. Adaptation may result when one of the
perceptual processes becomes modified in such a way that the resulting parameter values become more alike. "May" is used here deliberately, because this process-assimilation may take different forms.
Only modification of that process which results from the altered cue
will amount to adaptation. If process-assimilation is achieved by
modification of the other process, such modification will be in a
nonveridical direction. Such modification (of the unaffected process)
would ordinarily remain undiscovered because we do not usually
test for it.

II. Adaptation as a Result of a Normative Perceptual Process

Before turning to the principal topic of this chapter, I should discuss
briefly the possible role of normative processes in the explanations
of some cases of perceptual adaptation. This type of explanation was
first proposed by James J. Gibson (1933) in connection with adaptation to the curving of straight contours by wedge prisms. "When a
curved line has been perceived for a considerable length of time it
becomes phenomenally less curved" and afterwards "a straight line
appears distorted with an opposite curvature." Gibson attributes this
change to a "tendency of a perceptual quality toward the norm of its

series," the norm here being straightness, the "neutral quality" where decreasing curvature toward one side changes into increasing curvature toward the other (Gibson, 1937a; Gibson, 1937b). Whether this is the correct view of adaptation to prismatically caused curvature remains to be seen. There is, however, a group of perceptual functions where normative concepts are more obviously applicable, namely, the constancies. It is part of the notion of a constancy that a perceptual process operates in such a way that it results in a distinct state. Examples are size constancy, where, up to a point, the perceived size of an object is the same no matter what the observation distance and hence its image size; or the constancy of visual direction (Wallach & Kravitz, 1965), where a stationary object appears to be stationary when its visual direction is altered by the observer's own movements. If compensating processes account for the attainment of the distinct state and if these processes result from perceptual learning, it is conceivable that the distinct state functions as the selective principle toward which this learning is oriented. And if the compensating process turns out to be modifiable, that is, to adapt to the stimulation changes caused by interposed devices, the same selective principle can be assumed to govern this adaptation. I do not mean to propose such normative conceptions as ultimate explanations. On the contrary, I believe that they will be superseded when the underlying processes are understood in detail.[1] But they are of value as preliminary explanations and can serve as guides in the search for novel kinds of perceptual adaptation.

THE IMMEDIATE EFFECTS OF CUE DISCREPANCY

What is actually perceived when, due to cue discrepancy, two converging processes determine different values of their parameter? The perceptual results of cue discrepancy are as widely varied as the nature of the perceptual processes involved. A brief survey of some important examples follows:

The perception of the vertical is perhaps the most widely known example of cue discrepancy. When Asch and Witkin (1948) turned a subject's visual field about its sagittal axis, thereby creating

---

[1]An explanation of the development of compensating processes that account for a stationary environment during the observer's own movements, in a way that does not appeal to simple normative conceptions, is presented in Chapter XI, selection 9.

a discrepancy between the visual and gravitational cues for verticality, the perceived vertical direction seemed to vary widely from subject to subject. Indicating what they saw as vertical by setting a rod into the apparent vertical orientation, a few subjects set the rod to the gravitational vertical and a few set it closely parallel to lines and edges in the tilted scene that in normal orientation of the scene fall into the gravitational vertical; but the great majority of subjects gave settings which fell into the intermediate range of orientations representing a compromise between the normal effects of the two cues. These large and apparently consistent individual differences are of great interest. They are likely to reflect pervasive differences in mental functioning and have been so regarded (Witkin et al., 1954). They also exemplify a general use of cue discrepancy. Because its results reflect the difference in the effectiveness of several perceptual processes, cue discrepancy can be used as a technique in the designing of more sensitive tests of individual differences.

Distance cues. Cue pairing was recognized as frequently occurring and hence as a concept of wide-ranging application by Wallach and Norris (1963). We proposed to investigate cue pairing "by creating artificial viewing conditions under which one of a pair of cues is altered and thus comes into conflict with its normal partner." We investigated a particular case of cue discrepancy, namely, a discrepancy between the distance cue of accommodation on the one hand, and perspective cues for distance on the other, by creating a deceptive scene analogous in some ways to an Ames room. A drawing was placed on a table representing the projection of a cube on a horizontal plane, and the subject viewed it through a peephole that forced his eye into the station point of the projection. Since under these conditions all subjects see a three-dimensional object instead of the plane projection, the area representing the top surface of the cube in that projection appears to be located at a distance short of its true position. Thus, a point on the projection of the top surface appeared to be nearer than a point on the plain table surface equidistant from the eye. There were large individual differences in the reports on the shape of the perceived three-dimensional object; a few subjects saw a regular cube but most reported seeing similar forms leaning backward to various degrees. This slanting was clearly due to accommodation functioning as a distance cue, because all subjects saw a regular cube when they looked through an artificial pupil.

Measurements reflecting the different apparent distances of the top surface when viewed with or without an artificial pupil were taken; they corresponded to the observed shape differences. The various backward slants observed or implied in these measurements represented the individual subject's way of dealing with this cue discrepancy, another instance of compromise between conflicting cues.

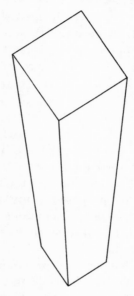

Fig. 1. Cube projection on horizontal plane

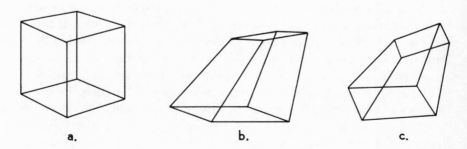

Fig. 2. Cube projection on space: *a,* as seen from station point yielding cube projection; *b* and *c,* side views.

Depth cues (1). In somewhat similar fashion, Wallach and Lindauer (unpublished data) studied discrepancy between perspective
depth cues and binocular vision. Deceptive depth was produced by
using a cube projection of another type. A three-dimensional wire
shape was designed that represented a projection of a cube on an
arbitrarily chosen space. This "projection body" shared its bottom
face with the cube from which it was derived, but the top corners
were displaced in various amounts away from the station point
which was nearly in the diagonal of the cube's top face and somewhat above it. This very skewed shape appeared to be a perfect wire
cube when seen with a single eye located at the station point, but its
true shape was perceived when the other eye was then opened and
binocular vision introduced. In this conflict between perspective and
stereoscopic cues the latter dominated initially in the case of all
subjects. But with prolonged binocular observation, nearly all subjects (30 out of 34) reported seeing a regular cube sooner or later
within the total observation time of five minutes. The median observation time until the cube made its appearance was 54 seconds; the
range was from 2 seconds to 4 minutes and 40 seconds. For 10 of the
30 subjects the cube report came in less than 20 seconds, and for 12
it took more than 1 minute. Once the cube was seen, subjects observed continuous fluctuations between the regular cube shape and
the true shape of the projection body, not unlike the spontaneous
fluctuations observed when a Necker cube reverses periodically,
except that they were more irregular than in the simple case of
depth inversion. Again, large individual differences were found.

Depth cues (2) A discrepancy has also been studied between
stereoscopic vision and another process of three-dimensional form
perception, the kinetic depth effect, *KDE* for short (Wallach & O'Connell, 1953; Green, 1961). These processes are paired under ordinary
circumstances when one moves about and looks with both eyes at
objects near one's movement path. Seen successively from different
directions, such objects turn in relation to the observer and give rise
to the *KDE*. The *KDE* has been studied by presenting to the subject
shadows of rotating solids or three-dimensional wire forms that
were produced by a point source of light and were visible on a
translucent screen; instead of the two-dimensional deforming
shadow, subjects perceived three-dimensional forms in rotation that
were in good agreement with the shadow-casting objects. Since this

effect is readily obtained with wire forms whose stationary shadows are normally seen as two-dimensional, it is apparent that the nervous system can use the information contained in such deformations to re-create the depth lost in the projection either on the shadow screen or, directly, in the image on the retina.

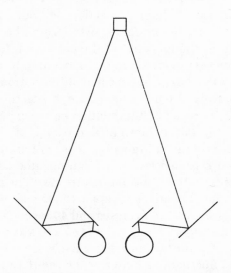

Fig. 3. Plan of the telestereoscope used by Wallach, Moore, and Davidson. Mirrors in the path between the object (small square) and each eye (circles) shift the optical vantage points of the eyes apart, enhancing vinocular parallax and therefore disparity.

Wallach, Moore, and Davidson (1963) brought about a discrepancy between the cues for the *KDE* and retinal disparity, the cue for stereoscopic vision, by using a mirror arrangement called "telestereoscope" to alter the disparity normally associated with a given three-dimensional shape. When a solid object is viewed through such a device, disparities are increased by a certain factor and stereoscopic depth is enhanced. Rotating the object will bring into play the *KDE,* which is not affected by the device, since this effect depends solely on the deformations of the object's retinal projection. Unfortunately for our present discussion, the result of this cue discrepancy has not yet been investigated as such. Most subjects reported that the rotating wire form appeared stretched in the depth dimension and as a consequence seemed to deform continuously (because a cross section is perceived veridically when it occupies the frontal plane, but its apparent width becomes enhanced when, turned into depth, it is given with increased disparity). But we do not know whether the perceived depth of the rotating wire form is as great as that of the stationary form—indicating a dominance of stereoscopic depth perception over the *KDE*—or intermediary between the depth of the stationary form and normal depth as represented by the image deformations. Such intermediary depth would result from a compromise between the normal effects of the two conditions of stimulation. Neither do we know whether there are fluctuations in the relative effectiveness of the competing cues during a lengthy observation period. The study (Wallach et al., 1963) was concerned solely with the adaptation resulting from prolonged exposure to these conditions of cue discrepancy.

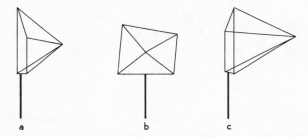

a   b   c

Fig. 4. A wire form used by Wallach, Moore, and Davidson in side view (a) and front view (b). When seen binocularly in front view, the perceived depth of this object is approximately that of its true shape as represented by the side view. When its front view is presented through the telestereoscope, perceived depth is enhanced as represented in the stretched side view (c).

Depth cues (3). Still another case of discrepancy of depth cues has been investigated by Wallach and Lindauer (unpublished data). The conflict in this case was between image deformation causing a *KDE* on the one hand, and perspective depth cues on the other. The latter were made deceptive by using a perpendicular projection of a tetrahedron fashioned as a wire form. In stationary presentation, this flat shape is seen as a pyramid by all subjects. How would it be perceived if a partial rotation gave rise to a *KDE*, which normally can bring about as accurate a veridical perception of a two-dimensional form as of a three-dimensional one? Such a presentation may lead to three different experiences:

a) If the *KDE* dominates perception, a plane figure (a triangle with internal lines) is seen to turn from the frontal into an oblique position and to return.

b) If perspective depth cues continue to cause perception of a pyramid, the image deformations are then reflected by the pyramid's deforming as a three-dimensional shape; the pyramid is seen to contract and expand horizontally, conforming thereby to the changes in width of the projection of the turning wire form.

Fig. 5. Projection of tetrahedron with supporting shaft

c) Finally, the two effects may occur simultaneously, with the subject reporting a three-dimensional shape of diminished depth turning and deforming. This combination seems to be the result of the *KDE* and perspective cues operating simultaneously.

Individual differences as to which of these three possibilities was preponderant were encountered in making the following measurements: From a starting point in which the pyramid projection was parallel to the shadow screen, it was turned about a vertical shaft by 26 degrees and then back into the frontal-parallel position. This rotation angle was chosen because it caused the shadow of the projection to narrow horizontally by 10 percent and then expand again. If after seeing three such oscillations the subject reported a pyramid changing its shape rather than a flat shape turning back and forth, the device that swiveled the wire form was set to turn it through an angle that caused the shadow to change in width by 20 percent. Three oscillations with this larger deformation were then presented, and if the subject still reported seeing a three-dimensional form, the deformation of the shadow was increased to 30 percent, and so on until either the subject saw a flat shape turning or the deformation reached 90 percent. We found very large individual differences. Among our 64 subjects, 4 saw the shadow as a flat figure turning into depth when its deformation was only 10 percent, while 10 subjects never perceived anything but the pyramid with its changes in shape. A few subjects (7) saw the shadow completely flat as soon as it appeared to turn, at whatever amount of deformation that happened; these subjects never experienced the above-mentioned combination of turning and form change. The remaining 47 subjects did perceive this for various numbers of trials, again with large individual differences prevailing. Eleven subjects observed the combination of turning and form change on only one trial, 7 reported it for two steps of deformation, and 12 of the remaining 29 subjects never saw the turning figure as completely flat. The onset of the *KDE,* the first report of turning, also showed wide variations. Table 1 gives the numbers of subjects whose first reports of turning occurred at the various steps of deformation. The individual differences encountered in this experiment certainly parallel those found by Asch and Witkin (1948). They show vividly how cue discrepancy may augment individual differences in perceptual responding which might otherwise not be measurable and may, in fact, be quite subtle.

TABLE 1
Amount of Objective Deformation at First Report of Turning

Deformation (%)	10	20	30	40	50	60	70	80	never
No. of subjects	15	9	5	6	5	6	3	5	10

Displaced visual direction as produced by a wedge prism may readily give rise to a cue discrepancy. For instance, when one views his own hand which rests on a table in front of him through a laterally displacing prism, a discrepancy results between visual and proprioceptive stimulation. The visual direction of the hand is altered by the prism, while proprioception represents the hand's location veridically. Hay, Pick and Ikeda (1965) have investigated what happens under these conditions. They recorded the seen and the felt locations of the hand in the following way: The subject's right hand rested on a horizontal board on whose underside was a row of pushbuttons arranged from left to right. By pressing one of the buttons with his left hand, which was kept out of sight, the subject could indicate the seen or the felt location of his right hand. Removal of the right hand revealed a target point on the board's upper surface whose apparent location could be recorded in the same way. The authors found that most subjects were unaware of any discrepancy between the seen and the felt locations of the hand, and that the recorded seen and felt location of the hand were the same. The mean location of this "fusion" of the seen and the felt hand was very little different from the apparent location of the target point (as affected by the prism), which, of course, was given visually only. The measured displacement effect of the prism on the target point was 10.9°, but when the subject's hand replaced the target point the mean change was less than 1°. The authors refer to this finding, that the location of the fusion of the seen and felt hand was in the visual rather than the proprioceptive direction, as "visual capture" and assume that it is the source of proprioceptive adaptation.

Dominance of the visual over the proprioceptive is, however, not always the outcome of a cue discrepancy resulting from a displacement of visual direction. When Wallach, Kravitz, and Lindauer (1963) had standing subjects look down on their feet through a laterally displacing prism, the subjects saw their legs initially at a slant corresponding to the displaced visual direction with which the legs approximately coincided. But after a 5-minute observation period, most subjects reported that their legs now appeared to be straight and remained so, unchanged, to the end of a 10-minute exposure. This apparent eventual dominance of proprioceptive stimulation may be due here to the circumstance that the legs of a standing person almost always represent a vertical direction and this may have to be considered as an additional cue, which in the present discrepancy is allied with proprioception. It may well be true that, in pure cases of discrepancy between vision and proprioception, vision dominates perceptual experience.[1] Such a view is supported by the experiment of Rock and Victor (1964) on *shape* simultaneously perceived in vision and touch. Here subjects viewed a small square plaque through a cylindrical lens which optically compressed it to one half its width while they simultaneously felt its

---

[1] An experiment by Rock, Goldberg, and Mack (1966), in which visual cues apparently counteract prismatic displacement, cannot be discussed because the experiment does not identify the veridical cues that may operate here.

shape with a cloth-covered hand. When tested in selecting a matching shape either visually or tactilely they always matched the visual shape, even when the selection was by touch. Vision proved to be "so powerful in relation to touch" that only one subject in five ever became aware of a conflict.

Visual motion. There is strong evidence that there are two conditions of stimulation leading to the visual perception of motion. Duncker (1929), who first proposed such a two-factor theory of motion perception, called the two conditions subject-relative and object-relative. The former consists in displacement of the moving object relative to the observer, a change in the object's visual direction; the latter in a displacement of the moving object relative to other visual objects, a change in the pattern of the content of the visual field. Seeing a single object in motion in an otherwise homogeneous field (such as a point of light in the dark) demonstrates the effectiveness of the subject-relative condition. But an object-relative displacement necessarily also involves a subject-relative one and is therefore not as obviously a stimulus condition for motion. Duncker argued that induced motion, an "illusion" of motion where a stationary object in a moving surround is seen to move (such as the moon among drifting clouds), is a manifestation of the effectiveness of object-relative displacement. Duncker also succeeded in isolating motion perception based on object-relative displacement by using displacement velocities below the threshold for motion perception based on subject-relative displacement. He found that under these conditions objectively stationary objects would just as readily appear to move as objectively moving objects and that, when either a surrounded object or its surround was displaced at a rate below the subject-relative threshold, the surrounded object always appeared to move while the surround appeared immobile, no matter which of the two was moving objectively. This finding also explained ordinary induced motion, where the surround is displaced with supraliminal velocity and is seen in motion on the basis of subject-relative displacement, while the surrounded object appears to move due to its displacement relative to this surround.

Further evidence for the effectiveness of object-relative stimulation conditions in motion perception comes from a consideration of the perception of speed. J. F. Brown (1931) discovered that the speed of motion, the impression of its swiftness or slowness, depends strongly on the size of the framework in relation to which an object is displaced, obviously a matter of object-relative conditions. Also, Wallach (1965) has pointed out that a number of interesting phenomena discovered by Gunnar Johansson (1950), where a given displacement leads to two simultaneously perceived motions, can be easily understood as effects of object-relative displacement. In one of Johansson's experiments two dark spots on a light background moved in straight lines, one downward and the other horizontally to the left, so that their paths converged on a point and thus formed the legs of a right angle. The spots were always seen to move straight toward each other while simultaneously they seemed to move as a group obliquely down to the left. They thus end up at the position where objectively they meet, but do so by simultaneously moving in two directions in such a way that a spot's perceived motions can be regarded as two kinematic components whose resultant is the spot's objective motion path. Why is this objective motion path split into two perceived motions? It is easy to see what goes on by imagining that the objective displacements of the spots be slowed down to a velocity below the subject-relative threshold so that only their object-relative displacement, their change of position relative to each other, is psychologically effective. They would then be seen only to move toward each other. But motion toward each other is precisely one of the two simultaneously perceived motion paths. And what is the other of the perceived motions? It is that component of the objective displacement that remains after the object-relative displacement that results in the motion toward each other has been deducted. Thus, of the two simultaneously present conditions of stimulation—of which subject-relative displacement represents the objective displacement as a whole, whereas object-relative displacement represents only a part—the effect of object-relative displacement is obviously prepotent, for it determines one of the perceived motions, while the other perceived motion corresponds to that part of the given displacement that is left unaccounted for by the first one.

This preponderance of the effect of object-relative displacement is also found in connection with the perception of motion speed. J. F. Brown (1931) discovered the framework dependence of motion speed mentioned above by having subjects make speed matches for transposed movement fields. They observed the passage of a black

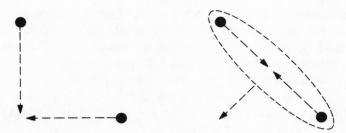

Fig. 6. Johansson's experiment

dot on a white ground through an oblong aperture cut into a black screen, and compared the speed of the dot's motion to that of dots in similar movement fields where the apertures and the dots were 2, 3, 4, 5, or 10 times larger. When this was done in the dark with only the area in the aperture illuminated, speeds appeared equal when the physical velocity in the larger movement field was nearly as much greater as its size. When the transposition ratios of the field sizes were 2:1, 3:1, 4:1, 5:1, and 10:1, matching velocities were found to be in the ratios 1.9:1, 2.6:1, 3.1:1, 3.5:1, and 6.8:1. The velocity ratios producing the same speeds approach the ratios of the field sizes to various degrees. If we assume for the moment ideal transposition ratios where matching velocities stand exactly in the same ratio as the sizes of the fields for which the matches are made, speed would depend on the rate of pattern change that the dots' displacements bring about. It would be totally independent of the objective displacement velocity which is given through subject-relative displacement. Rate of pattern change is clearly a matter of object-relative stimulation. Brown's finding held for a large range of objective velocities, all of which were above the subject-relative motion threshold. Since velocity of subject-relative displacement can only be defined as rate of change of visual direction, speed comparisons based on subject-relative stimulation conditions alone should reflect physical velocities. Recent work by Hill, Rock, and Fineman (1967) shows that this expectation is correct; it also shows that good speed matches can be made when only subject-relative displacement is given. Since in Brown's experiments the two movement fields to be compared were at the same distance from the subject, subject-relative stimulation caused by the displacement of the dots in the two fields was the same when the physical velocities were the same and should therefore tend to produce identical speed impressions; hence speed perception should be veridical. On the other hand, if Brown's discovery is to make sense at all, object-relative stimulation conditions as such should produce ideal transposition ratios. The fact that the transposition ratios actually obtained are close to the ideal ratios and far from veridical speed perception speaks for the relative potency of object-relative displacement in the perception of motion speed.

Little is known about the outcome of a cue discrepancy between subject-relative and object-relative stimulation. The one well-known instance, induced motion, has not been considered in this fashion and has not been appropriately investigated. Whenever an objectively (and therefore subject-relatively) stationary object appears to move because its surround is being displaced, and thus causes object-relative stimulation for the object's motion, the outcome of this cue discrepancy is either dominance of object-relative stimulation or a compromise between the cues. Which of the two it is, or how often one or the other occurs, we do not know, because no speed matches for objects in induced motion have yet been made. Nor do we know how often a stationary object whose surround is being displaced does appear to move. In recent work by Shaffer and Wallach (1966a), in which extent-of-displacement thresholds were measured under object-relative conditions, induced motion occurred only half of the time. These trials were, however, at threshold conditions and different results might have been obtained for larger and faster displacement of the surround.

How Do Paired Cues Come into Existence?

There are probably several answers to this question, because the nature of the perceptual content that is the end result of the converging perceptual processes put in operation by the two sets of cues differs from case to case. In depth perception, stereoscopic vision as well as the *KDE* result in an experienced three-dimensional array from which judgments concerning specific depth intervals are in turn derived. In the case of motion, on the other hand, stimulation causes an experienced quality quite similar to sensory qualities. Experienced motion is a property, though a temporary one, of an object just as color is a property of an object surface (Wallach, 1965).

And just like color, this motion quality is likely to be the experienced counterpart of an innate sensory process. There are grounds for assuming that subject-relative stimulation in the form of image displacement on the retina is the primary cause for the "sensation of motion." Object-relative displacement mediated by image displacement relative to other images is less likely to have a direct sensory connection to motion experience. The strongest support for this view comes from work by Krolik (1934), who demonstrated that under proper circumstances past experience has an influence on which of two objects in displacement relative to each other will be seen in motion. The two objects in his experiments were drawings of things, one always a vehicle and the other a normally stationary thing such as a building. There was a tendency to see the normally stationary object at rest, a fact that argues against a simple sensory connection between object-relative stimulation and motion experience.

If it is assumed that the primary stimulation in motion perception is subject-relative, how does object-relative displacement come to be a cue for motion also? I propose that simple associative learning accounts for this. In the great majority of ordinary cases of motion perception, subject-relative displacement is accompanied by object-relative displacement, for most physically moving objects are seen with stationary objects in the field. A process of stimulus substitution similar to classical conditioning may account for the capacity of object-relative displacement to evoke motion sensation. That the threshold for motion perception based on object-relative displacement is lower than the subject-relative motion threshold (Brown & Conklin, 1954; Shaffer & Wallach, 1966a) does not contradict this hypothesis. Once the connection between image displacement relative to other images on the one hand, and the motion "sensation" on the other, has been established through frequent pairing with image displacement on the retina, the operation of this connection should depend directly on the sensitivity to pattern change. The hypothesis can also account for the rule that in object-relative motion perception an object that is displaced relative to other objects forming its surround is seen to move, while the surround tends to appear stationary. It is this rule which causes object-relative motion perception to be veridical, because in the great majority of cases ordinarily encountered the objectively moving object is seen against a stationary background which forms its visual surround. The same, however, is true when an object is simultaneously given in object-relative and subject-relative displacement, the condition presumably responsible for object-relative displacement becoming a cue for motion perception.

ADAPTATION RESULTING FROM CUE DISCREPANCY

Prolonged exposure to cue discrepancy may lead to perceptual adaptation. It may cause one or both of the evoked perceptual processes to become modified in such a way that their results differ less than they would if they took their normal course. If such a modification occurs in that process evoked by the cue that is altered by the device causing the discrepancy, the modification amounts to adaptation. Three examples of perceptual adaptation where this concept of process assimilation appears applicable will be examined.

III. Adaptation in Stereoscopic Depth Perception

An exposure to discrepancy between retinal disparity and the image deformations that give rise to the *KDE* (described above under *"Depth Cues 2"*) will lead to modification of stereoscopic depth perception. Since the discrepancy is caused by a device which renders retinal disparity nonveridical, assimilative modification of the ensuing process of stereo vision amounts to adaptation. Wallach, Moore, and Davidson (1963) found that a 10-minute exposure to a rotating wire form with disparity enhanced by 110 to 130 percent by means of a telestereoscope led to decreases of up to 20 percent in estimates of depth in the observed stationary wire form and to somewhat smaller adaptation when the effect was transferred to a different wire form. Changed estimate of depth, however, was only one manifestation of an alteration in depth perception; when at the end of the exposure period subjects observed the rotating wire form directly, most of them saw it deform as it turned, a result of its diminished perceived depth. By using a device that diminished the disparity with which a three-dimensional form was given, an opposite modification of stereo perception could be obtained; after exposure, depth estimates were enhanced.

Process assimilation is, however, not the only plausible explanation for this adaptation; a normative interpretation appears also feasible. The distinct state which perception might here tend to achieve would be rigidity of the perceived rotating shape. When, due to enhanced or diminished stereoscopic depth, the wire form seems to undergo deformations as it rotates, a tendency to perceive rigid shapes may cause compensatory changes in stereo vision. This alternative explanation of the adaptation experiments does not involve the conditions of stimulation that give rise to the *KDE*; rather, it starts with the fact of a three-dimensionally perceived object in rotation—whether it is based on the *KDE* or on changing retinal disparities is of no relevance. It is this last feature which makes it possible to distinguish experimentally between the normative explanation and the interpretation in terms of process assimilation, which, of course, depends on the presence of stimulation that gives rise to the *KDE*. Conditions that cause perception of a three-dimensional form in rotation in the absence of cues for the *KDE* could be used to decide for or against the normative explanation. This strategy was employed by Wallach and Karsh (1963) when we compared the effect of exposure to rotating wire forms on adaptation to telestereoscopic viewing in the presence and absence of specific *KDE* cues. We made use of a result of an investigation of the *KDE* (Wallach & O'Connell, 1953) which showed that the *KDE* requires the presence of edges or lines in the deforming retinal projection of the turning object which simultaneously change, on the one hand, in length or in distance from each other, and on the other hand, in orientation; in the absence of the latter a true *KDE* is not obtained. Different objects were used in two adaptation experiments employing enhanced disparity. In one of the objects, the wires were either at right angles or parallel to the rotation axis, and when it turned only length or distances changed in its retinal projection. Wires in the other object were oblique to the rotation axis and their projections changed both in length and orientation when the object turned. Significant adaptation was obtained only for the latter. Inasmuch as both objects appeared to turn when they objectively turned during the exposure period, this result rules out the normative interpretation of the modification of stereoscopic depth perception.

It is inherent in the concept of process assimilation that a modification may also occur in that one of the converging processes which is not affected by the interposed device and therefore initially causes veridical perception. In the present case, this would be a modification in the *KDE*. Where adaptation of stereovision is to enhance disparity and where its modification causes a diminishment of perceived depth produced by a given disparity, a modification in the *KDE* would have to be in the opposite direction; i.e., a given deformation in the object's projection would come to lead to enhanced depth. Wallach, Moore, and Davidson (1963) tested for modification in the *KDE* and found none. While this result was not unexpected, it is of interest in connection with a fact reported earlier. Whereas the immediate effect of a cue discrepancy between retinal disparity and image deformation is that the former seems to dominate perceptual experience, it is also retinal disparity that undergoes rapid adaptation, whereas the *KDE* remains unaltered.

In ordinary perception, apparent stereoscopic depth depends not only on the given disparity but also on the distance from the eyes of the physical object or arrangement that causes the disparity. Since the disparity that corresponds to a physical depth interval varies inversely with the square of the distance of that depth interval, veridical stereoscopic depth caused by a given disparity also depends on this distance; the perceived depth would have to increase in proportion to the square of that distance. This has been shown to be approximately true for distances up to two meters. We obviously have here a constancy similar to that of size, where a compensation for variations in image size due to variation in distance takes place. In stereovision, the compensation is for the diminishment of disparity with increasing distance of the physical depth interval (Wallach & Zuckerman, 1963). The fact that stereoscopic depth perception can be modified experimentally suggests that this compensating process is learned and it may well be learned in the same fashion as the modification of stereoscopic depth perception under discussion, namely, through process assimilation.

IV. Adaptation to Displaced Visual Direction

A large variety of conditions have been found to lead to adaptation to displaced visual direction which is produced by wedge prisms, and more will undoubtedly turn up. Three kinds of tests have been used to measure adaptation, and they do not always yield the same amount of adaptation for the same exposure condition (Shaffer & Wallach, 1966b). The penetrating work of Hay and Pick (1966) has shown that adaptation can consist in a modification of visual as well as of proprioceptive processes. Things are further complicated by reports of seemingly contradictory results. This discussion will therefore be limited to showing that process assimilation can account for the established effects. Since Held and his co-workers have reported results supporting their theory that adaptation requires action on the part of the subject during the exposure period, the discussion can center about their results. Held and Bossom (1961) found that subjects adapted to lateral displacement of the visual direction only when they walked and did not when they rode on a wheel chair over the same path. The same result, however, is to be expected if process assimilation is made the explanatory principle. Unless an inactive subject looks at one of his limbs, conditions of lateral prismatic displacement do not provide a second set of cues representing the true visual direction. Only walking may produce a cue discrepancy; then the subject feels himself going in one direction, while the visual cues for his displacement relative to his environment indicate another direction of his locomotion. (The center of expansion of the visual field produced by the subject's locomotion, according to Gibson (1950), functions as a visual cue for the direction of his movement.) Passive locomotion will, in turn, eliminate the kinesthetic cues for the direction of his progress and hence cue discrepency.[1]

V. Adaptation to Visual Tilt

Process assimilation may also be responsible for adaptation to a prismatically rotated visual field. The underlying cue discrepancy is that explored by Asch and Witkin (1948), who presented upright subjects with a tilted visual environment. As stated above, the discrepancy consists in a conflict between the visual and gravitational cues for main directions of visual space, the vertical and the horizontal. Adaptation to the optically tilted environment is usually tested by having the subject set a luminous line to the apparent vertical or

[1]For a more detailed discussion and more experiments see Chapter X, selection 9.

horizontal in an otherwise dark room, before and after the exposure period. Asch and Witkin, who investigated the cue discrepancy condition itself, had such settings made with a rod seen against the background of a tilted visual environment. The visual environment represents one kind of stimulation for perceived verticality, through familiar field contents such as floors, walls, or trees that normally have a horizontal or vertical orientation. When the visual environment is tilted, these familiar field contents serve as deceptive cues for verticality. Postural cues, all ultimately related to the gravitational direction, provide the other basis for the perception of the visual vertical: normal subjects, with head upright, are able to set a luminous line to the vertical with great accuracy, even if that line is the sole visual object. It is this effect that postural processes have in vision that seems to be modified when adaptation to tilt occurs. This modification takes place under the influence of familiar field contents that are tilted by the prism; it can be regarded as a process assimilation serving to diminish cue discrepancy.

Changing the optical orientation of familiar field contents is, however, not the only effect of field tilting prisms which could account for adaptation. Ordinarily when one turns his head about the vertical axis, the environment is being displaced in relation to the eyes in a horizontal direction, and this causes a horizontal flow of images across the retinas when the eyes are not being moved in pursuit of the displacing field. When tilting prisms are worn, this displacement and the attendant image flow become slanted, and this could cause adaptation to tilt in its own way. In fact, there seems to be little doubt that it does. In the second of their experiments on tilt adaptation Mikaelian and Held (1964) eliminated all familiar field contents from the exposure condition by putting the subject in an environment of luminous spheres; they obtained a significant adaptation effect. Yet, this slant of the field displacement connected with head movements is not the sole condition leading to adaptation, for Mikaelian and Held obtained greater adaptation when subjects faced an ordinary environment with familiar contents representing verticality.

A similar conclusion can be drawn from the results of Morant and Beller (1965), who obtained significant adaptation to a tilted familiar environment when the subject was stationary and greater adaptation when the subject was also walking; presumably walking added slanted displacement of the environment during head rotation as a second condition of adaptation. No argument that tilt of the familiar field contents as such causes adaptation can, however, be derived from a recent experiment by Arien Mack (1967), whose subjects were prevented from turning their heads as they walked or were pushed along a corridor. Here, the rotation of the whole body that takes place when the subject is rounding a corner causes a displacement of the environment relative to the head, and this field displacement is slanted by the prism. While for active head movements proprioceptive as well as vestibular data provide the information about the true plane of the head rotation, only the latter can do so in Mack's experiment.

How important a factor the slanted field displacement is in the adaptation to prismatic tilt remains to be seen. In the meantime it may be pointed out that the operation of this factor may also be a case of process assimilation, with the direction of the field displacement being in conflict with kinesthetic stimulation representing the plane of the head rotation.

Afterthought

I have said more about the immediate effects of cue discrepancy than about its role in adaptation. One reason for this is that the former are a matter of observation, of perceptual fact, whereas, in connection with adaptation, cue discrepancy is a mere theory about antecedents. Moreover, the associated explanatory concept of process assimilation is still entirely hypothetical. It will probably remain so until we know more about how cue pairing comes about and then demonstrate that the development of paired cues—an issue discussed here only in connection with visual motion—and adaptation have common characteristics. Investigation of as many examples of cue pairing as can be found and of the evoked converging perceptual processes is therefore of great importance. Creating cue discrepancies, however, is not the only way to do so. We also need to know with what accuracy each of a pair of cues determines the common perceptual parameter, and this is possible where one can present each one of a cue pair without the other and measure its perceptual result. And in each case we must ask for the reason why the perceptual results agree: whether they do so because of a process of assimilation akin to that occurring in adaptation—stereoscopic depth seems to be an example—or whether this agreement is simply a product of the learning process responsible for the emergence as an effective cue of one of the pertinent stimulation conditions, as may be the case in the perception of motion.

In the meantime, the role here assigned to cue discrepancy can be used in the search for novel kinds of perceptual adaptation: take a case of cue pairing, create a discrepancy condition, subject observers to prolonged exposure to it, and test for possible process modification.

References

Asch, S. E., & Witkin, H. A. Studies in space orientation: II. Perception of the upright with displaced visual fields and with body tilted. *Journal of Experimental Psychology,* 1948, 38, 455–477.

Brown, J. F. The visual perception of velocity. *Psychologische Forschung,* 1931, 14, 199–232.

Brown, R. H., & Conklin, J. E. The lower threshold of visible movement as a function of exposure time. *American Journal of Psychology,* 1954, 67, 104–110.

Duncker, K. Ueber Induzierte Bewegung. *Psychologische Forschung,* 1929, 12, 180–259.

Gibson, J. J. Adaptation, after-effect, and contrast in the perception of curved lines. *Journal of Experimental Psychology,* 1933, 16, 1–31.

Gibson, J. J. Adaptation with negative after-effect. *Psychology Review,* 1937, 44, 222–244. (a)

Gibson, J. J. Adaptation, after-effect, and contrast in the perception of tilted lines: II. *Journal of Experimental Psychology,* 1937, 20, 553–569. (b)

Gibson, J. J. *The perception of the visual world.* Boston: Houghton Mifflin, 1950.

Green, B. F., Jr. Figure coherence in the kinetic depth effect. *Journal of Experimental Psychology,* 1961, 62, 272–282.

Hay, J. C., & Pick, H. L., Jr. Visual and proprioceptive adaptation to optical displacement of the visual stimulus. *Journal of Experimental Psychology,* 1966, 71, 150–158.

Hay, J. C., Pick, H. L., Jr., & Ikeda, K. Visual capture produced by prism spectacles. *Psychonomic Science,* 1965, 2, 215–216.

Held, R., & Bossom, J. Neonatal deprivation and adult rearrangement: Complementary techniques for analyzing plastic sensory-motor coordinations. *Journal of Comparative Physiological Psychology,* 1961, 54, 33–37.

Hill, L., Rock, I., & Fineman, M. Speed constancy based on size constancy. *Perception & Psychophysics,* 1968, 4, 37–40.

Johansson, G. *Configurations in event perception.* Uppsala, Sweden: Almqvist & Wiksells, 1950.

Krolik, W. Ueber Erfahrungswirkungen beim Bewegungssehen. *Psychologische Forschung,* 1934, 20, 47–101.

Mack, A. The role of movement in perceptual adaptation to a tilted retinal image. *Perception & Psychophysics,* 1967, 2, 65–68.

Mikaelian, H., & Held, R. Two types of adaptation to an optically-rotated visual field. *American Journal of Psychology,* 1964, 77, 257–263.

Morant, R. B., & Beller, H. K. Adaptation to prismatically rotated visual fields. *Science,* 1965, 148, 530–531.

Rock, I., Goldberg, J., & Mack, A. Immediate correction and adaptation based on viewing a prismatically displaced scene. *Perception & Psychophysics,* 1966, 1, 351–354.

Rock, I., & Victor, J. Vision and touch: An experimentally created conflict between the two senses. *Science,* 1964, 143, 594–596.

Shaffer, O., & Wallach, H. Extent-of-motion thresholds under subject-relative and object-relative conditions. *Perception & Psychophysics,* 1966, 1, 447–451. (a)

Shaffer, O., & Wallach, H. Adaptation to displaced vision measured with three tests. *Psychonomic Science,* 1966, 6, 143–144. (b)

Wallach, H. Visual perception of motion. In G. Kepes (Ed.), *The nature and art of motion.* New York: George Braziller, 1965. In the present volume, Chapter V.

Wallach, H., & Karsh, E. B. The modification of stereoscopic depth-perception and the kinetic depth-effect. *American Journal of Psychology,* 1963, 76, 429–435. In the present volume, this chapter, selection 4.

Wallach, H., & Kravitz, J. H. The measurement of the constancy of visual direction and of its adaptation. *Psychonomic Science,* 1965, 2, 217–218. In the present volume, Chapter XI, selection 1.

Wallach, H., Kravitz, J. H., & Lindauer, J. A passive condition for rapid adaptation to displaced visual direction. *American Journal of Psychology,* 1963, 76, 568–578. In the present volume, this chapter, selection 8.

Wallach, H., Moore, M. E., & Davidson, L. Modification of stereoscopic depth-perception. *American Journal of Psychology,* 1963, 76, 191–204. In the present volume, this chapter, selection 2.

Wallach, H., & Norris, C. M. Accommodation as a distance cue. *American Journal of Psychology,* 1963, 76, 659–664.

Wallach, H., & O'Connell, D. N. The kinetic depth effect. *Journal of Experimental Psychology,* 1953, 45, 205–217. In the present volume, Chapter II.

Wallach, H., & Zuckerman, C. The constancy of stereoscopic depth. *American Journal of Psychology,* 1963, 76, 404–412. In the present volume, Chapter VII, selection 3.

Witkin, H. A., Lewis, H. B., Hertzman, M., Machover, K., Meissner, P. B., and Wapner, S. *Personality through perception.* New York: Harper, 1954.

2. Modification of Stereoscopic

Depth-Perception

This is the first in a series of studies which explore artificial conditions that yield rapid perceptual learning and the nature of the effects obtained in learning. The following strategy for discovering conditions for rapid perceptual learning was employed: We selected two cues of different types which pertained to one and the same perceptual property, such as distance or depth; by means of an optical or mechanical arrangement one of the cues was so altered that the objective situation was misrepresented; and then O was exposed simultaneously to the two cues, which were now contradictory.

Method

The effect to be reported here involved the perceived depth of small objects. The cues which were opposed were retinal disparity and the conditions of stimulation that gave rise to the kinetic depth-effect *(KDE)*. The latter consist in changes in the retinal image of a three-dimensional object which, due to its rotation or the locomotion of O, alters its orientation relative to the eye; such changes are good cues for the object's shape and produce veridical three-dimensional perceptions of form.[1] For a given object, the two types of cue would, of course, tend under ordinary conditions to produce the same three-dimensional shape. We brought them into conflict by using a mirror-arrangement that increased all retinal disparities inherent in the

Written in collaboration with Mary E. Moore and Linda Davidson. Reprinted from *American Journal of Psychology,* 1963, 76, 191–204.

[1]Hans Wallach and D. N. O'Connell, The kinetic depth effect. *Journal of Experimental Psychology,* 1953, 45, 205–217. In the present volume, Chapter II.

two retinal images of an object. Such an arrangement is called a telestereoscope, and it enhances disparities by increasing, in effect, the interocular distance (Figure 1).

Various three-dimensional wire forms, which were made to rotate about a vertical axis, were observed through the telestereoscope. Under such conditions, the wire form appears to distort as it rotates. An imaginary line between two points on the object that lie in the same horizontal plane changes in length continuously during rotation; it appears shortest when it lies in the frontal-parallel plane and longest when it points away from the observer. When it lies in the frontal-parallel plane, its length is determined by the distance between the retinal images of these points; when it occupies the depth-dimension, its apparent length depends in addition on the disparity of its end-points and suffers the telestereoscopic enhancement. Thus, each cross-section of the wire form changes periodically in width; it is narrowest when it lies in the frontal-parallel plane and widest when it lies in the sagittal direction, and different cross-sections go through different phases of expansion and contraction simultaneously, depending on their momentary orientation to the sagittal direction.

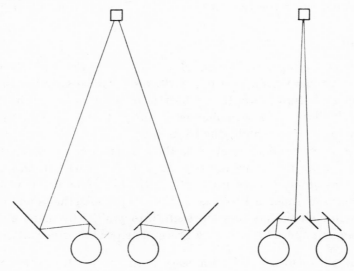

Fig. 1. Arrangements in enhancing (left) and reducing (right) retinal disparity. The light-paths from the target (square) to the eyes (circles) through the four mirrors of the telestereoscope are traced.

Viewing the rotating wire form through the telestereoscope for 10 min. changes the relation between disparity and perceived depth. This can be demonstrated in two ways. After the 10 min. "training period" the wire form has smaller apparent depth, and this is ascertained by having *O* estimate the perceived depth of the stationary wire form before and after the training period. The other demonstration consists in having *O,* after the training period, look directly at the rotating wire form. He will now see it distort, although ordinarily the directly viewed rotating form appears rigid. The distortion is the opposite to that observed through the telestereoscope; cross-sections will appear to decrease in width as they turn from the frontal-parallel to the sagittal orientation, indicating that the now normal disparity gives rise to a reduced depth. Although this latter demonstration of the training effect is simple and impressive, we used the estimation-procedure in most of our experiments because it yielded quantitative results. Unless otherwise reported, our telestereoscope increased the effective interocular distance in all experiments by 7.6 cm.; since the average interocular distance amounts to 6.5 cm., this more than doubled normal disparity. For each experiment, the telestereoscope was set in such a way that *O* viewed the wire form through the mirrors with the same convergence as he would view it directly. This produced a discrepancy between convergence-distance and accommodation-distance of 6.4 cm.,[2] which is equivalent to a negligible 0.15 diopters even for the shortest of the viewing distances used in our experiments.

Basic Experiments

A typical experiment employed a black wire cube with a 4.9-cm. edge, with one diagonal axis forming the extension of the vertical supporting shaft, about which the wire form could be rotated. The center of the cube was on a level with the *O*'s eyes and 63.5 cm. (25 in.) from the mirrors. Sixteen experimentally naive *O*s, previously tested for adequate stereoscopic vision, participated. The experiment began with *O* viewing, through the telestereoscope, the stationary cube which was so oriented that one of its diagonals fell into *O*'s

---

[2]This is the increase in the true viewing distance due to the detour of the light-path via the outer mirrors, which concerns accommodation but not convergence.

sagittal plane. O was instructed to adjust the length of a metal rod to equal the apparent height of the cube, along the diagonal. In making this adjustment, O looked alternately through the telestereoscope at the cube and downward at the metal rod, which he held in his hands. Then he made an estimate of the depth of the cube by adjusting the length of the metal rod to the apparent length of the sagittal diagonal. When these measurements were completed, O looked through the telestereoscope and watched the cube rotate at a speed of 12 r.p.m. for 10 min. At the end of the training period, O was asked to close his eyes while the rotation was stopped, and the cube was turned by hand into the same position it had before rotation started. O made another estimate of the cube's depth, and one of its height, in that order. The mean depth-estimate before rotation was 9.96 cm., while that for the height amounted to 5.71 cm. Since, objectively, the height and depth of the wire form were the same, the difference between measured depth and height (amounting to 4.25 cm.) is, of course, due to the telestereoscopic effect. After 10 min. of watching the cube rotate the mean depth-estimate was 8.36 cm., an average reduction of 1.60 cm. in perceived depth, a difference significant beyond the 0.1% level.

Similar results were obtained with a different wire form, a slightly irregular pyramid with a four-cornered base. (The edges of the base ranged from 5.1–6.3 cm. in length, and the four rods, rising to the apex, from 5.6–5.9 cm.) The perpendicular distance from apex to base was 3.8 cm., and, since estimates were made with the base in a frontal-parallel position, this distance also was the measured depth of this wire form. The rotating shaft was attached at right angles to one of the edges of the base. The mean estimate of depth (20 Os) was 6.93 cm. before the training period and 5.53 cm. afterwards. The mean change in depth, 1.40 cm., was significant beyond the 0.1% level. In this experiment, the diagonal of the pyramid's base also was measured before and after the training period. Since the diagonal lies in the frontal-parallel plane when measurements are taken, a change in its length reflects a change in perceived size. Mean estimates of the length of the diagonal were exactly the same before and after the training period, indicating that no change in apparent size accompanied the large change in perceived depth. In nearly all experiments to be reported, estimates of frontal-parallel size were made before and after the training period to assure that the changes in the depth-estimates obtained were not related to changes in over-all size.

Alternative Explanations

There are two other interpretations of the effect of the training pe-riod besides perceptual learning which need be discussed.

(a) One alternative is that the period of rotation reveals the true shape of the wire form and the final estimate of depth is influenced by the memory of this shape. This explanation does not apply to the qualitative demonstration of the effect of training (the distorting of the wire form in normal vision following training), but should be considered with regard to our quantitative method. It is easily re-futed by the fact that the training effect can be transferred to a different wire form.

In these experiments, the initial and final estimates of depth were made with one wire form while a different one was used in training. Except for this exchange of the objects presented, the proce-dure here was the same as in the basic experiments. Table 1 lists the magnitude of five effects of transfer and permits comparison with the results obtained when test- and training objects were the same. No conclusions should be drawn from apparent differences among the various effects of transfer; they do not approach significance. Most of the data were obtained early in our study before improved techniques were introduced; only Experiments *A* and *B* were done with groups of *O*s of whom none had previously served in teles-tereoscopic experiments and under conditions that afforded cues of perspective distance (see below). There can be no doubt that the training effect transfers to different objects, but it seems to do so with some loss.

(b) The second alternative interpretation of our effect is that the diminished depth after the training period is an effect of satiation. This term refers to the fact that prolonged exposure to the same pattern or the same continuous movement is apt to lead to a deterio-ration of the corresponding perceptual experience. Such spontane-ous changes can be observed when an outline-figure is fixated and becomes slightly smaller, or when stroboscopic motion between two spots which light up alternately is viewed for a prolonged period,

TABLE 1

The Results of Eight Experiments Compared

The diagonal cube (*A–D, G, H*) and the pyramid (*E, F*) have been described under Basic Experiments. The elongated pyramid (*G*) had a base identical with that of the pyramid, but a distance from apex to base of 6.4 cm. The perpendicular cube was in normal orientation and had an edge of 5.3 cm. The octohedron was regular and its edges were 6.3 cm. long. All decreases in depth were significant beyond the 1% level.

	Test object	Training object	N	Depth-decrease (cm.)
A	Diagonal cube	Diagonal cube	13	1.62
B	Diagonal cube	Perpendicular cube	18	1.24
C	Diagonal cube	Diagonal cube	16	1.60
D	Diagonal cube	Perpendicular cube	24	0.83
E	Pyramid	Pyramid	20	1.40
F	Pyramid	Diagonal cube	16	0.59
G	Diagonal cube	Elongated pyramid	14	0.73
H	Diagonal cube	Octohedron	21	0.68

conditions which lead eventually to cessation of the apparent motion. Diminished depth might conceivably be the result of a similar change.

Experiments with diminished interocular distance. We tested this explanation with experiments which involved the reverse training. The mirrors of the telestereoscope were so rearranged that, rather than increasing disparity, they reduced it (Figure 1) and therefore diminished perceived depth in relation to objective depth. Training with this device should lead to increased stereoscopic depth. If here, too, the training period should turn out to reduce perceived depth, an interpretation in terms of satiation would be indicated, whereas an increase in depth measured by the final estimate would point to learning as the cause of our effect. The new device reduced the effective interocular distance by 2.8 cm. Irregular pyramids, similar to the one used in the basic experiment, were the wire forms used. The base remained constant in all pyramids, but, since the new arrangement of the mirror reduced depth, the pyramids used in the present experiment had greater distances between apex and base; namely, 6.4 and 12.2 cm. For the former (25 in. distance from eyes, 17 *O*s) the mean depth-estimate before the training period was 3.03 cm.; after rotation it was 3.59 cm., the increase in depth of 0.56 cm. was reliable beyond the 0.5% level. For the latter (30 in. from eyes, 16 *O*s) the depth-estimate changed from 5.71 to 6.57; this difference of 0.86 cm. was significant beyond the 0.1% level. The increase in estimated depth due to the training amounted to 28% and 22% of the presumed decrement in depth caused by the mirror-arrangement. These relatively low values were probably due to the relatively small change in the effective interocular distance which the present mirror-arrangement produced. The telestereoscope used in the basic experiment augmented effective interocular distance by 7.6 cm., and increase of 117% (when the natural interocular distance is assumed to be 6.5 cm.), while the present mirror-arrangement reduced it by 2.8 cm., causing a comparable percentage change of only 74%. These considerations, together with the high reliability of the results obtained with fairly small groups of *O*s, make it clear that deterioration of depth-perception need not be seriously considered as an explanation for the major portion of our effect.

Dissipation of the Effect of Training

Once the new evaluation of disparity has become established through training, it should be possible to unlearn it—to relearn the former evaluation—by watching an object rotate in normal vision, without the telestereoscope. Since, after training, the object in normal vision is seen with reduced depth, stereoscopic depth-perception is in disagreement with the *KDE,* and the object seems to distort. The procedure we used was to have *O* look through the telestereo-

TABLE 2
Unlearning

N	Unlearning period (min.)	Depth decrease (cm.)	Reduction in learning effect (%)
20	0	1.40	—
18	0.5	1.08	23
12	2.0	0.58	59*
15	5.0	0.39	72*

* Significant beyond the 1% level.

scope at the pyramid, make a height- and a depth-estimate, watch the pyramid rotate for 10 min., and then, before making the final depth-judgment through the telestereoscope, watch another pyramid in rotation for a brief period, without the telestereoscope. This second pyramid had more depth than the original one in order to make it similar to the original pyramid as seen through the telestereoscope; the distance from apex to base was 6.4 cm. Table 2 shows the decreases in depth measured by this procedure with various durations of the unlearning period, as well as the difference between the depth-decrease in the learning experiment and the depth-decrease measured after each of the unlearning periods. Unlearning operated as expected, counteracting part of the depth-decrease that resulted from the original training, but, even after 5 min. of unlearning, the learning effect that remained was significantly different from zero beyond the 2% level.

More interesting than dissipation through unlearning is the dissipation of the training effect through mere lapse of time. If this dissipation were very rapid, it could be a source of considerable variance in our measurements of the training effect, for the time taken to make a depth-estimate varies from O to O. Information on the loss of the training effect with passing of time is, therefore, of practical concern in our experiments. It is also of theoretical interest; after having been modified, does the stereoscopic perception of depth return to normal only because it is again practiced under normal conditions, or is mere passage of time sufficient to reestablish the normal relation between disparity and perceived depth?

TABLE 3
Forgetting

N	Forgetting period (min.)	Depth-decrease (cm.)	Reduction in learning effect (%)
20	0	1.40	—
10	5	0.89	36
15	12	0.38	73*

* Significant beyond the 5% level.

We tried to answer this question by delaying the second estimate of depth. At the end of the training period, *O* sat quietly with eyes closed for either 5 or 12 min. before making a second estimate. The mean depth-changes obtained for the pyramid after these forgetting periods are given in Table 3. It might be added that the effect of 0.38 cm. remaining after the 12-min. intermission still is significant beyond the 0.5% level. The experiment with the 5-min. "forgetting" period was recently repeated under improved viewing conditions (see below) with the same wire form. With the second estimate made immediately after training, a group of 20 *O*s gave a mean depth-decrement of 1.28 cm., while from another group of 20 *O*s, who gave their second estimates with 5-min. delay, a mean decrement of 0.81 cm. was obtained; the difference of 0.47 cm. between the groups was significant beyond the 2% level.

Whether one wants to call the dissipation of the training effect with lapse of time "forgetting" depends on what view of the forgetting process one favors. If one assumes that forgetting usually consists in a replacement of a newly acquired habit by older habits, the term can be applied here. The discovery of a rapid modification of the relation between disparity and perceived depth makes it very likely that the original relation which *O* brings to our experiments also is an acquired on and is temporarily superseded by our training effect.

Cumulative Effect of Training

We consider our modification of stereoscopic depth an instance of learning. Perhaps the most important question to be asked in this context is whether it is a continuous process, that is, whether our training effect increases with the length of the training period. We did an experiment in which the training period was twice interrupted to obtain depth-estimates for shorter training times. The first post-training depth estimate was made after only 1 min. of observing the rotating wire pyramid through the telestereoscope. Immediately thereafter—no height estimate was made—observation of the rotating wire form was resumed and lasted for 3 min. A new depth-estimate was made, followed by another training period lasting 6 min., after which a final depth-estimate was obtained. The results are given on the left side in Table 4. They show that virtually the whole effect was produced in the first two training periods; the last period of 6 min. did not seem to add to our effect.

This seemed an unlikely result and we were unwilling to accept it as genuine, and this reluctance, in turn, led to an important improvement of our experimental conditions. This improvement has to do with the fact that perceived stereoscopic depth depends not only on the given disparity, but also on the distance of the object that causes the disparity; the greater the distance, the greater will be the apparent depth that results from the given disparity.[3]This means that a change in apparent depth of a wire form could come about through a change in the evaluation of a cue for distance. Our training effect is protected against such an interpretation by the finding that apparent size is not altered by the training period. If the training effect were produced by a change in the evaluation of distance cues, a size- as well as a depth-change should result. Changes in the *effectiveness* of available distance cues with prolonged observation could, however, account for our unlikely result. With two exceptions, all experiments thus far reported were done under conditions in which only convergence and accommodation operated as cues for distance; it seemed just possible that this kind of cue deteriorates with prolonged observation.

To strengthen the representation of the distance of the wire form, we introduced a further distance-cue—perspective—to the viewing condition. A wooden platform provided a horizontal surface stretching from *O* to the shaft supporting the wire form and 3 ft. beyond. This surface was only 16 cm. below the center of the wire form and started being visible approximately 15 in. from *O*. To strengthen its perspective effect, we covered it with a checkered oilcloth. The checkered surface was visible only to one eye in order to prevent telestereoscopic depth-perception of the pattern. A low screen in front of the left-objective mirror blocked the view of the horizontal surface for the left eye, while the wire form was visible to both eyes.

When the experiment was repeated under these conditions, each of the three training periods produced a clear and statistically

---

[3]J. Linschoten, *Structuranalyse der binocularen Tiefenwahrnehmung: Eine experimentelle Unterschung,* 1956, 180.

TABLE 4
Successive Determinations under Two Conditions

	Without perspective-cues (N = 24)			With perspective-cues (N = 41)		
	Mean depth (cm.)	Mean differ- ence	t	Mean depth (cm.)	Mean differ- ence	t
Depth prior to rotation	6.67			7.17		
		0.47	2.24†		0.37	2.46*
Depth after 1 min. rotation	6.20			6.85		
		0.45	3.46*		0.30	2.73*
Depth after total of 4 min. rotation	5.75			6.55		
		0.06	0.46		0.26	3.71*
Depth after total of 10 min. rotation	5.70			6.29		

*Significant beyond the 1% level.   †Significant beyond the 5% level.

significant effect (right side of Table 4). When the three training effects were plotted against a logarithmic time-scale, an almost straight line was obtained (see center curve in Figure 2). An analysis of variance showed significance beyond the 0.1% level for the total training effect ($F = 12.21$ with 3 and 120 df). For further comparisons, the assumption was made that the time-intervals between the four depth-estimates were "psychologically equal." When the mean depth-estimates were plotted against such a scale, it was found that again they nearly fell on a straight line. A linear trend was fitted to the group means, and the mean slope of the group curve was then tested against the variability among the slopes of the curves for the individual Os.[4] The linear trend was found to be significant beyond the 0.1% level. ($F = 14.97$ with 1 and 40 df). This indicates that the data for the individual Os as well as the group-data can be described as a linear function, and shows that our training effect is cumulative.

In addition to being highly significant, the linear component of the training effect accounted for virtually all the variance due to the

[4]D. A. Grant, Analysis of variance tests in the analysis and comparison of curves. *Psychol. Bull.*, 53, 1956, 141–154.

training conditions (99.87%). The minute residual (0.13) eliminates the possibility of any other systematic source of variance. This spoke well for the improved conditions under which the experiment was done. All further experiments were therefore done with the checkered surface visible, and the more important earlier experiments were repeated under these conditions.

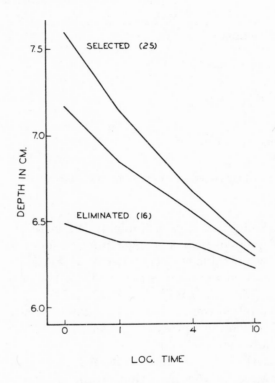

Fig. 2. Changes in depth as a function of time

Among them was one that had produced a surprising result. In addition to the two series of experiments on the dissipation of the training effect just reported, a third one had been done where O, during the interval between the end of the training period and the final depth estimate, looked steadily through the telestereoscope at the now stationary wire form. This condition apparently yielded a very fast dissipation of the training effect, as fast as the "unlearning" condition. This inexplicable result disappeared when the experiment was repeated under the improved viewing conditions; looking at the stationary wire form did not cause the training effect to dissipate faster than mere lapse of time spent with eyes closed. It looks as if prolonged inspection of the wire form with only oculomotor cues for distance present produced a slight effect of increasing depth which is superimposed on our training effect.

An inspection of the individual records that contributed to the right side of Table 4 made it appear that those Os who showed a larger initial depth also showed a larger training effect. We therefore divided the 41 Os who had participated in the experiment into two groups according to their initial depth and computed the mean effects for the three training periods for each group. A mean of 7.17 cm. had been obtained for the initial depth for all Os, and their mean height, a measure of frontal size, was 6.76 cm. We grouped Os according to whether their initial depth-estimates were higher or lower than their height-estimates. The groups thus constituted consisted of 25 Os with a mean initial depth of 7.60 cm. (selected Os) and 16 with a mean initial depth of 6.49 cm. (eliminated Os). The upper and the lower curves in Figure 2 show the mean training effects of the two groups plotted against an abscissa of log time in sec. plus one. The curve for the eliminated Os shows a very small training effect indeed—only 0.27 cm. for the three training periods combined— while the corresponding figure for the selected Os is 1.26 cm. Just why Os whose initial depth estimates were lower showed much less of a training effect is still a matter for speculation; but selection of Os according to their initial depth-estimates can be used to keep variance due to individual differences low, which becomes important where one tests for a difference in the amount of the training effect between different groups of Os.

We return now to the main result of the experiment, that our effect grows nearly linearly with the logarithm of the training time. This means, of course, that increments in the effect per unit of real time become smaller with elapsed total training time. If this relationship prevails for longer training times, as appears likely, little gain can be expected from prolonging the training period beyond 10 min. To be sure, the additional training effect produced during the last period seems somewhat more reliable ($t = 3.71$) than the one for the first period ($t = 2.46$), but this advantage appears small when weighed against increased fatigue and boredom of O. Thus far we have not worked with a training period longer than 10 min. A truly linear function of log time would predict that it would take 2 hr. to double the training effect that is obtained in 10 min. and that total elimination of the effect of the telestereoscope would be a matter of many days; but with a lifetime of practice in the normal relation between disparity and perceived depth opposing the training effect, it seems questionable that the latter could ever happen. It is also conceivable that stereoscopic depth-perception is not the only function which is changed in the training period; it is possible that the *KDE*, too, undergoes an alteration that serves to diminish the discrepancy which the telestereoscope produces. If this were the case, the modification of stereoscopic depth perception would be expected to halt before it fully compensated for the enhancement of disparity caused by the telestereoscope. The next experiment to be reported takes up this issue.

Modification of the Kinetic Depth-Effect

Just as it is possible to alter the relation between disparity and perceived depth, it is conceivable that the relation between the deformation of the image of a turning object and its perceived depth can be modified. This might possibly happen in our experiments, provided it is the contradiction between two sets of cues which is the cause of the training effect. According to this interpretation, learning diminishes the discrepancy between the perceptual result of the kinetic depth-effect *(KDE)* on the one hand and the artificially enhanced stereoscopic depth on the other. This diminution could be accomplished in two ways, merely by the change in the relation between disparity and perceived depth which was actually obtained, or by a simultaneous modification of the *KDE*. If the *KDE* were so changed that a given image-deformation gave rise to greater depth of the perceived object, this would serve also to diminish the discrepancy between the results of the two processes of depth-perception. The fact that, in our experiments, the *KDE* yields at the outset veridical depth, and stereoscopic vision does not, is irrelevant as long as there is no further kind of depth-cue in operation which provides independent information on the true depth. We attempted in the following manner to determine whether the *KDE* undergoes such a modification in our experiments.

The wire form used was the pyramid which, because of its irregular shape, does not yield perspective depth-cues. The training lasted an uninterrupted 10 min., and consisted in the usual binocular observation of the rotating wire form through the telestereoscope. It was in the depth-estimates that the present experiment differed. They were made while the wire form was in rotation and was monocularly observed.

The results for this experiment, in which 28 *O*s participated, did not show an adaptive modification of the *KDE*. Such an effect would have resulted in an increased depth of the monocularly perceived wire form after training. In fact, mean estimated depth decreased slightly, from 4.66 cm. to 4.44 cm., and this difference was reliable at the 5% level. This decrease turned out to be a matter of a small decrement in total size as indicated by a change in the height-estimate from 6.52 cm. to 6.16 cm. When the depth-change was compared with the height-change no significant difference was found ($t = 0.52$). Inasmuch as observation was monocular when the estimates were made, a change in total size after prolonged observation is not a matter for concern. It is most likely due to the absence of convergence as a distance-cue. The experiment makes it clear that our training period does not produce a modification of the *KDE*.

Modification of Stereoscopic Depth by Means of Perspective

There is a way to achieve a change in the relation between the given disparity and perceived depth which does not involve the *KDE*. In the case of regular orthogonal wire forms, stationary exposure during the training period also leads to such an effect. We demonstrated this with two such wire forms, a cube in normal orientation and a regular octahedron. They were attached to shorter shafts (the cube by means of a bar across the bottom face) in such a way that *O* saw them obliquely from above. In both forms, wire squares in horizontal orientation were visible, which might by the shape of their retinal projections give away the object's true depth. That this was the case could be inferred from the fact that many *O*'s initial depth-estimates failed to show the enhanced depth that the telestereoscope usually brings about. This same fact causes difficulties for demonstrating the effectiveness of perspective cues in modifying stereoscopic depth. The Os whose initial depth-estimates did not show the telestereoscopic effect could not be expected to produce evidence of a training effect. Yet, being presented with two sets of conflicting cues, they might well develop a modified stereoscopic depth perception.

We circumvented this difficulty by casting our demonstration in the form of a transfer experiment. Each of the wire forms mentioned was presented in a stationary position for 10 min. viewing through the telestereoscope, but the depth estimates before and after this inspection period were made with the diagonal cube. The experiments were done before perspective cues for distance were introduced. Inspection of the stationary octahedron caused an average reduction of 0.41 cm. in the apparent depth of the diagonal cube (18 Os); for the cube in normal orientation, the mean difference in estimated depth before and after the inspection-period amounted to 0.47 cm. (20 Os). Both differences were significant at the 1% level. This effect has not yet been further investigated. It is mentioned here because in certain contexts it may be necessary to control for the operation of perspective depth-cues.

Summary and Conclusions

Experiments yielding rapid perceptual learning were described. By having Os view rotating wire forms through a telestereoscope for periods of 10 min., a change in the relation between the given retinal disparities and perceived depth was obtained which partially compensated for the depth-enhancing effect of the telestereoscope. This change became evident when, during a subsequent direct viewing of a rotating wire form, Os perceived it distorting. The change could be measured by having Os make estimates of depth before and after the training period. By using an arrangement of mirrors that diminished disparities, an opposite training effect could be obtained, which caused given disparities to produce greater than normal depth. It was possible to present one wire form for the training period and use a different one for the estimation of depth, but in this transfer situation the training effect seemed to be diminished. The training effect dissipated quickly with mere passage of time, but not as rapidly as it was acquired. When the growth of the effect during training was studied, it was found to be cumulative, not only for a group of *O*s but also for individual *O*s.

These findings raise many problems. What is the ultimate cause of our training effect: the fact that enhanced stereoscopic depth implies a distortion of the rotating object or the contradiction between the two sets of depth cues present, disparities on the one hand and conditions of stimulation for the *KDE* on the other? Why is the training effect diminished when it is transferred to another wire form? Why is it possible that a sizeable modification of stereoscopic depth-perception can be obtained in so brief a training period? Work on these questions is in progress.

3. Why the Modification of Stereoscopic Depth-Perception Is So Rapid

Experiments have been reported in which extraordinarily rapid perceptual learning was obtained. By viewing a solid object in rotation through a telestereoscope (an instrument that enhances retinal disparity), the relation between disparity and perceived depth can be changed in a matter of minutes. This modification of stereoscopic perception of depth manifests itself in purely perceptual experiences, and it can be measured by having O make estimates of depth before and after the period of exposure to the experimental conditions.[1] The effect appears to be due to the discrepancy between the two sets of cues—those for the kinetic depth-effect and those for retinal disparity.[2] Since the relation between disparity and experienced depth can be modified by what appears to be a learning process, it seems likely that the normal relation between disparity and depth, which O brings to the experiment, is also a learned one. For the perception of depth to be veridical, this relation must change during the years of growth, as interocular distance increases, and remain the same afterward. Our Os' interocular distances had been constant for a number of years when they participated in the experiment, and the particular relation between disparity and depth that

Written in collaboration with Eileen B. Karsh. Reprinted from *The American Journal of Psychology,* 1963, 76, 413–420.

[1] Hans Wallach, M. E. Moore, and Linda Davidson, Modification of stereoscopic depth-perception. *American Journal of Psychology,* 1963, 76, 191–204. In the present volume, Chapter X, selection 2.

[2] Hans Wallach and E. B. Karsh, The modification of stereoscopic depth-perception and the kinetic depth-effect. *American Journal of Psychology,* 1963, 76, 429–435. In the present volume, Chapter X, selection 4.

was in existence when our training-procedure changed it had a learning period of several years in back of it. One may then ask why it is that our experimental procedure can rapidly change the quantitative aspect of a perceptual process which has presumably been learned years ago and has been practiced ever since. This paper explores two possible reasons for the rapid learning that is obtained in our experiments.

One explanation makes the assumption that our experimental procedure affords very concentrated learning compared to the learning that takes place in ordinary life. When *O* views the rotating object through the telestereoscope, every turn of the object by, say, 90° gives rise to a discrepancy between the potential result of the kinetic depth-effect and the enhanced stereoscopic depth that is caused by the telestereoscope. With the object rotating at approximately 10 r.p.m., the 10-min. training period is packed with occasions which can contribute to the learning of the new relation between disparity and depth. Compared to this, the learning occasions that offer themselves under the conditions one encounters in ordinary life may indeed occur much more rarely, which could account for the fact that a process that undoubtedly has been established for a long time and for which there have since been many learning occasions can be modified in a matter of minutes.

The second explanation assumes that the learning product on which the quantitative aspect of stereoscopic depth-perception is based is not very durable and that in the course of time it has frequently to be reacquired. The training for normal depth-perception would be cumulative only in a limited way and its effect less potent than its long duration would suggest.

Experiment I A

We tested for the first explanation, which hinges on the temporal concentration of learning occasions in the experimental training, by giving normal depth-perception the same presumed advantage. Prior to the usual training procedure, during which *O* saw the rotating object with artificially enhanced disparity, he observed the rotating object under normal viewing conditions also for a period of 10 min. Such pretraining provides the same kind of training in support of the *normal* relation between disparity and depth which the subsequent telestereoscopic presentation provides for an adaptation to the experimental conditions. Should we find that this pretraining of normal depth-perception strongly diminishes the effect of the telestereoscopic training, the first explanation would be confirmed.

METHOD

Training and tests proceeded in essentially the same fashion as previously described.[3] The telestereoscope increased the interocular distance by 7.6 cm. For the wire-form, we chose the irregular pyramid previously used. It was four-sided with a nearly square base (the diagonal was 8.5 cm., and the distance from the apex to the base was 3.8 cm.). Presumably this form does not provide perspective-cues for depth when its base occupies the frontal-parallel plane and the apex points toward O, the position in which depth-estimates were obtained. It was placed 32.5 in. from O's eyes, with a checkered table-cloth which covered a horizontal platform 16 cm. below the center of the pyramid providing perspective-cues for distance. This table-cloth, stretching from the vicinity of O toward the wire-form and 20 in. beyond to a white background-screen, was visible to one eye only. The speed of rotation during the training-period was 10 r.p.m. Depth-estimates were given by adjusting a measuring rod which could be extended to nearly twice its shortest length. O held the rod in his hands and looked down at it while using it to represent perceived depth. To make it possible to vary the length of the rods that were given to O before and after training, four rods were used that differed from each other in basic length in steps of 1 cm. As in previous work, estimates of size in the frontal-parallel plane were obtained together with the depth-estimates to make sure that the training period did not produce a decrease in total size which might account for part of the measured change in depth. In the case of the pyramid, estimates of the diagonal of the base were obtained.

Two groups of 20 Os were used. One was given the pretraining, which consisted in observing a rotating wire-pyramid under normal viewing conditions, followed by the usual training with the telestereoscope. For the other—the control group—the pretraining was omitted. To make the wire-pyramid presented in pretraining (where

[3]Wallach, Moore, and Davidson, *op. cit.*

it was given with normal disparities) look as much as possible like the pyramid seen through the telestereoscope, the former was larger in its distance from apex to base. While the bases of the two pyramids were identical, the pyramid used for pretraining had a distance from apex to base of 6.2 cm.

The Os were selected for good stereoscopic depth-perception and for consistency in their estimates. The following criteria were used: Os were eliminated (1) whose initial depth-estimates.were more than 0.5 cm. smaller than their estimates of the diagonal; (2) who failed to see the pyramid distort when seen in rotation through the telestereoscope; and (3) whose initial and final estimates of the diagonal of the base differed by more than 0.7 cm.

In detail, the procedure was as follows: All the Os were first shown the deeper of the two pyramids, and the particular distances for which they would have to give estimates were pointed out to them. Then they looked through the telestereoscope for 1 min. at the shallower pyramid, which was stationary with its apex pointing toward O. A size and a depth estimate were then made, in that order. O was instructed to base his estimates solely on the appearance of the figure at the time the judgment was given. After the initial depth-estimates, the Os of the pretraining group watched the deeper pyramid in rotation under normal viewing conditions, and then made a second depth-estimate of the shallow pyramid seen through the telestereoscope. These two steps were omitted in the case of the Os of the control group. Then all the Os had the usual training period during which they observed through the telestereoscope the shallow pyramid in rotation, and the experiment ended with the final estimates of depth and size, in that order.

RESULTS

The results are given in the first two rows of Table 1. They show a trend in line with the explanation which this experiment tests. The effect of the usual training period on perceived depth was indeed diminished for Os in the pretraining group, who showed a depth-decrement of 0.81 cm., while the mean depth-decrement for the control group was 1.28 cm.; this difference was reliable ($t = 2.58$, $p < 0.02$). The effect of pretraining on the modification of stereoscopic

TABLE 1
Mean Estimates of Size and Depth (in cm.) for Two Increments in
Interocular Distance (Experiments IA and IB)

Increment in interocular distance	Group	Size			Depth			
		initial	final	change	initial	second	final	decremer
7.6	Pretraining	6.325	6.465	0.140	6.690	6.530	5.880	0.81
	Control	6.450	6.510	0.060	6.595	—	5.315	1.28
12.8	Pretraining	6.255	6.305	0.050	7.495	7.055	6.165	1.33
	Control	6.345	6.255	-0.090	7.425	—	5.525	1.90

perception of depth was not, however, large enough to establish temporal concentration of learning occasions as the only explanation of the rapid learning produced by our usual training period. To do so, the pretraining should have had a major effect on the depth-decrement, which it did not.

Experiment I B

Experiment I B, a replication of Experiment I A with a greater increase in interocular distance, served a double purpose. First, we wished to see whether pretraining with the normal relation between disparity and depth would produce a larger change in the usual effect of training when that effect itself became greater. This we hoped to achieve by increasing further the disparity produced by the telestereoscope. Secondly, we wished to find out whether the usual effect of training would indeed become greater when disparity was increased, and, if it did, whether this alteration of our basic procedure would be preferable from a technical point of view.

METHOD

The arrangement of the mirrors of the telestereoscope was changed to increase each O's interocular distance by 12.8 cm., which, assuming that the mean interocular distance of our Os was 6.4 cm., would increase interocular distance by a factor of three. In the previous experiment, interocular distance was increased by 7.6 cm., or, on the average, by a factor of 2.2. To avoid any concomitant enhancement of retinal disparity which, in the case of some *O*s, might result in failure of some part of the wire-form to be binocularly fused, we compensated for the enhancement in interocular distance by increasing the distance from *O* of the form. Since disparity decreases with the square of the distance of the object from the eyes,[4]a moderate increase of that distance from 32.5 cm. to 42.5 cm. was sufficient to achieve such a compensation.

RESULTS

The results (last two rows in Table 1) reveal the expected increase in the effect of training; the control group showed a depth-decrement of 1.90 cm., as compared with the decrement of 1.28 cm. in Experiment I A. An additional increase in the interocular distance of 66.6% caused an increase in the effect of training of 48%. The effect of pretraining on training did not, however, increase proportionally with the training effect. Whereas in Experiment I A the depth-decrement after pretraining was 37% less than in the control experiment, the comparable loss in Experiment I B was only 30%. An analysis of the combined results of the two experiments showed a reliable effect of pretraining in reducing depth-loss ($F = 7.90$; $df = 1, 76$; $p < 0.01$), but the difference between the two experiments was not reliable.

To be sure, the enhancement of the average interocular distance from 2.2 times to 3 produced a greater training effect, and the difference was reliable ($F = 9.49$; $df = 1, 76$; $p < 0.01$), but this advantage was offset by a great increase in variability. While the *SD* of the initial estimate of depth in the case of the smaller interocular distance was 0.93 cm., it amounted to 1.63 cm. for the larger interocular distance, and this difference was significant ($F = 3.05$; $df = 59, 79$; $p < 0.01$). Consequently, the loss in depth-decrement due to pretraining in Experiment I B was larger but less reliable.

The larger variability connected with the greater interocular distance is also apparent when the differences between the initial and the second depth-estimates are compared. With only the pretraining period separating the two estimates, there is no reason to

[4]C. H. Graham, Visual perception, in S. S. Stevens (ed.), *Handbook of Experimental Psychology*, 888.

expect a systematic change in depth. While for Experiment I A the two mean estimates differ only slightly and not significantly (0.16 cm., $t = 0.96$), the results for Experiment I B show a sizable decrement of 0.44 cm., a difference which was not quite significant ($t = 1.86$, $p < 0.09$). A difference of similar magnitude (0.47 cm.) obtained in Experiment I A between the two depth-decrements was significant, although it pertained to different groups of Os. It is clear that the tripled interocular distance represents no technical advantage.

Experiment II

The second explanation for the rapidity with which a modification of stereoscopic depth perception can be achieved assumes a limited durability of the learning product responsible for the quantitative aspect of normal stereoscopic vision. Such limited durability could be demonstrated by showing that a period of disuse makes normal stereoscopic depth-perception less potent and hence less resistant to alteration. We proceeded by restricting Os to monocular vision for 24 hr. before the experiment. Originally, we attempted to show that wearing an eye-patch for a day prior to the usual training procedure would enhance the training effect. Such a result would have been an indication of diminished potency of normal depth-perception after a period of disuse and would have served as a demonstration of the specific relation—assumed in our explanation—between the modification of depth-perception and the depth-perception which O brings to the experiment. Pilot studies showed that 24-hr. disuse had more serious consequences for stereoscopic vision than was anticipated and that, as a result, our original plan would not succeed. After wearing an eye-patch for 24 hr., Os noticed spontaneous changes in depth of a binocularly viewed wire-form. The object would appear alternately deeper and shallower, and, perhaps as a consequence, mean depth-estimates were considerably smaller than normal. This being so, it is not suprising that a subsequent training procedure, while it did result in sizable training effect (that is, a *further* depth-decrement) did not by itself produce the postulated *enhanced* decrement. Accordingly, we altered the goal of the experiment to a mere demonstration of the deterioration of stereoscopic vision which is apparently produced by disuse.

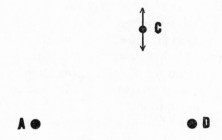

Fig. 1. Arrangement of the four rods used for depth-interval matching in Experiment II

METHOD

Two procedures were employed to obtain quantitative manifestations of this deterioration: *O* estimated the depth of a wire-form before wearing the eye-patch and afterward; two depth-intervals were repeatedly matched before and after disuse of binocular vision and the *SD* of each set of matches was determined.

Depth-estimates were given for the deeper pyramid described above. It was placed 42.5 cm. from *O*'s eyes with its apex pointing toward *O,* and it was viewed directly against a white screen. As in Experiment I A the table-surface was raised and covered with a pattern providing perspective-cues to distance. The arrangement for matching two depth-intervals consisted of four vertical rods, 12 in. long, placed according to the scale drawing of the ground plan shown in Figure 1. The centers of the Rods *A* and *D* were 4 in. apart and occupied *O*'s frontal-parallel plane 32.5 in. from *O*'s eyes. Rods *A, B,* and *D* were in fixed position; Rod *C* could be moved toward and away from *O* by a rack-and-pinion arrangement. Placed 5 in. in front of the Rods *A* and *D* was a screen with an aperture, 8 in. wide and 6 in. high, through which *O* viewed them, black against a well-illuminated background. *O*'s task was to match the depth between Rods *B* and *A* with the depth between Rods *C* and *D*. The depth-interval between Rods A and B (2.5 in.) was so chosen that all Os would see both rods fused when they looked at one of them. This was, however, not the case for the Rods B and C when the latter was in the matching position, that is, as much behind the plane of Rod A and D as Rod B was in front. Each O made 10 individual matches and the SD of these matches was computed for each O. Initially, Rod C was set either 2 in. in front or 2 in. behind the matching position. E slowly moved it toward the matching position. O was permitted to stop this motion to make leisurely comparisons and to ask for a shift in the opposite direction when the point at which the depth-intervals appeared equal seemed to have been passed. We deliberately used this flexible procedure rather than a rigid psychophysical method to keep it adaptable to the difficulties in depth-perception which Os have after the period of monocular vision.

Before they were selected, the Os were tested for good stereoscopic depth-perception. They were shown a wire-form derived from an octahedron by elongating one of its horizontal axes and asked to give a height- and a depth-estimate, the latter along the elongated axis which nearly fell into O's sagittal plane. This wire-form was 8.8 cm. high and 11.1 cm. deep. Only Os whose estimates of depth were 1 cm. greater than their height-estimates were used. The second test consisted of a depth-estimate of the pyramid used in this experiment. To be chosen for the experiment, O's estimate had to be at least 5.5 cm. Os who found it difficult to use either eye in monocular vision were eliminated. These were rigorous criteria; of the 60 undergraduates tested, only 20 were used in the experiment.

The sequence in the experiment proper was as follows: O made one estimate of the diagonal of the base of the pyramid, and one of its depth. Then he made a group of 10 depth-matches with the vertical bars. One day before the scheduled time for the second test, O put on an eye-patch, switched it from one eye to the other every 2–3 hr., and wore it during all his waking hours while he engaged in normal activities. Upon O's return to the laboratory for the second test, the eye-patch was removed, and O immediately made a depth-estimate for the pyramid, followed by an estimate of the diagonal of the base. After this, he made another set of 10 depth-matches with the vertical bars.

To get a first idea of the persistence of the deterioration, another set of estimates for the pyramid was obtained from half the Os after the matching, which took approximately 7 min. Then the *O*s had to look steadily at the pyramid for 5 min. and make another estimate of depth and of the diagonal. After a rest-period of 1 min., during which the *O*s sat with their eyes closed, they viewed the pyramid again for 5 min. and thereafter made a final set of estimates.

Results

There was a strong decline in the apparent depth of the pyramid after the 24-hr. period of monocular vision. The initial mean depth-estimate was 6.77 cm., while, after wearing the eye-patch, the mean was 5.36 cm. The depth-decrement, which amounted to 20.9% of the original depth was highly significant ($t = 9.19$, $p < 0.001$). There was also a small decrement in size; the mean estimate of the diagonal of the base decreased from 7.26 cm. before to 7.07 cm. after the monocular period, but the difference did not approach significance ($t = 1.64$, $p < 0.20$). The matches of two depth-intervals showed a sizeable increase in variability after the period of monocular vision. The mean *SD* rose from 0.50 cm. before to 0.71 cm. after disuse of stereoscopic depth-perception; this increase was significant beyond the 1% level ($t = 3.00$).

The 10 *O*s used in studying the persistence of the deterioration showed an initial mean decrease of 1.62 cm. in the depth of the pyramid. After the matching test, the mean depth of the pyramid had increased by 0.56 cm.; after the first 5-min. observation of the stationary pyramid, its depth had increased by an additional 0.47 cm., and another 5-min. observation-period produced a further increase of 0.27 cm. At that time, approximately 20 min. after removal of the eye-patch, all but 0.32 cm. of the original depth-decrement had been recovered.

Summary and Conclusion

Two possible explanations for the rapidity with which a modification of stereoscopic depth-perception can be achieved have been tested. One of them assumes that veridical stereoscopic vision is based on a somewhat unstable learning product which must continuously be reacquired on the learning occasions which occur in normal use of binocular vision. We found evidence for a deterioration of stereoscopic depth-perception after a period of 24 hr. of monocular vision, but we have not yet been able to obtain proof of a connection between the striking effect of disuse and the effectiveness of our training procedure.

The other explanation assumes that our training procedure is so effective in changing the product of previous learning in stereoscopic vision which O brings to the experiment because a high concentration of learning occasions is provided by our procedure as compared with the frequency with which ordinary life affords them. This explanation was tested by using the same procedure which had been employed to produce the modification of stereoscopic vision to strengthen *normal* stereoscopic perception before the modification was attempted: the Os observed a rotating wireform in direct view for 10 min. before they observed it through the telestereoscope. This experience did result in a diminished modification of stereoscopic vision, but the effect was not large enough to establish high concentration of learning occasions during the rotation as the sole explanation for the rapidity with which a modification of depth-perception can be obtained. To a great extent, this rapidity seems to depend on an inherent modifiability of stereoscopic depth-perception, and our evidence for its fast deterioration supports this view.

4. The Modification of Stereoscopic Depth-Perception and the Kinetic Depth-Effect

An earlier article described investigations of a novel process of perceptual learning, the modification of stereoscopic depth-perception by means of slow rotation.[1] In viewing a rotating three-dimensional wire-form through a telestereoscope, the normal relation between disparity and apparent depth was modified in a matter of minutes. A "training period" of 10 min. produced a reduction of perceived stereoscopic depth by as much as 20%. Evidence for such a change was obtained by having Os make estimates of depth before and after the training period, or by obtaining descriptions of a rotating wire-form seen directly; the form appears to distort as it turns as a result of a shortened depth-dimension. This training effect transfers to different wire-forms in diminished amount, and it dissipates with mere passage of time. The effect grows in steady fashion with the length of the training period not only for the group as a whole but also for the individual Os.

Among the problems that remained unanswered was in what way rotation causes the training effect. We see two possible answers:

Hypothesis 1. Rotation makes the enhanced depth caused by the telestereoscope immediately noticeable through the ceaseless distor-

Written in collaboration with Eileen B. Karsh. Reprinted from *American Journal of Psychology*, 1963, 76, 429–435.

[1]Hans Wallach, M. Moore, and L. Davidson, Modification of stereoscopic depth perception. *American Journal of Psychology*, 1963, 76, 191–204. In the present volume, Chapter X, selection 2.

tion of the turning wire-form. Any cross section of the wire-form
that is parallel to the axis of rotation gains in width as it turns from
a frontal-parallel position to one in depth where the enhanced
stereoscopic depth affects it, and it becomes narrower again as it
returns to a frontal position where image-shape again determines its
width. A tendency toward invariant form might be postulated to
account for the training effect which, by diminishing the apparent
depth that corresponds to the given retinal disparity, diminishes
also the form-distortions that result from the enhanced retinal disparities.

Hypothesis 2. By providing the conditions of stimulation for the
kinetic depth-effect *(KDE)* which also mediates the perception of
three-dimensional form and hence of depth, the rotation of the wire-
form in our training situation produces a perceptual discrepancy,
and the training effect may be based on a tendency to reduce this
discrepancy. When there are two different conditions of stimulation
that cause or affect the same perceptual property, the two resultant
perceptual processes operate in such a way that, under normal conditions, they produce the same value of that perceptual property—
depth in our case. The two sets of stimulus-conditions considered
here are (a) retinal disparity and (b) deformations of the retinal
projection of the wire-form due to its rotation, which, owing to the
KDE, also give rise to the perceived object's depth. For an *O* with
adequate stereoscopic depth-perception, the two simultaneously operating perceptual processes will normally produce the same apparent depth; but, when one set of cues is manipulated to cause the
result of one perceptual process to differ from the other, as happens
in our training period where stereoscopic depth is enhanced, a perceptual discrepancy comes into existence. A tendency to reduce this
discrepancy through the modification of one of the two perceptual
processes may be postulated as the cause of the training effect.

How can one hope to obtain evidence favoring one of these
explanations over the other? It is important to note that Hypothesis
1 refers only to the objective fact of rotation, whereas Hypothesis 2
is concerned essentially with the psychological consequence of rotation—the *KDE*—which causes depth-perception in its own right.
According to Hypothesis 1, rotation "exposes" the telestereoscopic
effect by causing axial cross-sections to change in width as they
successively occupy a frontal-parallel and a sagittal plane. Accord-

ing to Hypothesis 2, there is a change in stereoscopic depth-perception because, with the involvement of the *KDE,* two different processes of depth-perception pertaining to the same form take place simultaneously and cause conflicting results. Proof of involvement of the *KDE,* therefore, would be the answer to our problem, and such proof could be obtained if some characteristic of the *KDE,* not shared by mere rotation, could be shown to influence our training effect. Such a characteristic emerged from a study of the *KDE* by Wallach and O'Connell.[2] One of the conclusions of the study was that not just any deforming retinal image produced by a rotating solid will cause a reliable *KDE.* Only images displaying edges that change simultaneously in length and orientation will produce the *KDE* regularly, unaided by set or expectation. Images whose edges are only parallel and perpendicular to the solid's axis of rotation, and which therefore do not undergo changes in orientation, will cause, without the aid of set, the experience of a turning three-dimensional form only for some *O*s. Some evidence was reported in support of this claim.

Exploratory experiments by Stollnitz done in our laboratory five years ago demonstrated very strong effects of set which emerged as a potent condition influencing whether or not solid forms will be experienced. Immediately preceding experiences with two-dimensional and deforming shapes often seem to be able to prevent the *KDE* from occurring, while a set for seeing three-dimensional forms in rotation will cause such forms to be perceived even when the given pattern displays only contours that change in length alone. The claim that only simultaneous changes in length and orientation of edges will reliably cause the *KDE* can apparently be demonstrated only under set-free conditions. Still, we believe that the claim is concerned with a genuine characteristic of the *KDE* and can, thus, be used as a criterion as to whether the *KDE* as such is involved in our training effect.

Our experiment, then, consists essentially in using, in the situation that yields the modification of stereoscopic depth-perception, two wire-forms which differ in whether they display edges that change simultaneously in length and orientation during rotation. If the training effect obtained with the wire-form displaying such

---

[2]Hans Wallach and D. N. O'Connell, The kinetic depth effect. *Journal of Experimental Psychology,* 1953, 45, 205–217. In the present volume, Chapter II.

edges is larger, a strong argument can be made for the participation of the *KDE* in our training effect. This conclusion, in turn, would support Hypothesis 2. If no difference were obtained, the experiment would be inconclusive. That result would, of course, follow from Hypothesis 1, but it could also occur because, in our training situation, set for the *KDE* to take place was maximal, since binocular disparity also provides cues for depth and rotation and can cause these experiences independently of the *KDE*.

METHOD

We made the wire-forms for this experiment as simple as possible. They consisted of flat arrangements of parallel wires attached to the supporting shaft like flags (Figure 1). When each figure was turned about the vertical shaft, the flag with the vertical wire arrangement produced a retinal image which deformed in such a way that mainly the length of the supporting horizontal wire and the horizontal distances between the parallel wires changed periodically. For the "diagonal" flag, however, the oblique wires underwent in addition simultaneous alterations in length and orientation, changing from a 45° tilt when the flag was in a frontal-parallel position to one approaching verticality as the flag approached the sagittal position. The curved upper edges of the flags were meant to minimize perspective cues for depth which the flag's shape might provide. It had previously been shown that a modification of stereoscopic depth perception can be obtained with stationary exposure of orthogonal wire-forms to telestereoscopic viewing; that is, perspective cues provided by the wire-form can, if only in a minor way, have an effect similar to rotation.[3] This fact also made it necessary to use control conditions where the training period consisted in viewing a stationary flag through the telestereoscope, in order to measure any contribution of perspective cues to the training effect obtained with the flags.

The apparatus was previously described.[4] The version with the checkered table cloth visible to one eye was used. The telestereoscope added 7.6 cm. to O's interocular distance. The flag was 32.5 in. from O's eyes and visible against a white screen 20 in. beyond. It was

[3] Wallach, Moore, and Davidson, *op. cit.*, 191–204.

[4] *Ibid.*, 191–204.

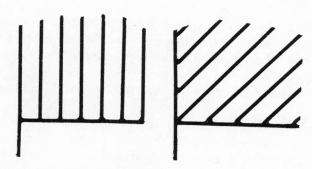

Fig. 1. Wire-forms used to test Hypothesis 2

not fully rotated, but was made to oscillate through an angle of 90°
at a rate of 17 c.p.m. between the frontal-parallel position and the
sagittal position pointing away from *O.* Depth- and size-estimates
were made with the flag fixed in a position 60° from the frontal plane
toward the rear. In making size-estimates, *O*s were asked to reproduce the apparent height of the flag by adjusting a brass measuring rod. Six rods of various lengths were used, each of which could
be extended to almost twice its shortest length. The *O*s gave depth-
estimates by reproducing the apparent length of the flag which in
its 60° position was, of course, enhanced by the effect of the telestereoscope.

There were four groups of *O*s; two groups saw their flag oscillate
during the training period and two (in the control condition) inspected it, through the telestereoscope, in the same fixed position as
for the depth-estimates. For all groups, the training period was
preceded by a 1-min. inspection-period, during which *O* looked
through the telestereoscope at the flag in the fixed position, and by
the first height- and depth-estimates, which were given in that order. The training period itself consisted of two observation-periods
of 2-min., separated by a 15-sec. rest-period. The training period was
immediately followed by the second depth-estimate and then the
second height-estimate.

Altogether 64 *O*s were used, 20 in each of the oscillation-groups
and 12 in each of the stationary-exposure groups. They were selected
for adequate stereoscopic depth-perception and for consistency in
their estimates. Stringent criteria were adopted, and 68 *O*s had to be

discarded, mostly for defects in stereoscopic vision. The criteria were as follows:

(1) Ability to see all parts of the flag fused simultaneously in spite of the enhanced disparities that the telestereoscope produces.

(2) A first estimate of the flag's length at least 1.5 cm. greater than the first height-estimate.

(3) No greater difference between the two height-estimates than 0.5 cm.

(4) Reports that the flag appears to change in length when its oscillation is observed through the telestereoscope. To make it possible to employ this criterion in connection with the stationary groups, Os of those groups, after completion of the procedure assigned to them, were given training with their flag in oscillation.

We believe that the high reliability of the results to be reported is due in part to the careful selection of Os.

RESULTS

The results are given in Table 1. The diagonal flag in oscillation produced by far the greatest training effect, a decrement in depth of 0.75 cm. which is very reliable ($t = 8.26$; $p < 0.001$). Compared with this, the effect obtained with the vertical flag in oscillation, a decrease of 0.205 cm., is almost negligible, although it is still reliable ($t = 2.15$; $p < 0.05$). As the height-estimates indicate, these depth-decrements cannot be attributed to decreases in total size. The height-estimates after training are on the contrary a bit larger than before ($F = 9.35$; $p < 0.01$) and are about of the same order of magnitude for all groups ($F < 1.0$).

An analysis of variance was performed on the depth-estimates of all Os before and after training. It showed that the training period caused a significant decrease in depth-estimates ($F = 26.56$; $p < 0.001$). The striking result was that the group with the diagonal flag in oscillation, when contrasted with the three other groups, accounted for 99.7% of the sum of squares of the interaction of treatments (the various training conditions) and training effect. Thus the training effect for this group differed reliably from that of the other groups ($F = 20.20$; $p < 0.001$). There were no differences between the group with vertical flag in oscillation and the stationary groups, as shown by a minute residual interaction. Thus the significant train-

TABLE 1

Mean Estimates of Depth and Height (in cm.) for Four Groups

Group	N	Depth			Height		
		before training	after training	decre-ment	before training	after training	incre-ment
Diagonal, oscillation	20	5.890	5.140	0.750	4.000	4.045	0.045
Vertical, oscillation	20	6.065	5.860	0.205	3.955	4.020	0.065
Diagonal, stationary	12	5.500	5.400	0.100	3.500	3.658	0.158
Vertical, stationary	12	6.158	6.092	0.066	3.875	3.950	0.075

ing effect obtained with the vertical flag is probably not due to oscillation which was absent from the training period of the other two groups. Rather, the small effect obtained with these three groups is likely to be due to a factor they have in common, probably some residual perspective-cue.

There is then strong evidence that the large training effect that, in the case of our flags, is obtained only through training with oscillation is connected with the *KDE.* Only the diagonal flag, which in oscillation produces those deformations of its retinal images that genuinely give rise to the *KDE,* yields the large training effect. The vertical flag, producing no such deformation, fails to do so. That is the result which, we stated, would confirm Hypothesis 2. Hypothesis 1, by contrast, would predict equally strong training effects for both flags in oscillation. By presenting a flag alternately in the frontal position where its length is given by means of its retinal projection and in depth where that length is given largely by means of retinal disparity, oscillation provides the information about the non-veridical stereoscopic viewing conditions, and it does this equally well for both flags. The training effect should therefore be the same for both flags. The fact that a training due to oscillation was obtained only with one of the flags is, therefore, not in agreement with Hypothesis 1.

DISCUSSION

Some readers may favor a third hypothesis that ascribes our training effect to the *experienced* distortions of our rotating wire-forms. Even without the present evidence we consider this a most unlikely explanation. Perceptual processes are generally inaccessible to awareness, and only their results may come to be represented in experience. That an experienced fact, by virtue of being a matter of awareness alone, should be a causal link in some perceptual process, as this hypothesis proposes, is thus rather unlikely. Quite apart from such considerations, there does not appear to be any reason why oscillation of the diagonal flag should lead to experienced distortions and oscillation of the vertical flag should not. To check whether, inexplicably, this did occur, we asked all our *O*s if they noticed a change in length while the flags were oscillating and found that most of them did. It will be remembered that report of distortion during oscillation was one of the criteria for the selection of *O*s. Of all *O*s tested in selecting the two oscillation-groups, only five were eliminated because they did not report changes in length during oscillation; of these, two were tested with the diagonal and three with the vertical flag.

Once it is clear that the *KDE* is involved in our training effect in a decisive manner, the notion of perceptual discrepancy follows. Stereoscopic vision on the one hand and the *KDE* on the other represent two parallel but separate routes to the perception of three-dimensional form and of depth. The former is strictly a matter of binocular stimulation. The latter is based on a kind of stimulation which is totally effective in a single eye. Whereas, in stereoscopic vision, near and far are strictly determined, the *KDE* leaves the sagittal dimension of visual space undetermined: in the absence of other cues for depth, monocularly given rotating wire-forms readily invert, and reverse depth is as frequently perceived as true depth. When, due to the effect of the telestereoscope, retinal disparity misrepresents objective depth, the outcomes of the two perceptual processes will be in disagreement and perceptual discrepancy results.

One might object to the concept of perceptual discrepancy on the ground that it is too far removed from facts, that it is concerned with the hypothetical outcome of hypothetical processes. This is true enough; as stated, the concept does not concern stimulation. Nor is it a matter of perceptual experience; as far as we know, a discrepancy is never experienced as such. The perceptual result is either experience being dominated by one of the competing processes—as seems to be true of our case in which stereoscopic vision dominates —or experience representing a compromise between the expected results of the two processes—Asch and Witkin's findings seem to

provide an example of this.[5] The concept is soundly based nevertheless, since our discrepancy is the normal outcome of clear-cut facts
of stimulation. With contradictory sets of sensory cues at the root of
the perceptual discrepancy, one might, in fact, speak of cue-discrepancy instead. We are perfectly happy with this formulation as long
as it remains clear that cue-discrepancy is defined here by the normal results of the ensuing perceptual processes and not in relation
to the physical object. That one set of cues represents the objective
situation correctly while the other does not is totally irrelevant,
unless a third set of cues that also mediates the objective situation
is given.

Since there are a number of perceptual properties that are dependent on more than one set of cues, cue-discrepancy may have
wide application in perceptual learning. It may, in many cases, replace current explanations of perceptual learning which ascribe an
essential role to motor activities. According to this view, the perceptual result of action would provide the information needed to make
perception more veridical. Needless to say, such feed-back is not
involved in the modification of stereoscopic depth, simply because
O remains inactive during the training period.

Relevance of the Results for the *KDE*

Our demonstration that the kinetic depth-effect *KDE* plays an essential role in the modification of stereoscopic depth-perception is of
importance also in connection with the *KDE* itself, for our experiment corroborates the older claim that only those rotating objects
will give rise to the *KDE* whose deforming retinal images have
edges that change simultaneously in length and orientation. To be
sure, this claim was originally supported by an experiment in which
these conditions *always* produced rotation in depth, whereas change
in length alone had this effect only in the case of one-third of the
*O*s; but a different kind of evidence is of great value. It is provided
by the result of our experiment in which the diagonal flag gave rise
to perceptual learning due to oscillation, while the vertical flag did
not. The two flags differed in that the projection of the former provided the stimulus-pattern claimed to be essential in producing a
KDE, while that of the vertical flag showed only changes in length.

[5] S. E. Asch and H. A. Witkin, Studies in space perception: II. Perception of the
upright with displaced visual field and body tilted. *Journal of Experimental Psychology,* 1948, 38, 455–477.

5. Adaptation in Distance Perception
Based on Oculomotor Cues

The experiments by Wallach and Floor (1971) showed that accommodation and convergence in conjunction operate as fairly adequate cues for shorter distances of objects from *S*. This made feasible an attempt to change through adaptation the relationship between these oculomotor adjustments and the distances they denote. The spectacles we used for this purpose changed accommodation and convergence by corresponding amounts at all object distances.[1] There were actually two spectacles that had opposite effects. One consisted of –1.5-diopter spherical lenses and 5-diopter prisms with bases in temporal position. They caused the eyes to accommodate 1.5 diopters more than the object distance would warrant and converge by an additional 5 prism diopters. These are oculomotor adjustments that corresponded to a shorter than the true object distance. Hence, these spectacles will be called "near glasses." The "far glasses" consisted of +1.5-diopter lenses and 5-diopter prisms with base nasal, and forced the eyes into adjustments equivalent to a larger object distance. Inasmuch as the change in accommodation and the change in convergence caused by such glasses are always equivalent,[2] all our considerations will be conducted in terms of the forced lens adjustments, implying a corresponding adjustment of convergence.

Written in collaboration with Karl Josef Frey. Reprinted from *Perception & Psychophysics*, 1972, 11, 77–83.

[1]Optical arrangements that changed accommodation and convergence in equivalent amounts were previously used by Leibowitz and Moore (1966).

[2]This is due to the fact that both accommodation and convergence are inversely proportional to viewing distance. Five prism diopters correspond to 1.5 lens diopters accurately only for *S*s whose interocular distance is 6.67 cm., approximately the mean of our *S* population.

Two facts about the effect of these glasses need to be kept in mind. They do not change oculomotor adjustment proportionately but additively. By causing the eyes to change adjustment to a given object distance by the equivalent of 1.5 lens diopters, they force an increase in accommodation and convergence corresponding to this diopter value in the case of the near glasses and an identical decrease in the case of the far glasses. An increase in accommodation and convergence corresponds to a shorter distance of the point on which the eyes are focused and converged, and a decrease corresponds to a larger object distance. Besides, there is the general fact about the diopter measure that the viewing distance that corresponds to a certain oculomotor adjustment is the reciprocal in meters of its lens diopter equivalent. Thus, the dioptric change caused by the glasses corresponds to vastly different changes in viewing distance, dependent on the distance of the object. For instance, normal oculomotor adjustment to a distance of 1 m. is equivalent to 1 lens diopter. With the near glasses in place, the adjustment amounts to 1.5 diopters more, i.e., 2.5 diopters, for the same object distance. An oculomotor adjustment amounting to 2.5 diopters, in turn, corresponds to a distance of 40 cm. An object at infinity, on the other hand, whose distance is equivalent to 0 diopters, will, through the glasses, be seen with an adjustment of 1.5 diopters, which corresponds to a distance of 66.7 cm.

Henceforth, we shall call a distance that corresponds to an oculomotor adjustment forced by our glasses "equivalent distance."[3] The near glasses do not only diminish the equivalent distances with which objects are viewed; they also contract the range of equivalent distances. Because the near glasses force the eyes to accommodate and converge an additional 1.5 lens diopters, oculomotor adjustment cannot be less than 1.5 diopters, and the largest equivalent distance possible is 66.7 cm. when objective distances comprise the entire range. Since the far glasses diminish oculomotor adjustments to all object distances by 1.5 diopters and increase the equivalent distance with which objects are viewed, they do not limit the range of equivalent distances, which thus can vary from infinity to the near point of accommodation. But they severely limit the object distances to which the eyes equipped with these far glasses can adjust. Since they

[3]This term was introduced by Leibowitz and Moore (1966).

force the eyes to look at objects with an adjustment that is 1.5 diopters less than their objective distance would warrant, an object 66.7
cm. distant will be viewed with an oculomotor adjustment for infinity. Thus, the largest possible object distance is 66.7 cm. This limits
the possible depth of space around an *S* wearing the far glasses to
66.7 cm.

What perceptual effects do such spectacles produce and what
effect of adaptation can be expected from wearing them? These
glasses alter the oculomotor adjustment with which objects are seen
and hence their distances insofar as these distances depend on
oculomotor adjustments. Among the several consequences of the
altered distances, the following is the most important: Where distance cues other than accommodation and convergence are largely
absent, the apparent sizes of objects should be altered, and this is
indeed the case. Seen through the far glasses, objects appear larger
than without them and through the near glasses, smaller. This is a
consequence of the rule of size perception, that perceived size depends on the size of the retinal image of the object and the cues that
are received for the object's distance. More accurately, perceived size
is equivalent to image size times registered distance (Emmert's law),
where registered distance is the representation of distance in the
nervous system, usually the result of the various distance cues available. Thus, the alteration of oculomotor adjustment caused by the
glasses amounts to an alteration of registered distance and a change
in perceived size results. An adaptation to our glasses would mean
that the relation between oculomotor adjustment and registered distance is so altered that the latter is in better agreement with object
distance. With adaptation complete, registered distance based on
oculomotor adjustment and hence size perception would become
veridical when the glasses are worn. Thus, some measurement involving size perception, once before and once after the adaptation
period, should measure the adaptation effect.[4]

[4]One would expect that the altered oculomotor adjustment caused by the glasses
would result in changed perceived distance, but such an effect is not clearly obtained.
An object seen through the far glasses, though it looks larger, will not also look farther
away. We ascribe this to an effect of perceived size on perceived distance. When it
is seen through the far glasses, an object's equivalent distance is larger than its true
distance, but the effect of this is counteracted by its increased perceived size. At any
rate, we concluded that perceived distance was not a good indicator of registered
distance and did not use estimates of distance to measure adaptation.

We measured adaptation with two such tests, both involving the role that registered distance plays in Emmert's law. In one of these tests, *S* gave estimates of the apparent length of the diagonal of luminous diamond shapes seen in the dark, by selecting and by adjusting the length of small metal rods using the sense of touch only (size estimation test). These estimates represented perceived size, which was thus the dependent variable in this test. The other test utilized the fact that certain objects occur in standard sizes only. A color slide of such objects was projected on a screen, and *S* was asked to adjust the size of the projected images until the size of the objects shown appeared normal to him (normal size adjustment test). In this test, a different use was made of Emmert's law. In the case of an object of standard size, the perceived size is fixed and, at the time of the test, supplied by memory. The size of the retinal image is here the dependent variable. Varying this image size (by changing the size of the projected image) until the size of the object appears normal therefore measures registered distance. If *S* adjusts the size of the image on the screen so that it is the true size of the object, registered distance agrees with the true distance of the screen. An adjustment of the projected image to smaller than normal means that registered distance is larger than the true distance, because a smaller size of the screen image and hence a smaller retinal image means, in the case of an object of normal size, that the object is farther.

The limitation of the equivalent distances inherent in the near glasses made it desirable to do the tests without them; the glasses were worn only during the period of adaptation. Thus, adaptation was not measured as a decrease in the change that viewing objects through the glasses causes, but as an error in natural vision. After adaptation to the near glasses, when registered distances were expected to be enlarged, estimated sizes would be, by Emmert's law, larger than they ordinarily are and adjustments to normal size, smaller, since adaptation to near glasses causes changes in the direction of those produced by wearing far glasses. For the far glasses, the opposite effects were expected. The mentioned limitations also prompted us to place the test displays at various distances from *S*. In the size estimation test, figures were presented at 25, 50, 100, and 200 cm. from *S*, and in the normal size adjustment test the screen distances were 25, 50, 100, and 150 cm. In the case of the near glasses, the two larger test distances were outside the range of equivalent distances possible when the glasses are worn, since then oculomotor adjustments of less than 1.5 diopters cannot occur. So the question arose as to whether an adaptation acquired with oculomotor adjustments of more that 1.5 diopters could manifest itself at distances corresponding to less than 1.5 diopters, that is, at the two larger of the four test distances. This question did not arise for the far glasses where the whole range of oculomotor adjustments could occur during adaptation.

Where adaptation is to a device that alters cues so that they misrepresent objective conditions, as is the case with our glasses, adaptation consists in a modification of the perceptual process evoked by these cues such that veridicality of perception is partly or completely restored. However, such a modification obviously can take place only when other cues are given that represent the true objective condition. In the case of the cues affected by our glasses, namely, oculomotor adjustment, there are several cues and conditions that can do this, such as perspective cues for distance, cues for distance produced by S's locomotion and his manipulations, and perhaps the image sizes of familiar objects. Since we wanted to obtain large adaptation effects, we tried to make as many of these cues available in the adaptation period as was feasible. Because of the limitation of object distances to 66.7 cm. required by the far glasses, two different conditions for adaptation were used in the case of the near glasses, one that was easily altered to conform to the limitations set by the far glasses (Condition A) and another one that promised optimal conditions for adaptation (Condition B). Since we aimed at as strong an adaptation effect as compatible with adaptation periods of feasible length, 15 min. for each, we gave S Condition A, tested for adaptation, and continued immediately with Adaptation Condition B, followed by another postadaptation test. In this fashion, the effect of Condition B was added to what adaptation was left at the end of the test for Condition A. In the case of the near glasses, two experimental sessions were run, one in which the normal size adjustment (NSA) test followed Condition A and the size estimation (SE) test followed Condition B, and another where the test order was reversed. The sequence of adaptation conditions was not varied. Only one experimental session was run with the far glasses. Here the NSA test always followed the first adaptation period and the SE test, the second.

Apparatus and Procedure

THE ADAPTATION PERIODS

Our spectacles consisted of one meniscus lens for each eye, ground to provide both the spherical lens action of ±1.5 diopters and the prism action of 5 diopters. The lenses were 49 mm. in diameter and fitted into welder's goggles where they replaced the glass filters. There was room inside the goggles to accommodate ordinary eyeglasses, and Ss who needed minor corrections could thus participate in our experiments. We only excluded Ss who wore strong corrective glasses.

The adaptation periods for the near glasses were as follows: In Condition A, S sat at a table covered by a white cardboard panel, on a stool 51 cm. high. His task was to move by hand or with a small rake 10 differently shaped wooden blocks back and forth across the table. To make this task a bit more interesting, one or another panel marked with the 10 outlines of the bases of these blocks covered the table and S had to fit each block into the outline of its base. In Condition B, S walked for 15 min. a long, narrow hallway that provided clear perspective depth cues. Four stands on which white cardboard squares, 30 cm. large and mounted approximately at eye level, were evenly spaced along the path of S, who would naturally look at each square as he approached it. E accompanied S on this walk.

In the case of the far glasses, Condition A was as described above, except for the discussed spatial limitations. A large cardboard box of cubic shape and 80 cm. in size was placed on the table so that its far wall was 60 cm. from the edge at which S sat. This enclosure, the inside of which was papered with richly patterned material, was so placed around S that his view was in all directions restricted by walls whose distance nowhere exceeded 65 cm. In Condition B, S sat in the same enclosure and worked for 15 min. on wooden block puzzles.

THE SIZE ESTIMATION TEST

As mentioned, the diamond-shaped test objects were presented at four distances. Their sizes were chosen so that they produced identical retinal images. At the distances of 25, 50, 100, and 200 cm. their diagonals were 3, 6, 12, and 24 cm., respectively, when adaptation was to the near glasses. In that case, an increase in the apparent size was expected after the adaptation period. Because adaptation to the far glasses would manifest itself in a decrease in apparent size, larger test objects were used; they measured 6, 12, 24, and 48 cm. along the diagonal. A lightbox on wheels and movable on a track was used to present the various test objects by means of a diamond-shaped aperture of variable size (Aubert diaphragm) over a milk-glass face. To allow *S* to move his head during the lengthy test period, we assured the proper location of *S*'s head while the test object was visible in the following manner: *S* wore a headgear that could be attached to a vertical shaft which turned in a bearing mounted above *S*'s seat. When *S*'s head was so positioned that its median plane was intersecting the center of the test object, the shaft was held in position by a stop and simultaneously operated a microswitch that caused the test object to light up; when the head was in any other position, the test object was not visible. This arrangement prevented movement parallax from operating as a distance cue.

Black drapes on either side of the track and a screen in front of the lightbox prevented *S* from seeing any part of the test arrangement while the room was lit. Only after *S*'s head was attached to the shaft and the room had been darkened was the screen lowered to the point where *S* could see the whole diamond shape, but none of the light reflected by the tracks beneath it. In short, all known distance cues other than accommodation and convergence were eliminated from the test conditions. Had any been operating, they would have provided veridical information about the distances of the test objects and would have counteracted the adaptation effect in the postadaptation test.

There were 12 metal rods which *S* used to give his size estimate. Each one could be extended so that its length was nearly doubled or quadrupled. They measured from 1.5 to 12.7 cm. in their unextended state. Size estimates using only the sense of touch were required, because had the rods been visible the changed size perception caused by adaptation would also have affected the apparent size of the rods in the postadaptation tests. Single estimates were given for each of the four test diamonds at the four test distances, one before and the other after the adaptation period, with the order of presentation varied from *S* to *S*. For a given *S*, the test order was the same in the pre- and postadaptation tests.

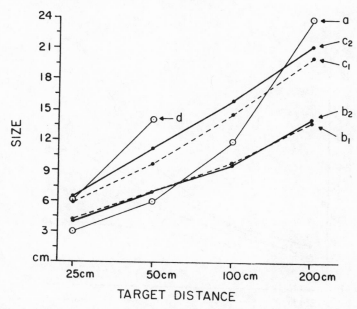

Fig. 1. Mean size estimates made before and after adaptation to near glasses. Curve a represents the objective target sizes. In Curves b_1 and b_2 the means of the preadaptation size estimates made in two experiments are given. Curve c_1 shows the mean size estimates after 15 min. of adaptation and Curve c_2 after 30 min. of adaptation. Curve d gives the sizes predicted for complete adaptation, based on preadaptation size estimates taken at the distances representing complete adaptation.

Since, in the tests, only accommodation and convergence were available as distance cues, the preadaptation size estimates fall considerably short of constancy. A comparison of Curve b, representing preadaptation size estimates, with Curve a, representing object sizes in Figure 1 or Figure 2, shows how greatly the sizes of the more distant test objects were underestimated. This fact becomes important when we want to compare the adaptation effects that were actually obtained with the size estimates to be obtained under the assumption that adaptation was complete. The theoretical distance of a test object under the assumption of complete adaptation is easily computed. The near glasses, for instance, force the eyes into an oculomotor adjustment that is 1.5 lens diopters greater than the object distance would require. Complete adaptation to this condition involves compensation for the whole amount by which the equivalent distance is shorter than the true object distances and means that the registered distance that corresponds to such an oculomotor ad-

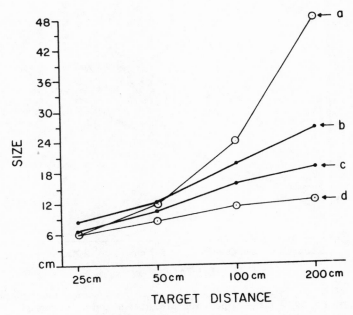

Fig. 2. Mean size estimates made before and after adaptation to far glasses. Curve a represents the objective target sizes. In Curve b the means of the preadaptation size estimates are given. Curve c shows the mean size estimates after 30 min. of adaptation. Curve d gives the sizes predicted for complete adaptation, based on preadaptation size estimates taken at the distances representing complete adaptation.

justment is larger by the equivalent of 1.5 diopters than it would normally be. Thus, to compute the theoretical adaptation distance that corresponds to a given test distance, we subtract 1.5 diopters from the diopter equivalent of that test distance and reconvert the result into distance. While the theoretical distance corresponding to complete adaptation is thus easily derived, a theoretical postadaptation size estimate expected to result from the theoretical adaptation distance must be empirically determined. We therefore obtained, prior to adaptation, size estimates at the theoretical adaptation distances that correspond to our test distances. This we did immediately after the preadaptation size estimates at the four normal test distances had been obtained. In the case of the far glasses, the theoretical adaptation distances were 18.2, 28.6, 40, and 50 cm. for the test distances of 25, 50, 100, and 200 cm., respectively. In the case of the near glasses, only two of the theoretical adaptation distances were meaningful, namely, 40 cm. for the test distance of 25 cm. and 200 cm. for the distance of 50 cm. For the larger test distances, theoretical adaptation distances were at infinity. Curves d in Figures 1 and 2 give the size estimates produced at the theoretical adaptation distances. The estimates are represented in the graphs not at the distances at which they were actually measured, but at the main test distances to which they refer.

The Normal Size Adjustment Test

A color slide was made of five standard-sized objects: a 12-in. ruler, a BIC pen, a dollar bill, a matchbook, and a wrapped piece of chewing gum. A Kodak Carousel 800 projector equipped with a 3-in. lens projected it from the rear on a translucent plastic screen, 70 cm. wide and 60 cm. high. Projector and screen were mounted on separate four-wheel carriages, both of which rode on a 4-m.-long track. At one end of the track, an adjustable chinrest and a horizontal bar above it, against which S leaned his forehead, located S's eyes at the height of the projector lens and thus of the center of the slide image. The size of the projected image could be varied by changing the distance between the projector and the screen. A black metal disk with a concentric opening 25 mm. in diameter was fitted into the front end of the projector lens to insure a sharp image at all projection distances. S controlled the size of the projected image by turning a crank which, by means of a looped cord and a system of pulleys, caused the projector carriage to move toward or away from the screen. Every effort was made to eliminate all distance cues other than oculomotor adjustments from the test conditions. There was one flaw: internal reflections in the projector lens produced a faint glow on the whole screen which, thus, became an object of fixed size at all test distances.

For each screen distance, S made two normal size adjustments, one where E had placed the projector so that the size of the image on the screen was clearly too large, while for the other the initial image size was made to look too small. The average of these two settings, whose order was randomized, constituted an individual score. Again, the order of the four screen distances was varied from S to S. For a given S, the same order was used in the pre- and postadaptation adjustment, and it was identical with the order employed in the *SE* test.

SUBJECTS

The same *S*s were used in all three experiments, the two versions of adaptation to the near glasses and one concerned with adaptation to the far glasses. The time interval between two experiments was at least 3 weeks, and adaptation to the far glasses preceded the second near-glasses version. *S*s, paid undergraduates, were selected for good distance perception based on oculomotor adjustment. To be employed, an *S* had to give, in the preadaptation *SE* test, four size estimates that increased with increasing size of the diamond shape, and in the first *NSA* test the adjustment produced for the 150-cm. screen distance could not exceed the true size of the objects by a factor larger than 1.5. To select our 24 *S*s, a total of 48 had to be given the preadaptation tests.

Results

Large and highly significant adaptation effects were obtained with these selected *S*s. In the case of the *SE* test, which yielded the strongest effects, not a single postadaptation score failed to differ from the corresponding preadaptation score in the direction of adaptation, and the same was true of the *NSA* test results for the near glasses—a total of 432 individual scores.

THE SIZE ESTIMATION TEST

Results of the near glasses. It will be remembered that adaptation to the near glasses was twice performed with the same group of 24 *S*s. In one experiment the *SE* test followed Adaptation Condition A, which always preceded Condition B, and in the other it followed Condition B. The *SE* results for both experiments are presented in Table 1. Since the two experiments were done some time apart, the preadaptation estimates were taken twice also. The close agreement between the means of the two sets of scores presented in Lines 3A and 3B demonstrates the repeatability of these measurements. The

TABLE 1

Adaptation to Near Glasses With 15 Min. of Block Moving (A) and With
15 Min. of Block Moving Plus 15 Min. of Walking (B) Measured
(in Centimeters) With the Size Estimation Test. N = 24

			25	50	100	200
1	Test distance		25	50	100	200
2	Target size		3	6	12	24
3	Preadaptation size estimate	A	4.19	6.98	9.92	13.98
		B	4.14	7.00	9.65	14.30
4	Postadaptation size estimate	A	5.91	9.82	14.70	20.30
		B	6.45	11.28	16.01	21.46
5	Difference between pre- and postadaptation size estimates	A	1.72	2.84	4.78	6.32
		B	2.31	4.28	6.36	7.16
6	Adaptation effect as size increase	A	41.81%	41.24%	47.63%	43.15%
		B	58.07%	61.79%	65.34%	50.62%

difference between the preadaptation and the postadaptation size
estimates (Line 5) represents, of course, the adaptation effect. The
means of these difference scores are given as percent size increase in
Line 6.

The means given in Line 5 of Table 1 show that the differences
between the pre- and postadaptation size estimates increased with
greater test distances. But this was merely due to the fact that the
objective sizes of the test diamond increased in proportion to the test
distance. Expressed as proportional size increase (Line 6), the effect
of adaptation on size was approximately the same for all distances.
Analyses of variance on the means of Lines 6A and 6B yielded no
significance as a function of the distance of the test object ($F = .41$
and $F = 1.38$, respectively). There was a difference in the mean effects
on size provided by Condition A and Condition B (compare Lines 6A
and 6B), with the latter yielding a significantly larger adaptation
effect ($F = 15.38$; $p < .005$). Our data provide no means for determining whether the larger effect measured after Condition B was due to
the greater effectiveness of Adaptation Condition B as such or due to
a cumulative effect of the two adaptation periods.

That an effect of adaptation was measured at the two larger test
distances represents a transfer of adaptation to oculomotor adjustments that never occurred during the wearing of the near glasses.
But the fact that the adaptation effects expressed as proportional size
increases are approximately the same at all test distances does not

necessarily mean that this transfer of the adaptation effect to the "unpracticed" oculomotor adjustments was complete. Inasmuch as our glasses force the eyes to change oculomotor adjustments by the equivalent of 1.5 diopters at all object distances (while the changes in distance that correspond to these changes in oculomotor adjustment vary widely with object distance), it seems plausible that adaptation, that is, the change of the registered distance that belongs to a given oculomotor adjustment, should also be of constant diopter value at all object distances. To find out whether this was the case, we transformed the size changes due to adaptation into their diopter equivalents. The size changes were transformed into distance changes by a method that took the underestimation of the sizes of the more distant test objects into account.[5] The diopter equivalents of these distance changes were found to decrease strongly with increasing test distances. At the test distances of 25, 50, 100, and 200 cm., the dioptric changes for Condition A amounted to 1.44, 1.00, .53, and .30, respectively. To be sure, adaptation effects larger than 1 and .5 diopters cannot be expected for the test distances of 100 and 200 cm., respectively, because such changes would correspond to objects at infinity. But the obtained values of .53 and .30 diopters are considerably smaller than these limitations, and a diminished transfer of the adaptation effect to oculomotor adjustments that did not occur during the adaptation period is a possibility.

Results for the far glasses. These results are listed in Table 2, whose arrangement is identical with Table 1.[6] Here the *SE* test was given only once, at the end of the second adaptation period. A comparison of Line 6 in Table 2 with Line 6B in Table 1 shows that the proportional size changes due to adaptation to the far glasses—here the changes were, of course, decreases—were not as homogeneous as those to the near glasses; the effect at the 50-cm. test distance was, in fact, significantly smaller than that at the 200-cm. distance. On the whole, the size effects obtained with the far glasses were signifi-

[5]We derived the registered distances that corresponded to the postadaptation size estimates from a curve where the preadaptation size estimates were plotted against test object distances. The values of the postadaptation size estimates were found on this curve, and the corresponding distance values were read.

[6]While in Table 1, Line 6, the adaptation effect on size is given as the ratio of mean postadaptation estimate over mean preadaptation estimate minus one, Line 6 in Table 2 gives mean preadaptation over mean postadaptation estimate minus one.

TABLE 2
Adaptation to Far Glasses With 15 Min. of Block Moving and 15 Min. of
Doing Wooden Puzzles Measured (in Centimeters) With the
Size Estimation Test. (N = 12)

1	Test distance	25	50	100	200
2	Target size	6	12	24	48
3	Preadaptation size estimate	8.43	12.39	19.71	26.51
4	Postadaptation size estimate	6.73	10.43	15.77	18.80
5	Difference between pre- and postadaptation size estimates	1.70	1.96	3.94	7.71
6	Adaptation effect as size decrease	27.11%	18.70%	27.44%	40.43%

cantly smaller than those due to the near glasses ($F = 22.67$; $p < .005$), but this result is probably immaterial. It can be ascribed to the fact that in the case of the far glasses adaptation caused registered distances to be diminished rather than enlarged, and identical dioptric changes would be expected to correspond to smaller distance and hence size changes.

The Normal Size Adjustment Test

The results for the *NSA* tests are presented in Tables 3 and 4. Here the mean pre- and postadaptation scores (Lines 2 and 3) are given as ratios of the size adjustments that *S* had made over the true sizes of the objects represented, multiplied by 100. Thus, a 100% entry would mean that *S* had succeeded in adjusting the image size on the screen to the true size of the object. As the preadaptation values in Line 2 show, surprisingly accurate adjustment means were obtained at all four test distances. In the case of near glasses (Table 3) the postadaptation adjustments are diminished in size, and this is in agreement with an increase in registered distance which adaptation to these glasses consists in. Under the assumption of complete constancy, the product of a retinal image size and registered distance is, for an object of standard size, a constant. Hence, when the registered distance increases as it should, the retinal image size should decrease. Since the objective distance of the screen remains unaltered, the size of the screen image must be made smaller to produce a smaller retinal image.

TABLE 3

Adaptation to Near Glasses With 15 Min. of Block Moving (A) and With 15 Min. of
Block Moving Plus 15 Min. of Walking (B) Measured With the
Normal Size Adjustment Test. N = 24

			25 cm.	50 cm.	100 cm.	150 cm.
1	Screen distance		25 cm.	50 cm.	100 cm.	150 cm.
2	Preadaptation normal size adjust-	A	98.40%	100.92%	102.71%	111.09%
	ment in percent of true normal size	B	93.90%	96.89%	99.98%	104.63%
3	Postadaptation normal size adjust-	A	88.62%	87.93%	84.31%	91.63%
	ment in percent of true normal size	B	83.88%	79.94%	76.08%	81.20%
4	Mean ratio of preadaptation score	A	1.1128	1.1537	1.2229	1.2239
	over postadaptation score	B	1.1220	1.2202	1.3351	1.3075
5	Adaptation effect	A	11.28%	15.37%	22.29%	22.39%
	as size decrease	B	12.20%	22.02%	33.51%	30.75%

In Line 4, the mean ratios of preadaptation adjustments over postadaptation adjustments are given, and in Line 5, the mean adaptation effects are listed as percentage size decreases; the latter, then, corresponds to Line 6 in Table 1. As was the case with the results obtained with the *SE* test, the size changes were significantly greater for Condition B than for Condition A (F = 18.79; p < .005). But the results differed from those of the *SE* test in that the size changes increased significantly with test distance (F = 18.99 and 32.54; p < .005 for each).

The results for the far glasses are presented in Table 4. Here adaptation provided an increase in size adjustments because it caused smaller registered distances, which, according to Emmert's law, require larger image sizes on the retina and on the screen in order to produce the same (normal) perceived sizes. Though small, the adaptation effects were quite significant. They serve to demonstrate that significant adaptation effects in both directions can be obtained with the *NSA* test also.

THE DIFFERENCE BETWEEN THE SE TEST AND THE
NSA TEST RESULTS

A comparison of Table 1 with Table 3 shows a striking difference in the amount of adaptation measured with the two tests. The size effects measured with the *SE* test were about 2.7 times larger. This difference was highly significant for both conditions, A and B (F = 54.8 and 44.3). When each test distance was separately considered,

TABLE 4
Adaptation to Far Glasses With 15 Min. of Block Moving Measured With the
Normal Size Adjustment Test. N = 12

1	Screen distance	25 cm.	50 cm.	100 cm.	150 cm.
2	Preadaptation normal size adjustment in percent of true normal size	93.20%	93.23%	97.34%	97.74%
3	Postadaptation normal size adjustment in percent of true normal size	96.21%	98.31%	103.33%	104.61%
4	Mean ratio of preadaptation score over postadaptation score	1.0323	1.0516	1.0592	1.0683
5	Adaptation effect as size increase	3.23%	5.16%	5.92%	6.83%

Duncan's new multiple range test showed that each difference between the two tests was significant at the .005 level.

This was, however, not the only difference between the results of the two tests. The means of the preadaptation scores obtained with the *NSA* test (Table 3, Line 2) show much better size constancy than those of the SE test (Table 1, Line 3). When the means for the 25-cm. and the 100-cm. test distances were compared and constancy quotients were formed for the two types of tests, a quotient of .6 was found for the *SE* test and one of .96 for the *NSA* test, where a quotient of 1.0 would stand for complete constancy. We ascribe this much more correct size perception in the *NSA* test partly to the fact that the images of the objects on the screen provide fine lines, absent in the test diamonds, that serve as more distinct marks for accommodation and convergence. We demonstrated this fact by collecting size estimates using the *SE* test method and the projection equipment of the *NSA* test for two kinds of test objects: (1) the projected images of a dollar bill, one 25% smaller and the other 25% larger than normal, or (2) the projections of a luminous diamond duplicating the bill's image sizes. Two screen distances, 75 and 150 cm. were used. Averaged over the two sizes, mean size estimates at these distances ran 12.6% and 21.1% larger for the bill images than for the diamonds ($p < .01$). Moreover, the loss in constancy from the 75-cm. distance to the 150-cm. distance was significantly larger for the diamond than for the bill ($p < .01$).

The other fact accounting for the better size perception in the *NSA* test is the presence of extraneous distance cues, probably provided by the faint glow on the screen mentioned above. We demonstrated the effect of extraneous distance cues in the *NSA* setup by obtaining size estimates and normal size adjustments under three viewing conditions: without glasses, with near glasses, and with far glasses. The test distances under these three conditions were so chosen that the test distances where no glasses were worn were the same as the equivalent test distances based upon the action of the spectacles. We selected two actual test distances, 33.3 cm. and 66.7 cm., because they were 1.5 diopters apart. Therefore, a test display 66.7 cm. distant would be seen through the near glasses with an oculomotor adjustment for 33.3 cm. distance, while a display actually 33.3 cm. away and seen through the far glasses would be at an equivalent distance of 66.7 cm. By comparing size estimates and size adjustments made under these two conditions with measurements taken without glasses at these display distances, the effectiveness of the glasses could be assessed. Since extraneous distance cues are veridical and thus interfere with the effect of the glasses, which, of course, alter only oculomotor cues, their presence would cause registered distances to deviate from equivalent distances, and size judgments obtained with and without glasses at equivalent and actual distances should reflect this. If, on the other hand, only oculomotor cues were present in the test situation, then the results of tests taken with the glasses should be predictable from tests without glasses, where the actual distances of the displays were the same as the equivalent distances with glasses. This prediction is simple in the case of the *SE* test because, as before, we chose the sizes of the test objects so that they produced equal retinal images: 6 cm. for the diamond at 33.3 cm. and 12 cm. for the one 66.7 cm. distant. Agreement of registered distance with equivalent distance should therefore cause identical size estimates where equivalent distance and actual distance are the same. As *SE* test data in Table 5, Lines 1 and 2, show, this was true of the two mean estimates obtained at the 33.3-cm. distance and nearly so for those at the 66.7-cm. distance. (The small difference between the mean estimates listed for this distance was not significant.) It is obvious that we had succeeded in excluding extraneous distance cues from the *SE* test conditions.

In the case of the *NSA* test, the assumption of an agreement of registered distance with equivalent distance leads to a different prediction about the measured sizes. For a pair of distances, one equivalent and the other actual, this assumption predicts normal size

TABLE 5
Mean Size Estimates and Mean Size Adjustments Made
With and Without Glasses Compared

Actual and Equivalent Distances at	Size Estimation		Normal Size Adjustment	
	33.3 cm.	66.7 cm.	33.3 cm.	66.7 cm.
1 Actual	8.02	12.76	.9548	.9917
2 Equivalent	8.03	12.17	1.5607	.5959
3 Corrected Equivalent			.7804	1.1918
4 Ratio	1.0	1.048	1.223	1.202

adjustments that correspond to equal retinal image sizes. But since for such a pair the screen distances are different, corrections have to be made in the means of the adjusted sizes to make them comparable. In the case of the pair concerned with the far glasses, the adjustment without the glasses was made with a screen distance of 66.7 cm., while the equivalent distance was produced by a screen image at 33.3 cm. seen through the glasses. A normal size adjustment made at the latter distance would have to be half as large as one made at the equivalent distance of 66.7 cm. in order for the two to produce the same retinal image size. To correct for this, a measured size adjustment made with the far glasses had to be doubled before it was compared with a size adjustment made at the actual distance. In the case of the near glasses, the actual distance was 33.3 cm., and the equivalent distance was produced when the glasses were worn and the screen distance was 66.7 cm. A normal size adjustment made under the latter condition, then, had to be halved to be comparable with one made at the actual distance of 33.3 cm. The mean size adjustment ratios obtained under the actual and equivalent conditions are given also in Lines 1 and 2 of Table 5, and the corrected values for the equivalent condition in Line 3. A comparison between the values in Lines 1 and 3 shows a considerable discrepancy, significant at the .01 level of confidence, for the near glasses as well as for the far glasses. To obtain percentage values for this discrepancy, ratios were formed between the two mean normal size adjustments obtained at each pair of test distances (using the correction) in such a manner that the influence of extraneous distance cues caused them to be larger than one (Line 4). These ratios show that adjustments made with glasses deviate on the average by 20% or more from the adjustments made without glasses at the corresponding distances.

This is a considerable effect and, together with the effect of the more distinct marks present in the *NSA* test display earlier reported, accounts for the much more correct size perception under the conditions of the *NSA* test.

Discussion

The presence of extraneous distance cues, in turn, furnishes an explanation for the smaller adaptation effects measured with the *NSA* test. Because extraneous distance cues are veridical, they would be in conflict with the altered registered distances based on oculomotor cues and caused by adaptation. The extraneous cues could, therefore, be expected to inhibit the manifestation of the adaptive modification that the processes connected with oculomotor adjustment had undergone. The presence of extraneous distance cues made the *NSA* test a less valuable tool in the investigation of our adaptation, but it provided us with an interesting result of a different kind: Our adaptation can become manifest in the presence of extraneous and, hence, conflicting distance cues.

Throughout this presentation, one basic assumption has not been questioned, namely, that changes in perceived size due to adaptation result from changes in registered distance. While this assumption is plausible, it need be specifically tested. Experiments to do this have by now been completed and have confirmed this assumption. They will be reported in connection with an investigation where the nature of the veridical distance cues present in the adaptation conditions was systematically varied.

References

Leibowitz, H., & Moore, D. Role of changes in accommodation and convergence in the perception of size. *Journal of the Optical Society of America,* 1966, 56, 1120–1123.

Wallach, H., & Floor, L. The use of size matching to demonstrate the effectiveness of accommodation and convergence as cues for distance. *Perception & Psychophysics,* 1971, 10, 423–428. In the present volume, Chapter IV.

6. The Nature of Adaptation in Distance Perception Based on Oculomotor Cues

The experiments here reported answer two questions raised by previous work on adaptation in distance perception based on accommodation and convergence. Such adaptation was presumably demonstrated by Wallach and Frey (1972) by means of changes in size perception. Size estimates of abstract shapes served as tests for such changes, as did adjustments of the images of familiar objects to their true sizes, with either kind of test performed under conditions where accommodation and convergence were the only available cues for distance. Ss were given these tests before and after an adaptation period during which glasses were worn that caused an alteration of the accommodation and convergence with which objects were viewed. Adaptation to glasses that increased accommodation and convergence resulted in an increase in perceived size, and a decrease in these oculomotor adjustments during the adaptation period caused a size decrease later on. One of the issues yet to be dealt with concerns the interpretation given by Wallach and Frey to these changes in size perception. They assumed that the size changes were manifestations of changes in distance perception. The other issue is concerned with the conditions under which adaptation to such glasses can be obtained. The conditions employed by Wallach and Frey involved an active S, namely, his locomotion or his manipulation of objects. In the present work, in Experiments 4 and 5, an attempt was made to produce adaptation under conditions where S remained immobile during the adaptation period.

Written in collaboration with Karl Josef Frey and Katharine Anne Bode. Reprinted from *Perception & Psychophysics*, 1972, 11, 110–116.

A. Size Changes as Manifestations of Changes in Distance Perception

Wallach and Frey adapted Ss to eyeglasses that altered, in corresponding fashion, the accommodation and convergence with which objects were viewed. One pair of spectacles consisted of meniscus lenses that were at once prisms of 5 diopters placed with their bases in temporal position and spherical lenses of —1.5 diopters. The lens action forced the eyes to increase accommodation by 1.5 diopters at all viewing distances, and the effect of the prismatic lens component was to increase convergence by an equivalent amount. These spectacles thus caused oculomotor adjustments that corresponded to distances shorter than the true object distances by the equivalent of 1.5 lens diopters (near glasses). A second pair of spectacles (far glasses), forcing oculomotor change of the same amount but in opposite direction, were also used.[1]

The immediate effect of these glasses was to change the apparent size of the object seen through them. Under conditions where distance cues other than accommodation and convergence were largely absent, the near glasses made objects look smaller. This was due to the operation of Emmert's law, according to which the perceived size of an object is equivalent to the size of its retinal image times its registered distance. The latter is the representation of object distance in the nervous system, usually the result of the available distance cues. Since accommodation and convergence can serve as cues to distance of the viewed objects, a change in these oculomotor adjustments will have an effect on registered distance. The near glasses, for instance, caused an increase in accommodation and convergence, which meant, of course, a decrease in the distances these oculomotor adjustments implied. Hence, to the degree to which they depended on accommodation and convergence, the registered distances also decreased. This, in turn, caused perceived size to diminish.

Adaptation, consisting in a compensation for the error produced by the spectacles and causing perception to change back toward

[1]For a more detailed description of the effects of the two pairs of glasses, see Wallach and Frey (1972).

normal, would tend to do away with the loss in size that the near glasses initially produced. As long as the adaptation effect lasts, accommodation and convergence would cause larger apparent sizes than they would normally produce, and this is what Wallach and Frey found. After adaptation to the near glasses, estimates of object sizes were 50%–60% larger than before. The far glasses, by forcing the eyes to decrease accommodation by 1.5 lens diopters and to change convergence by an equivalent amount, caused oculomotor adjustments to correspond to distances that were larger than the object distance by the equivalent of 1.5 lens diopters. This, in turn, caused perceived sizes to increase. Adaptation to the far glasses, then, consisted in a decrease of perceived size.

Two interpretations of such effects of adaptation on perceived size are possible. Wallach and Frey believed that, in essence, adaptation consisted in an altered relation between oculomotor adjustments and registered distance. While normally a particular oculomotor adjustment, serving as cue to distance, produced one value of registered distance, after adaptation it produced another value, resulting in turn in an alteration of perceived size. This interpretation is an analogue to the manner in which the glasses affect perceived size when they are initially worn, that is, through the operation of Emmert's law. The other interpretation assumes a direct compensation for the error in size perception produced by the glasses. When, e.g., the near glasses are first worn, perceived sizes are abnormally small. Adaptation, in tending to reestablish veridical perception, causes a compensating change in size perception: perceived sizes become more veridical as the glasses are worn, that is, larger than normal; this is the effect measured by Wallach and Frey.

We resolved this issue by obtaining evidence in favor of the interpretation by Wallach and Frey. If the change in registered distance they postulated could be shown to have manifestations other than in size perception, it would be established as the primary result of adaptation, and this we were able to do. The two further manifestations of changes in registered distance we demonstrated were (1) adaptation in stereoscopic depth perception and (2) an effect of adaptation on the representations of distances by a body movement.

Experiment 1. Simultaneous Adaptation in Size and Stereoscopic Depth Perception

There is a striking analogy between stereoscopic depth perception and size perception. Just as the size of the retinal image varies with the distance of the object that causes it, so retinal disparity, the condition of stimulation that produces perceived stereoscopic depth, depends on the distance from the eyes of the depth interval that causes the disparity. There is one difference: the size of the retinal image is inversely proportional to the first power of object distance, while the amount of disparity caused is inversely proportional to the square of the distance of the depth interval from the eyes.[2] Just as in the case of size, perception compensates for the decrease in retinal disparity with viewing distance: Perceived depth is roughly equivalent to the given retinal disparity times the viewing distance squared. Wallach and Zuckerman (1963) have demonstrated this in a number of ways and have shown that, just as in size perception, different kinds of cues for distance may represent the objective distance of the depth interval. They thus established the existence of a constancy of stereoscopic depth that corresponds to the constancy of size and is probably based on the same information about distance as is size constancy. To be sure, compensation for the decrease in retinal disparity with increasing distance of the corresponding depth interval is by no means as accurate as the compensation for the decrease in image size with increasing object distance that causes size constancy, and individual differences are large.[3] But there can be no doubt that compensation for the decrease in disparity is much larger than merely proportional to the first power of distance, and this fact has several easily observed consequences. One occurs in connection with displays, such as three-dimensional motion pictures that present the viewer with a left-eye picture and a right-eye picture of a three-dimensional scene. Here, apparent depth increases

[2]Geometrical proof for these relations may be found in Stevens (1951) p. 888, an explanation in Wallach and Zuckerman (1963).

[3]The relation between the perceived depth that results from disparity and the distance of the corresponding depth interval from the eyes was discussed by Foley (1967a), who also referred to previous work concerned with this relation. It seems possible that the differences between Foley's results (see also Foley, 1967b) and those obtained by Wallach and Zuckerman are related to the amount of disparity employed, small disparities by Wallach and Zuckerman and larger ones by Foley.

with the viewer's distance from the display.[4] Similarly, in demonstrations of the Pulfrich effect by means of depth perception, the apparent depth observed increases with increased distance of S from the display.[5] Finally, anyone who observes a loss in depth when viewing a scene through binoculars is witness to the fact that compensation for loss of disparity with increase in distance is greater than proportional.[6]

If adaptation to our glasses produces a change in size perception because it alters the relation between accommodation and convergence on the one hand and registered distance on the other, it may also have an effect on stereoscopic depth perception. But in that case, the effect of our adaptation on depth perception should be larger than its effect on size perception. This is so because, according to Emmert's law, perceived size depends on the first power of registered distance, whereas, according to the rule stated above (Zuckerman's law), perceived depth should be equivalent to the square of objective distance as represented by distance cues. Unlike the increase in perceived size due to adaptation to the near glasses, which is proportional to the increase in registered distance that results from its changed relation to accommodation and convergence, perceived depth should increase by an amount in keeping with Zuckerman's law. This means that adaptation to our glasses should produce a larger effect on perceived stereoscopic depth than on size. Such a result would favor the interpretation of Wallach and Frey that adaptation to our glasses consists in the first place in an alteration of registered distance. Registered distance, in turn, would affect both perceived size and depth.

[4]Whereas perceived depth is larger than proportional to registered distance, disparity in such stereoscopic displays is inversely proportional to the first power only of S's distance from the display. Compensation for distance is therefore in excess of disparity loss with distance. Hence perceived depth increases with increased distance from the display, ideally in proportion to distance but actually somewhat less.

[5]When a pendulum, moving in a frontal plane of S, is binocularly observed and a filter dark enough to delay neural transmission is placed over one eye, the pendulum bob appears to move on an elliptical path. With other conditions remaining the same, the apparent depth of the path will increase with increased distance of S from the pendulum. The explanation is similar to that for the analogous effect observed with stereoscopic displays (Note 4).

[6]For an explanation in terms of the constancy of stereoscopic depth of this effect of binocular optical magnification, see Wallach and Zuckerman (1963).

PROCEDURE

We demonstrated an effect of adaptation to near glasses on depth perception that was larger than the corresponding effect on size perception by obtaining size and depth estimates before and after the same adaptation period. As in the size estimation test used by Wallach and Frey, *S*s gave size and depth estimates using the sense of touch only and under conditions where only accommodation and convergence operated as distance cues. Test objects were two regular four-sided wire pyramids, their bases placed in *S*'s frontal parallel plane and their apexes pointing away from *S*. Size estimates were given by reproducing the length of one of the diagonals of the base with one of a series of small brass rods which *S* could select and whose length could be adjusted by him, and depth estimates were made by reproducing in the same manner the apparent distance between base and apex. Pyramids were presented at only two distances from *S*, one of the reasons being that in the present experiments two estimates were given for every test object, one of size and the other of depth. The two distances were 33.3 and 66.7 cm. They were chosen because they fell, in terms of the diopter scale, in the middle, between the 25- and 50-cm. distances and the 50- and 100-cm. distances, respectively, which had been used by Wallach and Frey, and because the difference between the 33.3-cm. and the 66.7-cm. distance was equivalent to 1.5 lens diopters. Inasmuch as, according to our hypothesis, complete adaptation would involve a change in registered distance amounting to 1.5 diopters, preadaptation estimates made at a 66.7-cm. distance could serve as norms for the effects of complete adaptation on a test object at 33.3 cm. distance. This was possible because the size of the bases of our pyramids were so chosen that they produced equal retinal images, although they were placed at different distances from *S*. Also, the distances between apex and base of the two pyramids were such that they produced equal retinal disparities. To achieve this, the pyramid that was twice as far from *S* had to be four times as deep as the nearer pyramid. Then, if complete adaptation to the near glasses were achieved, with accommodation and convergence evaluated by the nervous system as 1.5 diopters less than normal, the perceived size and depth of the pyramid at 33.3 cm. should be the same as the size and depth measured prior to adaptation for our properly transposed pyramid at 66.7 cm. distance.

Specifically, the diagonals of the square pyramid bases measured 5.5 and 11.0 cm., and the distances between apex and base amounted to 2.5 and 10 cm., respectively. The diagonals of the bases, which, incidentally, were in the diamond position, were represented by thin wires. This was done because Wallach and Frey had found that the presence in test objects of thin lines improved size perception when only accommodation and convergence served as cues for distance. The thickness of the wires of which the pyramids were made was also properly transposed. These wires were 1/16 and 1/8 in. in diameter, and the thickness of the diagonal wires was .3 and .6 mm., respectively.

The pyramids were placed inside wooden lightboxes whose black front panels measured 18 X 18 in. A diamond-shaped aperture was cut in the center of each panel and framed the pyramid's base, which was centered in the aperture and whose sides were parallel to its edges. These apertures measured 2.5 and 5 in. square, respectively. Beyond the apex inside each box was a translucent white plastic sheet that evenly diffused the dim light of four 7.5-W bulbs lit by a 40-V current and located in the rear of the box. Against this bright background, the wires comprising the pyramid appeared clearly outlined. The purpose of the box was to prevent the light needed to make the pyramid visible from illuminating the rest of *S*'s field of vision. Black cloth drapes were used to block excess light escaping from the apertures. The boxes were placed one behind the other on a platform that brought the apertures to the level of the eyes of *S* who was seated before them on an adjustable chair. The box with the nearer pyramid was hinged to the platform. By tilting it out of the way, *E* could expose the distant pyramid to *S*'s view. A biteboard was used to keep *S*'s head in a fixed position at the proper height and proper distance from the pyramids. Built into its mounting was a microswitch which operated the light bulbs in both boxes. By lightly pressing the biteboard forward with his teeth, *S* could turn on the box lights and make the exposed pyramid visible. *S*s thus made their estimates from a constant position and never saw a pyramid while moving their heads. The order in which the two pyramids were exposed for testing varied from *S* to *S,* but was the same in the postadaptation test as before the adaptation period. Both the size and the depth estimates, always in that order, were given for one pyramid before the other pyramid was presented.

Since Wallach and Frey had already demonstrated that adaptation could be obtained in opposite directions using near as well as far glasses, and since, with the shorter test distances that were also employed in the present work, the near glasses had produced stronger adaptation effects, only the near glasses were used in the first four experiments here reported. In all experiments the adaptation period lasted 20 min. In Experiment 1, E led S on a walk through a college building—the halls, lecture rooms, laboratories, a library, and up and down stairs. On the way, S saw many familiar objects, watched people approach and recede from view, and was exposed to scenes providing good perspective cues for depth.

Sixteen Ss, paid undergraduates, completed Experiment 1. They were selected for good size perception based on accommodation and convergence and for good stereoscopic depth perception. The following selection criteria were applied: When Ss were tested without glasses, the size estimate given for the 66.6-cm.-distant pyramid had to be at least 1.4 times as great as that for the nearer pyramid, and the corresponding ratio of depth estimates had to be at least 1.7. A total of 29 Ss had to be tested to yield the 16 experimental Ss.

RESULTS

The means of the preadaptation estimates for size and depth are given in the columns headed "Experiment 1" of Table 1 in Row 3, and the mean estimates after the adaptation period, in Row 4. The differences between corresponding mean estimates, which measure the adaptation effects, are found in Row 5, and the proportional size and depth increases after adaptation, in Row 6. All mean postadaptation estimates were changed in the direction of the expected adaptation effect: both mean size estimates and both mean depth estimates were larger after the adaptation period than before. Moreover, there was not one individual pair of estimates by any S that did not change in this direction. At both test distances, the increases in the depth estimates were considerably higher than the increases in the size estimates. The differences between these increments were highly significant; for the test distance at 33.3 cm., the depth increase was larger than the size increase for all *S*s except one, and for the 66.7-cm. distance 14 out of 16 *S*s gave this result. That the effects of adaptation on perceived size and depth differed in amount showed the effect on depth to be independent of the effect on size, and the fact that the effect on depth was larger supported the hypothesis that both resulted from a change on registered distance.

To be sure, the effect on depth is not as much larger as the difference between Emmert's law and Zuckerman's law would predict. The depth increases amounted to 103% and 101%, while, theoretically, based on the size increases actually obtained, they could be expected to be 134% and 186%. This discrepancy is, however, easily explained. A comparison of our preadaptation estimates for size and depth shows that stereoscopic depth constancy does not hold as well as size constancy under the conditions of our test. Whereas the ratio of the objective sizes of the pyramid bases at the two test distances amounted to 2.0, the corresponding ratio of the the mean size estimates was 1.7 (while the ratio of the retinal image sizes was 1.0). The ratio of the actual depth of the two pyramids, on the other hand, was 4.0 and the corresponding ratio of the mean depth estimates amounted to 2.32 (with the ratio of retinal disparities 1.0). Made comparable to the ratio of size estimates of 1.7 by taking the square root, the ratio of depth estimates amounted to 1.52 only.

Experiment 2. Adaptation under Conditions That Do Not Produce Retinal Disparity

There is still another way in which one can show that the effects of adaptation on size and depth perception are due to a changed relation of registered distance to accommodation and convergence: by eliminating stereoscopic depth perception entirely from the adaptation period. If postadaptation depth estimates are again higher than before adaptation, this cannot be ascribed to adaptation of stereoscopic vision itself. It rather must be the result of a change of an antecedent of perceived depth, i.e., of registered distance.

We created conditions of adaptation that were free of disparity-producing depth intervals, having *S* walk back and forth between two flat luminous surfaces, located at either end of a darkened room and the only objects visible to him. One of the surfaces was the screen of a TV set adjusted to a low brightness, and the other the translucent surface of a lightbox that was covered with ¼-in. wire screening. S's glasses were equipped with blinders that prevented him from seeing the dim reflections of the two bright objects from floor and ceiling. Under these conditions, the only possible information about distance besides that supplied by accommodation and convergence, derived from the growth of the retinal images of the luminous surfaces during S's approach and from S's walking toward these objects.

There are several ways in which such information may be effective in causing adaptation. (1) Kinesthetic information about walking cannot serve as cues for distance, but it can mediate distance change. Because accommodation and convergence are inversely proportional to distance, there is, when the glasses are worn, an alteration in the relation between these oculomotor adjustments and distance change provided by kinesthetic information. Normally, for instance, a change in oculomotor adjustment from an equivalent of 1.5 lens diopters to one of 2.5 lens diopters corresponds to a distance change from 66.7 to 40 cm. and would be produced by a small step forward. When the near glasses are worn, however, about the same change in the oculomotor adjustments is produced when S walks from the far end of the room to within 1 m. of the TV set.[7] (2) In conjunction with information about distance change, image size change may serve as a distance cue. Because the size of its image is inversely proportional to the distance of the object from S, the rate of image growth varies with the distance at which a certain change in distance is made. The larger the distance of the object from S, the smaller will be the change in image size that one step taken toward the object will produce. (3) Finally, there is, when the glasses are worn, an alteration in the normal association between the changes in image size and oculomotor adjustments. With both, image size changes and oculomotor adjustments, in an inverse relationship to distance, such an alteration should produce a striking discrepancy.

During S's 20-min. walk back and forth between the TV set and the light box, he was entertained by the TV broadcast. The pre- and postadaptation tests were identical with the tests in Experiment 1; 16 Ss, of whom 14 had participated in Experiment 1, took part.

---

[7]To be exact, the near glasses cause the eyes to view an object at infinity with an oculomotor adjustment corresponding to 1.5 lens diopters and an object 1 m. away with one of 2.5 lens diopters.

The results are presented in Table 1 under the heading "Experiment 2." Here, the mean changes in size and depth estimates were only half as large as those we obtained in Experiment 1. This is not surprising given the comparative paucity of veridical distance cues that were available during the adaptation period. Nevertheless, there was a highly significant increase in the depth estimates due to adaptation. At both test distances, every S gave a larger depth estimate after adaptation than in the preadaptation test. This is the answer to the main issue of this experiment. It happened although no practice of stereoscopic depth perception was possible during the adaptation period. Again, mean increases in depth estimates were greater than the mean changes in size, and these differences were, proportionally, equal to or larger than those obtained in Experiment 1. (They were also significant, with $p < .005$ for the pyramid at 33.3 cm. and $p < .02$ for the 66.7 cm. distance.)

Experiment 3. Adaptation Measured by a Movement Response

Up to this point, adaptation to glasses that alter oculomotor adjustments had been demonstrated only by effects on size and depth perception. When these effects had been shown to be indirect, mediated by alterations of registered distance, an attempt to demonstrate an effect of our adaptation on visual *distance* seemed appropriate. Because experienced distances of objects often do not only seem to depend on the given cues for distance, but also on the objects' perceived sizes, no test consisting in distance estimation appeared likely to succeed. We therefore used a bodily response to express the distance at which a target appeared to be located.

The target was a vertical black wire, .6 mm. thick. It was made visible by a dimly luminous area, 30 cm. high and 1 cm. wide, just behind it. Otherwise, the room was completely dark. The wire was located 33.3 cm. from S's eyes and in his median plane, with S's head kept in position by a head- and chinrest. S's task was to make the index finger of his right hand point to the left and, by moving it to the apparent distance of the wire, make it point at the wire from the side. Then S was to move the finger leftward toward the wire. A vertical board, parallel to S's median plane and 3 in. to the right of the wire prevented *S*'s finger from actually reaching the wire. *S*, who could see neither his hand nor the board, was instructed to point at the wire from the side and to move his hand toward it until his finger made contact with the board and to keep it there until E had marked its position. For each *S* a fresh piece of paper was clipped to the board on which to make these marks.

*S*s made three such depth pointings before and three after the 20-min.-long adaptation period. Unlike the tests in all our other experiments, this one was made with *S* wearing the glasses. That is ordinarily the preferred procedure. The reasons our other tests were made without glasses were set forth by Wallach and Frey. The conditions of adaptation were the same as in Experiment 1. Care was taken that *S* keep his hands in his trouser pockets or on his back throughout the adaptation period. This was done to prevent *S* from seeing his hands move while he wore the glasses and from perhaps developing an adaptation of motor processes related to the arm that was later employed in pointing. Twenty-five selected *S*s participated,[8] all except two of whom were new to our adaptation experiments.

RESULTS

The mean distances to which *S*s were pointing before the adaptation period amounted to 27.6 cm. This was significantly larger than the distance for which *S*'s eyes were actually accommodated and converged behind the glasses, which amounted to 22.2 cm.[9] The preadaptation pointings made by individual *S*s varied only moderately; the mean difference between the shortest and largest among the three individual pointing distances was only 1.96 cm. The variability among *S*s of the preadaptation pointing distances was larger; its standard deviation amounted to 3.67.

[8] *S*s for this experiment were selected on the basis of a normal size adjustment test (see Wallach and Frey, 1972). *S*s whose settings were larger than 150% of normal size were eliminated.

[9] Normally, the oculomotor adjustments to an object distance of 33.3 cm. correspond to 3 lens diopters. With the glasses causing an increase by 1.5 diopters, the eyes behind the glasses are adjusted for a distance of 22.2 cm., corresponding to 4.5 lens diopters.

The pointing distances after adaptation had a mean of 38.9 cm. For every one of our 25 Ss all his postadaptation pointing distances were larger than any of his preadaptation pointing distances. The mean proportional increase in pointing distance amounted to 40.9%.[10] It may be compared with a result obtained at a similar test distance by Wallach and Frey. They found after an adaptation period of similar length, that is, 15 min. as against our 20 min., a size increase of 41.8% for a test object at 25 cm. distance. This test distance was nearly the same as the distance of 22.2 cm. for which, behind the glasses, the eyes of our Ss were adjusted. Since, according to Emmert's law, changes in perceived size are proportional to changes in registered distance, our proportional increase in pointing distance should be comparable to proportional size increases. The obtained values, 40.9% by us and 41.8% by Wallach and Frey are in good agreement.

Since Ss neither moved their arms nor saw them during the adaptation period, we conclude that the increase in pointing distance after the adaptation period was not the result of an adaptation in kinesthesis but a change in visual distance. The apparent agreement between this change in pointing distance and the distance change implied in the increase in size estimates of an object at a similar test distance would support the view that the change in pointing distance was also a manifestation of registered distance.

B. Adaptation in an Immobile Subject
Experiment 4.

Experiment 2 was one of a series in which we tried to restrict the variety of cues that represented veridical distance during the adaptation period. In that experiment, all of the cues that may have been responsible for the achieved adaptation were produced by S's locomotion, namely, growth of image size with approach of the object

---

[10]It is interesting that adaptation as such did not result in a larger variability in the individual postadaptation pointing distances. With the mean postadaptation pointing distance larger by 40%, one would, in the normal course, expect a corresponding increase in its standard deviation. That is what we found: it rose from 3.67 for the preadaptation scores to 5.09, an increase of 39%. But adaptation did not cause an independent increase in variability.

and kinesthetic information about his locomotion. *S*'s visual field was not structured in the depth dimension at all. In Experiment 4, we restricted the conditions of stimulation to the distance and depth cues available to an immobile *S*. We also excluded from his field familiar objects and those that occurred only in standard sizes. The tests were identical with those used in Experiments 1 and 2.

PROCEDURE

S sat on a high stool at the narrow end of a 5 x 2 ½ ft. table, his head held in position by a chin- and headrest. He looked down on the table top which was covered with an oil cloth. Its checkerboard pattern yielded excellent cues for perspective depth. Scattered over the table surface were 10 black wooden blocks, all representing solids of different geometrical shape. The retinal images of these blocks, by being distributed over the retinal projection of the table top, served as further cues for perspective depth. The scene on the table was well illuminated. The remainder of the room was blocked from *S*'s view by a tall screen of white cloth which surrounded *S* and the table.

During the adaptation period, which lasted 20 min., *E* gave *S* tasks to perform that, in effect, caused him to make a series of eye movements and frequently to refocus his eye for different distances. For instance, *S* received the instruction: shift your eye from a near to a far object and back; count the number of edges on the tetrahedron; invent a maze, of such and such specifications, among the objects; count the number of squares on the tablecloth between two objects, etc.

Twenty *S*s participated, of whom nine had taken part in one or more of our previous experiments. The results of the latter did not differ significantly from those of the new *S*s. The selection criteria had been relaxed for the present experiment, stipulating only that the size estimate prior to adaptation for the more distant pyramid had to be at least 1.4 times as large as that for the near pyramid.

RESULTS

As shown in Table 1 under Experiment 4, the mean adaptation effects here obtained were small. They were, however, highly sig-

TABLE 1
Mean Size and Depth Estimates (20 Min. Adaptation)

		Experiment 1 (N = 16)		Experiment 2 (N = 16)		Experiment 4 (N = 20)	
		33.3 cm.	66.7 cm.	33.3 cm.	66.7 cm.	33.3 cm.	66.7 cm.
1 Test distance							
2 Objective size and depth of pyramids (in cm.)	S	5.5	11.0	5.5	11.0	5.5	11.0
	D	2.5	10.0	2.5	10.0	2.5	10.0
3 Preadaptation size and depth estimates (in cm.)	S	6.29	10.72	6.82	11.58	6.40	10.03
	D	5.03	11.69	6.02	12.71	5.46	11.00
4 Postadaptation size and depth estimates (in cm.)	S	9.61	17.72	8.62	14.52	7.51	11.44
	D	9.93	23.16	9.10	18.10	7.10	14.49
5 Difference between pre- and postadaptation estimates (in cm.)	S	3.32	7.00	1.80	2.94	1.11	1.41
	D	4.90	11.47	3.08	5.39	1.64	3.49
6 Adaptation effect as increase in size and depth	S	53.35%	68.59%	27.17%	25.44%	17.84%	14.76%
	D	102.88%	100.79%	52.89%	43.95%	32.22%	31.19%

nificant. With each of 20 Ss giving four pairs of pre- and postadaptation size or depth estimates, there were only four cases of an individual pair not changing like the mean, three where the postadaptation size estimate was smaller instead of larger than the corresponding preadaptation estimate, and one where a depth estimate changed in the wrong direction. As in our previous experiments, the difference between the mean size increase and the mean depth increase due to adaptation was significant in the case of each pyramid, for the smaller pyramid at the .05 level of confidence and for the larger one at the .005 level.

In spite of the restrictions on depth cues, these are respectable adaptation effects. With the mean size increase for the smaller pyramid near 18% and the mean depth increases amounting to 32%, which means 31% and 30% of complete adaptation, respectively,[11] the effects are as large as any that have been obtained with brief adaptation periods in other kinds of adaptation. As far as we can see, only the perspective deformations in the retinal projection of the table scene and retinal disparities operated here as spatial cues. Whereas perspective distortions in the projection of the scene on the table top can serve as cues to veridical distances (Gibson, 1950, p. 176), we do not believe that retinal disparity alone could. In the first place, retinal disparity gives rise only to perceived depth between objects and is not a cue for distance from S. Neither is it by itself a veridical cue to depth, since the distance from S of the depth interval causing a disparity is needed in its evaluation (Zuckerman's law). With convergence and accommodation altered by the glasses, only perspective cues were thus available to represent these distances veridically.

[11] The mean preadaptation estimates for the pyramid at 66.7 cm. distance represent the expected mean postadaptation estimates for the nearer pyramid under the assumption of complete adaptation, because a distance of 66.7 cm. is 1.5 lens diopters less than the distance of the nearer pyramid, and the image sizes and disparities produced by the two pyramids are the same. With the mean preadaptation estimates for the nearer pyramid representing zero adaptation and the mean preadaptation estimates for the distant pyramid 100% adaptation, the mean postadaptation estimates for the nearer pyramid represent 31% for size and 30% for depth of complete adaptation.

Experiment 5

Our last experiment employed the familiar size of objects that only occur in standard sizes as the veridical distance cue. Such use of familiar size derives from the equivalence between perceived size, on the one hand, and the product of size of the retinal image times registered distance, on the other (Emmert's law). If familiar size, which is a given, is substituted for perceived size, and with image size given also because it is physically dependent on object size and objective distance, registered distance becomes determined and may function like a distance cue. Although the way in which familiar size is ultimately related to distance perception is still under investigation, we were encouraged in using objects of familiar size to represent veridical distance by the success which Wallach and Frey had measuring registered distance with the normal size adjustment test. In this test, the size of images of familiar objects was varied until they appeared normal; in short, with familiar size again a given, retinal image size was here the variable that was dependent on registered distance.

Previous work on adaptation to our glasses had left open the question whether an adaptation produced with one range of oculomotor adjustments would transfer fully to another range. We therefore saw to it that as much as possible the oculomotor adjustments caused by looking at the two test pyramids would also occur during the adaptation period, and this involved taking into account the effect of the glasses on accommodation and convergence. We therefore presented during the adaptation period familiar objects that occur in only one standard size at three properly chosen distances. In a completely dark room, they were put under illumination in alternation, in order to eliminate retinal disparities to which simultaneous presentation would have given rise. Whereas in Experiments 1–4 adaptation was only to the near glasses, in the present experiment two groups of *S*s were used, one adapting to the near glasses and the other to the far glasses. The latter, by causing accommodation and convergence to diminish, produce larger equivalent distances. By compensating for this, adaptation would cause a change in the relation between oculomotor adjustments and the distances they represent in the nervous system such that smaller than normal registered distances now correspond to accommodation and convergence of particular amounts. This, in turn, should cause smaller perceived size and depth.

PROCEDURE

The following objects were used during adaptation: a black card on which a 1 cent and a 5 cent stamp and a gum wrapper were mounted, a dollar bill, and a telephone receiver painted white. Three small spotlights, each consisting of a 5-W bulb mounted on the end of a 63-cm.-long cylindrical tube, 8.5 cm. in diameter, were used to illuminate these objects obliquely from the right front. Each was aimed at one object, with the excess light hitting a black cloth curtain on the wall to the left. A screen in frontal position to the left of the displays hid what little light was reflected by the black curtain from S's view. The supports for the three objects were concealed so that they appeared to float in space when illuminated. A switch under E's control operated the three spotlights, one at a time. During the adaptation period, which again lasted 20 min., E illuminated an object for a minute or two and then switched to another one in random order. S's head was held in fixed position by a chin- and headrest. S was asked to look at each object as soon as it appeared, but he was not instructed to fixate it. Inasmuch as the illuminated object was the only thing visible, we counted on S's gaze being on it most of the time. When adaptation was to the near glasses, the card with the stamps, etc., was at a distance of 33.3 cm. from S, the dollar bill at 66.7 cm., and the receiver at 133.3 cm. With the changes in accommodation and convergence caused by the near glasses, the equivalent distances, that is, the distances for which the eyes behind the glasses were adjusted, were 22.2, 33.3, and 44.4 cm., respectively. In the case of the far glasses, the distances to which the eyes behind the spectacles were adjusted were larger than the actual object distances. We therefore placed the familiar objects nearer to S than they were during adaptation to the near glasses. They were now 25, 33.3, and 50 cm. distant. This made the equivalent distances 40, 66.7, and 200 cm. The tests for adaptation were the same as in Experiments 1, 2, and 4, and the criterion for the selection of Ss was the one used in Experiment 4. Twenty Ss participated in the adaptation to the near glasses and 16 Ss to the far glasses.

TABLE 2
Experiment 5: Mean Size and Depth Estimates (20 Min. Adaptation)

		Near Glasses (N = 20)		Far Glasses (N = 16)	
1 Test distance		33.3 cm.	66.7 cm.	33.3 cm.	66.7 cm.
2 Objective size and depth of pyramids (in cm.)	S	5.5	11.0	5.5	11.0
	D	2.5	10.0	2.5	10.0
3 Preadaptation size and depth estimates (in cm.)	S	6.01	9.73	6.66	10.85
	D	5.21	10.96	6.07	12.54
4 Postadaptation size and depth estimates (in cm.)	S	6.91	11.72	5.87	9.41
	D	6.55	14.10	4.91	9.74
5 Difference between pre- and postadaptation estimates (in cm.)	S	0.90	1.99	−0.79	−1.44
	D	1.34	3.14	−1.16	−2.80
6 Adaptation effect as change in size and depth	S	16.24%	20.75%	14.52%	16.31%
	D	26.87%	28.94%	24.51%	28.18%
7 Significance of difference between effects on size and depth		p<.005	p<.01	p<.01	p<.005

RESULTS

The mean adaptation effects, presented in Table 2, show the same pattern as the results of Experiments 1, 2, and 4. Although the effects were smaller than those for our first two experiments, they were still highly significant. In the case of the near glasses there was among 80 individual pairs of pre- and postadaptation estimates only one where any estimate was not larger after the adaptation period, and for the far glasses there was also one individual case that failed to show the expected effect of adaptation, namely, a smaller estimate after the adaptation period than before. In the case of both glasses and for both test distances, the mean adaptation effects on depth were proportionately larger than that on size and all four differences were significant, as the values for p listed on Line 7 of Table 2 show.[12]

The results of this experiment are valuable in several respects:

(1) Consistent adaptation effects were obtained with Ss inactive, thereby confirming the results of Experiment 4.

(2) As in Experiment 2, changes in stereoscopic depth estimates were produced without any practice of depth perception during the adaptation period. With any depth lacking in two of the visible objects and with the third, the receiver, being a round object free of edges and lines at different depth, no retinal disparities occurred while the glasses were worn. Again, the adaptation in depth perception could only have been the result of changes in distance perception, that is, a recalibration in the relation between oculomotor adjustment and registered distance.

(3) This is the only experiment where we used both kinds of glasses and therefore obtained adaptation effects in both directions, decrease in size and depth as well as increase. Some alternative interpretations of our results were thereby eliminated, such as satiation or fatigue, which can be considered only when changes take place in only one direction. Since Experiment 5 confirmed the two main results of the present work, namely, proof that our adaptation effects operated via registered distance and that they could be brought about with S inactive, to have obtained here adaptation effects in opposite directions was particularly appropriate.

(4) Because familiar size was the only indicator of veridical distance available in the adaptation period and did produce an adaptation effect, we can assume that it functions as a perceptual cue to distance. This is interesting in view of the work of Gogel (1969) which leads him to conclude that judgments of distance are derived from the image sizes of familiar objects by an inferential process.

References

Foley, J. M. Binocular disparity and perceived relative distance: An examination of two hypotheses. *Vision Research,* 1967a, 7, 655–670.

[12]In the case of the far glasses, the proportional adaptation effects were computed as ratios of the preadaptation over the postadaptation estimates.

Foley, J. M. Disparity increase with convergence for constant perceptual criteria. *Perception & Psychophysics,* 1967b, 2, 605–608.

Gibson, J. J. *The perception of the visual world.* Cambridge, Mass: Houghton Mifflin, 1950.

Gogel, W. C. The effect of familiarity on the perception of size and distance. *Quarterly Journal of Experimental Psychology,* 1969, 21, 239–247.

Stevens, S. S. *Handbook of experimental psychology.* New York: Wiley, 1951.

Wallach, H., & Frey, K. J. Adaptation in distance perception based on oculomotor cues. *Perception & Psychophysics,* 1972, 11, 31–34. In the present volume, this Chapter, selection 5.

Wallach, H., & Zuckerman, C. The constancy of stereoscopic depth. *American Journal of Psychology,* 1963, 76, 404–412. In the present volume, Chapter VII, selection 3.

7. On Counteradaptation

There seem to be two kinds of perceptual adaptation, one connected with constancies and the other concerning cue evaluation. Our experiments deal with the latter kind. When spectacles or other devices are used that alter cues to some perceptual parameter, such as visual direction, verticality, distance, or depth, a modification of the psychological process, based on such an altered cue, that compensates in part or fully for the cue alteration and tends to make perception veridical again can often be demonstrated. It is this shift back to veridicality that we here call adaptation. It is a matter of course that such compensatory modification can take place only if veridical information concerned with the parameter in question reaches S. This is achieved in most cases of modified cue evaluation by means of other cues that have an effect on the same perceptual parameter and are not altered by the spectacles or devices to which S adapts. (Sometimes, but by no means in all cases, the veridical cues are produced by S's acting, such as reaching or pointing with opportunity to correct, or by his locomotion, active or passive.) In adaptation that consists of modified cue evaluation, then, we have an altered cue and one or more veridical cues, all related to the same perceptual parameter. A precondition for this sort of adaptation, therefore, is the existence of "paired cues," that is, two or more cues, all of which determine the same parameter, and this is true of each of the four perceptual properties mentioned. Normally, each member of a cue pair operating alone should cause the same value of the parameter they determine in common.[1] But when one is altered by

Written in collaboration with Karl Josef Frey. Reprinted from *Perception & Psychophysics.* 1972, 11, 161–165.

[1]This statement is not meant as a prediction always verifiable by direct tests. Different members of cue pairs may determine their parameter with different accuracy, or the processes they cause may yield more or less readily to opposing tendencies. Such opposing tendencies exist, for instance, in distance perception where, according to Gogel (1969), a specific distance tendency operates.

spectacles and a cue discrepancy results, the conditions for a possible adaptive change exist. At the beginning of the adaptation period, the altered cue produces a parameter value which is different from that caused by a veridical member of the cue pair.[2] Eventually a modification in the perceptual process caused by the altered cue develops such that the difference between the value that the parameter assumes as a result of the altered stimulation and the value caused by the veridical member of the cue pair is diminished. Such a process assimilation amounts to adaptation. This is the hypothesis of process assimilation first proposed by Wallach and Karsh (1963) and discussed in detail by Wallach (1968). The work to be reported here is based on this hypothesis and is meant to support it.

The critical feature of this hypothesis is that process assimilation merely tends to diminish the results of cue descrepancy; perceptual change in the direction of veridicality is only an incidental outcome. Only if a modification occurs in the process produced by the *altered* cue will veridicality increase, that is, will adaptation occur. But there is no intrinsic reason why this should always be so, because, as stated, process modification tends only to diminish the difference in the outcomes of the two processes caused by the paired cues. A modification may just as well occur in the process caused by the veridical member of the pair, or in both processes. But if it occurs in the process belonging to the veridical input, process modification will cause a shift away from veridicality, since it consists in an assimilation to the nonveridical process. Because the direction of process modification is away from veridicality, we call the result of this modification counteradaptation. The possible occurrence of counteradaptation is, thus, a necessary consequence of the process assimilation hypothesis. An occurrence of counteradaptation would support this hypothesis by furnishing confirmation for one of its essential features, namely, that adaptation is caused here by cue discrepancy. That counteradaptation has, so far, not been demonstrated is due to the fact that, with one exception (Wallach, Moore,

[2]Under conditions where both the altered cue and veridical cues are present, it cannot be predicted whether or not or to what degree perceptual experience will reflect the altered parameter value, and what is experienced seems to have little bearing on subsequent adaptation. The perceptual outcome of conditions of such cue conflict is also subject to strong individual variations. For details, see Wallach (1968).

& Davidson, 1963, p. 202), no one has looked for it.[3] To do so requires testing for perceptual changes in connection with cues that are not altered by the spectacles and therefore represent the environment correctly. Not much attention is usually paid to them.

The strategy for looking for counteradaptation is to select a cue (A) whose alteration by spectacles has led in the past to rapid adaptation. Then one subjects the other, the veridical member (B) of the cue pair involved in this previous adaptation experiment, to an alteration by a suitable device, while Cue A is now used veridically. In this way, the cue pair is being subjected to a discrepancy that is different in absolute terms but may be quite similar to the previous one, if the mere difference between the cues is considered only. Because, according to the hypothesis of process assimilation, only the discrepancy as such matters, a similar discrepancy should lead to a similar modification. Since in the previous adaptation experiment the process produced by Cue A was modified, the same should happen in our new experiment. But Cue A is here veridical, and modification of the process it produces amounts, therefore, to counteradaptation.

Our counteradaptation experiments consisted of a transformation of an earlier experiment, namely, Experiment 2 from Wallach, Frey, and Bode (1972). In their work, the evaluation of accommodation and convergence as cues to distance was modified by the use of spectacles that forced alterations of these oculomotor adjustments in equivalent amounts. In three of their experiments, the cues that functioned veridically were limited, that is, the conditions in the adaptation period were such that, out of the numerous possible cues mediating distance, only one or two were operating in the role of veridical input, and they were different ones in each experiment. In spite of such restriction of the veridical cues, rapid adaptation was obtained to glasses that caused an alteration in accommodation and convergence equivalent to additional 1.5 lens diopters and thereby decreased all distances represented by these oculomotor adjustments.[4] Adaptation to these glasses consisted in an increase in the

[3]When they tested for modification of the process caused by the veridical cue, Wallach, Moore, and Davidson found none.

[4]For a more detailed explanation of the effect of these glasses, see Wallach and Frey (1972).

distances these oculomotor adjustments represented in the nervous system. Such increases in registered distance[5] made themselves felt in an increase in perceived size and depth and an increase in distance as represented by arm movements, always under test conditions where only accommodation and convergence served as cues for distance. In Experiment 2 of Wallach, Frey, and Bode, S found himself in a dark room with only two luminous displays visible, one at either end of the room. S's task was to walk toward one and then turn around and approach the other and to continue this activity for 20 min. Two kinds of possible veridical cues were in operation here and could have been responsible for the resulting adaptation, those derived from S's walking and those arising from the growth of the retinal image of the approached display. Because of the nature of the glasses, changes in oculomotor adjustment of eyes that looked through them corresponded to a change in distance ranging from about 60 cm. to about 30 cm. as our Ss moved approximately from a point 600 cm. distant from a display to within 55 cm. of it. Where walking was concerned, the discrepancy between an oculomotor change corresponding to a distance change of 30 cm. and a walking distance 18 times as large, which was actually needed to bring about this oculomotor change, may have contributed to adaptation. As to the growth of the retinal image, the discrepancy was between (1) a change in oculomotor adjustment equivalent to a distance change that would cause doubling of image size, and (2) an actual change in image size five times as great, for it was caused by the walk from a distance of 600 cm. to a distance of 55 cm. from the display. The adaptation effect so produced was measured by size and depth estimates obtained before and after the adaptation period and amounted to a size increase of 25% and a depth increase of nearly 50%.

In the present experiments, to simplify matters technically, we kept S stationary and used only image size change as a potential distance cue. Our plan was, then, to manipulate image size change to make it nonveridical and to keep oculomotor adjustment normal by having S wear no glasses and yet obtain a change in the evaluation of oculomotor cues, i.e., a modified relation between accommodation and convergence on the one hand and registered distance as

[5]The concept of registered distance was explained and its application demonstrated by Wallach, Frey, and Bode (1972).

measured by some of its manifestations on the other. We moved, in the dark, a luminous figure toward and away from S and made it change its size in such a way as to simulate a longer motion path. As it approached S, the objective size of the figure increased to produce image size changes that would have been produced by a figure of constant size traveling over a larger distance toward S. When the figure receded, its size decreased in corresponding fashion.

Our procedure may alternatively be considered a simulation of the effect of the kind of glasses used in the experiments of Wallach, Frey, and Bode. For technical reasons, the glasses whose effect we simulated were somewhat weaker. They would, had they actually been used, have caused the eyes to increase accommodation by 1 lens diopter and convergence in an equivalent amount. The simulated motion path in our experiment ranged from 400 cm. to 33.3 cm. from S's eyes. If it were actually seen through the 1 diopter "near" glasses, an object at a distance of 400 cm. would have been viewed with an oculomotor adjustment for 80 cm.[6] and one at 33.3 cm. with an adjustment for 25 cm. Therefore, presenting to an S who does not wear such glasses an object that moves from a distance of 80 cm. to a distance of 25 cm. produces the same sequence of oculomotor adjustments as presenting an object moving from 400 cm. to 33.3 cm. to an S who wears the 1 diopter near glasses. The 80-cm. to 25-cm. motion path thus simulates a 400-cm. to 33.3-cm. path viewed through glasses, insofar as oculomotor adjustments are concerned. The shorter motion path was actually presented in our experiment and will be referred to with the term "actual," while the 400-cm. to 33.3-cm path. will be called the "simulated" path.

To make the simulation complete, the size of the figure that moves on the actual path must be appropriately manipulated. It is required to produce the same sequence of retinal image sizes as the figure would yield that moves on the simulated path. The constant size of the figure that moves along the simulated path will be called the simulated size, while the various sizes of the figure that moves

[6]A point 400 cm. distant from the eyes is normally viewed with .25 diopter accommodation. (1 lens diopter = 1/distance measured in meters.) The glasses, by forcing an increase in oculomotor adjustments equivalent to 1 lens diopter, cause the point to be viewed with 1.25 diopters. This corresponds to a viewing distance of 80 cm.

on the actual path will be referred to as actual sizes. They can be computed from the following equation:

$$\text{actual size} = \frac{\text{actual distance}}{\text{simulated distance}} \cdot \text{simulated size}^7$$

So computed, the actual size of the figure at the actual distance of 80 cm. is .2, and at 25 cm., it is .75 of the simulated size. Since the equation shows that actual size is a linear function of actual distance, no further sizes need be computed.

If we abandon the viewpoint of simulation and consider the actual conditions that our S will face, we find that he will be exposed to deceptive cues to distance where image size change is concerned and to veridical distance cues by the oculomotor adjustments, for he will observe without glasses. A modification of distance perception based on oculomotor adjustments that results from this exposure would therefore be a case of counteradaptation.

Method of Adaptation

Our apparatus presented S with a luminous figure, a diamond, that grew in size when it moved toward him and shrank as it receded. It consisted of a lightbox on grooved wheels that ran on a track. Its front was a translucent sheet to which an Aubert aperture was attached. This aperture consisted of two metal sheets, of which the left one was fixed to the box, while the other one was mounted in the fashion of a sliding door and was hence horizontally movable. With their cutouts, each in the shape of a right angle, the two sheets formed a diamond-shaped opening which became larger as the sliding sheet was moved to the right and smaller when it moved to the left. The size of the diamond-shaped aperture was controlled by a third rail, a guide rail, which was fixed to the track between the other rails. A small wheel in horizontal position, whose bearing was attached to the sliding sheet with rods forming a right angle, rested against the guide rail from the right side. A spring that pulled the

---

[7] The equation follows from the law of projection, image size = c • object size/distance. Because we want to make the retinal images produced by the actual sizes at the actual distances the same as the retinal images of the simulated sizes at the simulated distances, we make actual size/actual distance = simulated size/simulated distance.

sliding sheet to the left caused the wheel to stay in contact with the guide rail, which thus controlled the position of the sliding sheet and the size of the diamond.[8] By means of a loop of cord and a set of pulleys, a reversible motor pulled the lightbox alternately toward and away from S. Two trip switches along the track and a relay circuit reversed the motor when the lightbox had reached either end of its motion path.

Wallach and Frey (in press) had found that the presence in objects of thin lines improved size perception when only oculomotor adjustments served as cues for distance. Apparently thin lines are good targets for accurate accommodation and convergence. We therefore added a thin vertical line to our luminous diamond and, to make it an integral part of this figure, we made it its vertical diagonal. This presented a problem because the top and bottom corners of the diamond shifted to the right as it increased in size and to the left when it became smaller again. This shift was half as great as the motion of the sliding sheet. Thus the line had to move in relation to the lightbox in a horizontal direction to keep coinciding with the corners. Our solution consisted in mounting a thin coil spring under tension horizontally and symmetrically above the aperture, one end attached to the stationary sheet and the other to the sliding sheet. A black thread was tied to the center of the spring and was held in vertical position by a weight at its lower end. As the sliding sheet, and with it the right spring attachment, was displaced, the center point of the spring and the thread moved exactly half as much as the sliding sheet, and, since this was also true of the top and bottom corners of the growing or shrinking diamond, the thread, once it coincided with these corners, remained in that position throughout.

Because the relation between the size of the diamond and its distance from S is linear, the guide rail had to be straight. The simulated size of the diamond, i.e., its diagonal, was chosen to be 25 cm. From this, its actual sizes at 80 and 25 cm. from S were computed as 5 cm. (.2 times 25 cm.) and 18.75 cm. (.75 times 25 cm.), respectively, and the guide rail was fixed to the track accordingly. It formed then an angle of 14 deg. with the track. S sat at the end of the track, his head in a head- and chinrest. The exact position of the

[8]We thank Mr. Otto Hebel for designing and constructing this variable aperture.

headrest was adjusted for each S so that the location of the aperture at which it measured 5 cm. was 80 cm. from his eyes.

This arrangement, then, achieved what we set out to do: It presented S with the sequence of image sizes that a diamond of constant size, moving back and forth between the distances of 400 and 33.3 cm. from S, would produce, and it caused concomitant oculomotor adjustments that would have occurred had S viewed these motions through 1 diopter near glasses. But we achieved this without any glasses, that is, under conditions where oculomotor adjustments were veridical. A change in registered distance measured after exposure to this arrangement would therefore be an instance of counteradaptation.

The conditions of counteradaptation just described were employed in two experiments which differed only in the method of testing and, in a minor way, in the criteria of S selection. Both test methods had previously been used by Wallach, Frey, and Bode.

Experiment 1

In this first experiment, size and depth estimates were obtained before and after a 20-min.-long exposure period. The test objects were wire pyramids seen against a small luminous area in an otherwise dark room under conditions where accommodation and convergence were the only distance cues available. There were two test distances, 33.3 and 66.7 cm., and the pyramids at these distances were so constructed that they produced the same image sizes and the same retinal disparities, the latter providing the only cues for perceived depth under the conditions of the tests. This required that the more distant pyramid was twice as large as the nearer one where its base and the thickness of the wire were concerned and that its depth was four times as large as that of the nearer pyramid. These differences in depth were necessary because an objective depth interval produces a disparity that is inversely proportional to the *square* of its distance from the eyes. S gave his estimate of the diagonal of the base of each pyramid and of its depth by means of a series of small adjustable brass rods of different lengths. Using only his sense of touch, he selected a rod and adjusted its length to fit the distance he wanted to reproduce. The order in which the two pyramids were exposed was varied but was, for a given S, the same in the pre- and postadaptation test. The size and the depth estimates, always in that order, were given for one pyramid and then for the other. Twenty Ss, selected undergraduates, participated. The following selection criteria were applied: In the preexposure test, S had to give a size estimate for the 66.7-cm.-distant pyramid that was at least 1.4 times as great as that for the nearer pyramid. Also, the corresponding ratio of depth estimates had to be at least 1.7.

RESULTS

The results of these tests are reported in the first two columns of Table 1. The mean size and depth estimates for the two pyramids after exposure to the counteradaptation conditions were larger than the corresponding mean estimates before the exposure, and the four differences were highly significant: in each of the two size tests, 18 of the 20 individual pairs of pre- and postexposure estimates showed changes in the same direction as the means, and among the 40 individual depth estimates, there was only one case in which the postexposure estimate failed to be the higher one. At each test distance, the mean proportional increase in depth was significantly greater than the mean proportional increase in size, with p <.01 in either case (see Line 6 in Table 1). Corresponding results had been obtained by Wallach, Frey, and Bode, who had found increases in size and depth estimates as a result of adaptation to near glasses under conditions partly simulated in our experiment. They had concluded that the changes in size and depth brought about by adaptation had been due to an alteration in the relation between accommodation and convergence on the one hand and registered distance on the other, with the size and depth increases both the result of the change in registered distance. We can draw essentially the same conclusion from our results. Stereoscopic depth was again absent from our exposure conditions, and any change in stereoscopic depth perception must therefore have resulted from the changes in the diamond size to which our Ss had been exposed. Only a change in registered distance can conceivably mediate between these size changes of the diamond and the resulting modification of depth. Again this interpretation is supported by the fact that the effect on depth was larger than the effect on size, a result that would have to be expected if both the size and the depth increases were due to an increase in registered distance.

(As stated, perceived size is proportional to the first power and perceived depth proportional to the square of registered distance.) In fact, the only reason for including size estimates in our test was to obtain such a difference between the increases in size and depth, for the size increases, as such, could conceivably have occurred as an adaptation to the changing size of the moving diamond; it is possible to interpret them as a partial compensation for the diamond's smaller objective size at the larger distances.[9]

TABLE 1
Mean Size and Depth Estimates

			Counteradaptation		Walking	
1	Test Distance		33.3 cm.	66.7 cm.	33.3 cm.	66.7 cm.
2	Objective size and depth in pyramids in cm	S D	5.5 2.5	11.0 10.0	5.5 2.5	11.0 10.0
3	Preexposure size and depth estimates	S D	6.42 6.04	10.13 11.95	6.82 6.02	11.58 12.71
4	Postexposure size and depth estimates	S D	7.07 7.16	11.81 15.06	8.62 9.10	14.52 18.10
5	Difference between pre- and postexposure estimates	S D	.65 1.12	1.68 3.11	1.80 3.08	2.94 5.39
6	Effect as increase in size and depth	S D	10.11% 19.36%	16.28% 27.98%	27.17% 52.89%	25.44% 43.95%

When our results are compared with those of Experiment 2 of Wallach, Frey, and Bode, as reproduced in the last columns of Table 1, some quantitative differences emerge. In the first place, our size and depth increases were, on the average, only half as great as those obtained by Wallach, Frey, and Bode with glasses and with S walking. (These differences were significant, with $p < .01$ for size as well

[9] In 1947, the senior author experimented with an analogous setup, but he hoped to bring about changes in size perception. When he realized that the effects he obtained could have been changes in the evaluation of accommodation and convergence as cues for distance, he lost interest. Such is the impatience of youth.

as for depth.) There were two material differences between their Experiment 2 and our experiment that can account for this difference. In their Experiment 2, S wore 1.5 diopter near glasses, while in the present experiment, 1 diopter near glasses were simulated. It is possible that weaker glasses would produce smaller adaptation effects. The other difference was that in Experiment 2, Ss were walking toward stationary figures and obtained kinesthetic information for their appoach, while in our experiment, Ss remained stationary, the distance change being brought about by movement of the figure. This circumstance eliminated from the exposure conditions one set of possible cues for distance change, namely, kinesthetic cues from S's walking.

The results of our experiment differed in another way from those of Experiment 2 as well as of three other experiments of Wallach, Frey, and Bode. In those experiments, the size and depth increases were proportionally about the same for the two test pyramids. In our experiment, these increases were larger for the pyramid at the 66.7-cm. test distance, and this difference was significant ($p < .05$ in the case of size and $p = .05$ in the case of depth). But as far as the importance of our experiments is concerned, these quantitative differences between our results and those of Experiment 2 are of no concern.

Experiment 2

Some time after the experiment just reported had been completed, we found that adaptation to glasses which change accommodation and convergence can also be measured by having S indicate the distance of a target by pointing, and this finding was incorporated in the report by Wallach, Frey, and Bode as Experiment 3. Because the interpretation of our present experiment as a case of counteradaptation hinges on the demonstration that our exposure condition produces a change in distance perception, we repeated our experiment, replacing the size and depth estimations with the pointing test.

In this test, S was standing, with his head in a head- and chinrest, and faced in complete darkness a dimly luminous rectangle, 30 cm. high and 1 cm. wide. A vertical black wire .6 mm. thick was stretched lengthwise over the rectangle. About 7.5 cm. to the right of the wire and parallel to the median plane of S's head was a vertical panel. Its near edge was 8 cm. from S's eyes, and its far edge was 60 cm. beyond. S's task was to bring his right hand approximately up to eye level and some distance to the right of the wire and to point from that position with his index finger to the wire, moving his hand leftward until his finger touched the panel. While S kept his finger in place and had his eyes closed, E marked the position of the finger on a paper that was fastened to the panel and later obtained the pointing distances from these markings. Three such pointings were made before the exposure period and three after adaptation. Each group of three pointing distances was averaged, and these values were recorded as the pre- and postadaptation pointing scores. In order to see if we would find here, too, a larger effect for a greater test distance as had been obtained in Experiment 1, the pointing tests were made with the rectangle and wire at two distances, namely at 25 cm. and 33.3 cm. from S's eyes. Because of the limitation inherent in the length of Ss' arms, we could not use the same test distances as before. Twenty selected Ss participated. A new selection criterion was used; it was concerned with the exposure period. In order to be accepted, an S had to perceive the diamond as becoming larger and smaller as it moved toward and away from him. We assumed that these size changes were an indication that accommodation and convergence furnished more precise or effective distance cues.

The results are given in Table 2. Although a good performance in the pointing test was not a selection criterion, the mean pointing distances before adaptation were in good agreement with the objective distances of the wire. (Compare Lines 1 and 2 in Table 2.) After the exposure period, the mean pointing distances for the two targets were 12.1% and 10.8% larger; these changes were highly significant ($t = 7.3$ and 5.8, respectively). The slightly smaller adaptation effect that was measured at the larger test distance was not significantly different from the other ($p > .6$). Whereas in Experiment 1 with the size and depth estimation tests a significantly larger adaptation effect was measured at the larger test distance than at the smaller one, no such difference was found with the pointing test. But because the pairs of test distances used were not the same in the two experiments, we do not discuss this comparison. The distance of 33.3 cm., however, was used in both sets of tests, and here the results are in fair agreement. The mean proportional increase in size, which, according to Emmert's Law, is the same as a proportional increase in distance, amounted to 10.1% ± 4.0, and the mean increase in pointing distance amounted to 10.8% ± 3.9.

TABLE 2
Mean Pointing Distances in Centimeters

Test distances	25	33.3
Preexposure pointing distance	25.1	34.1
Postexposure pointing distance	28.1	37.6
Proportional increase in distance	12.1%	10.8%

Discussion

The main purpose of our experiment was to establish firmly the concept of counteradaptation and the closely related idea of cue discrepancy as a basis of perceptual adaptation. Exposure to a luminous object in the dark that grew as it moved toward S and shrank as it moved away caused changes in size perception and in stereoscopic depth perception that can only be interpreted as resulting from a change in registered distance. The same exposure also caused changes in apparent distance demonstrated by a pointing response. Since accommodation and convergence were the only distance cues available in these tests and since they operated veridically during the exposure period, our "adaptation" period resulted in a perceptual modification away from veridicality instead of one tending to reestablish veridicality. Whether, besides such counteradaptation, our exposure period also produced an adaptation we do not know because we failed to test for adaptation. In this, our experiments corresponded to most work in perceptual adaptation where hardly anyone has tested for the kind of change we call counteradaptation.

Inasmuch as the conditions of our exposure period produced abnormal changes in image size in conjunction with normal changes in accommodation and convergence, the modification in the relation between these oculomotor adjustments on the one hand and registered and apparent distance on the other must have been caused by these abnormal image size changes. Only the discrepancy between the information about distance provided by these oculomotor cues and information provided by the image size changes could have been responsible for the perceptual effects we obtained. That image size change can play this role is another result of our experiments. In Experiment 2 of Wallach, Frey, and Bode, not only change of image size but also cues of *S*'s locomotion were in conflict with the distance cues furnished by the oculomotor adjustments, but these kinesthetic cues were absent from our experiments. Our result, however, should not be taken to mean that image size change as such can serve as a cue for distance. By itself, change of image size is ambiguous; a given image size change may be produced by a small distance change of an object nearby or a large distance change by a far object. But if the change of image size is large compared to the change of distance implied in the oculomotor adjustments that simultaneously take place, it can still be in conflict with the distance cues derived from these oculomotor adjustments. This was the case in our exposure period where the object of changing size that was presented produced a retinal image whose size changed by a factor of 12. (It will be remembered that the objective size changes simulated an object of constant size moving between the distances of 33 and 400 cm.) Because ordinarily the shortest viewing distance is 25 cm., the smallest distance range that can accommodate a change of image size of 12 to 1 is from 25 to 300 cm. This is very different from the actual motion path of 25 to 80 cm. for which oculomotor adjustments were made.[10] Thus, even this shortest motion path that can accommodate the given image size changes comprised distances considerably larger than the actual distances to which oculomotor adjustments were made and provided the cue discrepancy that produced the obtained modification in the relation between oculomotor adjustment and registered distance.[11]

[10]Even in the case of the rare *S* whose visual habits involve a shortest viewing distance as small as 15 cm., the smallest distance range that can accommodate the given image size changes still reaches to 180 cm.

[11]This effect of image size changes implies that the nervous system attributes these changes, at least in part, to distance changes rather than to changes in object size. The often observed fact that size change of a stationary object gives rise to an apparent distance change seems to be another consequence of this tendency.

References

Gogel, W. C. The sensing of retinal size. *Vision Research,* 1969, 9, 1079–1094.

Harris, C. S. The nature of adaptation to displaced vision: Visual, motor, or proprioceptive changes? *Science,* 1963, 140, 812–813.

Hay, J. C., & Pick, H. L., Jr. Visual and proprioceptive adaptation to optical displacement of the visual stimulus, *Journal of Experimental Psychology,* 1966, 71, 150–158.

Wallach, H. Informational discrepancy as a basis of perceptual adaptation. In S. J. Freedman (Ed.), *The neuro-psychology of spatially oriented behavior.* Homewood, Ill: The Dorsey Press, 1968. In the present volume, this chapter, selection 9.

Wallach, H., & Frey, K. J. Adaptation in distance perception based on oculomotor cues. *Perception & Psychophysics,* 1972, 11, 77–83. In the present volume, this chapter, selection 5.

Wallach, H., Frey, K. J., & Bode, K. A. The nature of adaptation in distance perception based on oculomotor cues. *Perception & Psychophysics,* 1972, 11, 110–116. In the present volume, this chapter, selection 6.

Wallach, H., & Karsh, E. B. The modification of stereoscopic depth-perception and the kinetic depth-effect. *American Journal of Psychology,* 1963, 76, 429–435. In the present volume, this chapter, selection 4.

Wallach, H., Moore, M. E., & Davidson, L. Modification of stereoscopic depth-perception. *American Journal of Psychology,* 1963, 76, 191–204. In the present volume, this chapter, selection 2.

8. A Passive Condition for Rapid
Adaptation to Displaced Visual Direction

The work to be reported is part of a series of studies devoted to the discovery of examples of perceptual learning rapid enough to make detailed investigation possible. It deals with the adaptation to a displaced visual direction caused by a wedge-prism fixed in front of the eye. With one of its faces in the frontal-parallel plane and with its edge vertical, such a prism displaces the visual field laterally, toward the side of the prism's edge, and thus alters the direction in which objects are seen. With Os wearing a 20-diopter prism in front of each eye, Held and Bossom obtained such an adaptation in 1 hr. with 10 out of 15 Os; the mean adaptation for the 10 Os amounted to 17% of the prismatic displacement of the visual field.[1] The same authors obtained complete adaptation with 8 Os by having them wear these prisms for several longer periods, distributed over 2, 3, or 4 days and totaling from 11–21 hr.

Our attempt to obtain reliable and rapid adaptation to displaced visual direction under controlled conditions is based on a scheme which had previously been successful in yielding a rapid modification of a perceptual process.[2] It consists in exposing O simultaneously to two different conditions of stimulation which give rise to the same perceptual property and in so altering one of them that it

Written in collaboration with Jerome H. Kravitz and Judith Lindauer. Reprinted from *The American Journal of Psychology*, 1963, 76, 568–578.

[1]Richard Held and Joseph Bossom, Neonatal deprivation and adult rearrangement: complementary techniques for analyzing plastic sensory-motor coordinations. *J. comp. physiol. Psychol.*, 1961, 54, 33–37.

[2]Hans Wallach and Eileen B. Karsh, The modification of stereoscopic depth-perception and the kinetic depth effect. *American Journal of Psychology*, 1963, 76, 429–435. In the present volume, this chapter, selection 4.

misrepresents the objective situation. A discrepancy is thus produced between the perceptual processes that result from the two conditions of stimulation and may lead to a modification of one or both of these processes. To apply this scheme to the adaptation of visual direction, we paired displaced vision with a directional cue of another kind, the visual vertical, by making a conspicuously represented visual direction coincide with the vertical. This condition was achieved by having *O* tilt his head forward and look down at his legs. The legs then nearly parallel a visual direction while at the same time they visually represent a vertical. When *O* wears a prism, the slant with which his legs are now given will be in conflict with the vertical direction which his legs represent to a standing *O*. As will be reported in detail, an exposure of 10-min. duration to this condition produces a large adaptation to the displaced direction in all our *O*s.

When *O* viewed his legs through a prism whose edge was vertical and to the left, he initially perceived his feet displaced toward the left. His legs appeared to be on a slant, seemingly emerging from his torso at an angle. This apparent oblique position of his legs, however, did not last long; half way through the training period, on the average, *O*s reported that their legs now seemed straight and this state of affairs continued to the end of the 10-min. exposure. It would be a mistake to interpret this outcome as the result of very rapid and complete adaptation to the prismatic displacement. When two different conditions of stimulation conflict with each other, either one may determine the content of experience, they may do so alternately or experience may represent a compromise between the normal outcomes of the resulting perceptual processes.[3] It is much more likely that the change in the apparent position of the legs is due to a shift from the domination of perceptual experience by the directional cues to domination by the cues for verticality. True or not, it should be clear that measurements of the adaptation should be made under conditions that do not involve the vertical as a visual direction.

Two different tests of visual direction were used, a pointing-test and a determination of the apparent forward-direction.

[3]Hans Wallach and Cynthia M. Norris, Accommodation as a distance-cue. *The American Journal of Psychology*, 1963, 76, 659–664.

The "pointing-test" consisted in having *O* point at a visual target under conditions that prevented him from seeing his pointing arm. *O* was asked to stand near a testing table, a horizontal board, 34 X 22 in., which could be raised or lowered. Near the middle of its longer edge and 4 in. above it, was an attachment for a horizontal metal piece on which a mold of *O*'s teeth was fixed. When *O* had the mold between his jaws, the table was at the level of his neck and there was room underneath for his arm to point horizontally. A measuring stick fixed to the far edge of the table was used to read the position of *O*'s pointing finger. Attached to the top of this edge was a rim, 2.5 in. high, which prevented an *O* with long arms from seeing his pointing finger. It also served as a rail for a sliding fixture which carried a socket for a flashlight bulb whose filament was 7.5 in. above the surface of the table. Tests were performed under light or under dark conditions. Under the former condition, the target for the pointing was the edge of a cabinet 16 ft. distant across the room, while, under the latter condition, the target was the glowing filament of the flashlight bulb adjusted to form a clearly visible point of light but too dim to illuminate even its immediate environment. To make this pointing-test as different from the forward-direction test as possible, both targets were located 7° to the left of *O*'s forward-direction when, by means of the mold, his head's orientation was fixed relative to the testing table. The test consisted in one pointing response. *O* raised his arm into a horizontal position in such a way that he felt his finger pointing at the cabinet-edge, or, under dark-room conditions, vertically below the glowing filament. It seems to us that this test was in principle not very different from the test used by Held and Gottlieb, and by Held and Hein, who had *O*s who were unable to see their hands mark points on a plane on which the virtual image of a target-pattern was localized.[4]

The "forward-direction" test was used to determine the direction of a target when it appeared to *O* to be straight in front of him. When the test was given in the dark, the same point of light which served in the pointing-test was used. With its socket sliding on the rim of the testing table, the little bulb could be moved horizontally

---

[4]Richard Held and Norman Gottlieb, Technique for studying adaptation to disarranged hand-eye coördination. *Percept. Motor Skills,* 1958, 8, 83–86; Richard Held and Alan V. Hein, Adaptation of disarranged hand-eye coordination contingent upon re-afferent stimulation. *ibid.,* 8, 1958, 87–90.

in the frontal-parallel plane of O until the glowing point appeared to be straight ahead. In daylight, the target in the forward-direction test was a small black oblong visible on a vertical panel of white plastic which was bent to form a half cylinder, 45 cm. in radius. A horizontal slot 45 cm. long and 0.2 cm. wide was cut into the panel into which the target-piece was inserted and along which it could be shifted from left to right. The panel was simply placed on the testing table. This test was a modification of the egocentric test used by Held and Bossom.[5] They placed O on a rotating chair inside a homogeneous drum and asked him so to turn the chair and himself that a target appeared straight ahead of him. Either daylight or dark-room conditions were employed. Wanting to avoid the involvement of vestibular stimulation connected with O's actual rotation, we had the target move while O remained stationary.

An individual test consisted here of two settings, one in which E moved the target toward the position that O judged to be straight ahead coming from the left and the other in which he started the target from the right. The test began with the target clearly too far to one side. After a first judgment was obtained, E moved the target to a point closer to the middle, obtained the next judgment, which usually also rated the position of the target as lateral, and so on. When judgments became hesitant, indicating that the critical range was reached, smaller steps were taken. An instruction to move the target back a step was obeyed. Initially we used this informal procedure because we did not know how short-lived a rapidly produced adaptation might be and wished to keep the test as brief as possible; later we wanted to keep the results of different experiments comparable and avoided changing the procedure. Inasmuch as E could not read the position of the target in the dark, there was, under darkroom conditions, no danger that he might, through the particular procedure he used, influence the result. Only when O judged the glowing filament to be straight ahead was the position of the bulb read with the help of a dim flashlight. Always, the average of O's two settings became his score.

There was a good reason for the use of two so greatly different tests in connection with the same training procedure. If both gave

[5]Held and Bossom, *op. cit.*, 33–37.

evidence of an adaptation, and, particularly, if they measured adaptation of equal amount, the adaptation would be more likely to consist in the modification of a single *perceptual* process and the possibility of its connection with a particular testing *response* would be distinctly lessened.

Each test could be given under two conditions: while *O* wore the prism (correction-method) or with normal viewing (alteration-method). With the edge of the prism to the left, all objects appeared displaced to the left, initially by approximately 11°. It will be seen that a pointing-test measured this effect of the prism with fair accuracy; on the average *O*s pointed about 11° to the left of the target. After some adaptation had taken place, pointing was somewhat to the right of the initial direction, that is, pointing was shifted toward the true direction of the target, in partial compensation for the effect of the prism. Adaptation was, therefore, measured as a correction of the error which the prism caused—hence the name we have given to this method. Since our prism displaced all visual directions to the left, an object which was seen through the prism as straight in front was actually approximately 11° to the right. Thus, in the initial forward-direction test, the glowing filament set to appear straight ahead was actually 11° to the right. After some adaptation had taken place, the filament had to be set less than 11° to the right in order to appear straight ahead. Again, adaptation was measured as a reduction of the prism-error.

When the pointing-test was made *without* the prism, *O* pointed correctly at first, while adaptation made itself felt as a pointing error: *O* pointed to the right of the target. Since adaptation makes objects appear displaced to the right, the glowing filament viewed without prism was actually to the left of the true forward-direction when *O* perceived it as straight ahead. Without the prism, adaptation was measured on both tests as an alteration of the initial veridical measurement.

In the earlier work mentioned, adaptation was measured by what we call the "alteration-method." We used the correction-method in addition on the chance that it might yield a greater adaptation-effect. In his work with long adaptation-periods, Ivo Kohler discovered conditional adaptation: long after reversing glasses had been omitted and all adaptation-effects had disappeared, wearing the glasses' frames would cause some of the effects to occur again.[6] If, in our experiments, adaptation were partially conditional, the correction-method, where the prism was worn for the tests, should yield larger effects. We were concerned with this possibility, because prism-wearing is associated not only with the tactile sensations and the narrowing of the visual field produced by the goggles, but also with specific form-distortions such as the curving of contours parallel to the prism's edge. In our experiment, there was also a chromatic filter which put a strong green color across the visual field.

A prism of 20 diopters produces rather strong colored fringes along contours, and thus causes a serious loss in acuity. We eliminated these fringes and greatly improved acuity by using, along with the prism, a Wratten Filter 58 by Kodak which passes a fairly narrow band of frequencies near the center of the visible spectrum. A plastic prism, 4.8 cm. from edge to base and 3.7 cm. wide, and the filter were attached to welder's goggles from which the glasses had been removed. The goggles were slightly altered to bring the inner prism-surface into frontal-parallel orientation. The prism was always in front of the right eye with its edge to the left. O's left eye was always occluded by having the opening of the goggles for that eye covered and by having him wear an eye-patch when the goggles were not used.

Unless otherwise stated, adaptation was produced by having O stand relaxed with head bent forward looking down at his lower legs. Os had no trouble holding this position for 10 min., the length of the training period in the present series of experiments. At the start of each experiment, an impression of O's teeth was taken and fixed to the testing table. The table's height was so adjusted that the mold fitted O's mouth comfortably when he was standing straight at the testing table. O was instructed to hold the mold firmly between his jaws during all tests.

For easier reference the following abbreviations are introduced: P = pointing-test; F = forward-direction test; c = correction-method, test with prism; a = alteration method, test without prism; 1 = test taken before training; 2 = test taken after training; Tr = 10-min. training period. Thus, $Pa1$ means a pointing-test taken without prism prior to training.

[6]Ivo Kohler, Ueber Aufbau und Wandlungen der Wahrnehmungswelt, *SB Oest. Akad. Wiss.*, 1951, 227, 1–118.

Experiment I

The first experiment to be reported—an improvement on a number of preliminary pointing experiments—was done under daylight conditions. O was given a forward-direction test and a pointing-test, both without prism. Then the goggles were put on him and a pointing-test and a forward-direction test were given, in that order. There followed the training period and the four post-training tests, which were given in this order: $Fc2$, $Pc2$, $Pa2$, and $Fa2$. Four pairs of measures of a potential adaptation-effect were thus made, employing each test with both methods. In all, 15 Os participated. It is an essential feature of this sequence that the tests with prism immediately precede and follow the training period, and that O put on the goggles only once. Removing the prism between the pre- and the post-training tests might introduce an error, because the displacement-angle varies somewhat with the angle that the line of sight forms with the prism. A deviation of the line of sight toward the prism's edge will enhance the angle of displacement, while the opposite deviation will decrease it.

Results of the pointing tests. The adaptation to the prismatic displacement is measured by the mean difference between the pointing directions before and after training. Tested with prism, this difference amounted to 4.55°, and was significant beyond the 1% level ($t = 9.12$). It can be compared with the displacement-angle which the prism causes for the particular target-direction, which is computed as the mean difference in the pointing directions obtained prior to training without and with prism ($Pa1 - Pc1$). It amounted to 11.82°. Thus, adaptation in this group of Os was 39.3% of the initial prismatic displacement.

Measured by the alteration-method, the difference between the pointing-directions before and after training was somewhat smaller; namely, 3.88° ($t = 5.04$; $p < 0.01$). As mentioned earlier, a smaller training effect measured without the goggles could be explained as the result of a partial conditional adaptation. Although we obtained a corresponding difference of similar magnitude in our next experiment, it did not reach significance. In an analysis that combined the results of Experiments I and II, the difference in the adaptation-effects measured with and without prisms was not quite significant ($F = 2.136$; $df = 1, 28$).

The *forward-direction tests* did not succeed. The mean directions in which the target appeared straight in front did not differ appreciably before and after training. As the next experiment shows, this outcome was due to some characteristic of the daylight-conditions under which the tests were performed, and not to the nature of the test as such.

Experiment II

This experiment was a repetition of the preceding one, except that all tests were performed in the dark, with the glowing filament serving as target, and that a small change was introduced in O's posture during the training period. While in Experiment I, O was asked not to move his head after he had tilted it forward and started to look at his legs, no such instructions were given Experiment II. Instead, changes in the position of O's head were recorded by means of a small mirror attached to the head which reflected light from a projector upon a 5-ft. vertical scale attached to the wall. A reading of the position of the spot of reflected light was taken every 30 sec. during the training period.

The *results of the pointing-tests* were quite similar to those of Experiment I. The adaptation-effect measured with prisms was 4.15° and was significant beyond the 1% level ($t = 4.19$). With the initial prismatic displacement ($Pa1 - Pc1$) measured here as 11.52°, adaptation amounted to 37.4% of that displacement. When the test was done without the prism, the effect was again somewhat smaller; namely, 3.76° but highly significant ($t = 8.68$; $p < 0.01$).

The *forward-direction test* in the dark was completely successful. Moreover, it measured an adaptation of the same amount as the pointing-test. With the prism, the mean difference between the scores taken before and after the training period was 3.76° ($t = 4.0$; $p < 0.01$). While this value was slightly smaller than that obtained with the corresponding pointing test (4.15°), the mean change in the forward-direction due to the prismatic displacement ($Fa1 - Fc1$) also was slightly smaller; namely, 9.63°; expressed as a fraction of the initial prismatic displacement, adaptation amounted to 39.1%. About one half of this decrement in the measured prismatic displacement was due to the fact that, in the forward-direction test, the line of sight formed a different angle with the prisms than it did with the target for the pointing-test. Once more, the test without prism showed a smaller adaptation-effect (3.18°, $t = 3.57$; $p < 0.01$) than the one with prism, and again the difference was not significant.

Very slow changes in the position of O's head occurred during the training period when O had no instructions to keep the head still. They were found to be unrelated to the adaptation-effect. An average deviation of the 20 head-position readings taken during training was computed for each O and rank-order correlations were obtained between these measures and the adaptation-effects measured with the Pc and the Fc tests. No correlations were found. For the Pc test, $r' = -0.04$ ($N = 19$), and, for the Fc test, $r' = -0.08$ ($N = 12$).

Since the results of the forward-direction tests are in good agreement with those of the pointing-tests when they were performed in the dark, the question of why the forward-direction test in daylight was not successful becomes an issue. There are facts which suggest an explanation. The variability of the initial forward-direction scores was considerably smaller under daylight-conditions than in the dark; the SD for the former was 1.39°, while for the latter it was 3.46°, and this difference was significant at the 1% level. (No such difference between the conditions of daylight and darkness was found for the pointing-tests; the corresponding SD were 3.25° and 2.72°.) The variability of judgments within individual Os also was different under the two conditions. Since an O's forward-direction score was an average of two settings, judgments made by individual Os could be compared; they turned out to be more consistent under daylight conditions. The mean difference between the two settings in the initial forward-direction test amounted to 1.50° for daylight and 4.22° for darkness. There was probably a tendency operating to center the target in the visual field. This explanation is supported by the fact that the variability in the scores for the first forward-direction test *with* prism was quite high ($SD = 4.54°$). When the prism was worn, some content of the visual field probably was so displaced that its center did not coincide with the apparent forward-direction, and such a discrepancy could account for the enhanced variability. This interpretation is supported by the fact that in daylight the forward-direction test did not measure the prismatic displacement correctly. The difference between the mean settings with and with-

TABLE 1

Mean Adaptation-Effects Obtained in Experiment III A, B, and C,
Compared with the 2 Previous Experiments
(N = 15)

Averages	Pointing, daylight		Pointing, darkness		Forward-direction, darkness	
	Mean	t	Mean	t	Mean	t
All responses	3.55°	6.65	4.19°	11.21	3.15	2.94
First responses	4.18°	6.15	3.81°	7.56	2.39	2.42
Experiments I and II	3.88°	5.04	3.76	8.68	3.18	3.57

out the prism amounted to 6.15°, only 63% of the prismatic displacement measured in darkness.

Experiments III A, B, and C: With the Alteration-Method

In the preceding experiments, for the reason already stated, the tests without prism always followed the tests by the correction-method. If the adaptation that is produced in our brief training period dissipates rapidly, these experiments do not give a correct picture of the adequacy of the alteration-method. For this reason, we did three experiments in which a test without prism was made immediately following the training period, and the same test was repeated a number of times to check on the course of possible dissipation. Where the pointing-test was used, O made four pointing responses before and eight after training. In the case of the forward-direction test, O made the same number of individual settings, which means that two scores were obtained before training and four afterwards. The three experiments were done under the following conditions: Experiment III A, pointing-test in daylight; Experiment III B, pointing-test in darkness; Experiment III C, forward-direction test in darkness.

Table I shows the adaptation-effects obtained. They are computed in two ways: from the average of all the responses made before training and the average of all responses made after training (first row) and from the first response or score before and the first after training only (second row). The latter method corresponds to the one used in Experiments I and II, and the corresponding measurements from these experiments also are given (third row). The reasons for the differences in the results of the two methods of computation become clear from an inspection of Figure 1 where the results of the individual responses are represented. The plots also show that there was no appreciable decline in the adaptation-effect in the course of the repeated tests. A comparison of the means in the second and the last row of Table 1 show that the delay of the tests without prism in Experiments I and II did not cause a lowering of the adaptation-effect. The mean effects were not appreciably greater when these tests followed the training period immediately. The small and insignificant difference in the third column ($t = 0.61$) was in the opposite direction.

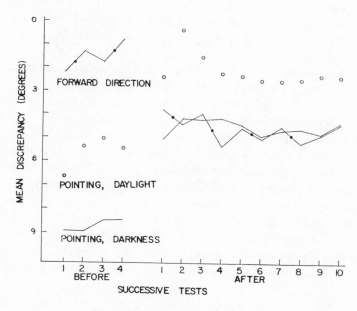

Fig. 1. Results of Experiment III

Experiment IV

Our final experiment was concerned with the cause of the adaptation. When O regards his legs through the prism, he is, as has been stated, exposed to conflicting cues. His legs nearly parallel a visual direction and they also represent the vertical direction. With the visual direction displaced by the prism, there is a discrepancy between cues representing the visual direction and the cues on which the perception of the vertical direction is based. This discrepancy can be eliminated by having O lie horizontally on his back, with his head raised to permit him to see his legs through the prism. Would adaptation occur under these conditions? We thought not. There would remain only a discrepancy between the displaced visual location of the legs and their location according to postural data. Results by Held and Hein seemed to indicate that such a discrepancy would be insufficient to cause an adaptation.

During the training period, O was lying flat on a day-bed, his head propped up by a firm cushion. While in the case of the standing O the prismatic displacement led, initially, to a vivid experience, the supine Os hardly noticed the displacement of their legs; in fact, 12 out of the 23 Os participating never reported it. Two tests were employed: a pointing-test in daylight and a forward-direction test in the darkness, both done with the prism. The sequence of events was the following: $Fc1$, $Pc1$, Tr, $Pc2$, $Fc2$.

Pointing responses were very little changed after training. The mean difference amounted only to 1.16° (compared to 4.55° in Experiment I under identical testing conditions) and was, in spite of the larger number of Os (23) and the high reliability of this test, insignificant ($t = 1.50$). The forward-direction test, on the other hand, measured an adaptation much higher than had previously occurred in our work. The mean difference between the pre- and the post-training forward-direction was 6.22° ($t = 9.69$; $p < 0.01$), about 65% of complete adaptation. It was significantly greater than the result of the corresponding test in Experiment II (where the mean change in the forward-direction amounted to 3.76°) with $t = 2.19$ and $p < 0.05$.

Because of its unexpected result, Experiment IV was repeated with the prism in reversed orientation. While in the experiments so far reported the edge of the prism was always to the left, the edge was now to the right and the prism displaced the visual field to the right. Under these conditions, the forward-direction test measured a similarly high adaptation, with the mean effect amounting to 5.46° (15 Os).

Discussion

One of the distinctive features of our experiments lies in the fact that two kinds of tests followed the same novel training procedure. One test required a physical response (pointing-test) and the other a perceptual judgment (forward-direction test). This confrontation of two kinds of test greatly different in nature yielded the most interesting results of our work. Previously, physical response-tests had been used in connection with training conditions which involved visually observed active movements of an arm,[7] and judgments of perceived direction in connection with *O*'s active locomotion.[8]

In our Experiment II, the two kinds of test measured adaptation in the same amount, and this result seemed to support the notion that the two tests were concerned with different manifestations of *one* perceptual-learning effect, an altered evaluation of the given visual direction; however, Experiment IV, in which *O* observed his legs through the prism while lying horizontally, contradicted this notion. While the forward-direction test showed a very high adaptation-effect, the yield of the pointing-test was very small and insignificant, the difference in the results of the two tests being very reliable ($t = 4.34$; $p < 0.01$). Having *O* lie down during training affected the results of the two tests so decisively that we must conclude that the tests measure the effects of different processes. In the light of Experiment IV, the fact that the two tests gave identical results in Experiment II becomes, in turn, a problem. A change in *O*'s position during training from supine to standing not only caused the pointing test to yield positive results, but also significantly *de-*creased the adaptation measured with the forward-direction test. An explanation of this peculiar combination of facts must be left to further study. Nor do we venture any statement concerning the nature of the two adaptation-processes which seem to be responsible for our results.

[7] Held and Gottlieb, *op. cit.*, 83–86; Held and Hein, *op. cit.*, 87–90. Recent work by Charles S. Harris (Adaptation to displaced vision: visual, motor or proprioceptive change? *Science*, 140, 1963, 812–813) also belongs here. The explanation Harris offers for his results—that adaptation consists in "a change in the felt position of the arm relative to the body"—is clearly not applicable to our results. During training our *O*s neither moved nor saw their arms.

[8] Held and Bossom, *op. cit.*, 33–37.

The other important result of our work has to do with the passive condition of our Os during training. Held and his collaborators maintain that adaptation to displaced visual direction can be obtained only when O visually observes the effects of his own active movements, and they have consistently obtained results supporting this view, with a test involving judgment of perceived direction as well as with a physical-response test. In our experiments, adaptation of high degree was obtained with both kinds of test under conditions in which O remained passive. A particularly striking result occurred in Experiment IV, where Os were supine and did not even have to maintain their equilibrium.

9. Counteradaptation After Exposure to Displaced Visual Direction

At this time, it seems useful to distinguish three kinds of perceptual adaptation: adaptation in the perception of shape in the frontal plane, adaptation consisting of the alteration of a constancy, and adaptation in the modification of cue evaluation. We are concerned here only with the latter. A modification of cue evaluation consists of a quantitative change in the relation of a cue to the perceptual property for which the cue provides the sensory information. Examples of such properties are distance perceived on the basis of accommodation and convergence, stereoscopic depth, visual direction, and the perception of verticality or slant. Devices that change accommodation and convergence, alter interocular distance, change visual direction by means of wedge prisms, or slant the visual field alter stimulation so that it misrepresents the objective conditions and nonveridical perception results. Eventually, a compensatory change in the perceptual process partially or totally corrects for the faulty sensory input—adaptation to the device takes place, with the result that veridicality of perception is partly or entirely restored. Such a compensating process change can, of course, take place only if veridical information about the pertinent objective conditions reaches the nervous system. Such information may be in a different modality from the altered stimulation, or it may be in the same modality provided it is not affected by the device to which S adapts. This veridical information must be contained in a sensory cue that per-

Written in collaboration with David Huntington. Reprinted from *Perception & Psychophysics,* 1973, 13, 519–524.

tains to the same perceptual property produced by the altered stimulation. In the case of adaptation in distance and in depth perception, sources of veridical information have been investigated (Wallach, Frey, & Bode, 1972, and Wallach, Moore, & Davidson, 1963, respectively). Where adaptation in distance perception is concerned, these sources consist of cues for distance other than accommodation and convergence, the altered cues. It seems, then, that in the kind of adaptation where cue evaluation is modified, we have an altered cue and one or more veridical cues all related to the same perceptual property. We believe that this is also true of adaptation to displaced visual direction and to visual tilt. We call different cues pertaining to the same perceptual property "paired cues." Under ordinary circumstances, each member of a cue pair operating by itself should produce the same value of the perceptual property which they both determine.[1] When one is altered by a device while the two perceptual processes resulting from the two cues still take their normal course, different values of the common property should result. Eventually, a compensating modification in one of the perceptual processes may take place such that the outcome of the two processes will again be in agreement. This is the process assimilation hypothesis first proposed by Wallach and Karsh (1965) and discussed in detail by Wallach (1968). According to this hypothesis, process modification serves to diminish the initial difference in the outcome of the two perceptual processes that results when one of a pair of cues is altered by a device.

It is an essential feature of this hypothesis that such process modification does not necessarily amount to a compensation for the effect of the device and hence to adaptation. Process modification will amount to adaptation only when it changes the process that is produced by the altered cue. If the process that is caused by the veridical cue is modified in order that the agreement in the ultimate outcome of stimulation by the cue pair be restored, no compensation for the device occurs, and veridicality is not enhanced. Instead, a process is so modified that perception based on a veridical cue becomes nonveridical. It is a consequence of the process assimilation hypothesis that such a change in perception toward nonveridicality

[1]This statement is not meant as a prediction always verifiable by direct test. See Wallach & Frey (1972). Note 1.

occasionally occurs when *S* is exposed to a cue-altering device. Wallach and Frey (1972) have introduced the term "counteradaptation" to refer to process modification of this sort.

Since the possible occurrence of counteradaptation is a consequence of the process assimilation hypothesis, demonstrating counteradaptation after exposure to a cue-altering device serves to confirm this hypothesis. But this is not the only reason why one might want to test for counteradaptation. Finding that counteradaptation develops along with a certain kind of adaptation or instead of it may solve certain problems that arise in connection with adaptation, such as failure of adaptation to develop where it would be expected to occur or an adaptation falling short of complete compensation for the effect of the cue-altering device. Figure 1 illustrates the various forms process assimilation may take. In the six sketches, the smaller vertical planes represent stimulation and the two horizontal lines, a cue pair impinging on a sensory surface. A point in the larger vertical plane represents the outcome of a perceptual process, experience or performance (such as judgment or pointing) or an intervening variable (such as registered distance). The lines connecting the planes represent the course the perceptual processes take. Sketch 1 shows the processes caused by the pair of cues producing the same value of their common perceptual property, the two process lines ending at the same point in the larger plane. This is what happens under ordinary circumstances. In Sketch 2, a device is introduced that causes a cue alteration so that it produces a different perceptual process with an outcome different from the process caused by the veridical cue. In Sketch 4, full process assimilation has occurred, with the process corresponding to the altered cue having undergone all the change; this is the case of complete adaptation, i.e., the outcome is the same as before the device was introduced (Sketch 1). Sketch 3 depicts partial adaptation. Full process assimilation has occurred also in Sketch 5, but here the process caused by the veridical cue has done all the changing and the value toward which the processes have assimilated is nonveridical. This is complete counteradaptation. It is a possible explanation where an expected adaptation fails to develop. Finally, Sketch 6 depicts the case of complete process assimilation due to simultaneous adaptation and counteradaptation. It can account for the case where adaptation develops but stops short of being complete, because counteradaptation has contributed to process assimilation becoming complete.[2]

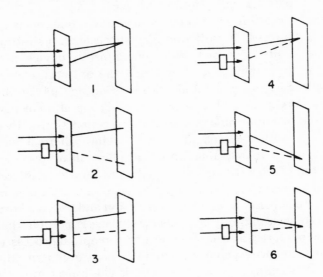

Fig. 1. Various forms of process assimilation

So far, few examples of counteradaptation are known, because specific testing is required to show that it occurred. Wallach and Frey (1972) caused a change in visual distance perception to take place as counteradaptation. They selected a condition where only one kind of cue served as veridical input in adaptation to glasses that changed accommodation and convergence with which objects were viewed. They transformed this condition in such a way that, while the cue discrepancy remained the same as before, the formerly veridical cue became nonveridical, and that accommodation and convergence now represented the objective facts correctly. Since the course that process assimilation takes supposedly depends only on the cue discrepancy when a simple cue pair is in operation, Wallach

[2]The term "counteradaptation" has recently been employed by other authors. Fischer and Hill (1971) used it in connection with a study of the effects of certain drugs on thresholds for form distortions. Franklin, Ross, and Weltman (1970) measured adaptation to the effect on distance and size produced by face masks under water. Like us, they used the term "counteradaptation" to refer to nonveridical changes obtained after the adaptation period; but they dealt with size perception, a constancy, and their concept of counteradaptation was not related to process assimilation.

and Frey obtained the same process change as before, except that, under the new conditions, it amounted to counteradaptation. Wallach and Smith (1972) demonstrated proprioceptive changes amounting to counteradaptation along with adaptation in visual distance perception after *S* observed his moving hands through glasses that changed accommodation and convergence. The present report is on two experiments in which counteradaptation in proprioception was obtained after exposure to displaced visual direction.

Experiment I

A condition often used to obtain rapid adaptation to displaced visual direction consists of having *S* walk with a wedge prism in front of one or both eyes. Here, a cue discrepancy exists between the proprioceptively and the visually given walking direction, the former veridical and the latter changed by 11 deg. by a 20-diopter prism. The visual walking direction is probably given primarily by the focus of expansion of the visual scene (Gibson, 1950, p. 128). The direction of this focus normally coincides with the walking direction, but when a wedge prism is worn and, together with the whole visual field, the focus of expansion is laterally displaced, a discrepancy between the visual and the proprioceptive walking direction results. A process assimilation that responds to this discrepancy can here either come about by a change in the relation between the cues for visual direction and the resulting visually perceived direction, a change that would compensate for the effect of the prism, or it can come about by a change in the evaluation of proprioceptive cues for the walking direction in a nonveridical direction. The former would amount to adaptation, the latter to counteradaptation. We expected that, if a change in the evaluation of proprioceptive cues developed, it would manifest itself in a discrepancy between an intended walking direction and the direction in which *S* actually walked. We probed for such a change in the actual walking direction with two tests. In one, *S* was asked to walk straight ahead in a totally dark room, and in the other test, also in the dark and after the prism had been taken off, he was asked to walk in the direction of a target point that had briefly lit up before he started to walk. In the latter test, an error in the walking direction would not only reflect a proprioceptive change, but also a change in the visual direction of the target point. But a third test that measured visual adaptation, as such, made it possible to demonstrate a proprioceptive change as the difference between the walking error and the measured visual adaptation. In the test for visual direction, S had the task of changing the position of a luminous target point in the horizontal dimension until it appeared straight ahead of him (visual forward-direction test).

What changes due to the exposure conditions can these tests be expected to turn up? If the prism causes an average shift by 11 deg. of all visual directions, for instance, to the right, the focus of the field expansion caused by S's forward motion will lie also 11 deg. to the right of the direction in which S walks. If S were conscious of the focus of field expansion, which he is not, he would see it lie 11 deg. to the right of his walking direction, provided he could experience this walking direction correctly, which he probably cannot.[3] Whether it is represented in conscious experience or not, this is the initial perceptual result of the cue discrepancy produced by the prism. If now process assimilation becomes effective, it diminishes this difference in the outcome of the two processes, with this difference, it will be remembered, being the normal result of the given discrepancy between the visual and the proprioceptive cues. Process assimilation may amount to a shift of the perceived visual directions to the left and to a shift of the proprioceptively perceived walking direction to the right of the actual walking direction. The former is, of course, the familiar visual adaption where a change in the relation between the given and the perceived visual direction compensates for the effect of the prism, enabling S, for instance, to point at a visual target with less of the error than the prismatic displacement of the target's direction would warrant. If, due to process assimilation, the proprioceptively perceived walking direction has come to be to the right of the actual walking direction, S, intending to walk in a certain direction, will actually walk a path to the left of the intended direction, and this will, of course, be counteradaptation. In the test in which S is asked to walk straight ahead, his actual walking direc-

[3]An S wearing a laterally displacing prism who, led by E, is walking straight ahead will, as a rule, not feel himself to be walking straight ahead but in the direction into which the prism displaces the focus of field expansion. This is in agreement with the other cases where visual and proprioceptive inputs are made to conflict with each other; the visual input seems always to dominate proprioceptive experience (Hay, Pick, & Ikeda, 1965; Rock & Victor, 1964).

tion will be to the left of forward, and when he has to walk in the direction of a previously exposed target point, it will be to the left of its visually perceived direction. The latter, because of visual adaptation, will, in turn, be to the left of the objective target direction, if the test is made without the prism. The effects of adaptation and counteradaptation will add, each having served in its way to compensate for the cue discrepancy caused by the prism.

PROCEDURE

During the exposure period, *S* wore welder's goggles with a 20 diopter wedge prism mounted in front of the right eye. His left eye was covered with a patch. For six *S*s, the base of the prism was to the left, so that the prism caused a displacement of the visual direction to the right, and for the other six, the base was to the right, causing a displacement of the visual direction to the left. The prism was covered with Wratten Filter 58 to eliminate color fringes and the attendant loss of acuity. During the exposure period, which lasted 20 min., *E* accompanied *S* on a walk through the building along wide hallways interspersed with climbing stairs and entering rooms. *S* was instructed not to look at any part of his body or to touch objects in his path.

All tests were made without prism in a darkened room. Here, too, *S*'s left eye was patched. For the visual forward direction test, the apparatus described by Wallach, Kravitz, and Lindauer (1963) was used, with one change—enabling *S* to change the target direction himself. *S* stood with his teeth in a mold, facing a horizontal frontal-parallel track, 58 cm. from his eyes. On it rode a sliding fixture with a dimly lit 2-V bulb at eye level. With the help of two strings, one for each hand, *S* could move the bulb along the track. He was instructed to move the bulb until it appeared "directly in front of you, straight ahead." After *S* was satisfied with his setting, he was asked to close his eyes and *E* read the position of the bulb from a scale in back of the track. A test consisted of two such settings, one starting from the extreme left and the other from the extreme right; their mean became *S*'s test score.

In the walking-straight-ahead test, *S* was put in a fixed starting position, with the orientation of his body controlled by a board on the floor against which *S* had to back his heels, his feet spread 40 cm.

apart. He was asked to walk straight ahead until he reached a string that was stretched across the 40 2 m. from his starting position and to stop there. *S*'s position was measured, and from it his walking direction was computed. This forward walking was repeated five times, and the mean of the five measurements became the test score.

A similar arrangement was used for the walking-toward-a-target test. A bulb at *S*'s eye level was located 2.5 m. from *S*'s fixed starting position, 50 cm. beyond the string barrier. The bulb was dimly lit for 2 or 3 sec. and, when it was extinguished, *S* was instructed to "walk to where you saw the light." *S* stopped at the string, and his position was measured. This procedure also was repeated five times in each test.

All three tests were given before and after the exposure period. The test order was varied from *S* to *S*, but was, for a given *S*, the same before and after the exposure period. Twelve *S*s were used to fill the six test orders twice.

Results

The mean differences between the walking directions before and after the exposure period and the corresponding angular differences in the target setting in the visual forward-direction test are given in Table 1. When the difference scores produced by exposures to right displacement and to left displacement were combined, the visual effect amounted to 3.1 deg., which is in line with previous results on visual adaptation.[4] The effect measured by the forward-walking test amounted to 4.5 deg., and this is counteradaptation in proprioception. The two effects are measured in combination in the walking-toward-target test, which showed a mean difference of 6.4 deg. There was no effect of test order, and the slightly smaller effects obtained with exposure to left displacement[5] were not significantly different either. The experiment, thus, yielded two demonstrations of coun-

[4]This result is slightly larger than one obtained by Shaffer and Wallach (1966) under similar exposure conditions and with an identical test. It is much larger, and significantly so, than one obtained by Held and Bossom (1961) in their Experiment I with a visual forward-direction test that differed from ours in that *S* varied his own orientation relative to the target.

[5]This effect may have been due to a difference in the displacement angle produced by a difference in the location of the prisms relative to the eye.

teradaptation in proprioception, the result of the forward-walking test and the difference of the results for the walking-toward-target test and the visual forward-direction test. This difference was significant ($p < .02$).

TABLE 1

Mean Differences Between Directions Measured by
the Pre- and Postexposure Tests in Degrees

Test	Exposure Displacement	Mean Difference Scores	p*
Forward	Right	5.0 Left	$< .05$
Walking	Left	4.0 Right	$< .05$
	Combined	4.5	$< .01$
Visual	Right	3.6 Left	$< .05$
Forward	Left	2.7 Right	$< .1$
Direction	Combined	3.1	$< .01$
Walking	Right	7.4 Left	$< .001$
Toward	Left	5.3 Right	$< .01$
Target	Combined	6.4	$< .001$

*All probabilities are for two-tailed tests.

Experiment II

With the proprioceptive counteradaptation after exposure to displaced visual direction thus demonstrated, it seemed worthwhile to examine a case where visual adaptation to wedge prisms has failed to occur. As stated, the process assimilation hypothesis suggests that a way to account for failure of an expected adaptation to occur is to demonstrate that counteradaptation develops instead. The experiment of Held and Hein (1958) and Held and Bossom (1961) are instances. In both cases, a visual adaptation to wedge prisms was obtained when *S*s moved and did not occur when *S*s remained passive during the exposure period. We believe, however, that the reasons for obtaining these results were different in the two experiments. In the experiment by Held and Bossom, *S*s walked during the exposure period or were pushed on a wheelchair over the same path. We explain the fact that adaptation failed to develop in the latter case by the absence of a cue discrepancy. Being leisurely moved on a wheelchair probably produced no proprioceptive stimulation carrying information about S's direction of motion.[6] Held and Hein, on the other hand, had S during the exposure period look at his arm and then tested for adaptation. When S moved his arm back and forth, an effect amounting to about 35% compensation for the visual displacement (a shift of 3.8 deg.) was obtained. But when the inspected arm remained stationary, no adaptation was measurable. In the latter case, the exposure condition does provide a cue discrepancy, the difference between the visual and the proprioceptive location of the arm. The failure of adaptation to develop when the arm remains stationary may well be attributable to counteradaptation in proprioception, a change in the felt location of the arm. We tested for a change in the felt location of the inspected arm by having the blindfolded S point with his other hand to an easily identified part of the inspected arm, first before and then again after the exposure period. If counteradaptation was responsible for Held and Hein's result, we would expect to find a change in the felt location of the inspected arm when it had remained stationary during the exposure period and a smaller change or none after observation of the moving arm. There were, then, two experiments, one with the arm stationary during the exposure period and the other with the arm continuously moving.

PROCEDURE

Throughout the experiments, S sat at a table with his left arm resting or moving on the black table top, with the hand closed in a fist, his head positioned by a teeth mold. During the exposure periods, S wore the same goggles as in Experiment I. In the stationary-exposure condition, the arm was so placed by E that the knuckle of the middle finger was located in S's median plane 44 cm. from his eyes, and S looked at his motionless fist for 10 min., with his right arm out of sight. In the moving-arm condition, S's elbow was in the same position on the table as in the stationary condition, but S was instructed to move his lower arm and hand back and forth between two marks on the table, 28 cm. apart, while looking at his fist. This exposure period also lasted 10 min.; this time, however, it was

[6]This explanation was proposed by Wallach (1968, p. 225).

broken midway by a 40-sec. rest period, during which S sat with eyes closed and arm stationary.

In the tests, the blindfolded S had to point with the index finger of his right hand at the knuckle of the middle finger of his left fist, the one that had been viewed during the exposure period. S's pointing finger, however, did not touch his left hand, but, instead, made contact with a Plexiglas plate that, for the test, was swung into position just above the left fist. When, before the preexposure test, S was instructed in this task, he was allowed actually to touch the knuckle a few times with eyes open "to get the feel of it." Then S bit into the mold, was blindfolded, and the Plexiglas plate was swung into place. E then moved S's arm into one of the two test positions so that the knuckle was directly beneath one of two marks on the transparent plate. These locating marks were 8.5 cm. to the left and 8.5 cm. to the right of S's median plane. To make a pointing, S brought his right hand into position above his left fist so that his index finger pointed to the spot where he felt the knuckle to be and then lowered his hand until the pointing finger touched the plate. E marked the position of S's finger on the plate, and S dropped his hand to the side. This pointing procedure was repeated two more times. Then E moved S's left arm and hand in the other pointing position, and three more pointings were made. Finally, E moved S's left fist into the exposure position midway between the two test positions, the plate was swung out of the way, and the blindfold was exchanged for the goggles: the exposure period began. The tests were repeated after the exposure period.

The same 16 Ss participated in both versions of the experiment, with an interval of at least a week between them. Half of the Ss wore prisms with base left in both versions, half wore them with base right.

RESULTS

The results of the pointing tests were as follows: For the condition with the arm stationary, there was a shift in the felt location of the fist in the direction of the visual displacement caused by the prism during the exposure period. Only a small, if any, shift occurred for the movement condition. With the results for the two fist locations employed in each test averaged and the results for the two displacement directions combined, the mean difference between the felt fist locations before and after the exposure with arm stationary amounted to 2.4 deg. (p < .005). When the moving arm was observed, the difference amounted to .5 ± 1.8 deg. The difference between the two means was significant (p < .025).

Discussion

Finding larger proprioceptive counteradaptation after viewing a prismatically displaced *stationary* arm than after observing active movements of the arm under the same conditions furnishes an explanation of Held and Hein's result; they found no visual adaptation under the first condition, but obtained it under the moving condition. In the case of the stationary arm, developing counteradaptation in proprioception seems to delay or to eliminate visual adaptation. Either one of these modifications amounts to process assimilation and can thus compensate for the cue discrepancy caused by the prism during the inspection period. There only remains the question of why little or no proprioceptive counteradaptation develops in the movement condition. This question is easily answered: When S moves his arm, proprioception is used to control the arm movement. This keeps the relation between proprioceptive cues and the perceived arm locations stable, and only the visual process can change to contribute to process assimilation. When the arm is stationary, proprioception has no such immediate function and is, so to speak, free to change. This explanation also accounts for Held and Hein's finding that passive arm movements as well as immobility failed to produce visual adaptation. Here, proprioceptive control of the arm need not operate either. Inasmuch as we found that inspecting the passive arm leads to a change in the proprioception of its position, the question may be raised as to why Held and Hein did not find evidence for a corresponding change when they tested for the effect of an exposure identical to ours. Unlike our test, theirs employed the same arm in the test that had been inspected in the exposure period. It would seem that a proprioceptive change concerned with the position of the stationary arm will not manifest itself in active movements of that arm.

Held and Hein attributed their result to the presence or absence of reafference, which consisted here of visual stimulation produced by the active arm movements. This stimulation provided visual signals that could be compared with the memory of reafferent signals that had, on earlier occasions, been produced by arm movements that were the result of efferent signals identical to the present ones. These earlier visual signals were, of course, different from those provided by stimulation altered by the prisms. Comparing them would bring about adaptation. This interpretation is supported only by other experiments, where absence of reafference also leads to failure of adaptation to occur, as in the work of Held and Bossom. Our experiments furnish a plausible explanation for Held and Hein's result, Experiment I by demonstrating that visual adaptation and proprioceptive counteradaptation to displaced visual direction can develop concurrently and Experiment II by demonstrating that proprioceptive counteradaptation results from that condition which, for Held and Hein, failed to produce visual adaptation.

That adaptation to displaced visual direction may lead to changes in proprioception is, of course, a well-known fact. It was first demonstrated by Harris (1963) in an experiment in which *S* observed for a brief period his pointing arm movements through laterally displacing wedge prisms. The compensatory change in pointing movements that resulted from this training did not transfer to the other arm and proved to be based on a change in proprioception concerned with arm movements. Harris's experiment is in some way analogous to our Experiment I, with his arm movements corresponding to our walking. But Harris failed to obtain visual adaptation: his forward-pointing test had the same result as his pointing-to-a-target test, while we found a significant difference between the results of the forward-walking test and the walking-toward-target test. Under our definition, the effect that Harris obtained has to be regarded as counteradaptation. Why no adaptation in vision was found along with the change in proprioception is not clear at this time.

The process assimilation hypothesis is meant merely to furnish a description of what happens when *S* is exposed to conditions that may lead to adaptation on the basis of cue alteration. It is not meant to be an ultimate explanation. The exact nature of the process change will probably turn out not to be the same in all cases of adaptation based on cue discrepancy, and hence the concrete causes will differ. In the meantime, the recognition that counteradaptation may develop along with adaptation or instead of it, as a matter of compensation for the discrepancy between paired cues, and that process modification will terminate when process assimilation has become complete has wide application in research on adaptation.

References

Fischer, R., & Hill, R. M. Psychotropic drug-induced transformations of visual space. *International Pharmacopsychiatry,* 1971, 6, 28–37.

Franklin, S. S., Ross, H. E., & Weltman, G. Size-distance invariance in perceptual adaptation. *Psychonomic Science,* 1970, 21, 229–231.

Gibson, J. J. *The perception of the visual world.* Boston: Houghton Mifflin, 1950.

Harris, C. S. Adaptation to displaced vision: Visual, motor, or proprioceptive changes? *Science,* 1963, 140, 812–813.

Hay, J. C., Pick, H. L., Jr., & Ikeda, K. Visual capture produced by prism spectacles. *Psychonomic Science,* 1965, 2, 215–216.

Held, R., & Bossom, J. Neonatal deprivation and adult rearrangement: Complementary techniques for analyzing plastic sensory-motor coordination. *Journal of Comparative & Physiological Psychology,* 1961, 54, 33–37.

Held, R., & Hein, A. V. Adaptation of disarranged hand-eye coordination contingent on reafferent stimulation. *Perceptual & Motor Skills,* 1958, 8, 87–90.

Rock, I., & Victor, J. Vision and touch: An experimentally created conflict between two senses. *Science,* 1964, 143, 594–596.

Shaffer, O., & Wallach, H. Adaptation to displaced vision measured with three tests. *Psychonomic Science,* 1966, 6, 143–144.

Wallach, H. Informational discrepancy as a basis of perceptual adaptation. In S. J. Freedman (Ed.), *The neuro-psychology of spatially oriented behavior.* Homewood, Ill: Dorsey Press, 1968. In the present volume, this chapter, selection 1.

Wallach, H., & Frey, K. J. On counteradaptation. *Perception & Psychophysics,* 1972, 11, 161–165. In the present volume, this chapter, selection 7.

Wallach, H., Frey, K. J., & Bode, K. A. The nature of adaptation in distance perception based on oculomotor cues. *Perception & Psychophysics.* 1972, 11, 110–116. In the present volume, this chapter, selection 6.

Wallach, H., & Karsh, E. G. The modification of stereoscopic depth-perception and the kinetic depth-effect *American Journal of Psychology,* 1963, 76, 429–435. In the present volume, this chapter, selection 4.

Wallach, H., Moore, M. E., & Davidson, L. Modification of stereoscopic depth-perception. *American Journal of Psychology,* 1963, 76, 191–204. In the present volume, this chapter, selection 2.

Wallach, H., Kravitz, J. H., & Lindauer, J. A passive condition for rapid adaptation to displaced visual direction. *American Journal of Psychology,* 1963, 76, 568–578. In the present volume, this chapter, selection 8.

Wallach, H., & Smith, A. Visual and proprioceptive adaptation to altered oculomotor adjustments. *Perception & Psychophysics,* 1972, 11, 413–416.

Compensation for movement-produced visual stimulation

1. The Measurement of the Constancy of Visual Direction and of its Adaptation

Introduction

When the visual field is displaced in relation to S's head while the head is kept still, the field is seen to move, but when a similar relative displacement is caused by a head movement the field appears stationary. This apparent rest of the environment during head movements seems to be the result of a compensating process in the nervous system through which the movement of the head is taken into account.[1] This interpretation is supported by the following

Written in collaboration with Jerome H. Kravitz. Reprinted from *Psychonomic Science,* 1965, 2, 217–218.

[1]For a summary of previous thinking on this matter, see Teuber, Perception, *Handbook of Physiology-Neurophysiology III,* p. 1647.

observation: When one wears left-right reversing goggles and turns his head, the visual field appears to swing with each turn at twice the angle of the head rotation. This fact is best understood by adopting the head as frame of reference and by describing the changes produced by head rotations as displacements of the environment relative to the head. Under ordinary conditions a head movement to the right causes a displacement of the environment to the left relative to the head. A nervous process which compensates for the effect of this displacement to the left causes the left-displacing environment to be perceived as stationary. That would mean that an environment that is not displaced in the relation to the head but revolves with the head rotation to the right should appear to move to the right at the rate at which the head turns. When left-right reversing goggles are worn, the normal displacement of the environment to the left is changed into an equally large displacement to the right. Since the compensating process causes the left-displacing environment to appear stationary, the optically caused displacement of the environment to the right should lead to an apparent motion of the environment to the right amounting to twice the angle of the head rotation.

The fact that the displacement between the visual field and the head is evaluated in such a way that the stationary environment is perceived as stationary during a head movement has been called constancy of visual direction (CVD). We measured the accuracy with which CVD operates with the help of a device designed to answer the question: How nearly must the visual field remain at rest during a head movement in order to be perceived at rest? Our apparatus enabled us to present a mobile target whose objective displacement was dependent on the S's head rotations. Because the target consisted of a luminous spot in a completely dark field, it represented the S's entire visual environment. Specifically, the target motion so depended on the head movements that it was possible to have the target direction become displaced in any ratio to the head's rotation. The sense of the target displacement in relation to the head's rotation could also be varied. Thus, the target direction could be displaced by any fraction of the head's rotation with or against the direction of this rotation. This made it possible to determine the range of the target displacement ratios that lead to experience of a stationary target or the range over which inconsistent judgments are obtained. Such measurements show the accuracy with which CVD operates.

Apparatus

The device that made it possible to have the target direction displaced dependent on the head's rotation consisted mainly of a variable transmission of the disc-and-ball type. It was located above the S's head, with its input shaft in vertical position and in line with the head's rotation axis. A light headgear served to connect the shaft rigidly with the head. The target consisted of a dim light spot of 7 cm. diameter on a homogeneous curved screen 2 m. from the input shaft. It was produced by a stationary projector whose beam was reflected by a small mirror which was fixed to a vertical shaft; the shaft, in turn, was connected with the output shaft of the transmission, thereby putting the direction of the target spot under control by the S's head. The control shaft of the transmission, which provided continuous variation of the transmission ratio, was operated by the experimenter, enabling him to set the device for any desired ratio of displacement of target direction to head rotation. The control shaft was connected to a mechanical counter which, once it was calibrated, made it possible to arrange the presentation of various transmission ratios according to a plan. A change of the counter by one digit corresponded to a change in the "target displacement ratio" of .28%.

Since our measurements concerned a function which takes head rotations into account and since only kinesthetic cues could mediate them, it seemed appropriate to keep the torque required to turn the input shaft small so as not to change appreciably the force normally necessary to achieve a head rotation. Starting the rotation of the input shaft of our device required a torque of 1.5 in.-oz. It resulted mainly from friction; gross changes in the transmission ratio did not alter it noticeably.

Procedure

Our experiments were concerned with displacement ratios, the ratio of the displacement of the target direction to the angle of the head rotation, for which our device provided continuous variation. Specifically, we wanted to measure the range of those displacement ratios which lead to apparent rest of the target. For this purpose we changed the displacement ratio (DR) in steps of .7%. Starting, for instance, with a DR which always caused apparent target motion with the head, the DR was varied stepwise toward objective target rest and beyond to target displacements that yielded judgments of motion against the head. After one set of limits of the "no-motion range" was thus established, we determined another one by running through the same steps in the opposite direction. We soon found that the no-motion range was not consistent: a certain DR that on one trial had led to apparent target rest might on another trial lead to experienced target motion. To get as exact information as possible on the accuracy with which CVD operates, we probed for the exact limits of those DR zones, which consistently elicited the same motion judgments, by repeated presentation of DR's near these limits, and determined for each *S* an "uncertainty range" comprising the whole DR range for which variable judgments or judgments of no motion had been obtained.

Results

For 22 randomly selected *S*s the uncertainty range had a mean width of 6.6% DR, and a median width of 5.4% DR. We also computed for each *S* the midpoint of the range of all his no-motion judgments. The mean of these "no-motion points" differed only negligibly from objective target rest; it fell on 1.5% DR with the head movement. Nevertheless, with as many as 22 *S*s involved, this value was significantly different from zero, that is, from the condition of objective target rest. One reason for such a deviation should be mentioned. It is connected with the fact that our target screen was at a finite distance from the *S*. The angular target displacement was therefore not only dependent on the given DR but also on the lateral displacement of the eyes caused by the head rotation, and the magnitude of this effect depends on the target distance. The role of target distance in connection with CVD will be investigated.

Measurements of CVD require that the target be given in an entirely homogeneous field. Marks that can serve as visual reference points for the target displacement alter the outcome radically. When a stationary pattern was projected on the screen, barely visible and consisting of vertical lines with gaps that formed a wide channel for the path of the shifting target, a displacement of only .28% DR in either direction from objective rest always caused a noticeable target motion.

Measuring Adaptive Changes in CVD

It is known that the compensating process which underlies CVD adapts itself to left-right reversal. When reversing goggles are worn for days, the swinging of the visual field with head movements, which was discussed above, diminishes gradually and stops altogether in about a week (Kohler, 1951). Being able to measure CVD, that is, to determine the center of the no-motion range, makes it possible to ascertain accurately partial adaptation where previously only complete adaptation yielded a well-defined experience.

Since reversing prisms cause nausea in most wearers, we used a different optical device to produce adaptive modification of CVD. Magnifying or minifying goggles, because they alter the size of visual angles, also cause the visual field to become optically displaced during head movements. We used minifying goggles of .66 power which displaced the visual field by one third of the angle of head rotation, i. e., equivalent to a DR of 33.3% with the head. After a S's uncertainty range had been measured, the goggles, which were made as light as possible and weighed including headgear 560 gm. were put on him. He was then sent out to do what he would ordinarily do when not studying. When he returned 6 hr. later, the goggles were taken off in the dark and another CVD test was given.

There was for all our 12 Ss a striking change in the no-motion point. It ranged from 10.2 to 34.5% DR, with the mean change amounting to 17.5% DR. Thus a target moving objectively in the direction of the head movement with a DR averaging 17.5% came to be perceived as stationary. No S showed an overlap of the uncertainty ranges measured before and after the adaptation period. This means that, had we presented to each S prior to adaptation a target with the DR of his no-motion point obtained after adaptation, he would have seen it move vigorously. With the rated power of the lenses corresponding to 33.3% DR, the change of the no-motion point amounted to slightly more than 50% of full adaptation. We also found that the uncertainty range after the adaptation period was not larger than it had been before; the mean uncertainty range amounted to 7.7% DR before and 6.7% DR after adaptation.

We are now studying the temporal course of the adaptation of CVD, how head rotation speed affects CVD and how rate and amount of target displacement are related in CVD measurements.

Reference

Kohler, I. Ueber Aufbau und Wandlung der Wahrnehmungswelt. *Sitz-Ber. Oesterr. Akad. Wiss. Philos. Histor. Kl.,* 1951, 227, 1–118.

2. Rapid Adaptation in the Constancy of Visual Direction With Active and Passive Rotation

Introduction

In a previous publication (Wallach & Kravitz, 1965) we reported a method of measuring the constancy of visual direction (CVD). It consisted in presenting to S a mobile target whose displacement was dependent on S's head rotation. Our apparatus made it possible to have the target direction become displaced in any ratio to the head's rotation. This arrangement enabled us to determine the range of displacement ratios that led to apparent target rest. This range included for almost all Ss the condition where the target was objectively at rest, as well as minor target displacements with and against the head rotation, that is, displacements associated with small displacement ratios (DR).

With the help of this technique we measured partial adaptation in CVD. Such adaptation occurs when optical devices are worn that alter the normal displacement of the visual environment relative to the head produced by head turning. We used minifying spectacles of .66 power which displaced the visual environment by one third of the angle of a head rotation (33% DR) in the direction with the head movement. After wearing these spectacles for 6 hr. our Ss showed a mean shift of the no-motion range of 17.5% DR; the no-motion range that before this "training period" had straddled objec-

Written in collaboration with Jerome H. Kravitz. Reprinted from *Psychonomic Science,* 1965, 3, 165–166.

tive target rest was now produced by displacement ratios which would normally yield vivid target displacements in the direction with the head movement. Unpublished data show that a 2-hr. training period also produced reliable adaptation; a mean change of the no-motion range of 12.5% DR was obtained for six *S*s (p=.05) amounting to 38% of full adaptation.

The present experiments demonstrate that very rapid adaptation in CVD is possible, provided the specific adaptation conditions are crowded into a brief time span. This strategy was used in the work on modification of stereoscopic depth perception (Wallach & Karsh, 1963) and we decided to apply it in another area of perceptual modification. In our previous experiments on the adaptation in CVD it had been left to chance how frequently *S* became exposed to the specific conditions that produce the adaptation as they wore the spectacles. On the assumption that a turning of the head while the visual field is abnormally displaced would constitute such a specific adaptation condition, we now arranged for *S* to turn his head continuously during a much shortened training period.

Procedure

The apparatus with which CVD was measured was described in the previous article. The procedure by which the no-motion range was measured also remained the same as in the previous work, except that DR was now varied in much larger steps of 2.6%. The small steps formerly used had made our measuring needlessly slow; besides, we had to consider the possibility that adaptation rapidly produced might also dissipate rapidly. Only the conditions under which adaptation was produced were new: no spectacles were used; *S* simply remained connected to the variable transmission with which the first measurement of his no-motion range had been taken, with the transmission now set to the largest DR that it would yield. This displacement ratio amounted to 150%. The sense of the target displacement was always against the direction of the head rotation. The target spot of 7 cm. diameter previously used was replaced by a much larger patterned field subtending a visual angle of 16 degrees and thus occupied a much larger part of the visual field than the spot. Thirty *S*s were divided into three groups. The 12 *S*s of Group I spent a 10 min. training period, which followed the initial measurement of the no-motion range, turning his head back and forth and observing the large target pattern which was being displaced by 150% DR *against* the head rotation. The second CVD measurement followed immediately. The 10 Ss of Group II were treated identically except that they went through the head movements of the training period with closed eyes. Group III (8 Ss) underwent passive rotation during training. In this case, S was seated on a turning chair whose rotation axis was aligned with the input shaft of the transmission and was turned back and forth by E through an angle of approximately 45 degrees. Here, too, the target displacement was against the head movement. In the case of half of the Ss of Group I, the measurements of the no-motion range were taken with the target spot substituting for the large patterned field which was still used in the training period.

Results and Discussion

As in our previous work, adaptation effects were measured as the difference between the midpoints of the no-motion ranges taken before and after the training period. A sizable change of the no-motion range was produced by continuous head turning; for all Ss of Group I the no-motion range had shifted after the training period in the direction of target displacement *against* the head rotation. The change in the no-motion point ranged from 5.2 to 21.8% DR, with the mean change amounting to 13.7% DR. It made no radical difference whether the measurements were taken with the patterned field or the target spot; the mean changes of the no-motion point happened to be identical for the two sub-groups (13.9 and 13.7, with the confidence limits at ± 5.3% DR).

Merely turning one's head back and forth without any visual stimulation proved to have an effect on some Ss of Group II. It caused a mean shift of the no-motion point in the direction *with* the head rotation. The change of the no-motion point ranged from 17.3% DR to none, with the mean for the whole group amounting to 4.8% DR ($p = .02$). It was on account of this exercise effect that we did our adaptation experiments with field displacements *against* the head rotation where the expected change of the no-motion point was in a direction opposite to that which continuous head moving can produce.

The passive training condition, too, produced a reliable adaptation effect. The no-motion range shifted toward field displacement against the head rotation for all *S*s; the change in the no-motion point ranged from 2.8 to 17.9% DR. It average 9.8% DR and was highly significant. This mean did not differ significantly from the mean adaptation effect obtained with active head movements (t = 1.36), but it would be a mistake to conclude at this time that proprioceptive stimulation from the neck region normally plays no role in CVD.

Our results proved the strategy of concentrating specific adaptation condition into a small time period successful. It enabled us to obtain in 10 min. an adaptation effect as large as that produced by a 2-hr. period of wearing minifying spectacles (13.7 as compared to 12.5% DR for the latter). This technique will make it possible to investigate this adaptation process in detail, the manner in which it grows and dissipates, and perhaps to determine its locus. A start has been made by showing that adaptation of CVD can be obtained with the *S* in passive rotation. This finding is relevant in the context of current debates on the importance of motor activity in perceptual adaptation.

References

Wallach, H., & Kravitz, J. H. The measurement of the constancy of visual direction and of its adaptation. *Psychonomic Science,* 1965, 2, 217–218. In the present volume, this chapter, selection 1.

Wallach, H., & Karsh, E. B. Why the modification of stereoscopic depth perception is so rapid. *American Journal of Psychology,* 1963, 76, 413–420. In the present volume, this chapter, selection 3.

3. Adaptation in the Constancy of Visual Direction Tested by Measuring the Constancy of Auditory Direction

In previous work on the subject of this article (Wallach & Kravitz, 1965a) we developed a method for the measurement of the constancy of visual direction. This term refers to the fact that the visual environment appears to be stationary when one turns his head. Such head movements bring about displacements between the environment and the head: turning the head to the right causes the environment to become displaced *relative to the head* to the left. As a condition of stimulation this displacement, taken by itself, is ambiguous; it can also be produced by an objective displacement of the environment to the left, and such an event normally causes veridical perceived motion of the environment. It is the presence or absence of the head movement during the displacement that determines whether the latter leads to perceived motion of the environment or to immobility. Our previous work shows that it is not the mere presence or absence of head turning that is here decisive; rather the amount of the head movement is, as it were, compared with the amount of displacement of the environment relative to the head. Only if that relative displacement closely approximates that which is normally produced by the head movement is the environment perceived as stationary. If it exceeds or is less than this normal amount, that is, if the environment is being objectively displaced during the head movement in the plane of the head's rotation, the

Written in collaboration with Jerome H. Kravitz. Reprinted from *Perception & Psychophysics*, 1968, 4, 299–303.

environment is seen to move. In other words, the amount of head turning is normally taken into account in the perception of motion or rest of the environment; hence the use of the term constancy. Ways of measuring the accuracy with which this constancy operates are the first concern of this report.

The considerations just presented are based on the fact that stimulation that results in motion perception always consists in a relative displacement, either between several environmental objects or between an environmental object and O. Here we are concerned with the latter kind, a displacement of the whole environment relative to O. It results from objective motion of the environment about O, causing a displacement of the environment relative to O's head, which, in turn, produces image displacement or pursuit eye movements. Identical conditions for visual stimulation, however, will result from head rotation with the environment objectively stationary; it also will cause a displacement of the environment relative to O's head. Therefore, displacement between environment and head, by itself, is an ambiguous condition of stimulation. Were it always to cause motion perception, one would see the environment move to the left when he turns his head to the right and vice versa. The only way in which this can be prevented is by resolving the ambiguity through the use of kinesthetic information about the movement or rest of the head. Then, when visual stimulation representing the environment as being displaced is received, it will depend on kinesthetic stimulation whether this results in perceived motion of the environment or in its perceived immobility. Therefore, the stimulation necessary to see the environment at rest during a turning of the head to the right is a twofold one: a displacement relative to the head of the environment in the opposite direction, that is, to the left, and kinesthetic stimulation representing the head movement of matching amount to the right.

Our concern here is with this matching of the amount of environmental displacement and the amount of head rotation. How accurate must this match be for the environment to be perceived as stationary during a head movement? Translated into concrete terms this means: How exactly must the visual environment as a whole be stationary during a head movement to be perceived as stationary? Or, in other words, how much may the visual field be displaced during a head movement and still be perceived as stationary? A procedure by which this question can be answered is in a sense similar to the one by which the accuracy of the perception of straightness of a line would be measured by presenting S with a series of, say, vertical lines, consisting of a straight line and a number of slightly curved lines varying in degree of curvature. S being asked to select those lines that appear straight to him would not only choose the objectively straight line but also a number of the physically curved lines from among those with the smallest curvature and call them straight. Gibson (1933) has observed that a straight line is part of "continuous series with two opposed kinds of experiences at the ends," namely curvature convex-to-the-right and curvature convex-to-the-left, and "a unique mental experience" namely, straightness, in the middle. As, objectively, curvature of one kind decreases from one end of the series, changes into straightness and then curvature of the other kind increases toward the other end, a range of apparent straightness can be determined that comprises the objectively straight line and a number of the least curved lines of either kind of curvature. In our measurements, a series of environmental displacements of different rates occurring during repeated head movements is presented which corresponds to the series of curved lines. The displacement series consists of motion to the left, immobility, and motion to the right when the head movement is, say, to the right, with the displacement rate arranged like the degree of curvature: one kind of motion decreasing in rate toward immobility and then the other motion increasing in rate. When presented, such a series yields a range of apparent immobility of the environment that comprises objective immobility and a number of the smallest displacement rates of either kind, motion to the left and motion to the right. Other displacement rates located in the series on either side of the range of apparent immobility, will be perceived as motion.

Such measurements were taken with an apparatus[1] that transmitted S's head rotation to a luminous target that, being presented in an otherwise dark visual field, stood for the visual environment. The amount of target motion in relation to the head rotation and the direction of the target motion in relation to the direction of the head

[1]The same apparatus was used in the present experiment; for a description see below under Equipment.

rotation were variable and under the control of *E.* Speed of the head rotation and its extent were left to the individual *S,* who was asked to turn his head back and forth in a natural manner. With a setting made by *E* the apparatus would displace the target direction by a constant *fraction* of the head rotation. Therefore, for a given setting, the *ratio* of the angle through which the target was displaced to the angle through which the head was turned was constant. The *absolute* amount of target displacement and its speed depended partly on the speed and extent of the head movements, but *E,* by setting the apparatus for particular ratios of target displacement to rotational head displacement, fully controlled the *relative* rate of target displacement. This proportion of target to head displacement was called displacement ratio (DR for short) and, transformed into percent by multiplying by 100, was the unit of all our measurements. This unit (% DR) corresponds to degree of curvature. There are two ways in which the target can be displaced in relation to a head movement: *with* the head rotation (target moves to right when head turns right) or *against* it. They correspond to the two kinds of curvature on either side of the straight line, which corresponds in our case to a motionless target.

Just as the range of apparent straightness which comprises the straight line and a number of the least curved lines of both kinds of curvature, measures sensitivity to objective curvature, so a range of displacement ratios that lead to perception of immobility measures the sensitivity to target displacement during head movements. Normally, such a "no-motion" range comprises objective target rest and small displacements with and against the head. We found a surprisingly narrow no-motion range; a target displacement of 4% DR to either side of objective target rest was on the average enough for target motion to be consistently reported.

Such measurements make it possible to investigate adaptation to spectacles that optically displace the visual field during a head movement. That such adaptation occurs has been known since Stratton in 1896 wore inverting lenses, which by switching optically left and right, cause a strong displacement of the visual field when the head is being turned. They change the normal displacement of the field relative to the head which is to the left when the head turns to the right into one to the right. Instead of the displacement of the field relative to the head *against* the head rotation, the optical dis-

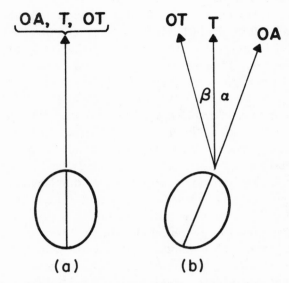

Fig. 1. Magnification causes field displacement during head movements. The enlargement of all visual angles in magnification causes a shift of all visual directions away from the optical axis (OA) in proportion to the angle they form with OA and to the power (p) of magnification. In (a) the arrow is at once the optical axis of the magnifier (OA), the objective target direction T, and the optical target direction (OT). (b) After a clockwise turning of the head in the amount of α, OA is in a new position. T, which is, of course, unchanged, now forms an angle with OA equal to α. This angle is being magnified ($\alpha \cdot p$) and this magnified angle is the one that the new optical target direction (OT) forms with OA. The difference between OT and T (β) is the optical displacement of the target direction due to the head movement. $\beta = \alpha \cdot p - \alpha$.

placement is *with* the head movement and results in a perceived swinging of the visual field when the head turns. Stratton found that such perceived swinging of the field with the head rotation eventually stops and that swinging against the head rotation is observed when the spectacles are taken off. For reasons previously explained (Wallach & Kravitz, 1965a), we avoided optical left-right reversal in our study of adaptation in the constancy of visual direction. Instead we produced optical displacement of the visual field during head movements by magnifying or minifying lenses.

Magnification causes field displacement during head movements in the following manner. A magnifier optically enlarges all visual angles in proportion to its power (p). When the head is turned by a certain angle, the direction of a stationary object normally becomes displaced relative to the head by the same angle (α). This angle, however, is being magnified ($\alpha \cdot p$). The excess of the magnified displacement ($\alpha \cdot p$) over the normal displacement (α) of a stationary object is the optical displacement (β) of the direction of the object. Hence $\beta = \alpha \cdot p - d$, or, $\beta = \alpha(p - 1)$. Thus, the field displacement during a head movement depends on the power of the magnifier and is proportional to the head rotation (see also Figure 1). It follows that the ratio of field displacement to the rotational displacement of the head equals the magnifying power minus one. A magnifier of 1.8 power, e.g., produces a target displacement of 80% DR. Inasmuch as the optical displacement is caused by the magnification enlarging the normal displacement between field and head during head movements and since this normal displacement is *against* the head rotation, the optical displacement (which is equivalent to an objective displacement) is also against the head movements. In minification where the power is smaller than one and the normal field displacement relative to the head is diminished, the optical target displacement is *with* the head movements.

Our first adaptation effects were produced by having Ss wear minifying spectacles of .66 power. They caused an optical displacement of the visual field by 34% DR *with* the head movement, i.e., the normal field displacement relative to the turning head, which equals the head rotation, is changed into one that amounts to only 66% of the normal displacement. This condition leads to a perceived motion of the environment with every head movement. Complete adaptation means, of course, that this motion is no longer seen, but this happened only to one of our 12 Ss within the 6 hr. adaptation period. The others still reported apparent field motions at the end of the adaptation period. That they had partially adapted could be shown after removal of the spectacles: facing again the normal displacement of the visual field relative to the turning head, they saw the field move *against* the head rotation. The degree to which they had adapted, however, could be ascertained only by a measurement of their no-motion ranges, which were now to be found somewhere among the displacement ratios *with* the head movement. Such a no-motion range could be compared with an earlier measurement taken before the adaptation period. The adaptation effect was computed for each S as the difference between the midpoints of these two no-motion ranges. The average adaptation effect for our 12 Ss amounted to 17.5% DR. For none of them did the two no-motion ranges overlap.

The following explanation will lead to a fuller understanding of this result. Since complete adaptation means that the field displacement of 34% DR with the head rotation caused by the spectacles produces perception of a stationary environment, after removal of the spectacles an objective target displacement of 34% DR *with* the head rotation produced on our measuring apparatus should also lead to perception of a motionless target. This was the case for the one *S* who had achieved full adaptation. Partial adaptation means that a target moving *with* the head rotation at some displacement ratio of less than 34% DR should appear to be motionless; the value of this displacement ratio can likewise be determined with our apparatus. (That our measurements typically yield a range of displacement ratios that cause apparent target rest does not change matters in principle.)

Being able to measure partial adaptation accurately has the advantage that the adaptation period can be shortened considerably and thereby make detailed experimental investigation of the adaptation process possible. We had six *S*s wear .66 power spectacles for 2 hr. and obtained a mean adaptation of 12.5% DR (Wallach & Kravitz, 1965b). A more radical shortening of the adaptation period was achieved by having *S* turn his head back and forth incessantly. We believed that exposure to displacement of the visual field during head movements is the immediate cause of the developing adaptation and assumed that an incessant exposure to this condition would lead to rapid adaptation. A corresponding strategy had proved successful in adaptation experiments on stereoscopic vision (Wallach & Karsh, 1963). It succeeded again when *S*, his head attached to the test apparatus, observed the target spot being objectively displaced with each head movement. With a strong target displacement against the head movement of 150% DR, an adaptation period of 10 min. produced a mean adaptation effect of 13.7%DR.[2]

There are two possible reasons for the very rapid adaptation that

[2]Such rapid adaptation makes it possible to test whether passive rotation also leads to adaptation. *S* was placed on a turning chair and, instead of turning his head, he was turned back and forth through an appropriate angle by *E*. This form of training produced a mean adaptation of 9.8% DR which was measured with *S* actively turning his head during the test.

occurred on these experiments: the high displacement ratio of 150% which was used here in the training period and the continuous head movements representing a concentration in time of the specific condition of adaptation. As yet unpublished work by Wallach and Frey rules out the high displacement ratio as reason for the very rapid adaptation. Rapid training was given under various conditions, with the displacement ratio one of the variables. No increased adaptation effect was obtained when the displacement ratio was raised from 40% to 80%. Continuous head turning seems to be the decisive factor. The brief and intensive training condition, however, has its disadvantages also: the adaptation effect does not last as long as one produced in a longer adaptation period, thus making an abbreviated measuring procedure necessary. In the present experiments the training period combined the advantages of continuous head turning and of a longer exposure.

The Problem

The experiments here to be reported represent a first step in an analysis of the nature of our adaptation process. We have seen that two kinds of sensory processes are involved in any measurement of the no-motion range: visual processes representing the displacement of the visual field relative to the head and kinesthetic processes representing extent and probably also rate of the head movement. The process modification which is the result of the adaptation may have, then, any one of three locations; the modification may be in the visual or the kinesthetic process, or there may be a modification of the interaction process where information about the head rotation is taken into account in the perception of motion or rest of the environment. The present experiments ask whether the adaptation we achieve consists in a modification of the processes concerned with kinesthetic stimulation. To answer this question we learned to measure the auditory analogue to the constancy of visual direction (CVD), namely, a constancy of auditory direction, and tested whether adaptation in CVD would transfer to the constancy of auditory direction. If our adaptation is a modification of the kinesthetic processes, that is, if there is a change in the evaluation of the kinesthetic stimulation representing the head rotation, such a transfer should take place.

Equipment

The apparatus with which the constancy of visual direction was measured consisted mainly of a variable transmission of the disk and ball type which was mounted above S's seat. The input shaft was vertical, pointing downward, and the horizontal output shaft forward. Attached to the control shaft, with which the position of the ball on the disk is set and hence the transmission ratio is determined, were a disk for turning the shaft and a rotation counter from which the ball position and, after calibration, the transmission ratio could be read. The output shaft terminated in a right angle gear whose vertical end shaft provided the mounting for a front surface mirror. In our apparatus a verticle shaft to which S's head could be fixed was connected to the input shaft of the transmission by a pair of gears which reduced the rotation rate by a factor of five. This was done to diminish the torque needed to operate the transmission. We have since determined that higher torques (of 8 in.-oz.) can be sustained and the head shaft may be attached directly to the transmission; down-gearing could then be provided on the output side of the transmission. This is preferable because the transmission is used more effectively at the higher input rate. Down-gearing by a factor of 10 is recommended. S wore a stripped down welder's headgear with a vertical plate fixed to the top in median orientation. This plate could be inserted into the slotted end of the input shaft, permitting the head to be shifted in the front-back dimension relative to the shaft until the latter coincided with the axis of S's head rotation before the plate was fastened in the slot.

A homogeneous white screen was erected 2 m. in front of S who was seated beneath the transmission. A small lantern aimed at the mirror that was connected to the output shaft projected via the mirror a luminous disk 7 cm. in diameter on the screen. When S turned his head back and forth the disk moved back and forth horizontally across the screen, at a rate relative to the head rotation (displacement ratio) that depended on the ratio for which the transmission was set. The lantern and the mirror were so arranged that the target disk was at S's eye level and straight in front of S when his head pointed straight ahead. The transmission could be set to shift the target disk either in the direction *with* the head rotation or *against* it. The calibration of the rotation counter, whose reading represents the input/output ratio for which the transmission is set, may be done empirically by measuring the rotation angle of the mirror shaft for one or more full rotations of the input shaft. The ratio of the two rotation angles of the shafts must be doubled to obtain the displacement ratio of the target disk because the reflected lantern beam shifted with twice the rotation angle of the mirror.

Except for the target disk and a small lamp illuminating the counter only, the room was completely dark during the CVD measuring. It is essential that no reference points for target displacement be visible, for they would cause veridical perception of target motion on the basis of object-relative displacement. The disk itself must be kept so dim that it does not serve as a source of illumination for objects in *S*'s visual field.

In our first experiment (Wallach & Kravitz, 1965a) adaptation training was with .66 power minifying lenses which were essentially reversed Galilean telescopes and were built in our shop. For a reason to be mentioned below, the present experiment employed adaptation to magnification. Commercial lenses of 1.8 power were attached to a welder's headgear with mountings that permitted adjustment to *S*'s interocular distance and made it possible to bring the lenses close to *S*'s eyes. During the training period *S* watched television broadcasts while turning his head back and forth more or less continuously. The TV set was almost 4 m. from *S*. The number of head movements *S* made during the training period was counted in the following fashion. Two photocells, each fitted into the end of a 4 cm. long tube to make their response more directional, were attached to the rear of the headgear. The tubes were positioned to form an angle of 25 deg. with each other, with the axis of the head rotation as the apex. A long box containing a fluorescent tube lamp behind a narrow slit which was parallel to the tube was placed in vertical orientation behind *S*. When he turned his head back and forth, light from the slit alternately activated the two cells. An arrangement of relays tripped an electric counter each time both cells had become activated in succession. A training period lasted 1 hr.

The device for measuring the constancy of auditory direction was quite similar to the apparatus used to measure CVD. An identical transmission, again equipped with a rotation counter on the control shaft, was used. Instead of turning a mirror which then caused the visual target to become displaced the output shaft of the transmission turned a rotary switch which would shift an auditory signal through a row of 30 small speakers, 1-1/4 in. diameter. To insure smooth shifting of the sound from one speaker to the next, the moving contact on the rotary switch was wide enough to connect with two speaker contacts during passage from one contact to the next. The speakers were mounted in a horizontal board 3 m. in front of S, in a staggered arrangement so that their angular distances as measured from S amounted to 1/2 deg. S's headgear was attached directly to the input shaft of the transmission. Thus, when S turned his head the signal was switched from speaker to speaker and E could hear it shift along the row of speakers. The rate of that shift relative to the head rotation was controlled by the setting of the variable transmission, and, after calibration, the ratio of the angular displacement of the signal to the angle of the head rotation could be ascertained by reading the counter. The signal consisted of a series of condenser-discharge clicks occurring at a rate of about 10 per sec.

The measurements of CAD took place in a soundproof room with floor and walls heavily padded so that reverberations were greatly diminished. Since our plan was to test for transfer of adaptation acquired by visual training to sound localization, CAD measurements had to be made in the dark. Preliminary measurements had shown that CAD deteriorates rapidly when S is kept in the dark for longer periods; therefore our measuring was frequently interrupted for lighting up the room. Ten sec. periods during which the click series was presented alternated with 6 sec. periods during which the room lights were turned on. The switching was done by a pair of tandem timers located outside the experimental room.

Measuring the Constancy of Visual Direction

As in our previously reported experiments, the constancy of visual direction and its adaptation were measured by determining the location and the extent of the uncertainty range before and after the adaptation period. The uncertainty range comprised those displacement ratios for which the responses of an S were inconsistent such that, for a given setting of the transmission, different responses were given on repeated trials. The computed midpoint of the uncertainty range was the no-motion point, and the difference between the no-motion points obtained before and after the adaptation period measured the adaptation effect.

The procedure for measuring the uncertainty range was as follows: Displacement ratios were varied in 1% steps, with each step representing a trial. On each trial, S had to turn his head back and forth three times and reported afterwards whether he had seen the target move or not, and, if he did, in which direction, *with* the head rotation or *against* it. The steps were presented in the sequence of the DR scale in two different orders. One order started with a displacement ratio that consistently produced reports of target motion in directions *with* the head rotation and the other with DRs producing the opposite reports. The initial step was followed by a trial sequence of diminishing DRs until the objective no-motion point was reached where the target spot remained physically stationary. Beyond that point DRs increased again, but now into the range of relative target displacements of opposite direction. To measure an individual uncertainty range S was presented once with both orders. Our procedure deviated from the method of limits at two points. On each run, after trials had produced a sequence of no-motion reports, the first trial that yielded a motion report with a reported direction opposite to the one with which the run had begun was repeated. If the repetition produced a no-motion report the next step was also presented twice, and so on until two motion reports in the right direction had been obtained for the same step. The same procedure was observed on the opposite run. The uncertainty range was computed by plotting the results of the two runs together, counting the steps for which inconsistent reports had been obtained, and adding one-half step for each end of the range.

After an adaptation had been achieved, no-motion reports no longer clustered about the objective no-motion point. In the case of adaptation to magnification, where field displacement is *against* the direction of the head rotation, no-motion reports after the adaptation period were for target displacements *against* the head rotation. Therefore, the two orders of trials employed to measure the uncertainty range consisted of target displacements of diminishing or of increasing DRs, both *against* the head rotation. The diminishing DR sequence was presented first. This was done because, on the post-adaptation measurement, the presentation of a displacement ratio leading to an apparent target displacement *with* the head would be an occasion for unlearning of the established adaptation. By starting the first sequence with displacement ratios resulting in apparent target displacement *against* the head, the range of no-motion reports could be mapped out with the presentation of displacement ratios leading to perceived target motion *with* the head rotation kept at a minimum.

Measuring the Constancy of Auditory Direction

It was possible to measure the constancy of auditory direction in a manner analogous to the measurement of CVD, that is, by determining an uncertainty range. This was, however, not sure at the outset, for a signal being displaced *with* the head rotation need not be perceived as a moving sound; a stationary source in an elevated direction may be perceived instead. This follows from the work by Wallach (1940) which shows that the change in the angle which the sound direction forms with the axis of the ears occurring during a head movement is a condition of stimulation in sound localization carrying information about the elevation of the source above the horizontal plane. With the source of sound remaining in the horizontal plane and for head rotation about a vertical axis, only displacement of the sound direction *with* the head, however, can produce perception of a stationary sound source. It is for this reason that the present experiment dealt with adaptation to displacement *against* the head rotation. If that adaptation were to transfer to sound localization, an auditory signal normally perceived in motion *against* the head would have been heard as stationary. The reason why in our experiment displacement of the auditory signal *with* the head rotation also resulted in apparent signal motion in the horizontal is probably that displacement ratios were small relative to those that had been found effective in sound localization and that the intermittently visible row of loud-speakers suggested localization in the horizontal plane.

Our procedure of measuring the uncertainty range in the constancy of auditory direction was identical with the CVD measurement described, except that the steps on which displacement ratios were varied were more widely spaced, namely, 2.2% DR instead of 1% DR. This was done because, understandably, the auditory uncertainty range was larger than the visual one. Care was taken that *S*s never turned their heads while the room lights were on, because seeing a stationary environment when the head turns serves to diminish the visually produced adaptation effect. For a similar reason, *E* never spoke to *S* while *S* was turning his head. At the end of the post-adaptation auditory test most *S*s were asked to turn their heads while the room was lighted. All of them reported apparent motion of the environment in the direction *with* the head rotation, an indication that the visual adaptation effect was still operative at the end of the auditory test.

The Plan of the Experiment

The constancy of auditory direction was measured for 24 *S*s and the individual uncertainty ranges were computed. Those *S*s with the largest uncertainty ranges were excluded from the transfer experiment. The remaining 14 *S*s first underwent adaptation to 1.8 power magnification and were tested visually. At this point, five more *S*s who had achieved only small adaptation effects were eliminated. The remaining nine *S*s later on repeated the adaptation training and were given the auditory test. In our previous work the effect of adaptation was measured as the difference between the no-motion points determined before and after the adaptation period. In the present experiment, the pre-adaptation measurement was taken at the end of a 1-hr. period of TV watching and of continuous head turning identical with the real adaptation training except that the magnifying spectacles were not over *S*'s eyes. Even the head gear was worn and the head movements were counted during these control sessions. The *S*s who completed the experiment attended a total of four experimental sessions which were spaced at least three days apart. The first was a control session that ended with the visual test. Then followed a training session culminating in the visual test. Next came again a control session leading to the auditory test. Finally there was a training session that ended with the auditory test.

During these sessions, which always lasted 1 hr., *S* was under instruction to watch the TV screen and to turn his head back and forth frequently. *E* checked the head movement counter from time to time and made sure that *S* moved his head often enough to complete a minimum of 2000 pairs of a left and a right turn during the session. Because our experiment involved an auditory test, the sound of the TV broadcast was not turned on. A conflict between the magnification-caused visual target displacement and the immobility of the auditory signal was thus avoided.

Results and Discussion

One hr. of more or less continuous head turning did not have a detrimental effect on the visual uncertainty range. The measurement taken after the first control session resulted in a mean of 3.86% DR (14 Ss), quite small in comparison with the previously obtained mean of 6.6% DR (Wallach & Kravitz, 1965a). The no-motion points, i.e., the midpoints of the uncertainty ranges, seemed also unaffected; their mean amounted to .58% DR in the direction *with* the head rotation. In our earlier work with rapid adaptation, where training had consisted in 5 min. of continuous head turning, a control experiment had resulted in a mean no-motion point of 4.8% DR *with* the head rotation (Wallach & Kravitz, 1965b). In that experiment, however, the control condition had prevented adaptation by having Ss keep their eyes closed while turning their head continuously, whereas in the control session under discussion Ss viewed television without the magnifiers that normally caused the adaptation. It appears that continuous head moving as such has no appreciable effect on CVD unless eyes are kept closed.

Next to be discussed are the results of the adaptation training measured visually. The mean uncertainty range measured after the first training session was 5.07% DR, larger by 31% than after the first control session, but not significantly so. The mean no-motion point after the training period was 9.39% DR *against* the head movement, and the adaptation effect measured as the mean difference between the no-motion points obtained after the training session and after the control session was 9.97% DR. For the nine Ss selected to complete the experiment, the uncertainty range after the first training session was 5.62% DR, the mean no-motion point was 12.65% DR, and the mean adaptation effect amounted to 13.22% DR.

For the constancy of auditory direction the uncertainty range was, expectedly, much larger than the one for CVD. Its mean for the initial measurement taken with the 24 unselected Ss amounted to 29.2% DR. If only the nine selected Ss who completed the experi-

ment are considered, the initial mean uncertainty range was 22.4%
DR. The measurement taken after the second control session showed
a still smaller mean uncertainty range of 17.27% DR, most likely the
practice effect of being tested a second time. There is a good reason
for the auditory uncertainty range to be from four to eight times
larger than the visual one. Auditory localization is very much less
accurate than visual localization. Pierce[3] found that the least percep-
tible extent of motion of a well localized auditory signal starting
from the median position was 2.5 deg., while Shaffer and Wallach
(1966) obtained visual extent-of-motion thresholds under comparable conditions (for a single luminous target in total darkness) that
ranged from 1.4 to 4.4 min., a sensitivity about 50 times greater.

   The auditory no-motion point did not coincide with objective
immobility of the signal. In the initial measurement on 24 *S*s it
amounted to 3.40% DR in the direction *with* the head movement,
significantly different from zero at the .05 level. A similar value of
3.15% DR was obtained after the second control session. We believe
that this result is due to the ambiguity, in our experiment, of signal
displacements in the direction *with* the head rotation, which we
mentioned above. Such displacements may lead either to apparent
target motion or to perception of a stationary sound source elevated
above the horizontal plane. The existence of the latter option should
have the effect of widening the mean range of no-motion judgments
in the direction of displacement *with* the head movement. In vision,
a similar failure of the no-motion point to coincide with objective
target rest has a different reason. There, an objectively stationary
target at a finite distance from *O* is being displaced relative to his
eyes in the direction *against* the head rotation (beyond the normal
displacement of a stationary object relative to the head) because the
eyes, being located forward from the head's rotation axis, become
displaced *with* the head rotation. This additional displacement of a
stationary target due to the location of the eyes is the greater the
nearer the target (Wallach & Kravitz, 1965a). It would cause the
no-motion point to be among the target displacement ratios *with* the
head rotation when the uncertainty range is measured. It does not
seem likely that our pre-adaptation measurements would show the
full effect of this additional displacement. The least that can be ex-

[3]Quoted in Robert S. Woodworth, *Experimental psychology* (1938). p. 519.

pected here is that Ss come to our experiment adapted to some finite field distance and that it is the difference between the latter and the target distance in the apparatus in which the uncertainty range is measured that causes the no-motion point not to coincide with objective target rest. Since the ears are not being laterally displaced by a head turning, this explanation does not apply to the auditory case.

The main question raised in this article, whether an adaptation in CVD transfers to the constancy of auditory direction, was to be answered by the auditory test that followed the second training session. Here, the mean no-motion point was .75% DR in the direction *against* the head rotation, while at the end of the control session the no-motion point had been 3.15% DR *with* the head rotation. The mean of the difference scores between these measurements amounted to 3.85% DR *against* the head rotation; it was, however, not significantly different from zero (p=.2). This mean is also quite small compared to the adaptation effect measured with the visual test. The latter amounted to 13.22% DR and was significantly different from the auditory difference of 3.85% DR at the .02 level.

We find, then, that partial adaptation in CVD to the effect of magnification was not reflected to an important extent in the measurement of the constancy of auditory direction. Little, if any, of the adaptation in CVD could be attributed to a modification of kinesthetic processes representing head rotation.

References

Gibson, J. J. Adaptation, after-effect and contrast in the perception of curved lines. *Journal of Experimental Psychology,* 1933, 16, 1–31.

Shaffer, O., & Wallach, H. Extent-of-motion thresholds under subject-relative and object-relative conditions. *Perception & Psychophysics,* 1966, 1, 447–451.

Wallach, H. The role of head movements and vestibular and visual cues in sound localization. *Journal of Experimental Psychology,* 1940, 27, 339–368. In the present volume, Chapter VI.

Wallach, H., & Karsh, E. B. Why the modification of stereoscopic depth perception is so rapid. *American Journal of Psychology,* 1963, 76, 413–420. In the present volume, Chapter X, selection 3.

Wallach, H., & Kravitz, J. H. The measurement of the constancy of visual direction and of its adaptation. *Psychonomic Science,* 1965a, 2, 217–218. In the present volume, this chapter, selection 1.

Wallach, H., & Kravitz, J. H. Rapid adaptation in the constancy of visual direction with active and passive rotation. *Psychonomic Science,* 1965b, 3, 165–166. In the present volume, this chapter, selection 2.

4. Adaptation in the Constancy of Visual Direction Measured By a One-Trial Method

In previous work on the constancy of visual direction,[1] a start was made in the investigation of adaptation to the regular displacements of the visual field during turning movements of the head such as occur when size lenses are worn. When such adaptation has taken place, it causes an objectively stationary visual field to appear to move during a head movement and this motion is in the direction opposite to the displacement to which S had fully or partially adapted. Measurements of this adaptation were made by presenting a target visible in the dark that could be displaced dependent on S's head movements and by finding that ratio of target displacement to head rotation at which the target appeared to be stationary. Such measurements have been taken for adaptation to minification, which causes field displacement in the direction *with* the head movement (Wallach & Kravitz, 1965a) and also for adaptation to magnification where the field displacement is in the direction *against* the head rotation (Wallach & Kravitz, 1968). But these two opposite effects have never been produced under otherwise identical adaptation conditions and their measurements were thus not comparable. Such a comparison is interesting, however, for the following reason. Since

Written in collaboration with Karl Josef Frey. Reprinted from *Perception & Psychophysics*, 1969, 5, 249–252.

[1]A lengthy explication of this concept, of the device used for measuring the constancy of visual direction, and of the effect of size lenses in causing displacements of the visual field is given in Wallach and Kravitz (1968).

the constancy of visual direction can be modified in as little as 5 min. (Wallach & Kravitz, 1965b), it seems reasonable to assume that the constancy which S brings to the adaptation experiment, i.e., the fact that the visual field appears stationary during head movements, is also learned; that, in other words, *experimental* adaptation is a modification of the result of a previous adaptation to the natural conditions of everyday existence. What are these natural conditions that everybody adapts to?

In answering this question we have, for the moment, to give up the ordinary way of thinking about motion and rest. This thinking is based on the perception of a stationary environment where objects that are perceived to be in motion are, in fact, being displaced relative to that environment. This way of perceiving is in agreement with the practical physical facts that matter in our ordinary dealing with the objects in our environment. But it is, nevertheless, true that a stationary environment is a product of our perceptual processes. In visual stimulation, the stationary environment is represented as stationary only as long as the head is kept still. When the head is turned—because the eye sockets shift with the head—stimulation conditions represent a stationary environment as being displaced relative to the head. Since, in the analysis of perceptual problems, conditions of stimulation rather than the physical environment are the primary facts, the displacement of the environment relative to eyes and head must be our starting point. With the head therefore taken as the frame of reference, a turning of the head to the right brings about a displacement of the visual field (relative to the head) to the left, and vice versa. Hence, the natural conditions to which everybody adapts consists in an environmental displacement in the direction *against* the head movement. Thus, the two kinds of experimental adaptation to artificially produced displacements of the optical, i.e., physical, environment differ in the way they relate to previous adaptation to the natural conditions; experimental adaptation to displacement *against* the head movement aims in the same direction as the previous adaptation, while the other kind, which occurs when minifiers are worn, develops in the opposite direction. A comparison between the two kinds of adaptation may, therefore, bear upon the relationship between experimental adaptation and previous adaptation whose result S brings to the experiment.

In the work to be reported, adaptation to displacement in the direction *with* the head movement and to displacement *against* the head movement was produced under conditions that were identical except with respect to direction. Also, the same group of *S*s was employed in both forms of the experiment. This was done because all previous work showed very large individual differences in the amount of adaptation achieved under identical training conditions. The amount of displacement relative to the head movement, termed displacement ratio, to which *S*s had to adapt was also varied; three different displacement ratios were used for each of the two directions, thus requiring each *S* to participate in six different adaptation experiments. Since the effect of rapid training disappears more quickly and is therefore likely to affect subsequent adaptation training less, should an aftereffect of experimental adaptation on subsequent adaptation exist, we used the rapid training technique previously employed (Wallach & Kravitz, 1965b).

The short-lived adaptation effects that result from rapid training present, however, a special problem: they are more difficult to measure in a uniform fashion, since they begin to deteriorate during the lengthy measuring procedures so far used by Wallach and Kravitz. A more rapid method of measuring adaptation was therefore developed for the present work; it consisted of a quantitative one-trial test. This test was based on the fact that an established adaptation effect causes a single stationary target to appear to move during a head turning in the direction opposite to the relative displacement to which *S* had adapted. The extent of this apparent displacement of a stationary target varies with extent of the head rotation and with the amount of adaptation attained. The latter follows from the manner in which adaptation was previously measured: the range of displacement ratios that lead to apparent immobility of the objectively moving target was determined (no-motion range) and its midpoint computed. The latter, the no-motion point, was the measure of adaptation. The larger the displacement ratio yielding this no-motion point, that is, the farther in the scale of displacement ratios (DR) the apparent no-motion point fell from the objective no-motion point (zero DR), the greater the adaptation measured. It is most likely that the larger the objective target displacement relative to the head movement that leads to apparent target immobility, the larger should be the apparent displacement of an objectively stationary target. And, since the *objective* target displacement resulting in apparent target rest is the larger the greater the adaptation, the *apparent* displacement of a stationary target should also increase with the amount of adaptation achieved. Furthermore, since the objective target displacement that leads to perceived target rest is relative to the amount of head movement, and is measured as a displacement *ratio,* it might be expected that the *apparent* displacement of a stationary target that occurs during head movements is likewise proportionate to the head movement; hence, our previous statement that the extent of the apparent displacement varies also with the extent of the head movement. Thus, if we want to use this apparent displacement of a stationary target as a measure of adaptation, we must either keep the extent of head movement constant or contrive to elicit an estimate that represents the ratio of the apparent displacement to the extent of the head movement.

We took the latter course. Instead of presenting S with a stationary target, the test was so arranged that S's head movements caused the target spot to become vertically displaced; when S turned his head to the right the target moved objectively upward, and left turning made the target move down. Thus, the same head movement that brought forth the apparent horizontal target displacement caused by the adaptation effect would simultaneously elicit an objective vertical displacement for the target. We had hoped, and indeed found, that the two displacements, although one was objective and the other apparent, add vectorially to produce an apparent oblique target motion: after the adaptation training Ss reported target motion at a slant, and they were able to reproduce the slant of the apparent motion path by setting a rod that could be turned in the frontal plane.

This slant estimate represents the extent of the apparent horizontal target displacement, because the tangent of the slant angle should equal the ratio of the extent of the apparent horizontal displacement over the extent of the objective vertical displacement. The apparatus used in this test was such that the angle of the extent of the vertical displacement was a constant fraction of the extent of the head rotation; in the present work it was always 40% of the latter. Since the same head movement that caused the apparent horizontal target displacement governed the objective vertical target displacement, the slant of the apparent path of the target motion represents the extent of the apparent horizontal target displacement also as a fraction of the head rotation, that is, as a displacement ratio.

Before the adaptation experiment proper, we explored *S*'s ability to detect deviation from verticality of the target's motion path and to make estimates of the slants of a number of different motion paths. Our apparatus was so modified that the target could objectively move at a certain slant when *S* turned his head. The apparatus would simultaneously displace the target vertically at a constant ratio of 40% of the angle of the head rotation and horizontally at a rate that could be varied from trial to trial. The resultant of the two simultaneous displacements was a slanted motion path whose slant angle depended on the rate of the horizontal displacement. When these trials had shown that variations in the displacement ratio in the horizontal motion component caused corresponding changes in the slant estimates, we proceeded to use this technique in tests of adaptation, where the horizontal component of the slanted motion path was supplied by the adaptation effect.

Apparatus

The measuring device previously used by Wallach and Kravitz (1968) was modified to produce vertical as well as horizontal target displacement. The projector beam that cast the target disk on the screen in front of *S* was successively reflected by two mirrors, a larger one that turned about a horizontal shaft and the one previously used that turned about a vertical axis and was mounted on the output shaft of the variable transmission. While the latter's angular displacement relative to the rotation of the input shaft was variable and controlled by setting the transmission ratio to a desired value, the larger mirror turned in fixed proportion to the shaft, causing a vertical target displacement of 40% of the head rotation. Either one of the mirror shafts could be disconnected from the turning parts of the apparatus and fixed in a constant position.

The ¼-in. metal rod used by *S* to indicate the slant of the target motion was 22.5 in. long. Attached perpendicularly at its midpoint was a short shaft that served as rotation axis for the rod. It had its bearing in the center of a white board 28 in. high and 22 in. wide. A long pointer was fixed on the other end of the shaft in the board's rear, permitting accurate reading of the rod position from a large scale. The board was mounted on a stand so high that the rod's shaft was at the level of S's eyes and was placed near the testing apparatus so that, by turning his head to the side, S could face the board and move the rod by hand.

Preliminary Experiments

(1) To test our Ss' ability to detect slanted target motion we followed the procedure used by Wallach and Kravitz in measuring the uncertainty range in the constancy of visual direction. Such measurements were concerned with the detection of objective, horizontal target displacements during head movements. In the present experiment an unchanging vertical displacement amounting to 40% of the head rotation angle was added to the variable horizontal displacement. As the displacement ratio of the horizontal target displacement was varied from displacement *with* the head movement through target immobility to displacement *against* the head movement, the resultant motion path of the target varied from slant to the right through verticality to slant to the left. Instead of reporting whether the target seemed to move or to be stationary as was done in the previous measurements, S was asked whether its motion path appeared vertical or slanted, in other words, judgments of verticality vs. slant replaced judgments of target rest or motion; in all other respects the procedure remained the same. The mean uncertainty range for perceived verticality of target motion was found to be 8.6% DR (14 Ss). This was 2% DR larger than the mean uncertainty range of 6.6% DR for apparent target rest obtained by Wallach and Kravitz (1965a) with naive Ss, and much larger than the mean of 3.86% DR obtained by the same Es with 14 practiced Ss (1968).

(2) We determined our Ss' ability to give estimates of the slant of the motion path by presenting them with eight different motion paths, of four different slant angles in each of the two slant directions, and had them reproduce the apparent slant of each motion path with the tilting rod. The different slant angles were produced by setting the horizontal target displacement to 5.3, 10.6, 15.9, and 21.2% DR. With the simultaneous vertical displacement a constant 40% DR, the resultant motion paths had slant angles of 7.5 deg., 14.8 deg., 21.7 deg., and 27.9 deg. The slant direction was controlled by causing the horizontal target displacement to be in the direction *with* or *against* the head movement.

Sitting under the measuring device, his head attached to its input shaft, S first turned his head to face the rod and adjusted it to the apparent vertical position. E read the setting and if it deviated from the true vertical, which happened only rarely, took down the rod position. Then, with the room darkened and the horizontal target displacement set to one of the predetermined values, S made three full head movements, thereby causing three up-and-down excursions of the target spot. He turned his head toward the rod, and, with the light turned on, made a rod setting. His slant estimate was the difference in degrees between his vertical setting and his slant setting. The sequence of presentation of the eight different motion paths was varied from S to S, but so that a slant in one direction was always immediately followed by a slant in the other direction. Each motion path was presented twice in the sequence of presentation and the average of the two estimates became S's score for that particular slant angle. In anticipation of a procedure followed in the main experiment, the starting position of the rod when S made his setting was always vertical.

The results are presented in Table 1. A comparison of the means of the slant estimates with the slant angles of the given target paths shows an underestimation of the slant angle. While this underestimation increased with the given slant angles, it was by no means proportional to them. Whereas the slant estimates given for particular motion paths by different Ss showed rather large variations, estimates by individual Ss showed good discrimination of the eight objective slants. For a total of 84 pairs of slant estimates given by individual Ss for adjacent objective slants, only two errors occurred such that the greater of the two objective slants was judged the smaller and vice versa.

Procedure in the Main Experiments

Rapid adaptation to field displacement *with* and *against* the head movement was compared for three rates of field displacement: 20, 40, and 80% DR. Thus, each of our 14 Ss, the same who had been used in the second preliminary experiment and therefore mastered the rod setting technique, participated in six adaptation experiments that differed in direction or rate of the field displacement.

TABLE 1
Mean Slant Estimates for Eight Motion Paths

Slant Direction Horizontal Displacement	Counter Clockwise Against				Clockwise With			
Displacement rate	21.2%	15.9%	10.6%	5.3%	5.3%	10.6%	15.9%	21.2%
Objective slant angle	27.9 deg.	21.7 deg.	14.8 deg.	7.5 deg.	7.5 deg.	14.8 deg.	21.7 deg.	27.9 deg.
Slant estimates	20.5 deg.	15.4 deg.	9.6 deg.	3.9 deg.	3.7 deg.	10.0 deg.	15.0 deg.	19.8 deg.

Each such experiment began with an initial rod setting. The mirror that caused the horizontal target displacement was arrested and the vertically displacing mirror was connected to the input shaft so that head turning produced objectively vertical target displacement. S had to make one rod setting that reproduced the apparent direction of this motion path. S was allowed two full head movements before setting the rod to the perceived target motion direction, and this procedure was followed throughout the experiment. The adaptation period, which now followed, was similar to the one used by Wallach and Kravitz (1965b) for rapid adaptation in that S simply remained in the test apparatus, which was set for a high displacement ratio, continuously turned his head back and forth and observed the moving target spot. It differed in that training lasted for exactly 100 full head movements and that the various displacement ratios for which the transmission was set were much smaller than the one ratio previously used. To change the apparatus to the adaptation conditions the vertically displacing mirror simply was disengaged and the variable transmission was set for one of the six displacement ratios stated above. After the room was darkened, S was asked to turn his head back and forth at a comfortable rate and pay attention to the moving target spot. When this adaptation period, which lasted on the average 3 min., ended, the apparatus was again arranged for objectively vertical target motion, with S sitting still and with eyes closed. Directly after this change-over, which took very little time, S made one slant setting. The difference in slant angle between this setting and the preadaptation setting is the measured adaptation effect.

Casual observations by Wallach and Kravitz had shown that after termination of the training period the adaptation effect gradually diminishes and disappears. The question arises whether encounters with normal field displacements during head movements are responsible for this or whether the mere lapse of time serves to diminish experimental adaptation and to reestablish the normal constancy of visual direction. Our one-trial measuring method is particularly suitable to answering this question, for it is uniform and takes little time. Therefore, following the postadaptation rod setting, *S* was asked to close his eyes and to sit still, with his head in normal position. After 5 min. another rod setting was made.

Immediately after this test for the decline of the adaptation effect with lapse of time, *S* was asked to turn his head back and forth five times while observing the target spot that was now objectively entirely immobile, and this was followed directly by another rod setting. This procedure gave us a rough idea of the effectiveness of a brief exposure to conditions that would tend to reestablish the normal constancy of visual direction.

An individual adaptation experiment ended here. *S* was asked to get up and move about freely for 20 min. After this rest period another one of the six adaptation experiments began. It was always the one with the same rate of field displacement that was used in the first adaptation of the day's session and in the opposite direction. Only two experiments were run on the same day; there were thus three experimental sessions in all; they were separated by at least 3 days. Except for the rule just stated, the sequence of adaptation was varied from *S* to *S* and satisfactorily balanced. When the initial rod setting of the second adaptation experiment of a given session raised doubt about whether all the effect of the preceding adaptation had disappeared, the experiment was broken off and was started at another time.

Results

The mean adaptation effects obtained under the six training conditions are listed in the first row of Table 2. In the case of both displacement directions, the effect increased as the displacement rate of the target rose from 20% to 40% of the head rotation, and this increase is significant at the .05 level. A further rise in the displacement ratio, to 80%, did not produce a comparable increase in the adaptation effect. Adaptation to target displacement in the direction *with* the head movement was consistently higher than adaptation to displace-

TABLE 2

Mean Effects of Six Conditions of Adaptation in Degrees of Slant and Decline of the Effects after 5 min. Rest and after Five Additional Head Movements (HM)

Adaptation Direction	With			Against		
Displacement Rate	20%	40%	80%	20%	40%	80%
Adaptation effect	6.82	8.65	9.42	4.28	6.68	6.29
Slant of rod setting						
after adaptation	6.71	8.61	9.46	4.21	6.68	6.04
5 min. later	3.86	5.43	5.18	1.18	3.39	2.43
Proportionate decline	42.5%	36.9%	45.2%	72%	49.2%	59.7%
Slant of rod setting						
after 5 HM	2.54	3.79	2.96	.79	2.07	1.50

ment *against* the head turning, a difference significant at better than the .005 level.[2]

There was a large and highly significant decline in the adaptation effect after the 5-min. period of rest, as shown by a comparison of the means of the slant settings made immediately after adaptation and of those made 5 min. later (second and third row in Table 2). In the fourth row of Table 2 this decline is given as a percentage of the effect measured immediately after the adaptation period. Presented in this fashion the decline is consistently greater in the case of adaptations to displacements in the direction *against* the head movement, and this difference is significant at the .01 level. The subsequent five head movements caused a sizeable further decline of what was left of the experimental adaptation (fifth row of Table 2). This brief exposure to conditions tending to reestablish the normal constancy of visual direction was quite effective (p < .001). It should be mentioned that our slant test also represented the conditons for the reestablishment of the normal constancy, because here, too, the target spot was stationary where the left-right dimension was concerned while *S* turned his head twice. (The vertical target displacement that occurred in these tests is not relevant.) Therefore, part of the decrease in the experimental adaptation measured

[2]It may be worth mentioning that there exists a correlation indicating that *S*s who showed a strong adaptation effect to displacement in the direction *with* the head movement also tended to show a strong effect when displacement was in the direction *against* the head movement; r = .54, p < .05.

after the 5-min. rest period must be ascribed to the additional test.

Discussion

The many significant differences that were obtained in these experiments are a tribute to the one-trial test used here for the first time. This test permits very brief and therefore more uniform training periods, which cause adaptation effects that decline rapidly and disappear completely, making feasible the use of the same Ss for all the experimental variations.

That experimental adaptation to target displacement *with* the head movement is consistently and very significantly greater than adaptation that goes in the opposite direction is the main result of our experiment. As explained above, the two kinds of experimental adaptation, which were here produced under corresponding conditions, differ in the manner in which they relate to the adaptation that Ss bring to our experiment. The latter, the adaptation to the normal field displacements relative to the head caused by head movements under natural conditions, is an adaptation to displacements in the direction *against* the head movement. Experimental adaptation to target displacement *against* the head movement is thus a development that goes in the same direction as adaptation to natural conditions and thus enhances it, whereas experimental adaptation to objective displacement *with* the head movement goes in the direction opposite to natural adaptation and diminishes it. That the greater experimental adaptation was obtained under the latter condition makes sense. It seems reasonable that a change that diminishes a previously established adaptation effect develops more rapidly than the opposite one that requires a further enhancement of the previously established adaptation. That experimental adaptation to objective displacement *against* the head movement declines more rapidly than the opposite adaptation is a finding that should probably be considered in the same context.

References

Wallach, H., & Kravitz, J. H. The measurement of the constancy of visual direction and of its adaptation. *Psychonomic Science,* 1965a, 2, 217–218. In the present volume, this chapter, selection 1.

Wallach, H., & Kravitz, J. H. Rapid adaptation in the constancy of visual direction with active and passive rotation. *Psychonomic Science,* 1965b, 3, 165–166. In the present volume, this chapter, selection 2.

Wallach, H., & Kravitz, J. H. Adaptation in the constancy of visual direction tested by measuring the constancy of auditory direction. *Perception & Psychophysics,* 1968, 4, 299–303. In the present volume, this chapter, selection 3.

5. Adaptation to Field Displacement During Head Movement Unrelated to the Constancy of Visual Direction

When the visual field is displaced relative to an S's head causing image displacement across the retina or pursuit movements of the eyes, the field is seen to move. But when the same kind of displacement causing similar stimulus processes is produced by a head movement of S, the field appears stationary. This is the result of a compensating process where the head movement is taken into account in the evaluation of displacements between the visual field and the head. We deal here with a perceptual constancy akin to size constancy, etc. This constancy of visual direction, as Wallach and Kravitz (1965a) have called it, operates with great accuracy; even small objective displacements of the visual field during head movements, which would increase or diminish the normal head-movement-caused displacement of the field relative to the head, will be perceived as field displacements. In other words, field displacements during head turning in the amount of the head rotation but in the direction opposite to it will be perceived as field immobility, while larger or smaller field displacements will be perceived as field motion. Field motion in the direction *against* the head movement direction will be perceived when the given field displacement is larger than normal and perceived field motion will be in the direction *with* the head movement when the given field displacement is smaller than normal.

Written in collaboration with Karl Josef Frey and George Romney. Reprinted from *Perception & Psychophysics,* 1969, 5, 253–256.

Previous work (Wallach & Kravitz, 1968) has shown that this compensating function can be easily modified. Partial adaptation to consistent abnormal field displacements can be readily produced. When *S* is exposed for some time to conditions that cause field displacements that are, say, smaller than normal in a certain amount, below-normal field displacements of some value can be found that lead to perceived field immobility, while normal field displacement will be perceived as field displacement in the direction *against* the head turning. The latter fact can be used as a qualitative test of adaptation, while finding the particular *ab*normal field displacement that is perceived as field rest measures the adaptation effect.

Stated in practical terms, normal field displacement during head movements is, of course, produced by objective field immobility, the normal condition of our lives. Below-normal and above-normal field displacements are produced by causing the visual field to be displaced during head movements and dependent on them. This can be done optically by equipping *S*s with minifying or magnifying spectacles or by mechanical means (Wallach & Kravitz, 1968). In the latter case the field is represented by a dimly luminous target spot in an otherwise dark environment. This target is projected via a reflecting mirror and will become displaced when the mirror is turned. Head turning is transferred to the mirror by means of a variable transmission, enabling *E* to present objective target motion in the direction *with* or *against* the head movement in any desirable ratio to the head turning. In order to represent below-normal or above-normal field displacement, such objective target displacement must be parallel to the plane of the rotation in which the head movement consists, and this is true of the mechanical device used so far in such experiments. It is true also of optical field displacements produced by power lenses.

The present report is concerned with adaptation to objective target displacements perpendicular to the plane of the head rotation rather than parallel to it. Inasmuch as in ordinary life such displacements between field and head never occur, adaptation to vertical target displacement would be unrelated to the constancy of visual direction. We demonstrated such adaptation in two ways: by rapid adaptation measured with the slant estimation technique developed by Wallach and Frey (1969) and by 1-hr.-long adaptation measured by Wallach and Kravitz' method (1968) of determining no-motion ranges.

I. Rapid Adaptation to Unrelated Target Displacement During Head Movements[1]

Adaptation was produced here by having S in a dark room observe a luminous target spot that moved up and down when S turned his head to the right and the left. The vertical displacement angle of the target was 40% of the angle of the head rotation. The measuring device used by Wallach and Kravitz (1968) and equipped with two mirrors by Wallach and Frey (1969) was employed. To create the adaptation conditions, the vertically displacing mirror was connected to the input shaft while the mirror that caused the horizontal target displacement was arrested.

Preliminary experiments had shown that, after an S had observed for some time a target being displaced upward when his head turned right and downward when his head turned left, a stationary target would appear to move down when the head turned right and up when it turned left. We made this adaptation-caused apparent vertical target motion measurable in a manner corresponding to that used by Wallach and Frey, namely, by transforming the extent of the apparent vertical target motion into the slant of an apparent oblique motion path. This was done by giving the stationary target spot an objective horizontal displacement of 40% of the head rotation. The adaptation-caused apparent vertical displacement added itself vectorially to the objectively given horizontal target displacement, resulting in an oblique apparent motion path, whose slant could be reproduced by S. This was done with the help of a metal rod attached at its midpoint to a horizontal shaft that turned in a bearing inserted in a large white board. The board was placed near S, somewhat to the side so that it did not obscure the target's horizontal motion path. The board and the plane in which the rod turned were in frontal-parallel position after S had turned his head toward it, and the shaft was at S's eye level. In reproducing the slant of the apparent target motion S turned the rod with his hand.

[1]This experiment was first reported at a colloquium of the Department of Psychology of Harvard University in April, 1967.

PROCEDURE

There were 16 *S*s and each participated in two experimental sessions at least 2 days apart. Each session began with a test in which *S*, sitting under the device previously used by Wallach and Frey, his head attached to the input shaft, had to turn his head toward the rod and set it to the horizontal. Then, with the vertically displacing mirror disconnected and the transmission set for the other mirror to cause a horizontal target displacement of 40% of the head rotation, *S* made three head movements and reproduced the direction of the target's perceived motion path by a rod setting. *S* made two such settings, one with the horizontal target in the direction *with* the head movement and the other *against* it. This was done because after adaptation also two tests were made that differed in the direction of the horizontal displacement.

Adaptation training consisted in 100 complete head movements during which the target moved vertically always upward when the head turned to the right and downward with left turning. The ratio of target displacement to the head rotation angle was 40%. When the 100 head movements were completed, which took about 3 min., the vertically displacing mirror was again disconnected and the other mirror set to produce an objective horizontal target displacement *with* the head movement. *S* was allowed three head movements during which he observed the slant of the apparent motion path and then reproduced that slant with a rod setting. Immediately thereafter the direction of the objective horizontal target displacement was reversed and, after another three head movements, *S* made another rod setting, now for horizontal displacement *against* the head movement. The difference in slant angle between corresponding pre- and postadaptation settings represents the adaptation effect. The second experimental session differed from the one just described only in that the horizontal target displacement in the first test was *against* the head movement and in the second test in the *with* direction.

RESULTS

The mean adaptation effects are listed in Table 1 under the heading "first adaptation test." Amounting to 6 deg., they approach the effects that Wallach and Frey (1969) obtained under very similar conditions

TABLE 1

Mean Adaptation to Vertical Target Displacement in Degrees of Slant
after 100 Head Movements

First adaptation test		Second adaptation test		Difference between first and second test	p
Direction of horizontal displacement	Adaptation effect; confidence limits at .05 level	Direction of horizontal displacement	Adaptation effect		
With	6.06 ± 1.76	Against	4.53	1.53	<.02
Against	6.03 ± 1.73	With	4.87	1.16	<.02

for adaptation to target displacement parallel to the plane of the head
rotation. The effects were highly significant as shown by the confidence limits also given in Table 1. The effect disappears rapidly as
demonstrated by the immediately following second test, which produced settings of significantly smaller slants. Since in a test the
target spot does not undergo vertical displacement—the horizontal
displacement of the target does not alter the matter in principle—the
test represents normal viewing conditions and is therefore an occasion that can cause undoing of the adaptation to the artificial displacement conditions of the experiment. A corresponding effect was
obtained by Wallach and Frey in connection with adaptation to
displacements parallel to the plane of the head rotation.

II. Prolonged Adaptation to Field Displacements Perpendicular to the Plane in Which the Head Turns

Adaptation to target displacement during head movements that is
unrelated to the constancy of visual direction is so important a fact
that we also demonstrated it with an hour-long adaptation period of
continuous head movements. This method yields a stabler effect and
therefore allows measurement of an uncertainty range. This is the
range of ratios of target displacement to head rotation angle over
which the target may appear stationary. Its shift after the adaptation
period measures the adaptation effect, but by its width it also tells
us something about the nature of the effect. Since power lenses
previously used for prolonged adaptation periods cause only field

displacement parallel to the plane of head rotation, vertical field displacement dependent on head turning was produced by a moving-mirror device. It could be changed to yield horizontal field displacement also, and we were thus able to produce adaptation to constancy-related field displacements, in the directions *with* and *against* the head movement as well as vertical field displacements under otherwise identical conditions. In the case of all three adaptation experiments, the displacement rate amounted to 50% of the angular displacement of the head.

APPARATUS

In the device used for adaptation training, S sat under a horizontal plate in which a vertical shaft was mounted. A thin vertical plate fixed in median position to the top of S's headgear could be inserted into the slotted end of this shaft. S's head could be adjusted to meet the shaft by raising the chair on which he sat. Three sets of angle gears and two additional shafts transmitted the rotation of the vertical shaft caused by S's head turning to a mirror mounted on a horizontal shaft. The mirror was close to S's face at the level of his eyes. It was slanted to form a 45-deg. angle with the vertical when S's head pointed straight forward, and it was under mild spring tension to take up the play in the various gears. A second larger, stationary mirror, also slanted approximately 45 deg. and its reflecting surface facing the movable mirror, permitted S to see a television set located straight ahead of him at a distance of 3.5 m. The stationary mirror was so adjusted that S saw the set straight ahead at eye level when his head pointed forward. This arrangement caused the set to be shifted optically up and down when S turned his head back and forth. Two gear arrangements were provided, one which caused the set to shift optically up when S turned his head to the right and the other for the set to appear to move down for the same turn direction. Always, the mirror turned at a rate of 25% of that of the head rotation, causing the set to become optically displaced at a rate of 50% of the head rotation angle.

To provide horizontal field displacement, the device was changed so that the movable mirror turned on a vertical shaft, making S see the TV set through a stationary mirror located at his side. The turning rate of the mirror remained the same and the ratio of the now lateral optical displacement of the set was again 50%. Apart from the mirrors, all surfaces of the device visible to S were masked with black tape. Except for a flashlight sparingly used by E, the room was kept dark throughout the experiment. The TV picture was dimmed to the point where its light was restricted to its immediate environment that was visible only in the mirror. Therefore, only those objects were seen during the adaptation period that underwent the appropriate displacements when S moved his head.

To count head movements, a rod was fixed at right angles to the vertical shaft to which S's headgear was attached. The end of this rod, which thus moved through an arc when S turned his head, operated two switches, one at each end of its motion path. An arrangement of relays tripped an electric counter each time both switches had been closed successively in one order and thus caused only completed movement cycles to be counted. The switches were so spaced that S had to turn his head through 30 deg. in order to activate both of them, and they provided stops that limited the head movements to 36 deg.

The measuring device used to determine the uncertainty ranges before and after the adaptation period was described in detail by Wallach and Kravitz (1968). It caused a circular target spot to become displaced horizontally when S turned his head. The displacement ratio, that is, the rate of target displacement relative to the head rotation, was variable and could be set by E, and the target spot could be made to shift in the direction *with* the head rotation or *against* it. In the work here reported we used this device to measure adaptation to horizontal field displacement.

To measure adaptation to vertical field displacement, the device was altered: The mirror that reflected the target spot was replaced by one that rotated about a horizontal shaft when S turned his head, causing vertical displacement of the target spot. Again, its displacement ratio was variable and the direction of the displacement of the target spot was also alterable; it could be upward for a turning of the head to the right, or downward.

PROCEDURE

Adaptation was measured by obtaining the uncertainty range of no-motion judgments before and after the adaptation period and by computing the difference of their midpoints. The manner of measuring the uncertainty range was similar to that previously employed and explained in the article by Wallach and Kravitz (1968). Again the rate of target displacement relative to the head rotation, the displacement ratio (DR) was varied. Where adaptation was to constancy related field displacement, that is, to displacement in the direction *with* or *against* the head rotation, one series of displacement ratios was presented that led, in that order, to perceived target displacement in the direction *with* the head movement, to apparent target rest, and to perceived target motion *against* the head rotation. The other series of trials covered the relevant part of the scale of displacement ratios in the opposite order. In the preadaptation measurements, the part of the DR scale presented comprised objective target immobility as well as displacement *with* and *against* the head movement. After adaptation had developed, causing target displacement of a certain DR range to be perceived as stationary, the trials to be presented were, of course, centered about this range.

Trials were spaced in steps of .8% DR, and the sequence of trials was presented twice, once in each direction, yielding altogether two limits at each end of the no-motion range. As in the previous work the uncertainty range was computed by plotting from the two sequences those trials that yielded no-motion reports or inconsistent ones; one-half step was added at each end of the range. When adaptation was to field displacements *against* the head movement—causing a range of displacement ratios *against* the head rotation to lead to perceived target rest—the first postadaptation sequence started with target displacement *against* the head movement of high DR leading to perceived target motion in that direction. This was done because the presentation of displacements leading to perceived target motion *with* the head rotation tends to diminish the established adaptation. By probing for the relevant DR range with trials yielding target motion against the head, the presentation of trials causing perceived target motion *with* the head was minimized. In the case of adaptation to displacement *with* the head rotation, the procedure was, of course, reversed. To give *S* practice with these measurements, the *pre*adaptation test was preceded by two trial sequences each of which determined only one of the two limits of the no-motion range, i.e., did not continue across the no-motion range to find the second limit, as happened in the subsequent actual test.

Adaptation to vertical field displacement was tested in a corresponding manner. Thus, there were two directions of vertical target displacement relative to the head rotation, one upwards when S's head turned right and downward when it turned left, and the other with reversed target displacements.

Subjects spent 1 hr. in the training device and made from 992 to 3046 complete head movements during that period. The same 12 Ss were at different times employed in all three conditions of the experiment. The order of adaptation to field displacements *with* or *against* the head rotation was randomized. In the case of vertical field displacement, six Ss adapted to upward displacement when the head turned right and the other six to relative displacement in the opposite direction.

RESULTS

As in our first experiment, adaptation to vertical field displacement yielded a sizable effect. The mean difference between the midpoints of the uncertainty ranges measured before and after 1-hr. adaptation amounted to 8.73% DR, and this effect was highly significant. There was no overlap of the uncertainty ranges taken before and after adaptation for any one of our Ss. As was to be expected, this effect is greater than the one obtained from a brief training period in our first experiment. The mean change in slant estimate in the amount of 6 deg. obtained there was equivalent to 4.2% DR. The difference between the two adaptation effects appears small when one considers that the large one results from 10 times more training than the smaller one. The comparatively small effect obtained after the long training of our second experiment cannot be attributed to a loss in adaptation gradually taking place during the much longer measuring procedure here employed. Such a progressive loss would have manifested itself in an enlarged uncertainty range measured after adaptation. The mean uncertainty ranges measured after adaptation show that no important enlargement occurred (Table 2).

The second experiment permits comparing adaptation to vertical field displacement with adaptation to constancy-related field displacement produced under closely similar conditions. For both conditions of horizontal field displacement mean adaptation was greater than adaptation to vertical displacement, but a significant

TABLE 2
Adaptation to Field Displacement in Three Directions Compared
All Means in % DR

Relative Field Displacement	Uncertainty Range Before	After	Mean Adaptation Effect	Difference	p
Vertical	2.39	2.65	8.73		
With head rotation	4.17	4.04	14.69	5.96	<.01
Against head rotation	3.31	4.51	10.14	4.55	<.03

difference was obtained only in the case of adaptation to displacement in the direction *with* the head rotation (p < .01). The mean uncertainty ranges for horizontal target displacement were larger than for vertical target displacement, both before and after adaptation. With the data for the two horizontal conditions combined, each difference was significant at the .05 level on two-tailed tests.

When the two constancy-related adaptation effects are compared with each other one finds that they confirm the result of Wallach and Frey (1969) who found that adaptation to field displacement *with* the head rotation was consistently greater than that to displacement in the opposite direction. We obtained a significant difference in the same direction (4.55% DR, p < .03).[2]

Discussion

The result of our work that partial adaptation to field displacements in an unrelated direction can be obtained as easily as adaptation to constancy-related displacements is confirmed by an experiment of John Hay (1968), conceived independently from ours. Employing an electronic technique he had *S*s adapt to horizontal displacements of a target point that were dependent on a nodding head movement, that is, on head rotation about a horizontal axis. Translated into the terminology used by us Hay's one quantitative experiment had the following result: Ten minutes of adaptation to horizontal target displacements of 70% DR when head movements were vertical yielded a mean adaptation of 8.4% DR; eight *S*s participated each of whom

[2]An interpretation of this finding is presented in Wallach and Frey (1969).

made a single no-motion setting, that is, one setting that fell somewhere within the uncertainty range.[3]

There are two ways in which to account for the existence of a
learned constancy such as the constancy of visual direction or, more
generally speaking, of instances of perceptual adaptation. They may
be due to specific learning capacities, each existing to meet its particular purpose. The assumption that they are based on specific learning processes would particularly fit such adaptive capacities that are
necessary to compensate for normal changes of the body as growth
of the skull (causing increase in interocular distance and hence in
retinal disparity)[4] or changes in ocular optics that produce shape
distortions in the visual field. It could, however, also apply to such
seemingly vital functions as the constancy of visual direction. Alternatively, some adaptation processes may be manifestations of general principles that can underlie a variety of cases of perceptual
learning.[5] The finding that adaptation to field displacements unrelated to the constancy of visual direction can be obtained at a
magnitude comparable to constancy-related adaptation favors the
latter view.

In constancy-related adaptation, an adaptation to the normal
field displacements relative to the turning head that S brings to the
experiment, is modified; adaptation is to a condition where the nor-

[3]Hay attributes adaptation to head movement-dependent object displacement to
the occurrence of eye movements that follow the displacing object during the adaptation process. He supports this view by an experiment in which a stationary as well
as a displacing object are visible during the adaptation exposure. He found an adaptation effect such that a stationary object appeared to move when S nodded his head
when during the adaptation exposure S looked at the displacing object, but no such
aftereffect occurred when S fixated the stationary object. This outcome can be interpreted in a different way: the two objects provide conflicting information and selective attention causes the different outcomes of the adaptation exposure. The absence
of measurements that show that adaptation is as great in the presence of the stationary
object as without it makes this demonstration inconclusive.

[4]Rapid partial adaptation of stereoscopic depth perception to artificially altered
binocular parallax, which corresponds to change in interocular distance, was demonstrated by Wallach, Moore and Davidson (1963).

[5]An example is the hypothesis of process assimilation which would account for
adaptation that takes place when one of a pair of cues giving rise to the same perceptual property is artificially altered. This hypothesis was first proposed by Wallach
and Karsh (1963) in connection with adaptation of stereoscopic depth perception. A
more detailed discussion may be found in Chapter 13 of *The neuropsychology of
spatially oriented behavior,* 1968, Sanford J. Freedman, editor.

mal displacements of an objectively stationary field are either augmented or diminished. But when the objective field displacement is vertical, the normal horizontal field displacement is thereby made oblique, a direction that is the result of the two displacement components. (In our second experiment, for instance, where the objectively vertical field displacement amounted to 50% of the rate of head rotation this oblique displacement formed an angle of 26.6 deg. with the horizontal.) The adaptation effect that results, however, does not consist in a modification of normal adaptation. Rather, *S* retains the adaptation to the normal, head-rotation-caused field displacement and develops an apparently independent adaptation to vertical field displacement. This is indicated by two facts: After the adaptation period, an objectively stationary target spot appears to move vertically, and the uncertainty range for vertical target displacement remains small after adaptation has taken place, significantly smaller than that measured for horizontal target displacement. This independent adaptation to vertical field displacement is unique in kind in *S*'s life; never before was he exposed to the combination of vertical field displacement occurring with head rotation in the horizontal plane. Yet he easily and rapidly adapts to these conditions and this argues that some general principle is in operation here rather than a specific learning capacity related to the field displacements normally caused by head movements and responsible for the constancy of visual direction.

References

Hay, J. Visual adaptation to an altered correlation between eye movement and head movement. *Science,* 1968, 160, 429–430.

Wallach, H., & Frey, K. J. Adaptation in the constancy of visual direction measured by a one-trial method. *Perception & Psychophysics,* 1969, 5, 245–252. In the present volume, this chapter, selection 4.

Wallach, H., & Karsh, E. The modification of stereoscopic depth-perception and the kinetic depth-effect. *American Journal of Psychology,* 1963, 76, 429–435. In the present volume, Chapter X, selection 4.

Wallach, H., & Kravitz, J. The measurement of the constancy of visual direction and of its adaptation. *Psychonomic Science,* 1965a, 2, 217–218. In the present volume, this chapter, selection 1.

Wallach, H., & Kravitz, J. Adaptation in the constancy of visual direction tested by measuring the constancy of auditory direction. *Perception & Psychophysics,* 1968, 4, 299–303. In the present volume, this chapter, selection 3.

Wallach, H., Moore, M., & Davidson, L. Modification of stereoscopic depth-perception. *American Journal of Psychology,* 1963, 76, 191–204. In the present volume, this chapter, selection 2.

6. Differences in the Dissipation of the Effect of Adaptation to Two Kinds of Field Displacement During Head Movements

One of the important issues in perceptual adaptation concerns the relationship between the learning process that causes the adaptation and the product of previous learning that governed S's perception prior to adaptation. The latter may be considered the result of an adaptation process also, namely, an adaptation to the natural conditions of viewing or listening, which is then temporarily superseded by experimental adaptation. In the end, after the postadaptation test has been administered, S, who is exposed again to the natural conditions, readapts to them, and his perceptual performance becomes normal again. There are, however, numerous instances of experimental adaptation where normalization of perception occurs without exposure to the natural conditions. A mere lapse of time during which S remains passive and shut off from relevant stimulation suffices here to reestablish the normal perceptual function. It is obviously of great interest to know where such spontaneous dissipation of the effect of experimental adaptation occurs and in what kinds of adaptation it does not. It is, in fact, possible that all experimental adaptation dissipates spontaneously and that we deal here, rather, with differences in the rate at which perceptual

Written in collaboration with Karl Josef Frey. Reprinted from *Perception & Psychophysics*, 1972, 11, 31–34.

functions return to normal. The experiment to be reported is part of a project where the rate of dissipation of a number of different kinds of adaptation effects is being studied.

The present experiment compares the rate of spontaneous dissipation of three kinds of adaptation to field displacements during head movements, field displacements in the direction of the head movements, either *with* or *against* it, or at right angles to the head movements. In previous work (Wallach, Frey & Romney, 1969), we referred to the first two kinds of adaptation with the term "related to the constancy of visual direction," while we regarded the last one as unrelated to it. This distinction refers to the following considerations. With the visual field stationary, a head turning will cause a displacement of the field relative to the head. When an identical displacement is caused by moving the visual field, the displacement will be perceived as motion of the environment, but when it is caused by a head movement, the environment will appear stationary. This is due to a compensating process which we called constancy of visual direction, or CVD, which takes head movements into account in a most accurate manner where perceived motion or rest of the environment is concerned (Wallach & Kravitz, 1968). The field displacements for which this constancy process compensates take place in the direction parallel to the plane in which the head turns, and that is the reason for calling adaptation to objective field displacement in this direction, i.e., to field displacements *with* or *against* the head movement, constancy related. When such objective field displacements are described as displacements relative to the turning head, they subtract themselves from or add themselves to the displacement that the objectively stationary environment undergoes relative to the turning head. It is the latter displacement that CVD causes to be perceived as environmental rest, whereas even a small increase or decrease in this displacement (caused by an objective field displacement *against* or *with* the head movement) is perceived as environmental motion. In other words, CVD singles out a particular rate of displacement parallel to the plane of the head rotation and makes it the zero point of the perceived environmental motions such that smaller rates of displacement produce perceived environmental motions in the direction *with* the head movement and larger rates cause perceived motions of the field *against* the head turning. The particular rate of displacement relative to the head that leads to perceived rest is the one produced by the stationary environment. Adaptation to natural viewing conditions, which causes the development of this way of perceiving motion and rest during a head movement, is concerned with field displacements parallel to the plane of the head rotation, for that is the displacement of the stationary environment relative to the turning head. Experimental adaptation to objective field displacements parallel to the plane of the head rotation thus modifies the result of the adaptation to natural viewing conditions.

Experimental adaptation to field displacements at right angles to the plane of the head rotation is not so closely related to CVD. It amounts to a field displacement *relative to the head* that is oblique to the plane of the head rotation (namely, the resultant of the objective field displacement and the displacement of the stationary field relative to the turning head). Such an oblique displacement is not involved in the acquisition of CVD; it does not occur under natural conditions. Thus, experimental adaptation to field displacement parallel to the plane of the head rotation (Type A adaptation) modifies a product of a previously learned compensating process, while experimental adaptation at right angles to the plane of the head rotation (Type B adaptation) does not. When Type B adaptation has developed, the adaptation to the natural viewing conditions that *S* brings to the experiment still functions unaltered. For instance, partial adaptation to vertical field displacement during head turning in the horizontal plane causes that field displacement to be perceived at a smaller rate than the objective displacement would warrant, but the field motion that is seen is still in a vertical direction: CVD, which causes perceived field immobility as an alternative to perceived horizontal field motion, still functions fully. With the two types of adaptation thus differently related to the product of previous learning of CVD, it seemed possible that they differed with regard to spontaneous dissipation of the experimental adaptation. Wallach and Floor (1970) had obtained significant dissipation for Type A adaptation, which most likely was spontaneous, while the results for Type B adaptation were not clear.[1]

[1]The dissipation measured for Type B adaptation was actually smaller than that obtained for Type A adaptation, but the difference failed to be significant.

Procedure

The general plan of our experiment was to produce experimental adaptations to horizontal field displacement and to vertical field displacement, both during head turning and to monitor their spontaneous dissipation. We measured adaptation effects three times, immediately after the adaptation period and 10 and 20 min. later. Between tests, S sat quietly, his eyes closed. For obvious reasons, we used the one-trial method introduced by Wallach and Frey (1969). This method measured the extent of the apparent motion which a stationary luminous spot in the dark underwent as an effect of adaptation when S moved his head. This was done by combining the "subjective" motion caused by the adaptation effect with an objective motion of the target spot at right angles to the former. When the field displacement to which S adapted was horizontal and, say, in the direction *with* the head movement, the apparent motion caused by the adaptation effect was *against* the head movement (to the left when the head turned right). When this apparent motion was combined with a vertical displacement of the target spot such that it moved objectively upward when the head turned right and down when the head turned left, the perceived target motion was oblique, slanting counterclockwise with respect to the vertical. It was this slant angle which S reproduced in the test and which measured the adaptation effect. Apart from the ease with which Ss can make such slant estimates, the procedure has the following advantage: the extent of the apparent horizontal motion, which depends on the amount of adaptation achieved or, after partial dissipation, on the amount of residual adaptation effect, depends also on the extent of the head rotation. But since, because of the mechanism used to produce the objective vertical target displacement, the latter also varied with the extent of the head movement, the slant angle actually represented the ratio of the apparent horizontal target motion to the head movement. This measure therefore closely corresponded to the displacement ratio, that is, the ratio of the objective angular field displacement to the angle of the head rotation causing it, with which we had previously measured this kind of adaptation.[2] When S

[2]For a detailed explication of the displacement ratio measure, see Wallach and Kravitz (1968).

adapted to vertical displacements during head rotation in the horizontal plane (Type B adaptation), a stationary target would afterwards appear to move vertically, and this was combined with an objective horizontal target displacement. Here the estimated slant angle was measured as a deviation from the horizontal (Wallach, Frey, & Romney, 1969).

It was important that the conditions for the two types of adaptation to be compared be identical. We achieved this by adapting simultaneously to horizontal and vertical field displacements of equal magnitude, a 40% displacement ratio. The apparatus described in detail by Wallach and Kravitz (1968), equipped with two mirrors to provide horizontal and vertical target displacements by Wallach and Frey (1969) and improved by Wallach and Floor (1970) was used. Simultaneous vertical and horizontal field displacements of equal displacement ratio (DR) produced an oblique target displacement of 45 deg. as resultant. There were two conditions of adaptation: the horizontal field displacement was either *with* or *against* the direction of the head rotation while there was only a single combination of head turning and vertical field displacement; when *S* turned his head to the right, the target spot moved objectively upward, and when the head turned left the target moved down. Therefore, the resultant target motion was between upper right and lower left in the case of the horizontal displacement *with* the head movement and of opposite slant when the horizontal displacement was *against* the rotation of the head. During the adaptation period, *S* remained attached to the test apparatus which was set to produce the simultaneous vertical and horizontal target displacements just described when he turned his head back and forth. The adaptation training consisted of 200 such cycles of head rotation.

Adaptation to the horizontal displacement component was tested by presenting *S* with an objective vertical target displacement of 40% DR, and a horizontal target displacement of 40% DR was used to test for Type B adaptation. Slant settings were made in the manner described by Wallach and Frey (1969). As in our previous work, tests were administered before and after the adaptation period. At the outset of the experiment, *S*s were given practice with slant estimation by following the procedure described by Wallach and Frey

(1969) under "Preliminary Experiments (2)"; Ss who performed poorly in this kind of test were eliminated at this point.[3]

Twenty Ss completed the experiment. For half of them, the test for adaptation to the horizontal displacement component always preceded the test for the Type B adaptation in the pre- and postadaptation tests as well as in the tests after the two dissipation periods. For the other half, the order of the two tests was always reversed. Half of the 10 Ss that made up each group adapted to horizontal target displacement in the direction *with* the head movement and the other half *against* it.

Results

The results are given in Table 1, where the listed mean slant settings are computed from the differences between the respective post- and preadaptation scores. The effects measured immediately after the adaptation period were approximately the same for the two types of adaptation.[4] The loss in adaptation effect after two 10-min. periods during which S sat with eyes closed was very different for the two types of adaptation. In the case of the adaptation to horizontal target displacement, there was a consistent decline in the measured effect. Nineteen out of 20 Ss gave a smaller slant estimate after the first 10-min. time lapse than immediately after the adaptation period, and the individual adaptation effects remaining after the second 10-min. time lapse were all smaller than those measured after the first 10-min. period of dissipation. The effect of adaptation to vertical displacement during head turning declined much more slowly. The first 10-min. lapse caused only a 5% mean decrease in the effect, which was not significant $(p > .1)$. The decline of 20% for the total dissipation period of 20 min. was significant $(p < .001)$. The differ-

---

[3] Ss who prior to adaptation gave slant-estimation scores with more than three reversals were eliminated.

[4] Two directions of target displacement were used in the case of Type A adaptation. Ten of our Ss adapted to horizontal target displacements *with* the head movements and 10 in the direction *against* them. No significant differences in adaptation or dissipation were obtained for these conditions. Previously, Wallach and Frey (1969) and again Wallach, Frey, and Romney (1969) had obtained a larger effect of adaptation when the field displacements were in the direction *with* the head movement. Then, the same Ss were, at different times, employed in the two conditions. In our experiment, with different Ss used in the two conditions and with only 10 Ss in each group, the difference failed to become manifest.

TABLE 1

Mean Effects of Adaptation to Oblique Target Displacement After 200 Head
Movements and After Two Periods of Dissipation

	Type A Adaptation		Type B Adaptation	
	In Deg. of Slant	*Percent of Full Effect*	*In Deg. of Slant*	*Percent of Full Effect*
After 200 HM	13.60	100	14.88	100
10 Min. Later	8.50	63	14.15	95
20 Min. Later	5.05	37	11.85	80

ences in the residual effects for Type A and Type B adaptation after
time lapse were highly significant. There was only one S who failed
to give a larger slant estimate in the test for adaptation to vertical
displacement than in the other test after the 10-min. dissipation
period, and, after the 20-min. time lapse, measured residual Type B
adaptation was larger for every one of the 20 Ss than the effect
remaining from adaptation to horizontal target displacement.

That the 20% loss in Type B adaptation effect after the 20-min.
time lapse represents spontaneous dissipation seems questionable.
Under very similar conditions, Wallach, Frey, and Romney (1969)
found an almost identical loss upon immediate retesting. In their
first experiment demonstrating adaptation to vertical target displacement during head turning, a test immediately following an
adaptation period consisting of 100 head movements yielded an
effect on slant estimation of 6.04 deg. A second test, which differed
from the first only in the sense of the objective target displacement
relative to the head turning, measured an effect of 4.70 deg., 78% of
the effect yielded by the first test. Since the second test followed the
first test immediately, this loss represents the effect of the first test.
It must be ascribed to the nature of the one-trial test employed,
which measured an apparent vertical displacement of a target that
was objectively stationary insofar as the vertical dimension was
concerned. (The objective horizontal displacement of the test target,
which served to measure the extent of the apparent vertical displacement as a slant, was here irrelevant.) Observing a stationary target
during a head movement, however, amounted to an exposure to
natural viewing conditions and should cause partial undoing of the
effect of experimental adaptation.

One might find difficulty in interpreting the loss in the effect of adaptation to vertical target displacement, which we found to amount to only 5% 10 min. after the first test and to 20% 10 min. after the second test in terms of the result of Wallach, Frey, and Romney just reported, on the ground that the latter obtained a loss of 22% without any time delay and after only one test. Two points should be considered here. The previous authors employed experimental adaptation amounting to 100 head movements, whereas we used 200; hence, the same test, consisting in an exposure to what amounts to an unlearning condition, could be expected to have a smaller effect in the latter case. And then there is the possibility that an analogue to reminiscence[5] for the effect of experimental adaptation operated to augment this effect when the test was delayed and thus counteracted the loss due to the unlearning effect of the preceding test.

At any rate, Wallach, Frey, and Romney unquestionably obtained from a one-trial test an unlearning effect that exceeded in magnitude the decrease in the adaptation effect with the time lapse we obtained for Type B adaptation, and that makes it likely that this decrease was due to the intervening test or tests (two tests preceded the last one) and not to the time lapse as such.

Discussion

Our experiment had two results: Type A adaptation in CVD dissipated spontaneously, and Type B adaptation probably did not, and if it did, it did so much more slowly than Type A adaptation. For the spontaneous dissipation of Type A adaptation we offer the following explanation: We make the plausible assumption that CVD, the way of perceiving that S brings to our adaptation experiment, is also the product of an adaptation process, an adaptation to the natural viewing conditions, and that, as a learning product, it survives in the nervous system the experimentally produced adaptation while the latter dominates S's perception. As during the dissipation period, the encounters with the conditions that produced experimental adaptation gradually recede into the past, CVD, the product of adaptation

[5] A discussion of reminiscence may be found in C. E. Osgood, *Methods and Theory in Experimental Psychology.* New York: Oxford University Press, 1953, pp. 509–513.

to the natural viewing conditions, becomes more and more manifest in *S*'s perception, which thus reverts to CVD: experimental adaptation gradually dissipates. This interpretation of spontaneous dissipation of Type A adaptation is supported by results obtained by Wallach and Floor (1970). They found that if CVD, that is, adaptation to natural viewing conditions, was strengthened just before experimental adaptation began, by exposing *S* for 200 head movements to a *stationary* target, experimental adaptation of Type A was retarded. This showed that CVD is, indeed, the product of an adaptation process and that this process interacts with experimental adaptation. Spontaneous dissipation is simply another result of such interaction.

It would be pleasant if it were possible to ascribe the failure of Type B adaptation to dissipate to the fact that, prior to experimental adaptation, no learning product existed of such a nature that it would be replaced by Type B adaptation. Such an assumption is, in fact, quite plausible. It seems, indeed, that there should be no learning connected with the fact that under natural viewing conditions the visual field does *not* move upward when the head turns right and down when it turns left. But this explanation is refuted by another result obtained by Wallach and Floor: Type B adaptation, too, is retarded when *S* is exposed for 200 head movements to a *stationary* target prior to experimental adaptation. Here, too, exposure to the natural viewing conditions just before experimental adaptation interfered with that adaptation process. Thus, it cannot be argued that exposure to natural viewing conditions leaves no learning effect that Type B adaptation would have to supersede. Instead, an explanation for the failure of Type B adaptation to dissipate spontaneously is needed that is compatible with the fact that practice with the natural viewing conditions interferes with Type B adaptation. What is here practiced under natural viewing conditions, must be different in nature from the learning process responsible for CVD, because the spontaneous dissipation found in the case of Type A adaptation does not occur in Type B adaptation. And that practice must be of such a nature that it can interfere with the process of vertical target displacement, because that practice subsequently retards such adaptation.

There seems to be only one kind of learning that fits these criteria, and that is connected with the eye movements that occur when one turns his head and looks at a point in the stationary visual field. Such eye movements are normally horizontal, but when, during Type B adaptation, the target is vertically displaced during head turning these eye movements become slanted.[6] In the experiment by Wallach and Floor, having S look at a stationary target during head turning just before adaptation to vertical target displacement amounted to practicing horizontal eye movements during head turning, and this, in fact, retarded adaptation to vertical target displacement, which involves slanted eye movements. It thus seems that learning to make oblique eye movements during head turning instead of horizontal ones is part of Type B adaptation.

Making horizontal eye movements during head turning is practiced throughout life. So is CVD, the adaptation to the natural conditions of having the visual field displaced relative to the head during head turning at the normal rate. In fact, the individual occasions for both practices are the same; each turning of the head provides one. Yet, the interaction between the two practices and the effects of experimental adaptation differs. Type A adaptation dissipates rapidly and S's perception reverts to CVD without practice. Experimental adaptation to vertical target displacement does not dissipate spontaneously or, if it does, reverts to normal much more slowly.

References

Wallach, H., & Floor, L. On the relation of adaptation to field displacement during head movements to the constancy of visual direction. *Perception & Psychophysics,* 1970, 8, 95–98.

Wallach, H., & Frey, K. J. Adaptation in the constancy of visual direction measured by a one-trial method. *Perception & Psychophysics,* 1969, 5, 249–252. In the present volume, this chapter, selection 4.

Wallach, H., Frey, K. J., & Romney, G. Adaptation to field displacement during head movement unrelated to the constancy of visual direction. *Perception & Psychophysics,* 1969, 5, 253–256. In the present volume, this chapter, selection 5.

[6]This is so because an objectively vertical displacement, when vectorially added to the horizontal displacement relative to the turning head of an objectively stationary point, amounts to a displacement relative to the head that is oblique to the plane of the head rotation.

Wallach, H., & Kravitz, J. H. Adaptation in the constancy of visual direction tested by measuring the constancy of auditory direction. *Perception & Psychophysics,* 1968, 4, 299–303. In the present volume, this chapter, selection 3.

7. Target Distance and Adaptation in Distance Perception in the Constancy of Visual Direction

Hay and Sawyer (1969) reported the discovery that the distance of the observed object is a factor in the constancy of visual direction. The latter is the compensating process which causes the apparent immobility of objects during head movements. It compensates for the angular displacement between a target point and the eyes caused by some rotating head movement. Such a displacement has two components. The main displacement is caused by a rotation of the head as a whole in relation to the stationary environment; every target in the environment will change its direction relative to the head by the angle by which the head is being rotated. The secondary displacement is related to the fact that the eyes are located forward of the various rotation axes of the head. This causes the eyes to be displaced relative to a target's main direction, which is the line that connects a target point with the particular axis of the head rotation. This displacement of the eyes has little effect on distant targets, but, for target distances of less than 2 m., the secondary displacement between a target point and the eyes attains appreciable amounts. Wallach and Kravitz (1965), who were the first to measure the constancy of visual direction (CVD), avoided dealing with the secondary displacements by using large target distances.[1] Hay and Sawyer measured CVD for a target 40 cm. distant, using the method intro-

Written in collaboration with Gary S. Yablick and Ann Smith. Reprinted from *Perception & Psychophysics*, 1972, 12, 139–145.

[1]Wallach and Kravitz (1965) obtained a small but significant deviation from ideal CVD and ascribed it to this secondary displacement of the eyes, but the senior author did not anticipate Hay and Sawyer's discovery.

duced by Wallach and Kravitz, and found complete compensation for the additional secondary displacement. They also tried to show that convergence of the eyes was the main cue mediating distance for the constancy of visual direction of near targets, but the results did not confirm this. The purpose of our work was (1) to show that the natural combination of accommodation and convergence employed as the sole distance cues would yield good CVD for near targets (Experiment 1), and (2) to find out whether CVD could be modified by adapting *S*s to spectacles that alter these oculomotor adjustments (Experiment 2).

The previous work of the senior author and his co-workers on CVD was concerned with the compensating process that causes the visual field and individual distant targets to appear stationary during a head rotation. If, for example, the head is turned clockwise through an angle, α, a distant target becomes displaced *in relation to the head* in a counterclockwise direction by the same angle. This main displacement of the target normally leads to the perception of a stationary target, while a displacement relative to the head that is not produced by an objectively stationary target, i.e., a relative displacement whose angle does not match the rotation angle of the head but is larger or smaller by a few percent, leads to the perception of a target that is seen to move during the head movement.[2] When the target is near and the displacement of the eyes in relation to the target's main direction matters, a clockwise rotation of the head through an angle, α, causes a change in the target direction from the vantage point of the eyes amounting to $\alpha + \beta$, where β is the additional target displacement caused by the displacement of the eyes relative to the target's main direction. The relation of β to α depends on the target distance (see Figure 1). The smaller this distance, the larger β will be for a given head rotation α. Such displacement ratios can be calculated from the following equation:

$$\beta/\alpha = d_E/(d_T - d_E) \qquad (1)$$

[2] Excellent compensation for the main target displacement due to head movements was measured by Wallach and Kravitz (1965 and 1968). The article of 1968 contains the more detailed description of CVD and its measurement. Measurements of CVD concerned with nodding of the head were reported by Wallach and Floor (1970). These three articles, as well as those by Wallach and Frey (1969) and Wallach, Frey, and Romney (1969), also report work on adaptation in CVD to conditions of abnormal field displacements during head movements.

where α is, as stated, the angle of the head rotation, β is the angle of the secondary target displacement (and hence β/α the ratio of the secondary target displacement), d_T the distance of the target from the rotation axis of the head, and d_E the distance of the eyes from the rotation axis.[3] Because of this dependence of the secondary target displacement on target distance, with this displacement ratio inversely proportional to the distance of the target from the eyes $(d_T - d_E)$, a process that compensates also for the secondary target displacement must take this distance into account, and thus depends on cues for the target distance. Such a process would be rather complex: as in CVD of distant targets, it takes into account information about the angle of the head rotation, and, in addition, it takes into account information about target distance.

Experiment 1. Measuring the Constancy of Visual Direction for Near Targets

Our first experiment resembled that of Hay and Sawyer in many ways. These authors measured CVD for three target distances, two of which were simulated by using artificial conditions that caused the eye to converge for the simulated distances. The values of CVD measured under these artificial conditions could then be compared with the measurement of CVD for the true target distance (which was 40 cm.), and the effects of the alterations of convergence on CVD could thereby be assessed. Though statistically very significant, these effects were small—18% and 16% of the effects predicted for the simulated distances. In our experiment, the true target distance was also 40 cm., measured from the eyes, and the simulated distances were produced by having S see the same target through spectacles that caused him to view objects with accommodation increased by 1.5 lens diopters and convergence increased by 5 prism diopters for each eye (near glasses) or through spectacles having the opposite

[3]This equation is an approximation derived from the following relation:
$$\tan \beta = \frac{\sin \alpha}{\cdot\, d_T/d_E - \cos \alpha}$$
The approximation is based on the assumption that head movements will not exceed 10 deg. to either side of the target direction. Under this assumption $\tan \beta$ and $\sin \alpha$ may be replaced by the respective angles and $\cos \alpha$ given the value one.

effect (far glasses).[4] The near glasses caused the target at the 40-cm. distance to be seen with an accommodation and convergence for a distance of 25 cm., and the simulated distance in the case of the far glasses was 100 cm.

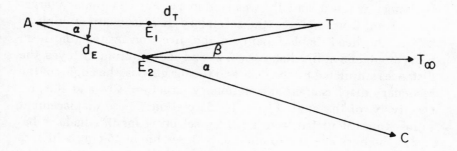

Fig. 1. A is the rotation axis of the head and T is a target. AT is, therefore, the main target direction. Initially, the head position is such that AT is straight ahead. Hence, the eyes (E_1) fall on AT; the main target direction and the true direction of the target, its direction from the vantage point of the eyes, coincide. After the head has been rotated clockwise through an angle, α, AC is the new direction straight ahead, and AT, the main target direction, will have been displaced relative to the head by α. E_2 is the position of the eyes after the head rotation, and E_2 T is the new true target direction, which now differs by the angle β from the main target direction, which is represented by E_2 T_∞. $(E_2 T_\infty$ is parallel to AT.) The angle CE_2 T is the total displacement of the true target direction relative to the head caused by the head rotation. It consists of α, representing the main target displacement caused by the head rotation, and of β, the secondary target displacement brought about by the displacement of the eyes relative to the main target direction. AT equals d_T and AE equals d_E.

As did Hay and Sawyer, we had our S use a nodding motion, a head rotation about a horizontal axis, and had his head connected to a potentiometer whose output controlled the vertical position of the spot on the screen of a cathode ray oscilloscope. Our setup differed in that S saw the oscilloscope screen directly and in that we varied the extent and direction of the motion of the spot in relation to the head movement by means of a variable transmission. Instead of the biteboard arrangement used by Hay and Sawyer to transmit the head movement to the potentiometer, we had S wear a headgear that

[4]For a description of these glasses and the way they operate, see Wallach and Frey (1972).

could be attached to the variable transmission. But these technical differences probably cannot account for the better results we obtained.

What are the results to be expected under the assumption that CVD completely compensates for the secondary displacement? When the spot is seen without glasses, it would be perceived as stationary when it actually was stationary. For a stationary target spot 40 cm. from the eyes, the secondary displacement amounts to 25% of the head displacement, in the direction against the head movement, and at the distances of 25 and 100 cm. from the eyes, the distances simulated by the near and the far glasses, the angles of the secondary displacement of a stationary target are 40% and 10%, respectively, of the angle of the head rotation. These displacement ratios were calculated from Eq. 1 by selecting for the distance between the eyes and the rotation axis the value of 10 cm., which is approximately correct for most adult Ss. All our calculations will be based on this value.

If the nervous system did not compensate for the secondary target displacement β/α at all, but still compensated for the displacement of the main target direction *relative to the head, S* would perceive a stationary near target as moving in the direction *against* the head rotation. In order that he see such a target as stationary, it would be necessary to give the target an objective displacement in the direction *with* the head rotation in the amount of β/α. Such an objective displacement would cause the near target to stay in the main target direction, i.e., it would simulate a target at infinite distance, for which the displacement of the eyes relative to the main target direction does not matter. If the nervous system were partially compensating for the secondary target displacement, a stationary near target would, during a head rotation, still appear to move *against* the head, but less so, and a smaller objective target displacement *with* the head would suffice to make the target appear stationary. This objective target displacement would therefore measure the degree to which the nervous system fails to compensate for the secondary target displacement, i.e., it would measure the lag in compensation for the secondary target displacement. If, for example, a target 40 cm. from the eyes, for which the secondary target displacement amounts to 25% of the angle of the head rotation, were to require a displacement in the direction *with* the head amounting to

10% of the head rotation angle ($\beta/\alpha = .1$) in order to appear stationary, we could say that a compensation occurs for 15% of the 25% of secondary target displacement. Such a lag, or an opposite error in CVD, can have two reasons: (1) *S* does not compensate well for secondary target displacement. (2) The cues giving information about the distance of the target are inadequate.

Measurements of this sort, while *S* wears one or the other of the mentioned spectacles, permit an assessment of the roles of accommodation and convergence in our experimental conditions. To the degree to which our measurements taken with glasses in place confirm the theoretical predictions given below, accommodation and convergence alone were responsible for the difference in the results obtained under our three experimental conditions.

The theoretical predictions for the measurements with glasses are derived in the following manner. When the near glasses are worn, and the oscilloscope screen is 40 cm. from *S*'s eyes, the oculomotor adjustment of the eyes is for a distance of 25 cm.[5] This is the target's equivalent distance.[6] But the secondary displacement of the target is still 25% in the direction *against* the head movement, because the actual distance of the spot on the screen remains 40 cm. and its secondary displacement depends on the actual distance. Since, theoretically, a target at an actual distance of 25 cm. has to undergo a secondary displacement of 40% of the head rotation in order to appear stationary, the spot at 40 cm. distance must be made to displace during every head movement in the direction against it at the rate of 15% in order to appear stationary, because this brings its displacement ratio up to 40%. Since the far glasses produce an equivalent distance of 100 cm., and since the secondary displacement ratio at that distance is 10% in the direction against the head movement, the spot on the screen must be given a displacement ratio of 15% in the direction *with* the head to diminish its 25% displacement ratio normal for its objective distance of 40 cm. to one of 10%.

[5]A distance of 40 cm. from the eyes is equivalent to 2.5 lens diopters. The glasses cause the eyes to increase accommodation by 1.5 lens diopters (and cause a corresponding change in convergence) to a total of 4 lens diopters, and that value corresponds to a viewing distance of 25 cm.

[6]The term "equivalent distance" was introduced by Leibowitz and Moore (1966) for the distance for which the eyes are adjusted behind devices that alter accommodation and convergence in corresponding amounts.

Equipment

The S wore a welder's headgear with a mounting extending on the right side down to the level of his upper neck. There, an aluminum rod was attached in a position perpendicular to the median plane of S's head. The mounting had to be adjusted for each S in such a way that the rod formed the extension of the rotation axis of the nodding movement S had to perform.[7] The rod could be attached to the input shaft of a variable transmission, which was mounted on a heavy stand on the right of S's seat. With this arrangement, S's head was rigidly coupled to the transmission so that his nodding movements turned the input shaft. This attachment served also to position S's head so that his eyes were at the level of the oscilloscope screen and 40 cm. from it. The height of S's seat was adjusted to bring his head to the proper level. The transmission was of the ball and disk type. By means of a large knob mounted in front and to the right of S at the level of his lower chest and of an arrangement of shafts, gears, and angle gears, S could turn the control shaft of the transmission and change its ratio and the direction of rotation of the output shaft in relation to that of the input shaft. A Veeder counter also attached to the control shaft permitted E to read the transmission setting. The output shaft of the transmission was connected with the shaft of a potentiometer used as a voltage divider of a 25-V dc source. A pointer fixed to the potentiometer shaft permitted E to read the potentiometer setting whenever necessary. The output of the potentiometer controlled the vertical position of the spot on the oscilloscope screen. Initially, E also could position the spot by using the controls on the oscilloscope. A special tube with minimal afterglow was used. To eliminate the faint glow of the face of the tube when it was in operation, the intensity of the target spot was made low. Also, the tube was covered with black cardboard, except for a vertical gap through which the path of the target spot was visible, and testing was done in total darkness. Work with CVD requires absence of lines or boundaries which could serve as a visual framework for the target displacements to be presented.

When his head was attached, S could, by nodding it up and down, cause the spot to shift up and down, or down and up, depending on the transmission setting which he controlled. From a center

[7]A description of the headgear may be found in Wallach and Floor (1970).

position at which the rate of transmission was zero and the spot remained at rest, *S* could gradually increase the ratio of the motion of the spot in relation to his head movement, and, depending on the direction in which he turned the knob from this center position, the spot would move *with* or *against* the direction in which the head movement displaced the eyes. The resulting ratio of the angular displacement of the spot γ (measured from a point behind the eyes in the vertical plane of the input shaft) and of the angle of the rotation of the input shaft (representing the angle of rotation of the head α) was the γ/α-displacement ratio, the unit of measurement that our equipment yielded. Once the gain control on the oscilloscope was adjusted, these displacement ratios were in a fixed relation to the readings on the Veeder counter, and that relation was empirically determined.

The displacement ratio that is measured by our device is not the same as the displacement ratio β/α discussed earlier. The latter measures the secondary target displacement, the displacement of the direction between a stationary target and the eyes caused by a head rotation; this change in the target direction is due to the fact that the head rotation displaces the eyes relative to the main target direction. The displacement ratio γ/α measured by our device is concerned with the objective target displacement produced by that device, and is geometrically different from the β/α ratio. The angular displacement γ of the target spot is measured from the rotation axis of the head and is, thus, geometrically the same as the angle of the head rotation α, whereas the apex of the angle β is at *S*'s eyes. Whereas our equipment measures the objective target displacement needed to compensate for the stationary target's apparent displacement in γ/α ratios, the theoretical predictions for the effects of the glasses on CVD were made in terms of β/α ratios. The following equation can be used to transform a γ/α ratio into a β/α ratio:

$$\beta/\alpha = \gamma/\alpha \cdot d_T/(d_T - d_E)$$

where, as before, d_T is the distance from the rotation axis to the target and d_E the distance from the rotation axis to the eyes, i.e., 10 cm. Our results will be transformed in this fashion and presented as β/α ratios. To correspond to the units of measurement used in earlier papers on CVD, these ratios will be multiplied by 100 and given as percent β-displacement ratios, abbreviated %β-DR.

PROCEDURE

Our tests were designed to determine the limits of the range of displacement ratios that did not cause S to report apparent target displacements during his head movements (no-motion range). But we did not employ the procedure developed by Wallach and Kravitz (1965, 1968), because work by Wallach and Frey (1969) and by Wallach and Floor (1970) had demonstrated very rapid adaptation in CVD. To keep to a minimum exposure of S during the test to target displacements that might cause small adaptation effects, we let S change displacement ratios, and determined only one upper and one lower limit of the no-motion range. The average of the two limits was recorded as S's no-motion point. E made a setting of the transmission that produced small apparent target displacements in one of the two vertical directions and told S in which sense to turn the control knob to diminish the target motion caused by his head movements. S was instructed to stop changing the transmission setting as soon as the target no longer seemed to move. If S thought he had overshot the limit, E reset the transmission to cause mild target motion in the former direction and asked him to make his changes more slowly. When S had found one limit, he closed his eyes and E read the transmission setting from the Veeder counter with a small flashlight. E then set the transmission to produce target motion in the opposite direction and asked S to find the other limit. With half the Ss, the limit for apparent target motion in the direction *with* the head rotation was found first, and for the other half, the limit of target displacement *against* the head movement was first determined. For all Ss, the no-motion point was first measured without glasses and then with the near and the far glasses, in that order. No instructions were given to fixate the target spot, because we wanted S to behave as naturally as was compatible with the test conditions. As in our previous publications on CVD, the question of whether target displacements relative to the head are registered by the eyes through image displacement or through taking pursuit movements into account is not raised here. Research designed to answer this question is in preparation.

Thirty-one paid undergraduate Ss participated. Of these, 20 Ss completed the experiment. Eight Ss were eliminated because their no-motion point for the directly viewed target differed from objective immobility by a displacement larger than 2% of the head rotation in one or the other direction. For three other Ss, the upper limit of the no-motion range taken with the far glasses could not be determined, because these Ss tried to use a displacement ratio that was beyond the range of the transmission.

RESULTS

The mean midpoint of the no-motion range for all 31 Ss amounted to .67±.89% β-DR in the direction *with* the head movement for the directly viewed target spot 40 cm. from the eyes. That is, for randomly selected Ss, the target spot had to be given a displacement *with* the head movement of .67% of the head rotation to appear stationary.[8] This deviation of the mean no-motion point from objective immobility was, of course, smaller for the 20 selected Ss, namely .19±.42%β-DR. When the near glasses are worn and the head is moved, a stationary target spot will appear to move in the direction *with* the head movement, and an objective target displacement in the direction *against* the head movement is needed to compensate for this apparent target displacement. The mean no-motion point measured with the near glasses amounted to a target displacement of 6.90% ± 1.58% of the head rotation in the direction *against* the head movement. As explained above, a target displacement in the direction *against* the head movement of 15% β-DR was expected to compensate for the effect of the near glasses on a target objectively 40 cm. away. Our result shows that even with selected Ss, compensation for the secondary target displacement is incomplete for a distance as small as 25 cm. This interpretation of the result is justified by the quite different result for the far glasses. To appear stationary, the target at an objective distance of 40 cm. had to undergo a mean β displacement of 15.76% ± 2.52% in the direction *with* the head movement when the far glasses caused an equivalent distance of 100 cm. from the eyes. This result agrees well with the difference between the secondary displacements of targets at objective distances of 40 cm. and of 100 cm., which amounts to 15%β-DR and shows that

[8]This result represents a lag in compensation for the secondary displacement of a stationary target. A displacement of the target spot in the direction *with* the head movement compensates objectively for an apparent target displacement *against* the head movement, and when an S sees that, his nervous system fails to compensate for the secondary target displacement.

accommodation and convergence suffice as distance cues when CVD compensates for secondary target displacements.

DISCUSSION

The experiment just reported shows that, in the case of near targets, the constancy of visual direction compensates not only for the main target displacement brought about by a head rotation as such but also for the secondary target displacement. CVD is virtually complete in the case of the target distances of 100 cm. and 40 cm., whereas compensation for the secondary target displacement was incomplete in the case of the 25-cm. distance. There are two possible reasons why, in the case of simulated distances, our results differed so much from those obtained by Hay and Sawyer. These authors manipulated only convergence, whereas our glasses altered convergence and accommodation in corresponding fashion. It seems unlikely, however, that this alone could account for so large a difference. Hay and Sawyer probably failed to keep the surround of the target spot completely dark. Visual landmarks cause an objective target displacement to be noticed that otherwise would not be perceived (Wallach & Kravitz, 1965).

Since the amount of secondary target displacement becomes larger as target distance decreases, compensating for it means taking target distance into account. The measurements of CVD with the far glasses show that accommodation and convergence, in combination, can here serve as potent distance cues. We therefore adapted Ss to our near glasses and tested for changes in CVD in the same manner in which we had tested for the effect of wearing the near and the far glasses in Experiment 1. If we succeeded in obtaining a change in CVD on the basis of adaptation to near glasses, we might thereby demonstrate still another manifestation of adaptation in distance perception[9] and contribute to the investigation of the role that registered distance plays in the operation of CVD.

[9]Wallach and Frey (1972) and Wallach, Frey, and Bode (1972) measured adaptation in distance perception in three ways: by having S indicate apparent distance by pointing and by the effect that a change in distance perception has on perceived size and on perceived stereoscopic depth. They also demonstrated the existence of an intervening variable, called registered distance, that results from cues for distance, whose relationship to these cues can be altered by adaptation, and which, in turn, manifests itself in size and in depth perception.

Experiment 2. Adaptation to Near Glasses

There are two ways in which such an adaptation might operate. The glasses may alter the relation between these oculomotor adjustments and the distance they denote in perception, i.e., the registered distance, as they were shown to do by Wallach and Frey (1972) and by Wallach, Frey, and Bode (1972). After such an alteration of registered distance, CVD should be altered also. Wallach, Frey, and Bode found that, when such an adaptation had taken effect and was tested under conditions where only oculomotor cues operated, a change in registered distance manifested itself when S represented the perceived distance of a target by pointing to it, as well as by changes in perceived size and stereoscopic depth. If such a change of registered distance alters CVD also, complete adaptation to near glasses would eliminate the apparent target motion in the direction *with* the head movement observed when these glasses are worn. Inasmuch as adaptation to the near glasses consists in increased registered distance, its effect on CVD when no glasses are worn would be the same as that of wearing our far glasses. Such adaptation would cause a stationary target nearby to be registered as farther than it actually was and make it appear to move in the direction *against* the head movement, because the target's actual secondary displacement is larger than its secondary displacement at the registered distance would be. An objective displacement of the target in the direction *with* the head would be needed to make it appear stationary and would, thus, measure the effect of adaptation on CVD.

Another form that adaptation to our glasses might take is a modification of CVD itself. When the near glasses are worn, objects at all distances are given with oculomotor cues that place them nearer to S than they objectively are. The secondary displacements the objects actually undergo during a head rotation are smaller than would be warranted by the registered distances that these oculomotor cues normally produce. This discrepancy between distance cues and the given object displacements during head movements may cause an adaptation such that apparent target immobility will result from a different combination of secondary displacements and oculomotor adjustments than the normal one. An adaptation produced by this discrepancy may take one of two forms: It may consist in a modification in distance perception such that oculomotor cues will produce registered distances more in agreement with the given object displacements caused by head movements. This would be the same kind of adaptation we discussed above; it would, however, be caused by field displacements during head movements. The adaptation may, however, also consist in a modification within CVD such that the process that compensates for the object displacements relative to the eyes caused by head movements is altered. This is the same kind of modification that results from exposure to objective target displacements or from optical field displacement during head movements, produced, for instance, by wearing magnifying or minifying glasses (Wallach & Kravitz, 1968). Since the near glasses cause registered target distances smaller than the true distances, the secondary displacements of any target due to head movements would be smaller than that shortened distance would warrant, and apparent target motion in the direction *with* the head movement should result. When the target is a luminous spot in an otherwise dark field, this motion is observed; our first experiment is based on this fact. But when the whole field is visible, it does not appear to move when S nods or turns his head and S experiences no apparent field displacements during the adaptation period.[10] Nevertheless, S is exposed to a discrepancy between the actually given field displacements and distance cues that would warrant larger field displacements *against* the head movement than those actually given. If this were to cause an adaptation within CVD, it would be an adaptation to field displacement in the direction *with* the head movement and would cause an objective target displacement *with* the head movement to appear stationary. In the end, this is, of course, the same overt effect that a modification in distance perception resulting from wearing near glasses would produce in a CVD test; only the underlying processes are different.

How, then, can we distinguish between the two possible forms that adaptation to near glasses may take—an adaptation process within CVD and an adaptation in distance perception? One could prevent modification in CVD by keeping S's head stationary throughout the adaptation period, but this is difficult to do. We made it possible to distinguish between the two forms of adaptation by also testing for adaptation in distance perception in other ways,

[10]This is probably due to the fact that veridical distance cues are available when the whole field is given, in addition to the oculomotor cues, which the glasses modify.

using two of the tests Wallach, Frey, and Bode had employed. *S*s were given a pointing test and size estimation tests in addition to being tested for a modification in CVD. If the amount of adaptation measured by these tests corresponded to the change in registered distance implied in the CVD test results, adaptation would consist only in a modification in distance perception. If the change in CVD were larger than the changes in registered distance implied by the two other tests would warrant, it would seem likely that adaptation within CVD also occurs. Adaptation within CVD would account for that part of CVD adaptation that cannot be ascribed to the change in registered distance as measured by the other tests.

PROCEDURE

Because we planned to use a set of five tests, two tests for CVD, a pointing test, and two size estimation tests, we made the adaptation period longer than it had ever been in adaptation to our near glasses, and in order to gain information about the long-range growth of the adaptation effect, we interrupted the adaptation period for a set of tests. After the preadaptation tests, *S* wore the near glasses for 1.5 hr., was given a set of tests, and immediately resumed wearing the glasses. After this second adaptation period, which lasted 3 hr., another set of tests was given. Afterwards, *S* sat quietly with eyes closed for 15 min. and then was given still another pointing test and the two size estimation tests. This retesting was done to learn at what rate the adaptation effects would weaken with mere time lapse between exposure to the adaptation conditions and the tests. This information was needed because the three kinds of test were always given in the same order. The retesting after a time lapse would allow us to estimate the loss in adaptation effect due to the duration of the tests. We always gave the CVD test first, because our primary interest was in the effect of adaptation to our glasses on CVD, and because we believed that the test did not provide conditions tending to reestablish normal distance perception. Then came the pointing test that took very little time; it was taken with *S* wearing the glasses and therefore could not provide "unlearning" conditions either. Two size estimation tests followed, which had previously been used by Wallach, Frey, and Bode (1972). Wallach and Frey (1972) had found that the effect of adaptation does not decline during a sequence of four size estimation tests.

Because such long adaptation periods had never been used in connection with glasses that alter oculomotor adjustment, we had to envisage the possibility that distance adaptation might be complete. We, therefore, employed only two of the conditions of testing CVD we had previously used, namely, viewing a target 40 cm. from the eyes either directly or through the near glasses. We omitted testing with the far glasses, because they cause the target at 40 cm. to be seen with an oculomotor adjustment equivalent to 1 lens diopter. Complete adaptation to the near glasses, on the other hand, would mean an increase in registered distance equivalent to 1.5 lens diopters and could not become manifest when the test object was seen with oculomotor adjustments corresponding to 1 diopter of accommodation.

On all three occasions, the CVD test with direct viewing preceded the one with glasses. The test procedure was the same as before, except that each test started with a setting of the transmission that produced clearly visible target displacement *with* the head rotation. This is the target displacement associated with wearing the near glasses. When such a displacement occurs during the test, it cannot possibly weaken an established adaptation. After, under these favorable conditions, one limit—and thereby the approximate value of the no-motion range—was found, the other limit could be found by presenting S initially with a weak apparent target displacement *against* the head movement, avoiding a larger apparent displacement that might tend to diminish the adaptation.

The procedure for the pointing test and for the size estimation tests was as described by Wallach, Frey and Bode. In the latter tests, half of the Ss were always tested first with the test object at the distance of 33.3 cm. and then with the test object at 66.7 cm.; for the other half, these tests were given in the reverse order. The object sizes to be estimated were so transposed that they produced identical retinal images. During the two adaptation periods, Ss, paid undergraduates, spent their time as they pleased, accompanied by a guide. They were, however, asked to walk about for the last 20 min. before returning for a set of tests. Our 10 Ss were selected on the basis of two CVD tests, one without and the other with the near glasses, given on the previous day. To participate, an S's no-motion point measured without glasses could not deviate from rest by more than .5%β-DR in the direction *with* the head movement. Also, with the near glasses in place, the target displacement *against* the head movement needed to produce apparent rest had to amount to at least 7% β-DR.

RESULTS

The first two columns of Table 1 give mean no-motion points for the CVD tests. The results for the preadaptation tests, which are again given in %β-DR, differ from those reported earlier, because we employed a highly selected group of *S*s. Whereas previously the mean no-motion point amounted to 6.9%β-DR *against* the head rotation direction when the near glasses were worn, the present group gave a mean of 10.08%β-DR, which was considerably closer to the value of 15% expected for the near glasses under the assumption that compensation for the secondary displacement of a target 25 cm. distant is complete. The mean of .61%β-DR found with direct viewing of the target point was in the direction *against* the head movement and therefore does not represent a lag in compensation, it simply reflects the smallness of our sample, as do the high confidence limits of all means in the table.

In the case of tests without glasses, the means of 10.44%β-DR and 8.65%β-DR measured after 1.5 and 3 hr. of adaptation, respectively, amount to changes of the no-motion point of 11.04%β-DR and 9.26% β-DR in the direction *with* the head movement. These changes represent more than half of complete adaptation, since complete adaptation would have meant a change of the no-motion point by 15%β-DR in the *with* direction. The effect of complete adaptation to near glasses is the same as that of wearing the far glasses, since the far glasses diminish accommodation and convergence in the same amount as the near glasses increase it, i.e., by the equivalent of 1.5 lens diopters. We had found in our first experiment that the effect of far glasses on a target 40 cm. distant was not different from the theoretical value of 15%β-DR, namely, 15.76%β-DR. To find out whether adaptation to the near glasses was complete, we compared this value with the mean no-motion point of 10.44%β-DR and 8.65% β-DR, measured after the adaptation periods. For the 10.44 value, because of high variance, the difference from the value for full adap-

TABLE 1

Mean Effect of Adaptation to Near Glasses

Tested With	CVD Test in % β-DR		Pointing Distance in cm.	Size Estimation in cm.	
Test Distance	40 cm.	40 cm. with Near Glasses	33.3 cm. with Near Glasses	33.3 cm.	66.7 cm.
Preadaptation	.61 ± 1.49 Against	10.08 ± 3.30 Against	29.7 ± 3.10	6.36 ± 0.95	9.44 ± 1.52
After 1.5 hr. adaptation	10.44 ± 6.59 With	2.09 ± 3.11 Against	36.4 ± 2.20	7.84 ± 1.53	12.03 ± 3.21
Change from preadaptation	11.04	7.99	6.7	1.48	2.59
After 3 hr. more adaptation	8.65 ± 3.55 With	1.13 ± 2.21 Against	36.0 ± 1.81	7.67 ± 1.50	11.91 ± 3.18
Change from preadaptation	9.26	8.95	6.3	1.31	2.47
After 15 min. dissipation			37.0 ± 2.62	7.84 ± 1.73	12.15 ± 3.34
Effect ratio for 1.5 hr. adaptation		.89	.44	.47	

tation failed to be significant, but for the mean no-motion point obtained at the end of the period of 3 hr. this difference was signifi-cant (p < .01).

In the case of the test with the near glasses in place, adaptation consisted in a decrease in the target displacement needed prior to adaptation to compensate for the effects of the glasses; as reported, that compensating displacement amounted to 10.08%β-DR in the direction *against* the head movement. After the adaptation periods, the mean no-motion points were different by 7.99%β-DR and 8.95% β-DR, respectively. A comparison of these effects with those ob-tained when testing was without glasses shows that the effects mea-sured under the two test conditions were approximately the same. Further, a comparison of the adaptation effects measured after the first adaptation period (11.04%β-DR and 7.99%β-DR) with the effects measured after the second period (9.26%β-DR and 8.95%β-DR) gives no evidence of larger effects after the second and longer adaptation period.

Corresponding results were obtained with the two other tests; they are given in the last three columns of Table 1. Here, too, the effects of adaptation measured after the second adaptation period were not larger than after the first. Another striking result is the small adaptation effects measured with the pointing test and the two size estimation tests. They are about half as large as the effect ob-tained by Wallach, Frey, and Bode, in their Experiments 3 and 1, after 20 min. of walking with the near glasses in place. Whether this is due to the fact that we did not select our *S*s for good performance on these tests, as the previous authors had done,[11] or is the result of the much longer adaptation periods cannot be ascertained. Experi-ments are being planned to explore the course of adaptation to near glasses over extended periods.

To compare the magnitude of the adaptation effects measured with our three kinds of tests, we determined the degree to which each effect differed from complete adaptation. This was done by computing for each kind of test an effect ratio, the proportion of the adaptation achieved over the change representing complete adapta-tion. In the case of CVD, complete adaptation to our glasses means, of course, that *S*, with glasses in place, accepts the same target dis-

[11]Our *S*s were selected for good performance on the CVD test only.

placement as stationary which prior to adaptation appeared to him stationary without the glasses. Thus, for the mean of $10.08\%\beta$-DR measured prior to adaptation *with* glasses, the preadaptation mean of .61%β-DR obtained *without* glasses represents complete adaptation, and the difference of 9.47%β-DR between these means is the empirically determined effect of complete adaptation in the case of the test *with* glasses. This value can be compared with the actual adaptation effect measured with the glasses, which amounted to 7.99%β-DR. The effect ratio, therefore, is approximately 7.99/9.47. We computed such effect ratios for individual Ss and used them to compare the result of the CVD test statistically with our other two adaptation measures. The mean effect ratio for 1.5-hr. CVD adaptation measured with the near glasses in place and computed in this manner was .89.

The effect ratio for the size estimation test was computed in corresponding fashion. This was possible because the distances of the two test objects from S were 33.3 and 66.7 cm., and these distances differed by the equivalent of 1.5 lens diopters. Complete adaptation to the near glasses means that the registered distance that corresponds to a given oculomotor adjustment is greater by the equivalent of 1.5 lens diopters. Thus, in the case of a test object 33.3 cm. distant, the registered distance corresponding to complete adaptation is 66.7 cm. Because the sizes of the two test objects were so chosen that they produced identical retinal images, a size estimate of the object at 66.7 cm., given prior to adaptation, represents the postadaptation size estimate of the object at 33.3 cm. under the assumption of complete adaptation. The difference in the size estimates of the two test objects given prior to adaptation therefore represents the effect of complete adaptation measured at the 33.3-cm. test distance. This difference, thus, becomes the denominator in the effect ratio, with the difference between the post- and preadaptation size estimates of the object 33.3 cm. distant becoming the numerator. The mean of the effect ratios computed for individual Ss amounted to .47.

Because it had previously been found that pointing distances are approximately linearly related to object distances, effect ratios could here be computed in a different manner. The pre- and the postadaptation pointing distances of individual Ss were changed into their diopter equivalents, and the ratio of the difference between these diopter equivalents over 1.5, the diopter value of complete adaptation, was computed. The mean effect ratio amounted to .44, and was thus quite similar to that computed for the size estimation test.

Both these mean effect ratios were smaller than the effect ratio for the CVD test. In spite of the small sample, the difference between the effect ratios for the pointing test and the CVD test was significant at better than the .01 level, and for the corresponding difference between the size estimation test and the CVD test, we found $p < .025$. These differences cannot be ascribed to the test order. As the fifth line in Table 1 shows, retesting with pointing and size estimations 15 minutes after the second postadaptation tests revealed no dissipation of the adaptation effect as a result of the preceding tests and of the time lapse. All means were the same (or insignificantly higher) in this retest as in the two preceding tests.

Discussion

Above, we have stated that an adaptation effect measured with CVD may represent two different adaptation processes, an adaptation within CVD and an adaptation in distance perception, the latter measurable also by other tests for adaptation in distance perception. Our finding that adaptation measured with the CVD test was significantly greater than the effects measured with the pointing test and the size estimation test shows that part of the effect measured with the CVD test resulted from adaptive change within CVD. If this inference is correct, we have obtained a modification of CVD by means of an adaptation period in which S was not aware of field displacements during head movements. Only the conditions of stimulation necessary to bring about such an adaptive modification were given: Object displacements relative to the head as normally produced by head movements (and normally leading to a stationary experienced field) were paired with oculomotor adjustments that corresponded to object distances normally associated with larger object displacements. When a single target is observed in the dark, displacements are experienced that are warranted by the oculomotor adjustments. But no such object displacements were experienced during our adaptation periods. It seems that conscious experience of object displacements during head movements is not necessary for adaptation and that only the conditions of stimulation—the discrepancy between the given object displacements and the given oculomotor adjustments—matter.

References

Hay, J. C., & Sawyer, S. Position constancy and binocular convergence. *Perception & Psychophysics*, 1969, 5, 310–312.

Leibowitz, H., & Moore, D. Role of changes in accommodation and convergence in the perception of size. *Journal of the Optical Society of America*, 1966, 56, 1120–1123.

Wallach, H., & Floor, L. On the relation of adaptation to field displacement during head movements to the constancy of visual direction. *Perception & Psychophysics*, 1970, 8, 95–98.

Wallach, H., & Frey, K. J. Adaptation in the constancy of visual direction measured by a one-trial method. *Perception & Psychophysics*, 1969, 5, 249–252. In the present volume, this chapter, selection 4.

Wallach, H., & Frey, K. J. Adaptation in distance perception based on oculomotor cues. *Perception & Psychophysics*, 1972, 11, 31–34. In the present volume, Chapter X, selection 5.

Wallach, H., Frey, K. J., & Bode, K. A. The nature of adaptation in distance perception based on oculomotor cues. *Perception & Psychophysics*, 1972, 11, 110–116. In the present volume, Chapter X, selection 6.

Wallach, H., Frey, K. J., & Romney, G. Adaptation to field displacement during head movement unrelated to the constancy of visual direction. *Perception & Psychophysics*, 1969, 5, 253–256. In the present volume, this chapter, selection 5.

Wallach, H., & Kravitz, J. H. The measurement of the constancy of visual direction and of its adaptation. *Psychonomic Science*, 1965, 2, 217–218. In the present volume, this chapter, selection 1.

Wallach, H., & Kravitz, J. H. Adaptation in the constancy of visual direction tested by measuring the constancy of auditory direction. *Perception & Psychophysics*, 1968, 4, 299–303. In the present volume, this chapter, selection 3.

8. The Compensation for Movement-Produced Changes of Object Orientation

It is a well-known fact that the projection of a solid object in rotation is in most cases perceived as a three-dimensional shape, often in good agreement with the shape of the object that causes the projection. Wallach and O'Connell (1953) investigated the conditions under which this happens. They also pointed out that this so-called kinetic depth effect plays a role in ordinary life, namely, when we move forward and pass a solid object. Under these conditions, the object is seen successively from different directions just as if the object were turning. Hence, a retinal projection is produced that, together with changes in size, undergoes the same form changes that the projection of the same object would undergo if the object were in partial rotation. The deformations of the retinal image that give rise to the kinetic depth effect are, therefore, the same whether O moves past a stationary object or whether a stationary O sees an object in partial rotation. No matter how these deformations are produced, the same three-dimensional object should be perceived. In another respect, however, the two conditions produce different results: In the case where the object is stationary and O moves, the object is not perceived to rotate. This happens in spite of the fact that the same conditions of stimulation, if produced by object rotation, would give rise to perceived rotation. Moreover, the perceived rota-

Written in collaboration with Linda Stanton and Dean Becker. Reprinted from *Perception & Psychophysics,* 1974, 15, 339–343.

tion that would result would not merely be the product of the kinetic depth effect. Since moving past an object results in seeing it successively from different directions and since this amounts to a rotation of the object relative to the eyes, all sensory processes that mediate the perception of rotation are in operation, in particular the processes of binocular depth perception. The present paper is concerned with the reasons why, in the end, we are not aware of this rotation.

The problem is analogous to that which is raised by the perceived immobility of the visual field when the head is rotated. Turning the head to the right causes the visual field to become displaced to the left relative to the head, and this displacement is identical to one caused by the visual field revolving about the stationary head. Although the objective revolving of the field would be perceived as such, the relative field displacement caused by head turning and providing identical visual stimulation conditions is not. It has been shown that this is due to a very accurate compensating process in which the neural effects of the visual displacement are matched up with proprioception of the head rotation (e.g., Wallach & Kravitz, 1968).

There appear to be two ways to account for the nonrotation of the objects we pass. (1) Since these objects do not really turn, they maintain an unchanging orientation in relation to objects that surround them, and since we perceive the visual surround usually as stationary and rigid when we move at moderate speeds, individual objects will appear stationary also. This is the context explanation. For many years, the senior author believed it to be correct. (2) The apparent unchanging orientation of an object we pass is the result of a compensating process that matches up information about O's changing location relative to the object with the object's visually given rotation and causes its apparent immobility.

Inasmuch as the context explanation is perfectly plausible, an explanation that postulates a compensating process seems unnecessary complex. Yet there are simple observations that argue for the operation of such a compensating process. When one walks past a realistically rendered oil portrait, the head appears to turn as if to keep looking at the person that passes by. Or better yet, when one passes a large painting of a landscape with good depth, the whole landscape appears to turn, with the foreground apparently moving with the onlooker. This is because a real head or a real three-dimensional scene would rotate relative to the moving *O* and would be perceived at rest, whereas the painted head or the picture landscape does not undergo such a rotation relative to the moving *O*. For the context explanation to account for the apparent rotation in the pictures, the nonrotation of the painted head or scene would have to make itself felt in relation to three-dimensional objects surrounding the painting that do rotate relative to the moving *O*. This condition is usually not present.

According to the compensation explanation, the apparent rotation in pictures results from a matching up of information about *O*'s change in location with the visually given rotation. When the latter is the normal one, that is, produced by a stationary object, no rotation is seen. But if the rotation is abnormal, a rotation of the object would be perceived. If, for any reason, the object's rotation relative to the moving *O* were less than normal, a rotation of the object should be seen in the direction *with* *O*'s progress, i.e., clockwise when the object is on *O*'s right. The nonrotation of a picture content is an instance of such abnormal rotation *with* *O*'s progress; a rotation in the direction *with* *O*'s progress should be perceived.

A somewhat more unusual condition provides an even stronger argument. When one suspends a translucent plastic mask at eye level and observes it monocularly from the hollow side, it has a strong tendency to invert and look convex. When that has happened and one moves, the mask appears to turn with about twice the angle by which one gets displaced relative to the mask. This happens because a reversal of rotation direction accompanies an inversion of the rotating object. This reversal of rotation direction also occurs when the original rotation remains unnoticed. If an object is, e.g., to the right of *O*'s motion path, *O*'s displacement relative to the object brings about a counterclockwise rotation of the object relative to *O*, counterclockwise as seen from above. Inversion and the associated reversal of rotation will cause the object to appear to rotate clockwise relative to *O*, and since an *O*-produced counterclockwise rotation in some amount would have led to the object's apparent immobility, the inverted object will appear to rotate in approximately twice that amount. It is easy to show that the context explanation is insufficient. One can darken the room and illuminate the mask with a narrow beam from the side. Although the mask is now the only object visible, it will still appear to turn with the moving O through an angle larger than that of O's displacement.

We measured the accuracy of this compensating process with a device that is an analogue to the apparatus with which Wallach and Kravitz (1968) measured the constancy of visual direction. The object that was to be observed by the walking S could be made to rotate objectively, in any amount and in either direction, dependent on S's change in position relative to the object. This was done by a device that variably coupled S's progress with the object's rotation. The object was fixed to a vertical shaft that was connected to the output shaft to a variable ratio transmission, while the change of S's position relative to the object caused the input shaft of the transmission to turn. Dependent on the setting of the transmission, the output shaft, together with the object, could either remain objectively stationary, or it could turn during O's passing so as to enhance the normal rotation of a stationary object relative to O in various proportions, or, by turning in the other sense, it could diminish that normal rotation in some proportion chosen by E. How much of such an enhancement or diminishment would be needed for O to perceive the object in rotation? Or, conversely, how wide a range of enhancing or diminishing of the normal rotation relative to O of a passed stationary object would go undetected? The width of such a range of undetected objective rotation would represent a measurement of the inaccuracy with which the compensation for movement produced changes of object orientation operates. If, e.g., the object is on the right of O's path, it will, if objectively stationary, rotate counterclockwise relative to O, in the amount of O's angular displacement in relation to it; this is the object's normal rotation. An objective counterclockwise rotation of the object, caused by passing on to the input shaft of the transmission O's angular displacement relative to the object, will enhance this normal rotation, and an objective clockwise rotation will diminish it. The setting of the transmission will determine the ratio of the object rotation to O's angular displacement relative to the object. This rotation/displacement ratio (RDR) will be our unit of measurement. The smaller the RDR at which the rotation of the object is perceived, the more accurate is the operation of this compensating process (COO). Thus, the range of undetected object rotations, the no-rotation range for short, will be stated in terms of RDRs.

If the object is on the left of O's path, it will, if stationary, rotate clockwise relative to O, the opposite of its rotation direction when it is on O's right side. In both cases, however, a point on the object that faces O will move in the direction *against* O's progress, while an objective rotation in the opposite direction on either side will cause the facing surface to move objectively in the direction *with* O's forward movement. Since in our experiment O moves back and forth past the object and therefore has the object alternately on his right and on his left, rotation *with* or *against* O's progress will be the terms used for the two rotation directions. The RDR will be either in the direction *with* or *against* O's movement. Our measurements were concerned with determining the no-rotation range, the range RDRs between the points at which object rotation in the *with* direction and object rotation in the *against* direction will be just noticed. The extent of the no-rotation range measures the accuracy with which COO operates.

There were two experimental conditions, one in which the object was observed in total darkness and the other in which, also in the dark, the object was seen against a background of a pattern of vertical luminous lines. The latter condition was employed to find out whether the object's orientation relative to a visual surround has an influence on the accuracy of the COO.

Equipment

Suspended from the ceiling was the supporting structure for four pulleys that turned on vertical shafts. The shafts were located at the corner of an oblong, 300 cm. long in front and in the rear and 112 cm. long on each side. Over these pulleys ran a closed loop of cable in the shape of an oblong. It was kept under tension by a fifth pulley that pulled the cable inward on one of the sides. Fastened at right angles to the cable on the front side was a 10-cm.-long piece of metal tubing, into which a light hollow rod could be fitted. This rod was rigidly attached to a welder's headgear from which the glasses had been removed. When the headgear was worn, the rod rose vertically from O's forehead. When the rod was inserted into the piece of tubing, it caused the cable to move along with O when he walked underneath it, sliding up and down in the tubing as O's head rose and fell with each step.

A variable ratio transmission was mounted in the center of the oblong. Attached to the vertical input shaft was a horizontal lever, a piece of metal tubing 160 cm. long. It was inserted in a connector fixed to the cable in the rear, exactly halfway around the cable oblong from the tubing underneath which O's eyes were located. When the cable moved, the connector took the lever along and turned the input shaft of the transmission. The connector was designed to slide on rollers along the lever, as its distance from the input shaft shortened and then lengthened while it approached and passed beyond the midpoint of the 300-cm. stretch of cable. Underneath the transmission, fixed to its output shaft, was the experimental object, its height above the floor adjustable to the level of O's eyes. A handrail, 100 cm. above the floor, ran parallel to the front cable to aid O in walking underneath the cable.[1]

Two different objects were used. One was a four-sided irregular wire pyramid, 6 x 7 cm. and painted to to glow in ultraviolet light. The other object was spherical and consisted of a hollow glass bulb, 10 cm. in diameter, that was painted white and was illuminated by a small light source inside. On its surface, an irregular pattern was created with 1-cm.-wide black tape. It was bright enough to be clearly visible, but did not illuminate its surround.

The pattern of vertical stripes consisted of a panel of black cardboard, 4 m. long and 56 cm. high, to which strips of photoluminescent tape, 1.8 cm. wide, were attached 18 cm. apart. This panel was illuminated by three hidden sources of ultraviolet light and was placed parallel with O's motion path 40 cm. beyond the shaft to-which the object was fastened.

Experiment I

PROCEDURE

We measured the no-rotation range under two conditions, in total darkness or with the object seen against the striped background. The sphere was used here because we were afraid that during the lengthy measurement procedure O would, in the case of the pyramid, learn to use the spatial relations between the object and the

[1]We thank Otto Hebel for designing this apparatus.

striped background in a deliberate fashion. The fact that the pyramid was a wire from whose lines could be seen crossing the stripe edges might make this possible. An abbreviated method of limits was used to measure each *O*'s no-rotation range. In each trial, *O* walked the length of the handrail with his head connected to the cable for its distance of about 300 cm., stopped, turned around, and walked back to the starting point, which for half the *O*s was on one end of the rail and for the other half on the other end. Only during the first half of his walk to the turning point could *O* see the sphere, for he was allowed to turn his head toward it, but not his shoulders; the same was true of the return walk. When the latter was completed, *O* reported whether the sphere had appeared to turn or not, and in which direction. A trial thus consisted of two passages. Initially, the transmission setting was such that *O* clearly saw the sphere turning as he walked past it. On subsequent walks, the objective rotation of the sphere was diminished in steps of .04 RDR. This procedure was continued until *O* reported no rotation on three subsequent trials. Then the transmission setting was changed to produce a clearly noticeable rotation in the opposite direction, and the other outer limit of the no-rotation range was determined in corresponding fashion. For half the *O*s, the procedure started with objective rotation *with O*'s progress, and for the other half in the direction *against* it. After the two outer limits of the no-rotation range were obtained, the inner limits were determined with two series of trials, which, starting with transmission settings that produced immobility of the sphere, increased the rotation rate by .04 RDR steps until *O*s reported rotation in three subsequent trials. One series determined the inner limit in the *with* direction, and the other was used to find it in the *against* direction.

Twelve *O*s, mostly high school students, participated in both conditions. Half of them first made the measurements with the striped background present and a week later in total darkness. For the other six *O*s, the reversed order was used.

RESULTS

Two methods of evaluating our raw data were used, and the results of both are presented in Table 1. The first method used all limits that

TABLE 1
Compensation for Changes in
Orientation Measured with the Sphere,
With and Without Stripes in its Background*

Method of Evaluation					
No Stripes			With Stripes		
With Limit	*Against* Limit	Range	*With* Limit	*Against* Limit	Range
No-Rotation Range					
.402	.240	.652	.359	.254	.611
Uncertainty Range					
.342	.297	.639	.367	.273	.635

*All means given in RDR.

were obtained. The limits of the no-rotation range were computed
for each S, one toward perceived rotation in the *with* direction and
the other in the *against* direction. Each of these limits was the
midpoint between the first no-rotation report occurring in the run
toward the no-rotation range and the first rotation report when the
trial series started with no-rotation judgments. The means of these
two limits and the mean no-rotation range are presented in the first
row of Table 1.

When we found that the inner limits, the change from no-
rotation to rotation reports, showed less variability than the outer
limits obtained in the first two runs, we made another computation,
using only the last two runs of the procedure, the trial series that
started with no-rotation reports. Here we used as limits the first
rotation report that was succeeded by two further rotation reports.
These results are presented in the second row of Table 1, headed
"uncertainty range." A comparison of the four ranges presented in
the table shows that the two methods of evaluation produced essentially the same results.

The important comparison is between the ranges obtained with
and without stripes. They were approximately the same for the two
conditions. The confidence limits at the .05 level for the two no-
motion ranges were .12 and .22. The presence of the stripes had not
much, if any, effect. Whether one concludes from this result that the
visual context provided by a well-lit environment does not contrib-

ute to the apparent immobility of an object one passes depends on whether one accepts the striped background as representative of a well-lit field. But, since our results leave no doubt that a COO operates, this is not an important issue. Moreover, it has no bearing on other discussions of our results.

Experiment II

The purpose of this experiment was to ascertain whether the sphere used in Experiment I was a representative object where our investigation was concerned. To this end, we compared its no-rotation range with that of the pyramid. Because the pyramid is a wire shape and its near and far edges are therefore simultaneously visible, its orientation relative to O is optimally given and is, in that respect, superior to any solid shape.

PROCEDURE

The procedure of Experiment II differed from that of Experiment I only in minor ways. To shorten the procedure, O reported what he had observed after each passage rather than after walking back and forth. A second change seemed necessary because of the use of the wire form: E changed the orientation of the object relative to the shaft on which it turned after each passage before O turned to walk in the other direction. He put it into one of four standard orientations that differed from each other by 90 deg. In the case of the pyramid, the four orientations were those where its axis formed an angle of 45 degrees with O's path. The starting orientation for each passage was randomly selected.

A different sample of Os, drawn from our undergraduate population, was used in the two experimental conditions. Measurements for the sphere were taken with 13 Os and for the pyramid with 19.

RESULTS

Mean limits and mean no-rotation ranges with their standard deviations are presented in Table 2. The mean no-rotation range for the sphere was somewhat larger than in the first experiment, but the difference was far from significant. No significant difference be-

TABLE 2
Mean Limits and Mean No-Rotation Ranges for
Pyramid and Sphere in RDR

	With Limit	Against Limit	Range
	Pyramid (N = 19)		
Mean	.480	.439	.910
SD			.379
	Sphere (N = 13)		
Mean	.376	.439	.815
SD			.254

tween the no-rotation ranges for the two objects was found. But since the mean range for the pyramid was somewhat larger than that for the sphere, it seems safe to conclude that the latter does not disfavor COO.

Individual differences were very large. The *with* limit for the sphere, which averaged .376, varied from .121 to .628. The no-rotation range, with a mean of .815, ranged from .344 to 1.49.

Discussion

The COO emerges from our measurements as a rather crude function. But it is accurate enough to account for the observation we want to explain. When one moves past a painting of a three-dimensional object, the object does not turn relative to O and is not given with an optical rotation. According to our explanation, the object is perceived to rotate because its normal optical rotation is absent. If the painted object were real, it would have to turn at 1.0 RDR in the *with* direction in order to produce this optical nonrotation. This is well beyond the mean limits of the no-rotation ranges we have measured and beyond any limit in the *with* direction we have encountered in individual Ss.

The question arises, what use is a compensating function with a no-rotation range of .8 or .9 RDR? Such a no-rotation range means that objective rotations that occur during O's locomotion and fall within that no-rotation range will not be perceived, although most of them could undoubtedly be perceived were O stationary. To be sure, we are not seriously disadvantaged by such an arrangement.

But, then, why does COO exist at all when it yields perception of existing rotation during locomotion only outside such a large no-rotation range? A simpler arrangement by which *all* optical rotations that occur during one's locomotion are prevented from causing perceived rotation would be as useful.

There is little hope that this question can be answered by further investigation of COO. To be sure, COO is very likely the result of an adaptation acquired some time in *O*'s past; it should therefore be possible to modify it through experimental adaptation, as has been done in the case of the constancy of visual direction. But such an approach does not appear feasible. One of the reasons why experimental adaptation in the constancy of visual direction can be so easily investigated is its very small no-motion range, which makes partial adaptation easily measured (Wallach & Frey, 1969; Wallach, Frey, & Romney, 1969; Wallach Floor, 1970). The very large no-motion range of COO makes this impossible.

The answer to the question may eventually be found in connection with the investigation of a class of adaptation processes that resemble each other. In all of them, the perceptual effects of those exteroceptive stimuli which are caused by *O*'s own movements are eliminated. Such sensory inputs do not carry useful information, i.e., information about genuine environmental events. They are easily detected by the nervous system because they always occur when the movements that cause them to take place. They are therefore covariant with certain kinesthetic processes, namely, the proprioceptions of those movements. Once a connection between these correlated exteroceptive and proprioceptive inputs has been established, a compensating process can develop that eliminates the normal effect of the exteroceptive stimulation. This class of adaptation processes is thus based on a covariance principle. COO can be regarded as the result of such an adaptation developed in *O*'s past. The exteroceptive input whose perceptual effect has been eliminated results from the optical rotation of an object past which one moves. The kinesthetic processes with which this input is covariant are either the proprioceptions of the movements that cause one to view objects from different vantage points or, more likely, the movements made necessary by one's changing location relative to the object. The latter consist of the gradual turning of one's eyes and one's head out of the direction in which one walks (that is, out of the primary position), a combination of rotary movements that take place when one moves past an observed object. The covariance between this combination of rotary movements and the object's optical rotation is not a simple linear one but of a higher order, because, for both, the rotation rate increases as one approaches the object.

The constancy of visual direction also fits this scheme. Here, the rate of displacement of the visual field caused by the head rotation varies with the rate of the head rotation. Both the original adaptation process that caused this constancy and the experimental adaptation that modifies it obviously belong to this class. We know of at least one other type of experimentally produced adaptation that develops only when the sensory events whose perceptual results are being diminished by the adaptation are covariant with O's head movements. It is interesting that this case of adaptation is not related to a normally existing compensation process (Wallach & Barton, reported in next selection).

References

Wallach, H., & Floor, L. On the relation of the adaptation to field displacement during head movements to the constancy of visual direction. *Perception & Psychophysics*, 1970, 8, 95–98.

Wallach, H., & Frey, K. J. Adaptation in the constancy of visual direction measured by a one-trial method. *Perception & Psychophysics*, 1969, 5, 249–252. In the present volume, this chapter, selection 4.

Wallach, H., Frey, K. J., & Romney, G. Adaptation to field displacement during head movement unrelated to the constancy of visual direction. *Perception & Psychophysics*, 1969, 5, 253–256. In the present volume, this chapter, selection 5.

Wallach, H., & Kravitz, J. H. Adaptation in the constancy of visual direction tested by measuring the constancy of auditory direction. *Perception & Psychophyiscs*, 1968, 4, 299–303. In the present volume, this chapter, selection 3.

Wallach, H., & O'Connell, D. N. The kinetic depth effect. *Journal of Experimental Psychology*, 1953, 45, 205–217. In the present volume, Chapter II.

9. Theory and More Experiments

The constancy of visual direction and the compensation for movement-produced changes in object orientation have similar functions. Both prevent visual stimulation caused indirectly by one's own movements from being represented in perceptual experience. Without these compensatory processes, one would see the visual field swing about when one turns or nods one's head, and an object past which one moves would appear to turn.

There are two further visual changes that are brought about by one's own movements. When we tilt the head, e.g., clockwise, the visual field rotates counter-clockwise in relation to the head, through an angle equal to that of the head movement. This rotation is not perceived, and this fact is currently under investigation. That we deal here with a learned compensation process was demonstrated by altering it by means of experimental adaptation in a manner analogous to adaptation in the constancy of visual direction. After exposure to an arrangement that actually rotated the visual field dependent on head tilting, S perceived a stationary field turn in a direction opposite to the field rotation to which he had adapted, and this adaptation effect could be measured by compensation.

The fourth visual change brought about by our own movements occurs when we walk. Moving forward causes the retinal projection of the array of objects in front of us to expand, but this expanding is usually not perceived. Indirect evidence that this is the result of a learned compensatory process will soon be published.

There exist, then, at least four compensating processes that prevent those stimulations from having their normal perceptual results that are indirectly caused by our own movements. Together they result in a perceived environment that remains stable when we

move. Or, viewed in somewhat different fashion: Our own movements cause two kinds of stimuli, the proprioceptive stimulations of
kinesthesis and visual stimulators indirectly caused by our movements. With certain exceptions, the latter do not carry useful information, i.e., information about genuine environmental events.
Preventing them from producing perceptual experiences and being
represented in cognition is therefore desirable. (Exceptions are those
instances where visual inputs caused by our own movements have
an effect equivalent to that of kinesthesis, adding to the information
provided by proprioceptive sense organs. An example is the use of
visual information about head movements in sound localization; see
Chapter VI.) It is likely that all these compensating processes are
learned, although there exists, at present, no such evidence in the
case of the compensation for movement-produced changes in object
orientation. Furthermore, in the cases of the constancy of visual
direction, of the compensation for field rotation during tilting of the
head, and of the compensation for movement-produced changes in
object orientation, it was possible to show that the compensating
process, more or less accurately, matches up the visual inputs with
the proprioceptions of the movements that physically cause these
inputs. This was done by demonstrating the existence of limited
no-motion ranges.

Because the visual inputs are caused by one's movements, they
are covariant with the movements and with the proprioceptive processes that represent them in the nervous system. This covariance
is, therefore, by necessity present where our compensatory processes match up visual and proprioceptive inputs. In fact, it makes
the matching up process possible. It is my thesis that this is not the
only role that the covariance between the visual and proprioceptive
input plays in the development of these compensating processes.
The argument for this thesis comes from the investigation of two
novel adaptation processes.

Wallach and Barton equipped S with spectacles that, by means
of a stereoscopic effect, caused frontal planes to curve in depth. Essentially these spectacles consisted of wedge prisms, which cause
lines parallel to their base to curve slightly. Thus, when a pair of
prisms is placed in front of the eyes so that vertical lines reach the
two eyes with opposite curvature, the resultant retinal disparities
will cause a depth effect. The spectacles caused frontal planes to

appear to form part of a hollow cylindrical surface with horizontal axis. Adaptation to these glasses develops rapidly: a frontal plane viewed without glasses will then appear to form a bulging cylindrical surface. This effect was measured by compensation. In the test, *S* adjusted the cylindrical curvature of a frontal surface so that it appeared plane. Since after adaptation a plane frontal surface appeared to bulge, the bulge was compensated for by an objective concavity of the test surface. The difference between the concavity of the test surface required for it to appear plane after the adaptation period and a similar pre-adaptation setting measured the adaptation effect.

During adaptation, *S* faced a light plane surface covered with an irregular pattern of black dots. There were initially two adaptation conditions, one in which *S* nodded his head up and down while looking at the dot pattern and another in which he kept his head still in a head rest. When *S* moved his head, the concavity caused by the glasses also moved up and down, deforming the dot pattern, while, with head still, the pattern looked like a rigid hollow. Highly significant partial adaptation effects were found after head movements, but no adaptation was obtained when the head was stationary and the pattern was seen as a rigid concavity. The difference between the results for the two conditions was significant at the .01 level.

These findings caused us to ask which feature of the exposure condition with head movements was responsible for the adaptation, the pattern deformation as such or the conjunction between the pattern deformation and the head movement. Therefore a third adaptation condition was tried in which *S*'s head was stationary, but a dot pattern was moved vertically up and down through *S*'s field of vision. In this manner, the same pattern deformations were produced as those caused by head nodding. This condition yielded no adaptation, and this result was significantly different from that for the head movement condition at the .01 level. Thus, pattern deformation alone is not sufficient to produce this kind of adaptation; only the conjunction of pattern deformation with head movements will yield it.

An analogous experiment was performed by Wallach and Flaherty employing one of the form distortions caused by a wedge prism. This particular distortion resulted from the fact that the displacement of the visual direction caused by the prism is different when the line of sight passes obliquely through the prism; when it passes obliquely near the apex, the displacement is greater than normal and when it passes near the base, it is smaller. As a result, distances between evenly spaced points aligned in a frontal plane at right angles to the prism base appear to be smaller than normal where they are viewed through the base part of the prism and larger where they are viewed through the prism near its apex. This form distortion is most clearly seen when a pattern of evenly spaced lines that are parallel to the prism base fill the field visible through the prism. Adaptation would here consist in a compensation for this form distortion with the consequence that an evenly spaced line pattern viewed with the naked eye would appear to have an opposite form distortion.

The attempt to obtain adaptation was made by making this form distortion vary with head movements. S wore over his right eye a 30 diopter wedge prism in vertical orientation and was asked to nod his head up and down while looking at the center of a large field of evenly spaced horizontal stripes. This caused the form distortion to shift through the line pattern in a manner similar to the previous experiment where a head movement caused a three-dimensional shape distortion, a hollow produced by the glasses, to shift up and down. Adaptation was readily obtained under these conditions. After a 20-minute exposure to the constantly shifting deformations, the line pattern viewed without the prism appeared to have a mild form distortion of the kind produced by the prism but of opposite direction. This adaptation was measured by compensation. A set of prisms running from 2 to 12 diopters in 2-diopter steps was used. A measurement consisted of the average diopter value of those prisms which compensated for any pattern distortion S might see. The set of prisms was presented twice, once in descending and then in ascending order. Such measurements were taken before and after the adaptation period, and their difference was the adaptation effect.

Highly significant adaptation effects were obtained after 10 and 20 minutes of exposure. They were significant at the .002 level, after the 10-minute period and at the .01 level after 20 minutes of adaptation.

As in the previous experiment, we went on to show that observing pattern deformation was not enough to obtain this kind of adaptation, that rather the deformations needed to be accompanied by

S's head movements. In a control adaptation condition, the form distortion shifted through the line pattern as well as across *S*'s retina as it had done in the experimental condition, but was not connected with head movements. *S* viewed the striped surface with head stationary through a prism which tilted back and forth, approximating the average angle and rate of tilt produced by the head movements in the experimental condition. If the cyclical pattern deformations produced by the tilting prism were sufficient to produce adaptation, this control condition should do so. If, on the other hand, adaptation depended on the conjunction between pattern deformations and head movements, no adaptation should take place.

Because, in this condition, it was necessary to test for adaptation while *S*'s head was stationary, the original experiment in which *S* moved his head during the adaptation period was repeated, with the difference that the tests were now conducted with head stationary. Again, partial adaptation was obtained after head movements, but no adaptation was obtained when the head was stationary and the shifting width distortion was produced by tilting only the prism. The difference between the mean effects for the two conditions was significant at the .02 level, showing that head movements were needed for adaptation.

In both of these new adaptation processes, the shifting of a deformation through a pattern produced adaptation only when it was caused by head movements and was, therefore, covariant with them. They have this characteristic in common with the four kinds of compensating processes that tend to keep the perceived environment stable. But there is this difference: In these compensating processes, movements are the only causes of the visual inputs whose perceptual effects are eliminated. Movement is the sole cause of the swinging or of the rotation of the visual field relative to the moving head, of the rotation of an object past which one moves, and of the expansion of the object array one approaches. In the two adaptation experiments, the deformations, whose normal perceptual effects are diminished by partial compensation, exist independently of *S*'s movements. Even the assumption that *shifts* of the deformation through a normally stable pattern are required for these adaptations to develop does not imply that head movements are necessary. That they, in fact, are, shows that they play an essential role in the adaptation process. They set up in the nervous system a covariance between the proprioceptive inputs representing them and some visual input, the shifting of the deformation. This covariance is a signal to the nervous system that the visual input does not represent genuine environmental facts or conditions and instigates the adaptation process that tends to prevent these visual inputs to be represented in experience.

I believe that we have here a principle that operates in a number of perceptual learning processes. That covariance functions as a signal to the nervous system to develop adaptation processes which eliminate the normal effects of certain visual inputs is an idea that is applicable to our four compensation processes. Covariance would play this role in their original development as well as in the experimental adaptations that we demonstrated in connection with two of them. This would make it unnecessary to see these compensating processes as related to a specific end, that of keeping the visual environment stable.

List of publications not included
in this volume

HANS WALLACH. Ueber visuell wahrgenommene Bewegungsrichtung. *Psychologische Forschung*, 1935, 20, 325–380.

HANS WALLACH. Ueber die Wahrnehmung der Schallrichtung. *Psychologische Forschung*, 1938, 22, 238–266.

HANS WALLACH. On sound localization. *Journal of the Acoustical Society of America*, 1939, 10, 270–274.

HANS WALLACH AND MARY HENLE. An experimental analysis of the law of effect. *Journal of Experimental Psychology*, 1941, 28, 340–349.

HANS WALLACH AND MARY HENLE. A further study of the function of reward. *Journal of Experimental Psychology*, 1942, 30, 147–160.

WOLFGANG KOHLER AND HANS WALLACH. Figural after-effects. An investigation of visual processes. *Proceedings of the American Philosophical Society*, 1944, 88, 269–357.

HANS WALLACH AND ALICE GALLOWAY. The constancy of colored objects in colored illumination. *Journal of Experimental Psychology*, 1946, 36, 119–126.

HANS WALLACH. Brightness constancy and the nature of achromatic colors. *Journal of Experimental Psychology*, 1948, 38, 310–324.

HANS WALLACH, EDWIN B. NEWMAN, AND MARK R. ROSENZWEIG. The precedence effect in sound localization. *American Journal of Psychology*, 1949, 62, 315–336.

HANS WALLACH AND PAULINE AUSTIN ADAMS. Binocular rivalry of achromatic colors. *American Journal of Psychology*, 1954, 67, 513–516.

HANS WALLACH. The perception of motion. *Scientific American*, 1959, 201, 56–60.

HANS WALLACH. On the moon illusion. Letter to *Science*, 1962, 137, 900–901.

HANS WALLACH AND CYNTHIA M. MORRIS. Accomodation as a distance-cue. *American Journal of Psychology*, 1963, 76, 659–664.

HANS WALLACH. The perception of neutral colors. *Scientific American*, 1963, 208, 107–115.

HANS WALLACH AND CHARLES LEWIS. The effect of abnormal displacement of the retinal image during eye movements. *Perception & Psychophysics*, 1966, 1, 25–29.

OLIVIA SHAFFER AND HANS WALLACH. Extent-of-motion thresholds under subject-relative and object-relative conditions. *Perception & Psychophysics*, 1966, 1, 447–451.

OLIVIA SHAFFER AND HANS WALLACH. Adaptation to displaced vision measured with three tests. *Psychonomic Science*, 1966, 6, 143–144.

JEROME H. KRAVITZ AND HANS WALLACH. Adaptation to displaced vision contingent upon vibrating stimulation. *Psychonomic Science*, 1966, 6, 465–466.

HANS WALLACH AND JEROME H. KRAVITZ. Adaptation to vertical displacement of the visual direction. *Perception and Psychophysics*, 1969, 6, 111–112.

HANS WALLACH AND LUCRETIA FLOOR. On the relation of adaptation to field displacement during head movements to the constancy of visual direction. *Perception and Psychophysics*, 1970, 8, 95–98.

HANS WALLACH AND ANN SMITH. Visual and proprioceptive adaptation to altered oculomotor adjustment. *Perception and Psychophysics*, 1972, 11, 413–416.

Index